D0944909

HELMUTH VON MOLTKE
AND THE ORIGINS OF THE
FIRST WORLD WAR

This book explores the influence of Helmuth von Moltke, Germany's Chief of the General Staff between 1906 and 1914. Based largely on previously unknown primary sources, it analyses the General Staff's role in military decision-making and Moltke's relationship with Kaiser Wilhelm II, as well as the genesis of the Schlieffen Plan and Germany's military and political reactions to the many pre-war crises. Moltke's influence on Germany's political decision-making is shown to have been decisive, helping to foster an increasingly confrontational mood.

The book takes specific issue with the common perception of Moltke as an ineffectual and reluctant military leader, remembered primarily for the defeat at the Battle of the Marne and his alleged adulteration of the Schlieffen Plan. It concludes that, on the contrary, he was both bellicose and ambitious, hoping for war 'the sooner the better' and playing a crucial role in the outbreak and early months of the First World War.

ANNIKA MOMBAUER is Lecturer in European History, The Open University.

NEW STUDIES IN EUROPEAN HISTORY

Edited by

PETER BALDWIN, University of California, Los Angeles
CHRISTOPHER CLARK, University of Cambridge
JAMES B. COLLINS, Georgetown University
MIA RODRÍGUEZ-SALGADO, London School of Economics and
Political Science
LYNDAL ROPER, Royal Holloway, University of London

This is a new series of scholarly monographs in early modern and modern European history. Its aim is to publish outstanding works of research, addressed to important themes across a wide geographical range, from southern and central Europe, to Scandinavia and Russia, and from the time of the Renaissance to the Second World War. As it develops the series will comprise focused works of wide contextual range and intellectual ambition.

Helmuth von Moltke at the time of his appointment as Chief of the
General Staff of the German Army, 1906

HELMUTH VON MOLTKE AND THE ORIGINS OF THE FIRST WORLD WAR

ANNIKA MOMBAUER

CAMBRIDGE
UNIVERSITY PRESS

PUBLISHED BY THE PRESS SYNDICATE OF THE UNIVERSITY OF CAMBRIDGE
The Pitt Building, Trumpington Street, Cambridge, United Kingdom

CAMBRIDGE UNIVERSITY PRESS
The Edinburgh Building, Cambridge CB2 2RU, UK
40 West 20th Street, New York, NY 10011-4211, USA
10 Stamford Road, Oakleigh, VIC 3166, Australia
Ruiz de Alarcón 13, 28014 Madrid, Spain
Dock House, The Waterfront, Cape Town 8001, South Africa

http://www.cambridge.org

© Cambridge University Press 2001

This book is in copyright. Subject to statutory exception
and to the provisions of relevant collective licensing agreements,
no reproduction of any part may take place without
the written permission of Cambridge University Press.

First published 2001

Printed in the United Kingdom at the University Press, Cambridge

Typeset in Monotype Baskerville 11/12.5 in QuarkXPress™   [SE]

A catalogue record for this book is available from the British Library

ISBN 0 521 79101 4 hardback

D511
M5525
2001

For my Mother

SEP 2 7 2001

Contents

List of illustrations   *page* x
List of maps   xii
Acknowledgements   xiii
Hierarchy of ranks for officers in the German army before 1914   xiv
List of abbreviations   xvi
General map of Europe   xvii

    Introduction   1

1   Military decision-making in Wilhelmine Germany   14

2   Alfred von Schlieffen and Helmuth von Moltke: 'military genius' and 'reluctant military leader'?   42

3   From crisis to crisis: the international background to military planning in the pre-war years   106

4   The July Crisis and the outbreak of war: the German perspective   182

5   The General Staff at war   227

    Conclusion. Myths and Realities: Helmuth von Moltke and the origins of the First World War   283

Bibliography   290
Index   318

Illustrations

Helmuth von Moltke in 1906 (Interfoto Pressebild-Agentur,
Munich)   *frontispiece*
1 Scenes at the annual summer manoeuvres, 1899   *pages* 60–64
   a 'The Garde du Corps on Parade' (Courtesy of the Imperial
   War Museum Photograph Archive, HU 68414)
   b The Kaiser (on horseback) talks to Archduke Franz
   Ferdinand (Courtesy of the Imperial War Museum
   Photograph Archive, HU 68471)
   c The Kaiser greets his staff officers. (Courtesy of the Imperial
   War Museum Photograph Archive, HU 68475)
   d The Kaiser with Moltke (left). (Courtesy of the Imperial
   War Museum Photograph Archive, HU 68472)
2 Army manoeuvres, 1904. (Süddeutscher Verlag-Bilderdienst,
   Munich)   65
3 Colmar Freiherr von der Goltz, postcard *c.* 1914   70
4 Kaiser Wilhelm II and Helmuth von Moltke, 1911
   (Süddeutscher Verlag-Bilderdienst, Munich)   89
5 North Sea cruise, 1912 (Süddeutscher Verlag-Bilderdienst,
   Munich)   123
6 Helmuth von Moltke, 1912 (Bildarchiv Preussischer
   Kulturbesitz, Berlin)   134
7 Archduke Franz Ferdinand and his wife Sophie, postcard
   c. 1914   183
8 Chancellor Theobald von Bethmann Hollweg in military
   uniform, postcard *c.* 1916   184
9 The mobilization order of 1 August 1914   217
10 The Kaiser, with hand-written declaration, postcard *c.* 1914 218
11 Wilhelm Groener during the First World War (Interfoto
   Pressebild-Agentur, Munich)   240
12 Alexander von Kluck, postcard *c.* 1914   241

13 Karl von Bülow, postcard *c.* 1914   242
14 Ludendorff with Hindenburg during the First World War
    (Interfoto Pressebild-Agentur, Munich)   262
15 Erich von Falkenhayn, postcard *c.* 1915 (Interfoto Pressebild-
    Agentur, Munich)   268

Maps

1. General map of Europe   *page* xv
2. The Schlieffen Plan   73
3. The German advance of 1914   239

Acknowledgements

Over the years that it took to research and write the doctoral thesis that became this book, I have been fortunate in the help and support that I have received from many friends and colleagues in Germany and England – too many to mention them all here. I hope I have thanked them in other ways.

My primary debt is to my supervisor, Professor John Röhl, whose advice, expertise and encouragement have been invaluable. It was his enthusiasm for the history of Wilhelmine Germany that first made me decide to pursue my studies into the origins of the First World War. Moreover, I cannot thank John and Rosemarie Röhl enough for their kindness and friendship over the years.

My thanks are also due to my examiners, Professor Hew Strachan and Professor Jonathan Steinberg, and to Beryl Williams at the University of Sussex, for their advice and interest in the subject.

I am most grateful for the financial support that I received from the British Academy. Without it, I could not have undertaken the research on which this book is based. My thanks also go to the archives and libraries I have visited, including the Bundesarchiv-Militärarchiv, Freiburg, the Bundesarchiv, Abteilung Potsdam, the Geheimes Staatsarchiv, Berlin-Dahlem, the Politisches Archiv des Auswärtigen Amtes in Bonn, the Bayerisches Hauptstaatsarchiv-Kriegsarchiv, Munich and the Sächsisches Hauptstaatsarchiv, Dresden. The Photograph Archive of the Imperial War Museum kindly provided some of the illustrations in this book. I should also like to thank Rose-Marie von Berghes and Marie-Liza von Bethusy-Huc, Helmuth von Moltke's granddaughters, for talking to me about their memories of their grandparents.

I am indebted to many friends and colleagues for reading parts of the manuscript at various stages, for their welcome suggestions for improvements, and for making additional material available to me. My particular thanks go to Dr Robert Foley, for his friendship, his military expertise, and his interest in discussing Moltke with a non-military historian like me. Konrad Donat in Bremen has helped me enormously over the last years, providing me with valuable material on Moltke and Steiner, and with insightful comments on draft chapters. Dr Paul Lawrence has read the text with incredible attention for detail and has made valuable suggestions for improvements. He has been a greater help than he realizes.

Finally, like many historians who come to dedicate their first book, I, too, am indebted to my parents for putting up with such an unusual choice of profession and for supporting me in every way. By way of thanks, woefully inadequate, this book is dedicated to my mother, Sybille Ulinski, to whom I owe the biggest debt of all.

Hierarchy of ranks for officers in the German army before 1918

Army ranks	*Approximate British equivalent*
Leutnant	Second Lieutenant
Oberleutnant	Lieutenant
Hauptmann	Captain
Major	Major
Oberstleutnant	Lieutenant Colonel
Oberst	Colonel
Generalmajor	Brigadier
Generalleutnant	Major General
General	Lieutenant General
Generaloberst	General
Generalfeldmarschall	Field Marshal

Abbreviations

AA	Auswärtiges Amt
AOK	Armee-Oberkommando (Army High Command)
BA-MA	Bundesarchiv-Militärarchiv, Freiburg
BayHSTA-KA	Bayerisches Hauptstaatsarchiv-Kriegsarchiv, Munich
BEF	British Expeditionary Force
DD	*Die deutschen Dokumente zum Kriegsausbruch*
GP	*Die große Politik der Europäischen Kabinette*
HJ	*Historical Journal*
HQ	Hauptquartier (military headquarters)
HZ	*Historische Zeitschrift*
KA	Kriegsarchiv
KGFA	Kriegsgeschichtliches Forschungsamt des Heeres
NL	Nachlaß (papers)
NDB	*Neue Deutsche Biographie*
MGM	*Militärgeschichtliche Mitteilungen*
MS	Manuscript
NCOs	Non-Commissioned Officers
OHL	Oberste Heeresleitung
Oberost	Oberkommando Ost
o.D.	ohne Datum (no date)
PA Bonn	Politisches Archiv des Auswärtigen Amtes, Bonn
PRO	Public Record Office, London
Sächs. HSTA	Sächsisches Hauptstaatsarchiv, Dresden
TB	Tagebuch (diary)

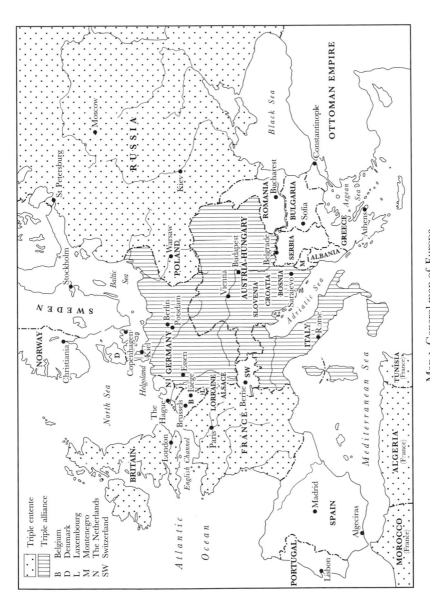

Map 1 General map of Europe

Triple entente
Triple alliance

B   Belgium
D   Denmark
L   Luxembourg
M   Montenegro
N   The Netherlands
SW Switzerland

Introduction

The origins of the First World War have been debated continually since its outbreak in August 1914. Every possible point of view has been advanced in trying to explain why war broke out, and the heated debates that surround the topic continue to fascinate historians and students alike. Since the Fischer controversy of the 1960s, some consensus has been reached and no one today would seriously support Lloyd George's famous dictum that the European nations had 'slithered into war', almost as an act of fate, an inevitable result of alliance policy for which no single government could be held responsible. Rather, many would argue that the fact that war proved unavoidable in 1914 was due to earlier developments and crises, some of which had been instigated or provoked by Germany, whose military and political decision-makers had embarked on *Weltmachtpolitik*. This intention of securing for Germany a position of dominance both within Europe and ultimately world-wide was at the heart of the origins of the First World War.

The culpability of Germany's political and military leaders can hardly be disputed, and yet the extent of their responsibility for creating a situation that would lead to war is still subject to debate. The importance and dominance of the military in Imperial Germany is almost proverbial, and their responsibility for bringing about war in 1914 can be clearly demonstrated with the help of archival sources that have only recently come to light.[1] These new documents support the thesis that German decision-makers consciously risked war in 1914, in order to improve the country's deteriorating position vis-à-vis her European neighbours. Some of the military went even further in their bellicose designs, and wanted 'war for war's sake'. In the not-too-distant future, Germany would no longer be able to wage a war against her neighbours with any real chance of success, their argument ran. As a result of this

---

[1] For more details, see the 'Note on Sources', pp. 6–13 below.

perceived urgency, their actions and demands were motivated by a desire to fight a war before it ceased to be a viable option.

In January 1906, Helmuth von Moltke became Chief of the Great General Staff. He was to occupy this important position for the next eight years – a crucial time, as we know with hindsight, during which he was responsible for developing Germany's war plans, and ultimately for leading her army into war. This book examines the role and importance of Imperial Germany's last peacetime Chief of the General Staff, and is based largely on primary evidence which has recently become available following the collapse of the Soviet Union. In offering a re-evaluation of that most highly rated of Prussian institutions, the Great General Staff, and its most poorly rated chief, the younger Moltke, several common myths and preconceptions can be dispelled.

Moltke's reputation as Chief of the General Staff was largely shaped by the fact that during the war the German army under his leadership fared less well than expected, culminating in the disastrous defeat on the Marne and his subsequent dismissal. His ultimate failure as a military leader has led to the view that Moltke's entire time in office was unsuccessful, especially compared to that of his predecessor, who would allegedly have been able to achieve victory where Moltke failed. He was unfortunate in succeeding Count Alfred von Schlieffen, a Chief of the General Staff who left behind a devoted 'school' of followers, and Moltke's achievements and failings have invariably been compared to those of his famous predecessor. Moltke's many contemporary and subsequent critics have pointed to the fact that he had not been an ambitious or well-qualified Chief of the General Staff, nor an obvious candidate to replace Schlieffen, and that his pessimism and lack of self-confidence impeded his decision-making.[2]

The deliberate attempt after the war to establish a favourable view of Schlieffen has clouded our vision of the pre-war years. We see Schlieffen and his famous deployment plan, as well as Moltke's subsequent strategic planning, through the eyes of a 'Schlieffen school' of German military commentators. Much of Moltke's role has been distorted by this biased perspective. The most outspoken critic of Moltke, and a dedicated believer in Schlieffen's abilities, was Wilhelm Groener, who had served on the General Staff under both Schlieffen and Moltke. Groener, more than anyone else, has to be regarded as the creator of the

---

[2] For a recent negative evaluation of Moltke, based on the views of the 'Schlieffen school', see Arden Bucholz, *Moltke, Schlieffen and Prussian War Planning*, Providence and Oxford 1991, p. 223.

'Schlieffen myth'. His papers in the military archive in Freiburg and his numerous publications created an idealized image of Schlieffen and bemoaned any changes made to Schlieffen's plan.[3] Another dedicated and outspoken supporter of Schlieffen and a strong believer in the Schlieffen Plan was Wilhelm von Hahnke, who was doubtless motivated by the fact that he was Schlieffen's son-in-law, as well as his adjutant and secretary. Indeed, it was to Hahnke that Schlieffen had dictated his famous memoranda of 1905 and 1912. After the war he became an ardent defender of the 'Schlieffen myth', whose post-war reminiscences testify to his devotion to Schlieffen: 'I trusted Schlieffen blindly and during my decade-long work with him as his first adjutant and secretary I was absolutely convinced of the truth and validity of his thoughts. [Schlieffen] accepted me as his son into his heart and his trust, and confided to me the labour of his whole life.'[4]

The following account is both a study of Moltke's role and an attempt to show that the picture painted in the immediate post-war years was tendentious and sometimes deliberately clouded the issues. A departure from the usual Schlieffen-centred perspective helps to shed new light on Moltke and German strategic planning in the pre-war years. Foremost among the myths, and most damaging to Moltke's reputation, has been the Schlieffen Plan and Moltke's alleged adulteration of it. Because Moltke has so often been accused of ruining the famous deployment plan, and of being an unworthy successor to Schlieffen, it is necessary not only to examine Moltke's appointment, but to go further back in time to investigate Schlieffen's time in office and the genesis of the Schlieffen Plan. Only then can the period of transition, from the alleged genius Schlieffen to the apparent epigone, the reputed 'reluctant military leader', be properly understood.

Because of the strong post-war 'school' of Schlieffen followers, it became almost impossible to criticize Schlieffen publicly in the inter-war years. This was particularly true once the Nazis controlled publishing, as Moltke's former adjutant Friedrich von Mantey found when he attempted to publish a manuscript on Moltke and the Schlieffen Plan. He

---

[3] See e.g. *Das Testament des Grafen Schlieffen. Operative Studien über den Weltkrieg*, Berlin 1927; *Der Feldherr wider Willen. Operative Studien über den Weltkrieg*, Berlin 1930; *Lebenserinnerungen. Jugend, Generalstab, Weltkrieg*, Göttingen 1957.

[4] Hahnke's letter to the Prussian Crown Prince, 2 April 1922, Bundesarchiv-Militärachiv (BA-MA), NL Hahnke, N36/10. After Schlieffen's death, it was Hahnke who passed the 1912 memorandum to Moltke. See Wolfgang Förster, 'Einige Bemerkungen zu Gerhard Ritters Buch "Der Schlieffenplan"', *Wehrwissenschaftliche Rundschau*, 1, 1957, p. 44. Other prominent Schlieffen defenders include Hermann von Kuhl, Erich Ludendorff and Wolfgang Förster.

complained that 'because one is not allowed to say anything against Schlieffen's plan, it has been impossible to find a publisher so far'.[5] Even today, voices hailing Schlieffen as a genius, and his plan as a potential miracle, have not fully subsided. Despite substantial critiques, especially by Gerhard Ritter,[6] many of the Schlieffen school's views are reiterated to this day.[7] According to Gotthard Jäschke, Ritter was a mere layman who should show more respect towards a man 'whom a whole generation of General Staff officers had considered a genius and whom many still honour as such today'. In other words, Ritter the civilian should not interfere in military affairs, a view that echoes the prejudiced military attitude towards civilians that was already prevalent during Schlieffen's time. Jäschke, unconvinced by Ritter's criticisms, values the plan highly. 'The memorandum is neither a recipe for victory nor a recipe at all, but a – perhaps desperate, but certainly ingenious – attempt to point the way for the uncertain Moltke.'[8] Rolf-Joseph Eibicht's monograph on Schlieffen is a more recent example of writings in the tradition of the 'Schlieffen school': there is no doubt in the author's mind that Schlieffen would have succeeded in 1914 where his hapless successor failed. Eibicht asserts that 'Schlieffen would, without a doubt and in an ice-cold manner, have attained the goal of a total and absolute defeat of the enemy, if he had had the opportunity to lead personally in 1914', adding confidently that 'Schlieffen would have achieved one of the biggest military victories for the German Reich in the First World War.'[9] This school of thought attributes the defeat of Germany in the First World War to Moltke's shortcomings. Against this background, Moltke's role as Chief of the General Staff in the first months of the war deserves particular attention. In what way were Germany's demise and Moltke's own fall from grace connected? The following account takes issue with the view that Germany would have fought successfully under Schlieffen in 1914: a view that stems from writers like Groener, who maintained that Schlieffen had possessed the secret of

---

[5] Mantey to Tappen, 9 March 1933. Mantey's manuscript on 'Moltke, Schlieffenplan und Eisenbahnfrage' was rejected despite positive feed-back from 'several high-ranking officers': BA-MA, NL Tappen, N56/5, p. 221.

[6] Gerhard Ritter, *The Schlieffen Plan. Critique of a Myth*, London 1958.

[7] A recent example is the readers' debate in the *Spectator*, March–October 1997, where an amateur historian, who claimed to be Schlieffen's granddaughter 'Alice von Schlieffen', staunchly defended the general's plan and reiterated the usual accusations against the epigone Moltke.

[8] Gotthard Jäschke, '"Schlieffenplan" und "Marneschlacht"' in Dermont Bradley and Ulrich Marwedel (eds.), *Militärgeschichte, Militärwissenschaft und Konfliktforschung*, Osnabrück 1977, pp. 187, 195.

[9] Rolf-Joseph Eibicht, *Schlieffen. Strategie und Politik. Aus der Unterlegenheit zum Sieg*, Lünen 1991, pp. 17, 34, 40.

victory, and that he would have achieved a 'massive strategic Cannae!' if he had been in charge of the army in 1914.[10]

In an in-depth analysis of the July Crisis of 1914, this study also investigates the degree of influence of military decision-makers in the management of the events that directly led to war. Focusing on the military during the July Crisis highlights the extent to which military concerns and thinking had become common currency. They were often accepted uncritically by civilians and increasingly determined their decisions. The short-sighted and narrow military planning of the pre-war years had tragic effects when war broke out, and the lack of alternative deployment plans to the Schlieffen/Moltke Plan significantly reduced political and military options at the end of July.

In re-evaluating Moltke's role and importance, the following account does not aim to rehabilitate Germany's last Chief of the General Staff – if anything, the conclusion drawn from this investigation must be that Moltke's influence was more decisive in pushing Germany into war than has previously been assumed. After all, the portrayal of Moltke as a weak and insignificant figure did more than emphasize Schlieffen's mythical genius. It also tended to minimize Moltke's responsibility, and thus, by implication, that of Germany, for the outbreak of war. Accounts that stress Moltke's reluctance to order mobilization during the July Crisis, for example, have argued that his hesitancy was proof that he did not want war.[11] The evidence available today makes such allegations untenable.

Because of his alleged weakness, Moltke's bellicose pre-war statements have sometimes been dismissed as the ranting of a weak man trying to give the impression of decisiveness. However, this study shows that his aggressive outbursts should actually be taken seriously. They occurred too frequently to be disregarded, and they were voiced with increasing conviction during his time in office. Moltke's importance lies in his consistent and desperate pressurizing for war before – as he saw it – time ran out for Germany and her only strategic plan.[12] It also lies in the substantial

[10] Quoted in Jehuda Wallach, *Das Dogma der Vernichtungsschlacht. Die Lehren von Clausewitz und Schlieffen und ihre Wirkungen in zwei Weltkriegen*, Frankfurt/M. 1967, pp. 97–98. Just like Schlieffen, Groener seemed unaware that the battle of Cannae did not lead to ultimate victory for Hannibal. Rather, it led to the ultimate destruction of Carthage when it was burnt to the ground by the Romans. Cf. Wallach, *Kriegstheorien. Ihre Entwicklung im 19. und 20. Jahrhundert*, Frankfurt/M. 1972, p. 106.

[11] Theobald von Schäfer, 'Wollte Generaloberst von Moltke den Präventivkrieg?', *Berliner Monatshefte*, 5/1, 1927, p. 552.

[12] Arden Bucholz, *Moltke*, p. 223, argues that Moltke is negligible in terms of his military skills, his input and influence on military planning. For a different interpretation, see Isabel Hull, 'Kaiser Wilhelm II and the "Liebenberg Circle"', in John C. G. Röhl and N. Sombart (eds.), *Kaiser Wilhelm II. New Interpretations*, Cambridge 1982, p. 212. For a dismissal of Moltke's belligerent statements, see e.g. L. C. F. Turner, *The Origins of the First World War*, London 1970, p. 21.

political pressure that he was able to exert, and in his considerable personal influence arising from his special relationship with the Kaiser. As the official German history of the war noted in 1924, 'in peacetime he [Moltke] had often been able to advocate army matters successfully and effectively vis-à-vis the War-Lord (*Kriegsherrn*), owing to the special relationship of trust that he had with the Kaiser'.[13] Given Moltke's political role, an area in which he wielded much more influence than Schlieffen had ever done, this study focuses primarily on Moltke in a political context. It asks how Moltke reacted to the international conflicts and crises that provided the background to his time in office, and it seeks to uncover his personal role in impressing on the civilian leadership that Germany's aggressive foreign policy could be backed up by strong force, and that Germany should fight a war – the sooner, the better.

A NOTE ON SOURCES

In view of the controversial role that Moltke played in the events leading up to the outbreak of war, it is unfortunate, although perhaps not surprising, that the availability of primary source materials is so limited. Documentary evidence from Moltke himself is scarce, and this lack of primary sources has meant that Moltke's role has been difficult to evaluate. His 'Nachlaß' in the military archive in Freiburg is relatively insubstantial and contains no private or personal accounts. His diaries have not survived, for the bulk of Moltke's papers were burned by his eldest son Wilhelm von Moltke in 1945 when the Russians reached Berlin. Even before this date, material among Moltke's papers had been selected and removed. Following Moltke's death in June 1916, his former adjutant Wilhelm von Dommes was seconded to 'select the important papers' from his possessions.[14] It is unclear what he was looking for and what he selected for removal, but it is likely that any documents relating to military matters would have been weeded out at that time. Fragments remained in the possession of Moltke's younger son Adam, and copies of some documents were made in 1933 for a planned new edition of Moltke's memoirs by Jürgen von Grone, who made this material available to the Bundesarchiv in Freiburg after the Second World War.[15]

---

[13] Reichsarchiv (ed.), *Der Weltkrieg 1914–1918*, vol. 1, *Die Grenzschlachten im Westen*, Berlin 1924, p. 180.

[14] BayHSTA-KA, NL Rudolf Ritter von Xylander, Kriegstagebücher II, HS2309, 19–20 June 1916, pp. 603–4.

[15] Egmont Zechlin, 'Ludendorff im Jahre 1915. Unveröffentlichte Briefe', *HZ*, 211, 1970, p. 318, note 10.

The edited letters and memoirs, published in 1922 by Moltke's widow under the title *Erinnerungen, Briefe, Dokumente*,[16] offer an insight into Moltke's personality, particularly in private letters to his wife. However, the edition is thoroughly unreliable. The material was both selected and heavily edited by Eliza von Moltke, and we cannot be certain how much she left out or altered. Published at a time when the question of war-guilt dominated the political agenda, it is likely that potentially 'incriminating' evidence was excluded and perhaps ultimately destroyed by Moltke's widow in an attempt to offer an apologetic account of her husband's activities. Where it is possible to compare original documents with the edition that Moltke's widow prepared, minor alterations are clearly noticeable, showing that, at best, she was no professional editor.[17]

After the death of Moltke's widow in May 1932, the papers in her possession were passed on to her daughter Astrid Gräfin von Bethusy-Huc (1882–1961), who in turn passed them on to Jürgen von Grone, a friend of the family and fellow Anthroposophist, under the condition that no material be passed on to the Anthroposophical Society in Switzerland or any other public or private institution. The documents later found their way to Thomas Meyer, who prepared an edition of the 1922 *Erinnerungen* with new additions, which he published in 1993.[18] The Rudolf Steiner

---

[16] Helmuth von Moltke, *Erinnerungen, Briefe, Dokumente 1877–1916. Ein Bild vom Kriegsausbruch, erster Kriegsführung und Persönlichkeit des ersten militärischen Führers des Krieges*, ed. Eliza von Moltke, Stuttgart 1922.

[17] Reichsarchiv, *Weltkrieg*, vol. 1, p. 63, cites one of Moltke's memoranda, and refers to the discrepancies in the *Erinnerungen* publication. That the 1922 *Erinnerungen* seem very heavily edited and contain little reliable information on the pre-war period is also emphasized by Holger H. Herwig, 'Clio Deceived', in Steven Miller *et al.* (eds.), *Military Strategy and the Origins of the First World War. An 'International Security' Reader*, Princeton 1991, p. 294. See also Isabel Hull, *The Entourage of Kaiser Wilhelm II 1888–1918*, Cambridge 1982, p. 366, note 21; John C. G. Röhl, *1914: Delusion or Design? The Testimony of Two German Diplomats*, London 1973, pp. 37–38.

[18] Thomas Meyer, *Helmuth von Moltke 1848–1916. Dokumente zu seinem Leben und Wirken*, 2 vols., Basel 1993. An English translation entitled *Light for the New Millennium: Rudolf Steiner's Association with Helmuth und Eliza von Moltke: Letters, Documents and After Death Communications* was published in 1998. Meyer made use of a several-month gap in Swiss copyright laws to edit material without seeking authorisation from surviving members of the Moltke family. In a meeting with the author in Brühl, Germany, in June 1997, Moltke's granddaughters Rose-Marie van Berghes and Marie-Liza von Bethusy-Huc expressed their outrage upon discovering that private papers, pertaining among others to their mother, Astrid von Bethusy-Huc, née Moltke, had been published without their consent. Most of Meyer's edition is of little value for historians. While a second edition of the Moltke *Erinnerungen* would be welcome (the first is very difficult to obtain today), the mistakes Meyer made in transcribing the text do not commend his edition and are evidence of the hurry he was in to meet the copyright deadline. The 'after-death communications' from Moltke to his widow via Rudolf Steiner are probably only of interest to Anthroposophists, although they shed interesting light on the link between Eliza von Moltke and Steiner. (The connection between Moltke and Steiner is more fully explored in Chapter 2 below.) Meyer further included documents from the Moltke Nachlaß in Freiburg, as well as unpublished material in family possession, making his two volumes – despite their obvious shortcomings – the most comprehensive collection of primary material pertaining to Moltke.

Nachlaß Verwaltung in Dornach, Switzerland, keeps a collection of letters exchanged between Eliza von Moltke and Rudolf Steiner, but this apparently contains no material on Helmuth von Moltke himself.[19] Because of the troubled history of the Moltke papers it is difficult to get access to what little material remains, or even to determine what is still available.

Moltke's published *Erinnerungen* replaced a pamphlet entitled 'The War-Guilt' – *Die 'Schuld' am Kriege* – written by Moltke in November 1914, which Eliza von Moltke had edited and intended to publish in 1919 with an introduction by Rudolf Steiner.[20] Steiner and Eliza von Moltke wanted to publish this justificatory account a few weeks before the Allies' meeting at Versailles. By demonstrating how chaotic military decision-making had been in the pre-war Germany, they aimed to undermine the 'war-guilt' thesis and hoped to be able to avoid the signing of the notorious paragraph 231, the 'war-guilt' clause.[21] When the contents became known to the German Foreign Office (Auswärtiges Amt) and the army, its members were anxious to prevent the publication of the pamphlet. Moltke's former adjutant, General Wilhelm von Dommes, was sent to advise Eliza von Moltke and Steiner that 'Berlin did not desire' Moltke's memoirs in print, and the publication was subsequently withdrawn. When Dommes met with Eliza von Moltke, she read the pamphlet to him and he recorded in his diary: 'Contains nasty stuff.'[22] The Auswärtiges Amt objected to the publication because of fears that details of the Schlieffen Plan, particularly regarding the violation of Holland, might be made public.[23] At a time when the Kaiser was living in uncertain circumstances in exile in Amerongen, his fate heavily dependent on continued Dutch refusal to extradite him to the Allies for trial, public knowledge of Germany's initial intention to violate not only Belgian but also Dutch neutrality could have been disastrous.[24]

---

[19] Information from Professor John Röhl, who was allowed access to the Rudolf Steiner archive and from Konrad Donat of the Steiner Nachlaß Verwaltung in Dornach, Switzerland.

[20] *Die 'Schuld' am Kriege – Betrachtungen und Erinnerungen des Generalstabchefs H. v. Moltke über die Vorgänge vom Juli 1914 bis November 1914.* The text of the pamphlet was later included in the 1922 edition of Moltke's *Erinnerungen*.

[21] See Eliza von Moltke's introduction to Moltke's *Erinnerungen*, p. VII; Jürgen von Grone, 'Zum Kriegsausbruch 1914', *Die Drei, Zeitschrift für Anthroposophie und Dreigliederung*, Herausgegeben von der Anthroposophischen Gesellschaft, Stuttgart, 1964/1, p. 3.

[22] Dommes's diary of May and June 1919, BA-MA, NL Dommes, NL512/4. Excerpts also printed by Meyer, *Helmuth von Moltke*, vol. 1, pp. 410ff., who claims that the diary is a new discovery (p. 409), when it has in fact been available in Dommes's Nachlaß in Freiburg and is no recent find.   [23] Wallach, *Dogma*, p. 127.

[24] On the Kaiser in exile following his flight from Spa on 9 November 1918, and the Dutch refusal to extradite him, see Sally Marks, '"My Name is Ozymandias". The Kaiser in Exile', *Central European History*, 16, 1983, pp. 122–170.

This lack of primary evidence is not restricted to Moltke's personal papers. Documentary source material for the German army before the First World War is in short supply, and this has impeded the work of military historians since the Second World War. Military documents relating to the Wilhelmine period are scarce, owing to the destruction of the military archive in Potsdam. However, during the last few years it has transpired that the archive was not, in fact, completely destroyed during the bombing of Potsdam in 1945, and that important military records and documents were seized by the Red Army and taken to Podolsk, south of Moscow, where many tons of material apparently still await inspection.[25] Some of these documents were returned to Potsdam in December 1988 (around 40 tons, including 3000 Prussian and German army files), and have been available to western scholars since the collapse of the GDR in 1989.[26] In 1993, the material was moved from Potsdam to Germany's military archive, the Bundesarchiv-Militärarchiv in Freiburg. The initial excitement with which scholars awaited this new material proved somewhat exaggerated: the substantial gaps in the primary source material relating to German military history of the period were not completely closed by the documents unearthed in Moscow. However, the files contain a wealth of evidence that can be used to shed light on Moltke and the General Staff during the time under investigation.

Among the files returned are those of the Kriegsgeschichtliche Forschungsanstalt des Heeres (Army Research Centre for Military History), founded in October 1919.[27] This institution consisted primarily of former members of the General Staff and the army (of the 65 members, 13 were civilians, and 52 active or retired officers),[28] and its aim was an

---

[25] Bernd Wegner, 'Deutsche Aktenbestände im Moskauer Zentralen Staatsarchiv. Ein Erfahrungsbericht', *Vierteljahreshefte für Zeitgeschichte*, 2, 1992, pp. 311–319. See also Horst Romeyk, 'Das ehemalige sowjetische Sonderarchiv in Moskau' and 'Die deutschen Bestände im Sonderarchiv in Moskau', *Der Archivar*, 45, Heft 3, July 1992.

[26] Uwe Löbel, 'Neue Forschungsmöglichkeiten zur preußisch-deutschen Heeresgeschichte', *MGM*, 51, 1992, pp. 143–149.

[27] For the history of the KGFA, see Helmut Otto, 'Der Bestand Kriegsgeschichtliche Forschungsanstalt des Heeres im Bundesarchiv-, Militärisches Zwischenarchiv Potsdam', *MGM*, 51, 1992, pp. 429–441; Adolf Brenneke, *Archivkunde. Ein Beitrag zur Theorie und Geschichte des europäischen Archivwesens*, bearb. u. ergänzt von Wolfgang Leesch, Leipzig 1953, pp. 304ff.; Karl Demeter, *Das Reichsarchiv. Tatsachen und Personen*, Frankfurt/M. 1969; Hans Schleier, *Die bürgerliche deutsche Geschichtsschreibung der Weimarer Republik*, Cologne 1975, pp. 128ff.

[28] Arden Bucholz, *Hans Delbrück and the German Military Establishment: War Images in Conflict*, Iowa City 1985, p. 142. However, according to Reinhard Brühl, 110 former officers were taken on by the archive in October 1919, 41 of whom had been members of the General Staff for over 20 years, and 54 for over ten years. Those who stayed were officially dismissed from their military duties on 31 March 1920 and became civil servants with civilian titles. Brühl, *Militärgeschichte und*

analysis of the war (preparation, planning, conduct, strategy, failures) along the lines of military history writing as it had been practised within the General Staff throughout the nineteenth century. Research was under-taken in order to publish Germany's official military history of the war. As early as in the autumn of 1914 it had been decided that a 'popular' history should be published as soon as possible, and in December 1914 the new Chief of the General Staff Erich von Falkenhayn ordered the establish-ment of a 'Kriegsnachrichtenstelle' to collect reports about various battles with the aim of using these after the war to compile an official history.[29]

After the war, the Reichsarchiv collected documentary evidence by approaching key military and political figures and assembling informa-tion based on their diaries and memoirs. The result of this work, the 'Weltkriegswerk' in 14 volumes plus two additional volumes of docu-ments, was published from 1924 onwards.[30] The archive's files, which have recently been returned to Germany, include copies and citations from documentary evidence that had been lost in the original. In addi-tion to this, they boast a collection of first-hand accounts and comments by leading military figures on controversial topics such as the outbreak of war and the lack of economic preparation for the war in peace-time, as well as major battles and certain individuals, such as Moltke. For an investigation of Moltke's role in the events leading to war in 1914, the eye-witness accounts and unpublished memoirs of his contemporaries, collected by the archive from 1919 onwards, are an invaluable source, especially in view of the otherwise limited evidence available.

footnote 28 (*cont.*)

Kriegspolitik. Zur Militärgeschichtsschreibung des preußisch-deutschen Generalstabes, 1816–1945, (East) Berlin, 1973, pp. 245–246. Even as late as 1939, of the 20 active officers that were employed as civil servants in the archive, 15 had been in the General Staff before 1918, 12 of those had been high-ranking General Staff officers. Memorandum Major a.D. Reymann, 'Wie es kam, daß wir äußerlich Zivilisten wurden', February 1939, BA-MA, W-10/50021, p. 3.

[29] See BA-MA, RH61/v. 20, KGFA, 'die Bearbeitung des Werkes "Der Weltkrieg 1914–1918"'.

[30] *Der Weltkrieg 1914–1918*, 14 vols.; *Kriegsrüstung und Kriegswirtschaft*, 2 vols. and documents, Berlin 1930. Other publications include *Die Schlachten und Gefechte des Großen Krieges 1914–1918* (1920) and *Forschungen und Darstellungen aus dem Reichsarchiv* (7 vols.) as well as the series *Schlachten des Weltkrieges* (38 vols.) and *Erinnerungsblätter deutscher Regimenter* (approx. 250 vols.). Although *Der Weltkrieg* was officially published by the Reichsarchiv and was often referred to as the 'Reichsarchivwerk', it was commonly also referred to as the 'great German General Staff work about the World War', clear evidence that the General Staff was still considered in charge of military history writing in the Reichsarchiv after Versailles. Major a.D. Reymann, February 1939, BA-MA, W-10/50021; Erich Murawski, 'Die amtliche deutsche Kriegsgeschichtsschreibung über den Ersten Weltkrieg', *Wehrwissenschaftliche Rundschau*, 9, 1959, 2 parts, pp. 513–531, 584–598; Markus Pöhlmann, 'World War Experience and Future War Images in the Official German Military History', paper delivered at the Shadows of Total War Conference, Bern, August 1999, forth-coming in Roger Chickering and Stig Förster (eds.), *The Shadows of Total War: Europe, East Asia, and the United States, 1919–1939*, Washington DC and Cambridge, Mass., 2001.

The task of the Potsdam Reichsarchiv was, in the words of one of its members, 'scientific research into and description of the period of history of the Reich that is behind us and that found its climax and its ending in the World War'.[31] In addition, it aimed to collect and administer the Reich's documents for the period since 1871 and to answer queries and give information based on that material. The source material contained in its files is not without its problems, particularly because the work of the Forschungsamt was shaped by a desire to write an apologetic history. The contributors were resentful of the Entente's victory and of the new democratic system of the Weimar Republic. They wanted to see both the monarchy and the army restored, and they were keen to prove German innocence in the events leading to the outbreak of war. In January 1919 the Potsdam archive described its purpose and intentions in a letter to the Kriegsarchiv in Munich, displaying a striking cynicism regarding Germany's future:

> To give to posterity an image of the reality of war in general, and of the events of the World War, for the glory and honour of the German people's army. They will urgently need it, when the dream of a League of Nations and of making mankind happy is over and done with, and when new problems and political crystallizations have developed which demand the conduct of that ancient form of fighting that we see around us daily. . . .[32]

Dreams of *Weltpolitik* had merely been postponed by Germany's military leaders. As August von Mackensen remarked in 1919: 'Germanness (*Deutschtum*) will not go under, but it will be a long time before it regains the position in the world that it deserves.'[33] The idea that war was the means by which Germany would regain its former powerful position is implicit in this thinking. One of the purposes of the archive was thus to keep the 'spirit of the General Staff' alive.[34]

The military influence over the newly founded archive was pronounced. Most of the archival material was of military origin, and the key positions were occupied by former members of the General Staff. The archive's first president was Hermann Ritter Mertz von Quirnheim (the last *Oberquartiermeister* of the war history section of the Great General

---

[31] Reichsministerium des Innern über Aufgaben und Entwicklung der Historischen Kommission des Reichsarchivs, quoted in Helmut Heiber, *Walter Frank und sein Reichsinstitut für Geschichte des neuen Deutschlands*, Stuttgart 1966, p. 125.

[32] Quoted in Bernd-Felix Schulte, 'Neue Dokumente zum Kriegsausbruch und Kriegsverlauf 1914', *MGM*, 1, 1979, p. 124.

[33] Theo Schwarzmüller, *Zwischen Kaiser und "Führer". Generalfeldmarschall August von Mackensen. Eine politische Biographie*, Paderborn, Munich, Vienna and Zurich 1995, p. 174.

[34] See Brühl, *Militärgeschichte*, p. 238.

Staff), and the director of the Historical Department, as well as Mertz's eventual successor, was Hans von Haeften (one of Moltke's former adjutants).[35] Although opposition to this military predominance was voiced by the Auswärtiges Amt, on the basis that history-writing should not be in the hands of the military and that political documents should be kept in a separate political archive, this was to no avail.[36] The military were adamant that the writing of military history should remain firmly in the hands of former generals, as Wilhelm von Dommes wrote to Gerhard Tappen in July 1924:

Haeften . . . wants to use the writings of the Reichsarchiv to erect a memorial to the old army – in strictest historical truth. . . . I consider it a great fortune for the old army to which we have dedicated our lives' work that the history-writing is [in his hands]. The government has caused him exceptional difficulties over the last few years. . . . The democrats want to influence history-writing along their lines (*in ihrem Sinne*). One can imagine what would have come from that.[37]

The Reichsarchiv took over research into military history from the former General Staff, and in 1924 the department was renamed 'History Department', dropping the 'war history' so as no longer to remind outsiders of the General Staff connection. Behind the scenes, however, it was openly admitted that this was merely a civilian disguise under which to continue military research and planning, despite the Versailles treaty restrictions on Germany's army.[38]

With its declared aim of maintaining the influence of Schlieffen's strategic thinking on future war planning, the Reichsarchiv became one of the main creators of the 'Schlieffen myth'.[39] In 1921, the Schlieffen Society (Schlieffenverein) was founded, consisting of former members of the General Staff, the élite of the officer corps. This 'Generalstabsvereinigung

---

[35] Hermann Ritter Mertz von Quirnheim (1866–1947) was president until 31 October 1931, and was replaced on 1 November 1931 by Hans von Haeften (1870–1937). The new director of the historical department in 1931 was Wolfgang Förster (1875–1963), who was the last president, from May 1937 until the end of the war, following Haeften's death. Otto, 'Kriegsgeschichtliche Forschungsanstalt', pp. 430ff; Brühl, *Militärgeschichte*, p. 245; Ursula von Gersdorff, 'Wolfgang Förster 85 Jahre', *Wehrwissenschaftliche Rundschau*, 10, 1960, pp. 439–440. On the history of the Reichsarchiv, see also Matthias Hermann, 'Das Reichsarchiv (1919–1945): Eine archivalische Institution im Spannungsfeld der deutschen Politik', 2 vols., Ph.D dissertation, Berlin Humboldt University 1994.   [36] See Heiber, *Walter Frank*, pp. 126–127.

[37] BA-MA, NL Tappen, N56/3, Dommes to Tappen, 22 July 1924. Groener also claimed that using the remaining General Staff officers in civilian public service positions was a way of keeping the General Staff going, if in a different guise. Groener to Ebert, 17 September 1919, quoted in Brühl, *Militärgeschichte*, p. 246.

[38] See e.g. BA-MA, W-10/50021, Major a.D. Reymann's memorandum of February, 1939, 'Wie es kam, daß wir äußerlich "Zivilisten" wurden', in which he describes the attempts at disguising the military character of the Reichsarchiv ('Die "Tarnung" im Reichsarchiv').

[39] Bucholz, *Delbrück*, p. 144.

Graf Schlieffen', as it was revealingly called by some contemporaries, was an ill-disguised attempt at getting around the Allies' prohibition of a General Staff. Under the presidency of Generalfeldmarschall von Mackensen its aim was, in his own words, to keep former members of the General Staff 'usable for war'.[40]

The files of the Reichsarchiv are thus interesting in more than one respect. Not only do they help to throw further light on German military history prior to and during the First World War, and provide much-needed documentary source material on the younger Moltke, they also shed new light on the continuity of military thinking between the Second and the Third Reich. In this context, the frequent references to a future war, in which the German army would have learned from past mistakes, make chilling reading:

Fate, in the end, denied us the right man at the right time in the decisive place and thus denied us victory. Lamenting this is no use. But we want to learn from the deeds and from the mistakes, so that we can emerge victoriously from this test when fate once again considers the German people, now purified and hardened through this trial, worthy of mastering its own fortunes.[41]

[40] Schwarzmüller, *Mackensen*, pp. 208/209.
[41] BA-MA, w-10/50951, Major von Nida, 'Der Sturm auf Lüttich nach eigenen Erlebnissen', October 1920.

CHAPTER ONE

Military decision-making in Wilhelmine Germany

The importance and extent of the role of the Chief of the General Staff can be understood only in the context of the complicated system of military decision-making that was characteristic of Imperial Germany. It was determined by two elements in particular: the Kaiser's extensive and almost unchecked power, and the polycratic structure of the army, in which rival centres of authority were often in direct competition with one another. This chapter will analyse the organization of the German army as essential background to an understanding of Helmuth von Moltke's role and the limitations of his position. Given his impressive title and the fact that historians have so often focused on the General Staff in their investigations of the German army, it is easy to form the impression that this post was the most important and most influential military position in the German Empire. Certainly, this is what contemporaries in the General Staff claimed.[1] However, the Great General Staff did not have sole control over the army. There were many competing bodies, each with their own wide-ranging authority, and ultimately any person's influence depended on his standing with the monarch. This important fact is vital in understanding the limitations and constraints of Moltke's position. The Great General Staff created Germany's strategy, it devised the annual mobilization plan and had to ensure that the army was ready for war at all times. However, military doctrine was created by the Ministry of War and the corps commanders, who had immediate access to the Kaiser. The structure of the armed forces was also ultimately decided by the Minister of War, who was responsible for presenting demands for army increases to the Reichstag. Important appointments were decided by the Kaiser's Military Cabinet, independently of both the General Staff and the Ministry of War. This chapter will examine the nature of the competition between these different

---

[1] Wilhelm Groener regarded the position of Chief of the General Staff as the most honourable in the world. *Der Feldherr wider Willen*, p. xii.

military bodies, before moving on to an analysis of the Great General Staff as a military institution.

Prussia and the military seem almost synonymous; it is difficult to think of one without the other. In Prussia, and from 1871 in the united Germany under Prussian suzerainty, the military played a prominent part in everyday life. For many Germans, it was thanks to the army and the victorious wars of unification that Germany had become a unified state and begun her ascent to the status of a major European power. During Wilhelm II's reign, this overemphasis on all things military became particularly pronounced, thanks not least to the Kaiser, whose upbringing had been steeped in military tradition, and who regarded himself as a second Frederick the Great, and as a result aspired to lead 'his' army personally.[2] Not suprisingly, Bismarck, the founding father of the new Reich, had considered it imperative to wear a uniform in public, as did many other high-ranking civilians at the time. The importance of the uniform in Wilhelmine Germany cannot be overstated, and the often-cited example of the 'Hauptmann von Köpenick' illustrates the extent of this.[3] While the military's role and fatal influence in the political system of Imperial Germany seem without parallel vis-à-vis her European neighbours (although, as Jacob Vogel emphasizes, comparative studies in this area are still lacking), the role of the military in public life, the importance of parades and military festivities, was as pronounced in parliamentary France as it was in monarchist Germany. The idea of a German *Sonderweg* seems problematic given such parallels. The overemphasis on the military was much less a 'specific phenomenon of German society' than the result of a process of nationalization and militarization which can be regarded as a general development of European society in the late nineteenth

---

[2] See e.g. Wiegand Schmidt-Richberg, 'Die Regierungszeit Wilhelms II', in Militärgeschichtliches Forschungsamt (ed.), *Handbuch zur deutschen Militärgeschichte 1648–1939*, vol. 5, *Von der Entlassung Bismarcks bis zum Ende des Ersten Weltkrieges (1890–1918)*, Frankfurt/M. 1968, p. 32, who argues, however, that this 'overestimation of the military' must not be confused with 'militant spirit'. 'The excesses of militarism, such as the exaggerated cult of uniforms, the overestimation and copying of military manners might have seemed bizarre and obtrusive to foreign onlookers', he maintains, 'but were really more trivialities (*Äußerlichkeiten*).' However, it could be argued that the effect and influence of such views on the public attitude as a whole was far more decisive than Schmidt-Richberg estimates, especially from 1911 onwards. Without such 'overestimation of the military', its decisive influence over political decision-making would not have been possible. On the Kaiser's childhood, see John Röhl, *Wilhelm II. Die Jugend des Kaisers, 1859–1888*, Munich 1993; English edition *Young Wilhelm*, Cambridge 1998.

[3] The story of the unemployed cobbler Wilhelm Voigt, who bought a second-hand uniform and managed to occupy the Köpenick town hall, based solely on the authority that the uniform lent him, captures perfectly the importance of military authority in Imperial Germany.

century.[4] Where Germany differed, and was perhaps even unique, was in the extent of the Kaiser's role: his exaggerated influence was seldom moderated by outside forces.

It was perhaps a bad omen that the second German Reich, the united Germany, had been founded on the basis of three wars. With hindsight it seems as if no peaceful existence could have resulted from such aggressive beginnings. The wars of unification allowed the military to assume an exaggerated role in the new Reich. They also paved the way for the General Staff's increase in power and importance, based on the successes achieved under the leadership of the elder Moltke.[5] The General Staff acquired an almost 'mythical status' and its officers were regarded as the 'crème de la crème' among the German military.[6] At the same time, officers who had taken an oath to their king conceived of themselves as a separate caste, above the ordinary civilian citizen. This position of perceived superiority in turn helped to ensure first that the military were largely regarded with great admiration, and secondly that they were able to fulfil the demands of their changing domestic role within Wilhelmine Germany. If need be, they would have to protect the monarch from external and internal threats.[7]

Article 63 of the new constitution of 1871 ruled that the previously separate German armies were to form one Imperial German army, the Reichsheer under the supreme command of the German Kaiser.[8] However, in peace-time some contingent armies retained their own military administration and jealously guarded this independence. Among them, the Bavarian army enjoyed the most wide-ranging special rights, such as organizational independence in peace-time and a separate General Staff, War Academy and Ministry of War. Regarding organizational matters, concessions had also been made to Württemberg,

---

[4] Jacob Vogel, *Nationen im Gleichschritt. Der Kult der 'Nationen in Waffen' in Deutschland und Frankreich, 1871–1914*, Göttingen 1997, pp. 11, 19, 28off.   [5] Otto, *Schlieffen und der Generalstab*, p. 18.

[6] Bucholz, *Moltke*, pp. 39, 13.

[7] Gotthard Breit, *Das Staats- und Gesellschaftsbild deutscher Generale beider Weltkriege im Spiegel ihrer Memoiren*, Boppard/Rhein 1973, p. 21. On the army's domestic role, see Wilhelm Deist, 'Die Armee in Staat und Gesellschaft 1890–1914', in Michael Stürmer (ed.), *Das kaiserliche Deutschland. Politik und Gesellschaft, 1870–1918*, Düsseldorf 1970, p. 318.

[8] For the following see Ernst Huber, *Deutsche Verfassungsgeschichte seit 1789*, vol. 3, *Bismarck und das Reich*, Stuttgart, 1963, p. 989, pp. 992–1002; Walther Hubatsch, 'Die Verwaltung des Militärwesens 1867–1918', in *Deutsche Verwaltungsgeschichte*, ed. Kurt G. A. Jeserich, Hans Pohl and Georg-Christoph von Unruh, vol. 3: *Das Deutsche Reich bis zum Ende der Monarchie*, Stuttgart 1984, pp. 316–317; Friedrich Hossbach, *Die Entwicklung des Oberbefehls über das Heer in Brandenburg, Preussen und im Deutschen Reich von 1655 bis 1945*, Würzburg 1957, pp. 36ff. The present book cannot address in more general terms the constitution of the Reich or its structures. A helpful summary can be found in Thomas Nipperdey, *Deutsche Geschichte 1866–1918*, 2 vols., Munich 1992, vol. 2, *Machtstaat vor der Demokratie*, pp. 85ff.

Saxony, Hessen and, to a lesser degree, other states.[9] Co-ordination among the contingent armies was achieved with the help of military plenipotentiaries, exchanged between the provincial capitals and Berlin. Between Prussia, Saxony and Württemberg this exchange of information was much more successful than between Prussia and Bavaria, again because the Bavarian army carefully guarded its independence. Actual unity of the German army was only finally achieved and consolidated on the battlefields of the First World War, although tensions remained throughout between Prussian and non-Prussian officers.[10] During the war, the Kaiser's right to supreme command over the Imperial army overruled any special peace-time rights that had existed for the contingents. As Prussia's army and military constitution provided the model for the Imperial army, and Prussian military law was introduced in non-Prussian contingents after 1871, the German army after 1871 was much more Prussian than German in character, and the Prussian army corps far outweighed the others.[11] In 1871, there were 14 army corps from Prussia, two from Bavaria and one each from Saxony and Württemberg. By 1914, these numbers had increased to 19 Prussian, three Bavarian, two Saxon and still only one from Württemberg – 25 in total. Prussia's share in the Reichsheer was over 75 per cent.[12] The predominantly Prussian character of the German army was further heightened by the fact that the Prussian King, in his role as German Kaiser, carried the title of 'Supreme War-Lord' (*Oberster Kriegsherr*) and possessed the right of supreme command over the army in times of war.

It was the Kaiser's role in military decision-making that determined how the different military institutions, the Great General Staff, the Prussian Ministry of War and the Military Cabinet, interacted with each other and conducted their business. The Kaiser's *Kommandogewalt* (power to command) was one way of reducing civilian interference in the army. Wilhelm II appointed key figures, such as the Imperial Chancellor, the Prussian Minister of War and the Chief of the Great General Staff, without having to consult anyone. He was in charge of all military appointments, usually acting upon the advice of his Military Cabinet.

[9] Friedrich-Christian Stahl, 'Preußische Armee und Reichsheer 1871–1914', in Oswald Hauser (ed.), *Zur Problematik 'Preußen und das Reich'*, Cologne 1984, p. 191. On the Bavarian Army, see Frederick Francis Campbell, 'The Bavarian Army, 1870–1918: The Constitutional and Structural Relations with the Prussian Military Establishment', Ph.D. Dissertation, Ohio State University 1972. See also BayHSTA-KA, MKr1, 'Deutsche Reichsverfassung mit den Sonderbestimmungen für Bayern'.   [10] See also Stahl, 'Preußische Armee', pp. 191, 238.
[11] Huber, *Deutsche Verfassungsgeschichte*, vol. 3, p. 994.
[12] Stahl, 'Preußische Armee', pp. 195–196.

In addition, he was entitled to make decisions on organizational matters concerning the army, such as training, discipline, promotions or deciding to what uses to put the troops.[13] It was his right to declare war and conclude peace, although both required the Chancellor's countersignature. Similarly, decisions relating to military administration and the budget, such as the size of the army, equipment, supplies and so on, required the countersignature of either the Chancellor or the Prussian Minister of War.

While the Kaiser was keen to exercise his influence in civilian as well as military matters, it was in the realm of the army that he was most involved. He considered himself primarily a military man, and valued his military staff highly. In contrast with the civilian leaders, who were ultimately answerable to the Reichstag, his military entourage were relatively free from such constraints. Ultimately, Wilhelm II had nothing but contempt for civilians, an attitude which was largely shared within the military. In his post-war memoirs, Wilhelm Groener came to regret this military disregard for politicians and diplomats, although he assumed that the attitude of French, English or German officers towards civilians would have been similar. 'However', he concluded, 'to our own detriment we allowed this military animosity against diplomacy and politics to become too pronounced before and during the war.'[14] Moreover, in a country where the military were able to influence policy and decision-making to such a large degree, such pronounced dislike was to prove more dangerous than, for example, in Britain and France.

Because of the Kaiser's determination to lead 'his' army personally, although he lacked the necessary skills to do so, the German army was in most matters dependent on his often whimsical and usually ill-informed opinions, and as a result clearly suffered from a lack of coherent leadership. Wilhelm II did not have the patience or skill to attend to matters of real importance, and instead occupied himself with superficialities, such as uniform changes and parades. As Count Zedlitz-Trützschler complained in his diary of 1904: 'We are currently, for example, occupied with the 37th change of uniforms since the accession to the throne!'[15] The Kaiser enjoyed interfering in army manoeuvres and exercises despite his obvious lack of talent and knowledge, and was

---

[13] Schmidt-Richberg, *Handbuch*, p. 62.   [14] Groener, *Lebenserinnerungen*, p. 60.
[15] Robert Graf von Zedlitz-Trützschler, *Zwölf Jahre am deutschen Kaiserhof*, Stuttgart 1924, p. 61 (English translation *Twelve Years at the Imperial German Court*, London 1924). Zedlitz-Trützschler was the Kaiser's *Hofmarschall* until his resignation in May 1910 on the grounds of irreconcileable differences with the Kaiser. His memoirs provide a critical insight into his time at court.

usually unopposed in this by his subordinates. This situation only improved after 1906 with the appointment as Chief of the General Staff of the younger Moltke, who made it a condition of his appointment that the army manoeuvres be transformed into a more useful exercise by limiting the Kaiser's involvement.[16]

Perhaps worse still, in order to retain his influence over military matters, the Kaiser actively encouraged the already existing division between the command and administrative structures in the army and even introduced the same dual system into the navy in 1889.[17] In place of the Admiralty Staff, the body that had so far been solely responsible for naval matters of command and administration, he created a Supreme Command (*Oberkommando*) for command, the Reich Navy Office (*Reichs-Marineamt*) for naval administration, and the Imperial Navy Cabinet (*Kaiserliches Marinekabinett*), modelled on the already existing Military Cabinet. Jörg-Uwe Fischer sees the reason for this in the Kaiser's desire to rule over 'his' army and 'his' navy personally, arguing that the Kaiser could not consent to allowing an influential position like that of Chief of the Admiralty Staff to exist 'between himself and his favourite creation'.[18] Because there already existed a similar division between the various military institutions, there was no danger of the Chief of the General Staff assuming such an important role, either. The Kaiser's desire to consolidate and extend his personal influence thus had a detrimental effect on both the army and the navy. Increasing fragmentation of the army's structure removed any unity from the military leadership.[19] As a result, co-ordination of strategy or policy between the

---

[16] The Kaiser's interferences in manoevres are detailed in Chapter 2.

[17] See Rudolf Schmidt-Bückeburg, *Das Militärkabinett der preußischen Könige und deutschen Kaiser, Seine geschichtliche Entwicklung und staatsrechtliche Stellung 1787–1918*, Berlin 1933, pp. 180–182. Caprivi resigned as leader of the navy when he failed to prevent the introduction of dualism into its leadership, for he recognized it 'immediately as a fateful mistake'. See also Jörg-Uwe Fischer, *Admiral des Kaisers. Georg Alexander von Müller als Chef des Marinekabinetts Wilhelms II.*, Frankfurt/M. 1992, p. 34; Walther Hubatsch, *Der Admiralstab und die obersten Marinebehörden in Deutschland 1848–1945*, Frankfurt/M. 1958, p. 49; idem, 'Verwaltung', p. 326. See Carl-Axel Gemzell, *Organization, Conflict, and Innovation. A Study of German Naval Strategic Planning, 1888–1948*, Lund, Sweden, 1973, p. 39 for a diagram of the naval hierarchy before and after Wilhelm II's changes.

[18] Fischer, *Admiral des Kaisers*, pp. 29–30. The Kaiser's Cabinet order of 14 March 1899 reveals how he conceived of his position: 'After having decided to exercise the supreme command over My navy, just as over My army, personally, I do not consider it practical that there should exist between Myself and the separate leaders a central institution of command, which would after all only have the purpose of delivering My orders.' Quoted in Ernst Huber, *Heer und Staat in der deutschen Geschichte*, Hamburg 1943, p. 358. See also Hubatsch, 'Verwaltung', pp. 310–332. Alfred von Tirpitz also describes the negative results of this 'Kabinettsregierung' and division of power in his *Erinnerungen*, Leipzig 1919, pp. 38–9.

[19] See also Schmidt-Bückeburg, *Militärkabinett*, p. 187.

army and the navy became impossible. Rivalries over the limited budget available to both institutions, and over the Kaiser's favour, impeded effective planning between the two. The Kaiser could have instigated co-operation, but, for reasons already described, he reinforced existing rivalries rather than trying to bridge the gaps.[20] Instead, owing to the Kaiser's influence, for many years Germany spent most of her defence budget on building a navy to challenge British supremacy, although she was a land power. Strategically, the naval expenditure made little sense, because a future war would be decided on land. However, as long as the Kaiser favoured the naval policy of Admiral von Tirpitz, no one was in a position to change his mind.

In an attempt to reduce the existing antagonism between the General Staff and the Admiralty Staff, the two institutions regularly exchanged officers. In practice, this did not always create the mutual understanding it was intended to achieve, nor did it reduce the rivalry between the two institutions. In 1906 *Korvettenkapitän* Freiherr von Keyserlingk was seconded to the deployment department of the General Staff, where he found himself facing criticism from members of the General Staff, who lacked any good will towards the navy. They reproached the navy for its apparent lack of 'offensive spirit', which, according to the General Staff, was in stark contrast to the large budget that the navy had been granted. Keyserlingk felt in turn that Schlieffen's influence, his insistence on the offensive even from a position of inferiority, and his repeated reassurances that all was well despite worsening military conditions, had impaired the General Staff's sense of judgement.[21]

Many of the leading officers were well aware of the Kaiser's shortcomings. Yet this never made them question their duties to the monarch or forget the oath 'With God for King and Fatherland' that every officer had taken, and that applied in peace-time as much as during the war. In particular the higher ranks of the army felt a strong sense of allegiance

---

[20] See also Wiegand Schmidt-Richberg, *Die Generalstäbe in Deutschland 1871–1945: Aufgaben in der Armee und Stellung im Staate*, Stuttgart 1962, p. 19. While Schmidt-Richberg asserts that only the Kaiser could have changed the situation, he stops short of saying that the Kaiser, by virtue of his personality, was entirely unable to do so.

[21] Keyserlingk's memorandum, 1 November 1906, quoted in Hubatsch, *Admiralstab*, p. 129. Ludendorff spent almost four months on the Admiralty Staff and in the navy in 1905. F. Uhle-Wettler, *Erich Ludendorff in seiner Zeit. Soldat, Stratege, Revolutionär. Eine Neubewertung*, Berg 1995, pp. 53–4. Groener also spent some time with the navy, having served on board S.M.S. *Pommern* for several weeks in the summer of 1908: *Lebenserinnerungen*, p. 123. Moltke's *Erinnerungen* offer no evidence that he might have spent time with the navy. Members of the Bavarian General Staff were also seconded to navy manoeuvres and journeys – although they had to meet their own expenses for these trips. See BayHSTA-KA, Generalstab, 324.

to their King (in Bavaria, Württemberg and Saxony it was to their own king that most allegiance was felt). In the more prestigious regiments (particularly the *Garderegimenter*), officers would have been in frequent touch with their monarch, thus re-emphasizing their special bond.[22] Generalfeldmarschall Erich von Manstein remembered the attitude in the Imperial Army in his memoirs, pointing out how inextricably linked the Prussian army and the monarch had been. The oath sworn by soldiers had created an ethical bond between them and their 'Supreme War-Lord'. Abstract concepts such as the state did not enter into the equation, and neither did the personality of the king. 'One did not serve Wilhelm II, one served the King.'[23] Thus, it was beside the point if the individual felt critical towards the monarch he was serving. Obedience was demanded vis-à-vis the institution of the monarchy, rather than to any individual king. Minister of War Karl von Einem's memoirs emphasize a similar view. While, for example, the military leaders regretted the dismissal of Bismarck and disagreed with the Kaiser's decision, they would never have voiced their criticism publicly:

We considered it a human and historic tragedy that the founder of the Reich, who had done so much for the army, was forced to leave his creation. But we were too firmly embedded in the monarchical conviction to have voiced our criticism publicly; after all, we were soldiers and furthermore we believed in our Kaiser.[24]

Even the highest-ranking military leaders were willing to accommodate the Kaiser, for reasons of loyalty that may be difficult to comprehend today. Interference from outside the military sphere was regarded as a threat to the military order, and from within the military criticism was unlikely, not only in the light of the feelings expressed in Manstein's illuminating memoirs, but also in view of the fact that one's army career would have been jeopardized by overt criticism of the system and its leader.

The Kaiser exercised his *Kommandogewalt* with the help of men, usually generals, in *Immediatstellen*, that is positions with direct access to the monarch. In the early days of the Reich, these had only been the Minister of War and the commanding generals of the army corps.[25] The

---

[22] See Breit, *Staats- und Gesellschaftsbild*, p. 21.

[23] Erich von Manstein, *Aus einem Soldatenleben 1887–1939*, Bonn 1959, pp. 51ff. Quoted in Breit, *Staats- und Gesellschaftsbild*, p. 21.

[24] Generaloberst von Einem, *Erinnerungen eines Soldaten 1853–1933*, 2nd edn Leipzig 1933, p. 40.

[25] Schmidt-Richberg, *Generalstäbe*, p. 16. The commanding generals occupied the highest peacetime command in the German army, and the importance of their position was both emphasized and heightened by their immediate access to the monarch. They were in charge of training and commanding the troops, and answered only to the King.

Chief of the General Staff was granted the right of direct access in 1883 – the year which marked the beginning of the rivalry between the Minister of War and the Chief of the General Staff. Until that date, the General Staff had been nominally subordinate to the Minister, being only a department within the Ministry of War.[26] However, Wilhelm von Hahnke complained after the war that Schlieffen, having been 'merely' Chief of the General Staff, had apparently never enjoyed sole access to the Kaiser, but that traditionally the Minister of War and the Chief of the Military Cabinet had always been present. In addition, Wilhelm II had often asked the commander of his Headquarters to attend.[27] *Immediatrecht* (the right of direct access) did not therefore necessarily equal private access to the Kaiser. Waldersee, Schlieffen's predecessor, had enjoyed the privilege of being alone with the Kaiser. It is likely that the same right was not granted to Schlieffen because he was not the Kaiser's friend. With Waldersee, on the other hand, the Kaiser had a close relationship that went back to the 1880s, when Waldersee had assumed a position of importance resembling that of a father figure.[28] The younger Moltke, too, was granted private and immediate access to the Kaiser on account of their close personal relationship. Personal patronage was thus in many ways as important as official authority.

The number of *Immediatstellen* had already been increased under Wilhelm I, but under his grandson it reached over 40 within the army alone (there was a similar number of *Immediatstellen* within the Navy).[29] In military matters, immediate right of access was granted to the Chancellor, the Minister of War, the Chief of the General Staff, the Chiefs of the Military and Naval Cabinets, the State Secretary of the Imperial Naval Office, the Commanding Admiral and the president of the Imperial Military Court, to name but the most important.[30] Further right to immediate access was enjoyed by the commanding generals of the army corps, who numbered 25 in 1912.[31] Not all the *Immediatstellen* conferred equal status, but where they did, rivalries often occurred.[32] Internal power struggles were frequent, as the various *Immediatstellen* vied for royal favours and regarded themselves as being in competition for

[26] See H. O. Meisner, *Militärattachés und Militärbevollmächtigte in Preußen und im Deutschen Reich*, Berlin 1957, p. 53.   [27] BA-MA, NL Hahnke, N36/12, pp. 3–4.
[28] On Waldersee's role in Prince Wilhelm's formative years, see Röhl, *Wilhelm II. Die Jugend des Kaisers*, pp. 495ff., 599ff.
[29] Schmidt-Richberg, *Handbuch*, p. 62; Hossbach, *Entwicklung*, p. 51.
[30] Schmidt-Bückeburg, *Militärkabinett*, p. 187.
[31] Huber, *Deutsche Verfassungsgeschichte*, vol. 4, *Struktur und Krisen des Kaiserreichs*, Stuttgart 1969, p. 524.
[32] Schmidt-Richberg, *Generalstäbe*, p. 17.

funds and prestige. They also 'competed' to determine what would be Germany's best military strategy for the future. Only the fact that certain holders of *Immediatstellen* had regular meetings with the Kaiser due to their special responsibilities (War Ministry, Military Cabinet, General Staff) prevented even more disjointed decision-making in this decentralized military structure.[33]

In addition to the *Immediatstellen*, the Kaiser's military entourage consisted of general adjutants, generals à la suite, aides-de-camp (*Flügeladjutanten*), the Chiefs of the Navy and Military Cabinet and the entire Military Cabinet,[34] that is, military men close to the Kaiser and with immediate access to him, often on a daily basis. The so-called military headquarters (*Königliches Hauptquartier*) was made up of those generals, adjutants and aides-de-camps who were in personal service to the Kaiser, plus the commanders of the *Schlossgardekompagnie*, the *Leibgendarmerie*, and the headquarters.[35] All in all, total numbers varied between 20 men in the military entourage when Wilhelm II acceded to the throne, and 44 in 1914.

Wilhelm's military entourage consisted largely of men whom the Kaiser had known personally prior to their appointment, for, particularly in positions close to him, his 'desire for the familiar face'[36] determined his choice. Helmuth von Moltke became one of the Kaiser's personal adjutants in 1891, and was from then on in almost daily contact with the monarch.[37] As Isabel Hull shows, the *Flügeladjutanten* had to adhere to strict codes of conduct. Even criticism of one's immediate superior was ruled out, and it was of course impossible for anyone to criticize the Kaiser, especially given the fact that one's position ultimately depended on his favour. Many of these officers occupied either military or diplomatic offices (as ambassadors, military plenipotentiaries or attachés), and as such helped to extend the Kaiser's self-centred style of governing from military to political matters. In particular his much-favoured *Flügeladjutanten* – whom Wilhelm II regarded as the élite[38] – considered themselves to be able to run politics better than the despised diplomats of the Auswärtiges Amt, and intervened frequently. Their close relationship with the Kaiser allowed them to report directly to the monarch, especially in the early days of his reign, when many of them had been his acquaintances from his army regiment. In later years, the

---

[33] Schmidt-Richberg, *Handbuch*, p. 62.   [34] Stahl, 'Preußische Armee', p. 202.
[35] For this and the following information, see Hull, *Entourage*, pp. 175ff.
[36] Ibid., p. 189.   [37] See also Chapter 2.
[38] Schmidt-Bückeburg, *Militärkabinett*, p. 195.

increasing age gap and decreasing familiarity led to less informality.[39] It was at the monarch's discretion whether or not to inform other authorities, such as the Minister of War or the Chancellor of their news. This *Adjutantenpolitik* significantly impeded the relationship of the Auswärtiges Amt with the Kaiser.[40]

By 1895, the aides-de-camp had become so involved in policy-making that they appeared, in Holstein's words, like 'an organized secondary government'. Count Münster at the German embassy in Paris asked sarcastically: 'Why is there still a Wilhelmstrasse if official business is to be divided up among the Aides-de-Camp?'[41] Wilhelm II's military entourage provided an important level of decision-making, both military and political, which was removed from the control of parliament or any civilian institution. For the Kaiser, this was one of the means by which he secured and extended his influence. At times, Wilhelm's *Flügeladjutanten* even helped determine his decisions against the advice of the Military Cabinet or the General Staff, as in the case of Moltke's appointment.[42]

Although the Kaiser was in theory the head of the army, there was no uniform army leadership. Instead, different military institutions and individuals vied with each other for influence and envied each other's positions. Apart from the three main military bodies, the Ministry of War, the Military Cabinet, and the General Staff, the commanding generals of the 25 army corps were an important, although often overlooked, part of military planning. They liaised directly with the Kaiser in questions of command, and they reigned supreme over the army corps that they commanded.[43] It was the corps commanders who commanded and trained the troops and who were at the forefront of developing new military doctrine. The commanding generals, rather than the General Staff, determined how the German army fought. Much of the debate about doctrine and tactics in German military circles was led by these generals, men such as Colmar von der Goltz, Friedrich von Bernhardi, Sigismund von Schlichting and others. Many of the tasks one would perhaps associate with General Staff work were actually part of

[39] Josef Stürgkh, *Im Deutschen Großen Hauptquartier*, Leipzig 1921, p. 25; Hull, *Entourage*, p. 205.

[40] Stahl, 'Preußische Armee', p. 202; Schmidt-Bückeburg, *Militärkabinett*, pp. 195–196.

[41] Both Münster and Holstein are quoted in John Röhl, *Germany without Bismarck. The Crisis of Government in the Second Reich, 1890–1900*, London 1967, p. 161.

[42] H. O. Meisner (ed.), *Denkwürdigkeiten des Generalfeldmarschalls A. Grafen von Waldersee*, 3 vols., Stuttgart 1923–1925 (cited as Waldersee, *Denkwürdigkeiten*), vol. 3, pp. 224–225. See Chapter 2 below.

[43] Ludwig Rüdt von Collenberg, *Die Deutsche Armee von 1871 bis 1914*. Forschungen und Darstellungen aus dem Reichsarchiv, 4, Berlin, 1922, p. 9; Paul Schneider, *Die Organisation des Heeres*, Berlin 1931, p. 66.

the domain of the commanding generals. By virtue of their direct access to the Kaiser, they added another layer to the complicated and deliberately multi-faceted decision-making structure of Imperial Germany. Co-operation and co-ordination of policy were difficult, if not at times impossible, in this system which allowed for secrecy and circumvention of even the most important decision-makers. While such a system might have benefited the Kaiser in his ill-fated desire to direct 'his' army, the various competing elements, examined in more detail below, suffered under the lack of coherent leadership.[44]

THE PRUSSIAN GENERAL STAFF ESTABLISHES ITS INDEPENDENCE

As part of Scharnhorst's military reforms in the early part of the nineteenth century, the body of military advisers that had been known as the '*Generalquartiermeisterstab*' (later Generalstab) had been integrated within the Prussian Ministry of War. However, by 1821 a process of separation from that body had begun: General von Müffling was appointed 'Chief of the General Staff of the Army' outside the Ministry of War. By 1825, the Staff was formally a separate institution, but its chief had no right of immediate access to the King, and all orders and suggestions of the Staff had to travel via the Ministry of War. The Minister of War remained the Chief of Staff's superior, and the main military adviser to the King until as late as 1864.[45] A letter from the elder Moltke, dated April 1864, outlines the position of impotence of the Chief of Staff at that time:

It often happens that my expert opinion in the most important matters is demanded suddenly, while on another occasion it is not considered necessary to inform me of an intended decision, or even one that has already been made. Therefore I have to attempt at least to keep myself informed of things by way of private correspondence.[46]

In the early stages of the war of 1866, Moltke succeeded in gaining control over military operations, and was authorized for the duration of the war to give orders directly to the troops, while merely informing the Minister of War of his instructions. For the first time, an immediate link of command between the Chief of Staff and the commanding generals had been created. His victorious campaigns helped Moltke to establish

---

[44] See Deist, 'Die Armee in Staat und Gesellschaft', p. 316
[45] See Huber, *Heer und Staat*, pp. 338ff. for this and the following.
[46] Moltke to Oberst v. Blumenthal, 28 April 1864, quoted in ibid., p. 340.

the authority that was needed for his 'usurpation' of military power and influence.

The wars of 1870–1871 finally consolidated the Chief of Staff's independence, not least because Moltke's victories thrust the General Staff into the limelight. He retained in peace-time the influential position he had gained during the war. He was solely responsible for the tactical and strategic preparations for war and for the training and education of the higher-ranking officers of the General Staff, and served as the Kaiser's immediate adviser in operational matters. However, in financial matters he was still required to co-operate with the Minister of War, for the latter remained responsible for negotiating the military budget in the Reichstag. In 1883, a permanent right of immediate access was granted to the Chief of Staff, extending his position of influence even further. The Great General Staff (*Großer Generalstab*) had emancipated itself from the Ministry of War.[47] This new position of importance also manifested itself in the increasing number of General Staff officers, and in the new General Staff building that was erected opposite the Reichstag behind the Brandenburg Gate.[48]

It was not Moltke, however, who increased the General Staff's powers even further, but his ambitious subordinate Count Alfred von Waldersee. Moltke made little use of his *Immediatrecht*. Waldersee, however, who came to undertake more and more of the day-to-day General Staff work as the ageing Moltke became less of a leader and more of a figurehead, arranged regular audiences with the Kaiser whenever Moltke was away from Berlin.[49] Because of his close friendship with Wilhelm II, first as Prince and then as Kaiser, Waldersee was able to win his support for his plans for the further development of the General Staff. After Wilhelm succeeded his father in 1888, Waldersee became the new Chief of Staff, and as such perhaps the most influential person around the Kaiser at that time, enjoying the confidence of both Wilhelm and his wife. Due to the Kaiser's dislike of attending to his 'duties', most ministers, with the exception of the Minister of War, found it difficult to get an opportunity to discuss their affairs with him. Waldersee, however, had no difficulty in arranging audiences.

[47] See e.g. Schmidt-Bückeburg, *Militärkabinett*, p. 150; Schmidt-Richberg, *Generalstäbe*, p. 16.
[48] Walter Görlitz, *Der Deutsche Generalstab. Geschichte und Gestalt*, Frankfurt/M. 1950, p. 123. When the elder Moltke became Chief of Staff in 1857, there were 64 General Staff officers. In 1877 that number had increased to 135 and by 1888 it had reached 239.
[49] Schmidt-Bückeburg, *Militärkabinett*, p. 152; Hossbach, *Entwicklung*, p. 48. On Waldersee, see also Görlitz, *Generalstab*, pp. 138ff.

As the Kaiser's special confidant, Waldersee's influence was not restricted to military matters. He was able to discuss and influence the Kaiser in political matters, and seems to have had some say in the developments leading to Bismarck's dismissal. During the 'Waldersee era' the General Staff was also able to consolidate its new position of influence.[50] Waldersee's scheming included first of all the appointment of a new Minister of War. A change of minister would increase Waldersee's own power as the new Chief of the General Staff, and he aimed to reduce the Ministry of War to an administrative body. Training and appointments to higher posts were to become the General Staff's domain.[51] Waldersee's short time in office provides a perfect example of the way power was exercised and important appointments were made in Wilhelmine Germany. Waldersee's preferred successor to Minister of War Paul Bronsart von Schellendorf was General Julius von Verdy du Vernois. Waldersee had ascertained during his negotiations with Verdy that he would not object to Waldersee's attempts to reduce the Minister's powers. After a few months in office, however, even the pliable Verdy began to object to further curbing of his responsibilities and to the Kaiser's independent decision-making.[52] In October 1890, the Kaiser replaced Verdy with Hans von Kaltenborn-Stachau. By this time the position of Minister of War had been thoroughly devalued, and even Waldersee became concerned that things might have gone too far, for the Kaiser increasingly seemed to want to become his own Chief of Staff.[53]

Waldersee's plotting to increase the General Staff's power ultimately back-fired. He had attempted to elevate the military above the political leadership, but his political aspirations eventually appeared threatening to the Kaiser. After Waldersee had criticized the Kaiser's performance during the 1891 manoeuvres, the monarch had him removed to a corps command in 1891.[54] The Kaiser did indeed desire to be his own Chief of Staff as well as his own Chancellor. He would not tolerate among his immediate subordinates a man who was trying to amass powers and establish the kind of position of authority to which Waldersee was aspiring. Rather than having one influential military figure beneath him, the

---

[50] Huber, *Heer und Staat*, p. 349; Schmidt-Bückeburg, *Militärkabinett*, p. 183.

[51] See ibid, pp. 165ff. for the following.

[52] One example of this was the Kaiser's decision to move an infantry brigade to Berlin to counter civil unrest, without consulting Verdy or the Chancellor. Ibid., p. 189.

[53] See e.g. ibid, pp. 191–192.

[54] Huber, *Heer und Staat*, p. 349. In 1900, Wilhelm had appointed him Commander-in-Chief for the China expedition following the Boxer Rebellion. Röhl, *Germany without Bismarck*, p. 268.

Kaiser preferred to divide powers among a number of generals. Of course, the Chancellor and Minister of War were also in favour of the dismissal of Waldersee, as they wanted to curb the development of any political ambitions within the General Staff, and to limit the powers that the Chief of the General Staff had acquired.[55] In 1891, Waldersee was replaced by Count Alfred von Schlieffen, who was a better candidate in the Kaiser's opinion, because he lacked all political ambition.[56] Before the work of the Great General Staff is investigated in more detail, its 'rival' institutions, the Prussian Ministry of War and the Military Cabinet, as well as the role of the commanding generals, must first be examined.

THE PRUSSIAN MINISTRY OF WAR

In this complicated system, dominated by the Kaiser's interference, the General Staff had to work alongside the Prussian Ministry of War, the longest established of Prussia's military institutions. Founded by Scharnhorst in 1809, it was originally the central body of the Prussian army. In 1809 it was responsible for the entire military administration, and was 'in all military matters the King's highest military institution'.[57] Decentralization of military power and pluralism of *Kommandostellen* (positions of command) had in part been blamed for Prussia's collapse in 1806, and Scharnhorst's reforms aimed to establish a more functional military set-up by providing a central military body which was equipped with all the necessary responsibilities. However, the system did not stay intact for long. In the first half of the nineteenth century the powers of the Ministry of War were already beginning to be eroded, shifting to both the developing Military Cabinet and the General Staff. While the Minister of War was still the King's key adviser in the war of 1864, when war broke out in 1866 the elder Moltke, as Chief of Staff, managed to gain independent power to command the army, establishing a position equal to that of the Minister of War.[58] After 1871, the responsibilities of the Ministry were further reduced, as the General Staff and Military Cabinet asserted themselves and claimed increasing shares in the Ministry's powers and responsibilities.

---

[55] See ibid, p. 350.
[56] His role in the General Staff will be examined in more detail in Chapter 2.
[57] *Publicandum* of 18 February 1809, quoted by Minister of War Bronsart in his memorandum on the position of the Prussian Minister of War, composed on the eve of his resignation in 1888. Quoted in Schmidt-Bückeburg, *Militärkabinett*, pp. 167–168. On the Ministry of War see also H. O. Meisner, *Der Kriegsminister 1814–1914. Ein Beitrag zur militärischen Verfassungsgeschichte*, Berlin 1940.
[58] Huber, *Heer und Staat*, pp. 322–323.

In Wilhelmine Germany the Prussian Minister of War was responsible for the army's organisation, equipment, armament, funds and related matters.[59] In conjunction with the General Staff he decided on training standards for troops and non-commissioned officers. The Minister of War was further responsible for the strength and military preparations of the German army. The Minister's responsibilities had initially included matters of both command and administration, but as part of the attempt to prevent the Reichstag from gaining influence over matters pertaining to the army's command, his influence had gradually been reduced to administrative matters only.[60] By the late nineteenth century, the Ministry had lost its original purpose of uniting the various military institutions under one roof. Although the Minister of War no longer possessed the right to command troops by this period, he nonetheless occupied a strong position owing to his responsibility for presenting the military budget to the Reichstag and administering it. The General Staff informed him of its demands and requirements, but it was ultimately up to the Minister of War to decide which army or navy increases were needed. Because of his important position in connection with the budget, both the General Staff and the Military Cabinet attempted to curb the Minister's powers in the 1880s and 1890s. The debate over army increases between the General Staff and the Ministry of War is of crucial importance throughout the period under investigation in this book, and provides the background to much of Moltke's peace-time work.

In the Reichstag, the Minister's position equalled that of a *Reichskriegsminister* (i.e. not just a Prussian minister, but in effect an Imperial Minister of War), although for several reasons such an office was never formally created. On the one hand, the Kaiser, whose concern was always to consolidate or expand his power and influence, would not have had the same authority over a *Reichskriegsminister* as he did over a Prussian one, who was necessarily also a Prussian general, and as such obliged under oath to obey his monarch. Bismarck, too, had feared for his influential position and had therefore deliberately not created such an important post.[61] On the other hand, Bavaria, Saxony and Württemberg were keen to preserve their military independence as much as possible, and would not have accepted the superiority of a *Reichskriegsminister*.[62] This constitutional peculiarity put the Prussian Minister of War in a difficult position. Legally, he was not a minister for

---

[59] See Schmidt-Richberg, *Handbuch*, pp. 64ff. for the following information on the Ministry of War.
[60] Huber, *Deutsche Verfassungsgeschichte*, vol. 3, p. 1000.
[61] Nipperdey, *Deutsche Geschichte*, vol. 2, p. 202.   [62] Stahl, 'Preußische Armee', p. 198.

the whole nation; Bavaria, Saxony and Württemberg had their own Ministers of War, theoretically of equal rank. Fortunately, the ministers worked together well and were in direct correspondence with each other, so that this unresolved and potentially troublesome situation generally had no negative consequences for the army.[63]

Vis-à-vis the Kaiser, the Minister of War's position was even more precarious. The Kaiser, as King of Prussia and leader of the Prussian army, appointed the Prussian Minister of War. As a general, he would have sworn an oath of obedience to his 'Supreme War-Lord', the monarch, while as a Prussian minister, he was bound by the constitution and obliged to object to orders that were in opposition or in conflict with it. If the two were irreconcilable, his only option was to resign.[64] The Prussian Minister of War was the only Prussian soldier who owed a duty of obedience both to his monarch and the Prussian Constitution of 1850.[65] That this was no enviable position is exemplified by Franz von Wandel's diary entry at a time when he was head of the General War Department (*Allgemeines Kriegsdepartement*) within the Ministry of War. He was contemplating retirement, partly for fear of being appointed Minister of War, which he considered 'would be the death of me, physically, spiritually, morally':

> I would wear myself out and yet would not contribute anything towards the good of army or country. No minister, other than the Reich-Chancellor, has as difficult a position as the Minister of War: on the one side the Kaiser, Military Cabinet, commanding generals, Chief of the General Staff, on the other [side] the Secretary of the Reich-Treasury and the Reichstag. The level of work, self-denial, trouble, fighting, that a Minister of War must suffer incessantly is only known to someone who has for years been working in the Ministry of War, and he would always say: under no condition do I want to become Minister of War.[66]

Seen in this light, it is not surprising that the position of Minister of War changed more frequently than any of the other influential military posts. Between 1871 and 1914, there were eight Prussian Ministers of War, compared to four Chiefs of the Military Cabinet, and four Chiefs of the General Staff.[67]

---

[63] Rüdt von Collenberg, *Die Deutsche Armee*, p. 9.   [64] Schmidt-Richberg, *Handbuch*, p. 66.

[65] Stahl, 'Preußische Armee', p. 199.

[66] BA-MA, NL Wandel, N564/4, diary entry, 14 October 1912, pp. 38ff. Excerpts from Wandel's diary also in Gerhard Granier, 'Deutsche Rüstungspolitik vor dem Ersten Weltkrieg. General Franz Wandels Tagebuchaufzeichnungen aus dem preußischen Kriegsministerium', *MGM*, 2/1985, pp. 123–162.

[67] See also Stahl, 'Preußische Armee', p. 200, and appendix 3, p. 242. Stahl calls the position of Minister of War 'probably the thorniest [office] within the higher echelons of the Prussian army', p. 199.

THE MILITARY CABINET

The Chief of the General Staff also had to negotiate his position vis-à-vis the Military Cabinet. As a 'department for personal matters' (*Abteilung für die persönlichen Angelegenheiten*), this institution had existed within the Prussian Ministry of War since 1824, and was responsible both for personnel questions and for matters directly related to the King. A relatively small institution, it had not gained independence from the Ministry of War until 1883, when it became answerable directly to the Kaiser.[68] The Military Cabinet prepared the Kaiser's orders and dealt with requests directed towards the monarch. All officer positions were filled according to its suggestions.

During Wilhelm II's reign, the importance of the Military Cabinet increased and it was criticized by many as unconstitutional and potentially dangerous. The Kaiser regarded the cabinet system as his 'personal' institution and a means by which he tried to escape the ties of constitutionalism.[69] Not surprisingly, there was a clear demand at the end of the war that the Military Cabinet be dissolved. The 'Workers' and Soldiers' Council' demanded its abolition, arguing that 'it is impossible for us to agree to the continuing existence of this notorious remnant of the old system'.[70] Even before this time, the Military Cabinet had many critics. It was feared that in this powerful military institution secret decisions were being made that no constitutional body could control or influence. No provisions for such a cabinet were made in the German constitution, so legally there was indeed reason for contemporaries to be concerned about the possibility of a shadow government (*Nebenregierung*) being exercised with the help of such extra-constitutional bodies.[71] The existence of the cabinet system was seen by critics as absolutism in its most pronounced form.[72] All military appointments, promotions and demotions of officers could be passed by the Military Cabinet without ministerial countersignature.[73] As Huber explains, the extent of the cabinet's influence resulted from the fact that its exact role was never

---

[68] In 1914, it consisted of its Chief and seven officers: Stahl, 'Preußische Armee', p. 205. The most important critical account of the role of the Military Cabinet is Schmidt-Bückeburg, *Militärkabinett*. See also Schmidt-Richberg, *Handbuch*, pp. 67ff.; Huber, *Heer und Staat*, pp. 69ff.; Hermann Granier, 'Eine Denkschrift des Generals Edwin von Manteuffel über das Militär-Kabinett', *Forschungen zur Brandenburg-Preußischen Geschichte*, vol. 47, Berlin 1935, pp. 172–181.

[69] Huber, *Heer und Staat*, p. 333.

[70] BA-Potsdam, files of the Reichskanzlei, R43, 12837, file 2019 (Militärkabinett), p. 42.

[71] 'Nebenregierung' in Schmidt-Bückeburg, *Militärkabinett*, p. 206; also Schmidt-Richberg, *Handbuch*, p. 68.   [72] Schmidt-Bückeburg, *Militärkabinett*, p. 224.

[73] Schmidt-Richberg, *Handbuch*, p. 68.

clearly defined, for 'an institution without a defined area of competence is potentially responsible for everything'.[74]

Not only the Military Cabinet, but the Naval and Civil Cabinets, too, were in positions of great influence, due to the trust that their chiefs enjoyed with the Kaiser. The chiefs of the cabinets could make themselves heard much more easily than any ministers, accompanying the Kaiser on his journeys and also having more regular access to him than those responsible to parliament.[75] It is very noticeable that all three cabinets gained increasing influence at the beginning of Wilhelm II's reign, when the young monarch was trying to establish his personal rule; and that during his struggle to gain more personal power, he came to rely more and more on his cabinets.[76]

Even apologists such as Huber and Schmidt-Richberg, who dismiss the notion of 'personal rule', do not dispute that the chief of the Military Cabinet was in a very influential position indeed. The Chief of the Military Cabinet was a '*vortragender Generaladjutant*', i.e. an adjutant with immediate access to the monarch, and he belonged to the Kaiser's closest military entourage. He travelled with him and was present at audiences with holders of other *Immediatstellen*. Schmidt-Richberg describes the position of Chief of the Military Cabinet as an 'exceedingly important and influential post',[77] although he modifies this by adding that the Chief of the General Staff was in a similarly powerful position. This is no doubt true, but only attests to the wide-ranging influence of the different military institutions under Wilhelm II. Their importance changed, depending on the individual who occupied a position at a particular time. Under Wilhelm II, the Chief of Military Cabinet was a less influential position when Dietrich von Hülsen-Haeseler occupied it than it had been under Wilhelm von Hahnke,[78] and the position of Chief of the General Staff was more important under Waldersee and the younger Moltke than it had been under Schlieffen. In Moltke's case, this was due in particular to his close friendship with the Kaiser. This is a clear indication that the personality occupying a position was more important than the position itself, and also illustrates

---

[74] Huber, *Heer und Staat*, pp. 333–334.

[75] This is very apparent in the time-table of *Immediatsvorträge* (personal audiences) that Schmidt-Bückeburg published in his study on the Military Cabinet: the majority of these audiences were with 'bodies not responsible to parliament', and within that there was a heavy slant towards the military. *Militärkabinett*, p. 178.

[76] See Röhl, *Germany without Bismarck*, p. 127.

[77] Schmidt-Richberg, *Handbuch*, p. 67; Huber, *Bismarck und das Reich*, p. 816.

[78] Wilhelm von Hahnke (1833–1912), Chief of the Military Cabinet from 1888–1912, father of Schlieffen's son-in-law Wilhelm von Hahnke (cf. Chapter 2).

the importance and influence an individual could gain if the Kaiser was favourably disposed towards him.

It is certainly undeniable that the Chief of the Military Cabinet had, through his close contact with the Kaiser, significant influence on the monarch and ultimately on military matters. However, the Kaiser did not always follow the Chief's advice, especially where appointments to leading positions within the army were concerned. The Kaiser felt more than able to make his own decisions, even against the advice of his closest and most trusted advisers. This is demonstrated most prominently in the appointment of Moltke as Chief of the General Staff in 1906, against the advice of the Chief of the Military Cabinet, Hülsen-Haeseler, who even threatened to resign over this issue.[79]

The Chief of the Military Cabinet's domain was primarily in the area of appointments. He did not have any influence on operational decisions, which were the Chief of Staff's domain. Where the two institutions might clash was over the appointment of army leaders and army chiefs of staff, as they did, for example, when it came to selecting the personalities to lead the German armies into war in 1914. From the General Staff's point of view, the Military Cabinet was an unwelcome rival. In a post-war, apologetic article on the work of the General Staff in the pre-war years, Georg Graf von Waldersee outlined how the younger Moltke's work had been much impeded because of the 'sad chapter' of appointing 'the personalities'. The Military Cabinet, Waldersee complained, had allowed Moltke 'only very modest influence' on appointments, and had frequently opposed General Staff suggestions. The result, Waldersee stated almost triumphantly, was that Moltke could not trust the cabinet, and that he had therefore been forced into secrecy vis-à-vis the Military Cabinet.[80]

Compared to 'constitutional' positions, the Chiefs of the Military Cabinet changed very infrequently. There were only four such chiefs in Wilhelm's reign; Wilhelm von Hahnke from 1888–1901, Dietrich Graf von Hülsen-Haeseler from 1901 until his tragic death whilst dancing for the Kaiser in 1908,[81] Moriz Freiherr von Lyncker until July 1918, and Ulrich Freiherr von Marschall until the end of the war. All (apart from

---

[79] Moltke's appointment will be examined in detail below.

[80] Georg Graf Waldersee, 'Von Kriegführung, Politik, Persönlichkeiten und ihrer Wechselwirkung aufeinander', *Deutscher Offizier Bund*, 11, April 1927, p. 444.

[81] Hülsen-Haeseler's bizarre death in November 1908 is described in Zedlitz-Trützschler's memoirs, *Zwölf Jahre am deutschen Kaiserhof*, pp. 216ff.

the fourth, who was in office for only the last few months of the war) remained in their position for an exceptionally long time.[82]

THE GREAT GENERAL STAFF AS A MILITARY ORGANIZATION

Before the First World War, it was commonly said that Europe was home to five reputedly perfect institutions: the Roman Curia, the British Parliament, the Russian Ballet, the French Opera, and the Prussian General Staff. In taking over the leadership of the latter organization, Helmuth von Moltke, Germany's last peace-time Chief of the General Staff, acceded to a position that he and his fellow officers regarded as the most honourable in the world.[83] The Great General Staff was the organizational centre of the German army. Its responsibilities in peace-time were, to name but the most significant, the preparation of the annual mobilization and deployment plans, the observation of military powers throughout the world, in particular the armies of possible opponents, the preparation and execution of the *Kaisermanöver* and other army manoeuvres and exercises, General Staff journeys and war games, the study of technical innovations and their possible application to operations and tactics, and the selection and training of General Staff officers.[84] The limitations to its responsibilities are as important as the tasks it did perform: the Great General Staff was the Kaiser's tool for leading the army, but its functions were to advise and prepare, not to command. The General Staff did not carry responsibility for the training or commanding of troops or for compiling field regulations, which were the domain of the Ministry of War and the commanding generals.[85]

---

[82] By contrast, between 1888 and 1918, there were altogether eleven Ministers of War and eight Chancellors. It is noticeable that the chiefs of the Civil and the Naval Cabinet were also of long standing in their posts. Hermann von Lucanus was chief of the Civilian Cabinet from July 1888 until his death in August 1908. His successor, Rudolf von Valentini, stayed in office until January 1918 when he was forced to resign. He was followed by two short-term chiefs, Friedrich von Berg, January to October 1918, and Clemens von Delbrück, October to November 1918. The Naval Cabinet, which had not been established until 1889, had only two long-serving chiefs: Gustav von Senden-Bibran, and, after he became too ill to continue in his post, Georg Alexander von Müller, who had been Senden-Bibran's deputy during the last two years of his illness. See Huber, *Bismarck und das Reich*, p. 818; Schmidt-Richberg, *Handbuch*, p. 67. See also Röhl, *Germany without Bismarck*, p. 205, who points out that members of Wilhelm's entourage stayed in office 'four or five times longer than the responsible members of the Government', usually until they retired or died.   [83] Groener, *Der Feldherr wider Willen*, p. XII.

[84] Stahl, 'Preußische Armee', pp. 210–211; Bucholz, *Moltke*, pp. 12–16, 158ff.

[85] Martin Samuels, *Command or Control? Command, Training and Tactics in the British and German Armies, 1888–1918*, London 1995, p. 30; Schneider, *Die Organisation des Heeres*, pp. 28ff.

Most of the work of the General Staff in peace-time was conducted behind closed doors, largely unnoticed by the general public. Except for the annual *Kaisermanöver*, and for publications of the Department for Military History, the outside world learned little about the activities in the General Staff building on the *Königsplatz*.[86] Unlike the Minister of War, the Chief of the General Staff had no obligation to justify his actions in the Reichstag or anywhere in the public sphere. He was answerable only to the Kaiser. As a result, very little information was passed on to other military or civilian institutions about the strategic planning conducted by the General Staff. As will be seen below, this was to have particularly serious consequences in connection with the deployment plan that was put into effect in 1914.

To some degree, and more than any other of the military institutions of Imperial Germany, the General Staff tried to bridge the differences that existed between the Prussian army and the contingent armies of Bavaria, Saxony and Württemberg. Officers from the latter armies were commanded to serve in the General Staff in Berlin, or participated in General Staff exercises, and Prussian General Staff officers also participated in Bavarian exercises. It is certainly true, as Stahl emphasizes, that such important links existed, and it is significant that it was considered important to forge them. Well-known non-Prussian General Staff officers of accepted standing included Wilhelm Groener (Württemberg) and Richard Hentsch (Saxony).[87] However, the acceptance of 'foreign' officers as equals by Prussian officers was not as complete as Stahl would contend. There existed a surprising amount of animosity between Prussian and non-Prussian officers, just as between ennobled and bourgeois officers.[88]

The German General Staff consisted of 625 officers in 1914 and was divided into the Great General Staff in Berlin and the Troop General Staff, in which officers served with the various army corps and divisions all over Germany.[89] The Berlin-based Great General Staff was made up of 13 departments, and was headed by the 'Chief of the General Staff

---

[86] Hermann von Kuhl, *Der Deutsche Generalstab in Vorbereitung und Durchführung des Weltkrieges*, Berlin 1920, p. 3.

[87] Stahl, 'Preußische Armee', pp. 214–215.

[88] See Breit, *Staats- und Gesellschaftsbild*, p. 14. See also Mark R. Stoneman, 'Bürgerliche und adlige Krieger: Zum Verhältnis zwischen sozialer Herkunft und Berufskultur im wilhelminischen Armee-Offizierkorps', in Heinz Reif (ed.), *Bürgertum und Adel im 19. und 20. Jahrhundert* (Berlin 2000). My thanks to Mr Stoneman for making his manuscript available to me.

[89] Bucholz, *Moltke*, p. 137, p. 225; Samuels, *Command or Control?*, p. 15. Of these 625 officers, 239 were available for service in the Troop General Staff, while 113 were assigned to the Great General Staff in Berlin. Ibid., p. 15.

of the Army'. The following list explains the departmental divisions as well as the internal hierarchy:[90]

Oberquartiermeister I (Germany)
Second Department: Mobilization, deployment and operations of the
    German army
Railway Department: Railway matters (expansion and maintenance)

Oberquartiermeister II (Foreign Armies) (so-called Language Section)
First Department: Russia and the East
Third Department: France, England and the West
Ninth/Tenth Department: Austria-Hungary, Italy, the Balkans

Oberquartiermeister III (Training)
Fifth and Eighth Departments: Training, Education
especially General Staff Journeys and War Academy

Oberquartiermeister IV (Foreign Fortifications)
Fourth Department: France, and the West in general
Seventh Department: Russia, and the East in general

Two or three departments were subordinated to one of four *Oberquartiermeister* (Chief Quarter Masters), usually of the rank of *Generalmajor* or *Generalleutnant*, while chiefs of departments were usually *Oberstleutnant*. Some departments were directly subordinated to the Chief of the General Staff. Those were the Sixth Department, responsible for the preparation, execution and evaluation of the *Kaisermanöver*; Department IIIb, in charge of secret intelligence information; and the Central Department, responsible for personnel matters. The Departments for Military History, κι for 1870/71 and recent history of warfare, and κ2 for earlier history of warfare, especially the wars of Frederick the Great and Napoleon, were subordinated to the fifth

---

[90] This list combines information from Santen and Bucholz. Santen, unpublished diaries in family's possession, Wennigsen, Hanover (courtesy of Professor John C. G. Röhl), 'Erinnerungen', vol. II, pp. 343ff.; Bucholz, *Moltke*, p. 137. See also Holger Herwig, *The First World War. Germany and Austria-Hungary 1914–1918*, London, New York, Sydney 1997, pp. 57–58. Bucholz and Herwig refer to 'sections' and 'bureaux', while Santen refers to 'Abteilungen', which is here translated as 'departments'. According to Schneider, *Organisation*, p. 29, the General Staff consisted of 11 departments. Details of the activities of the Second Department in Erich Ludendorff, *Mein Militärischer Werdegang*, Munich 1933. Walter Nicolai describes the activities of 'Sektion IIIb', the secret military intelligence department, in *Nachrichtendienst, Presse und Volksstimme im Weltkrieg*, Berlin 1920.

Oberquartiermeister, who was also in charge of the departments for topography, trigonometry and cartography, which together constituted the Land Survey Department.[91]

Aspiring officers would have required years of service, preparation and training before getting an opportunity to prove themselves in the General Staff. First they had to volunteer for the War Academy entrance examination. Of approximately 400 candidates per year, about 100 passed and were admitted to the War Academy in Berlin for training that lasted three years, with officers from Prussia, Saxony and Württemberg visiting the same academy. Bavaria had its own War Academy. Training at the academy was almost exclusively theoretical, with only brief periods spent with the troops. At the end of their time at the War Academy, candidates undertook a three-week training staff ride. Only a small percentage of the successful candidates of the academy actually became General Staff officers. The drop-out rate was between two-thirds and three-quarters. After a few months spent back with their regiments, the remaining 25–35 officers spent a probationary period of one to three years on the Great General Staff in Berlin, in which they had to prove their ability for General Staff work. After such a rigorous selection process, only about ten candidates per annual intake would finally end up as General Staff officers.[92] Once in the General Staff, however, officers enjoyed earlier and more frequent promotions than their non-General Staff colleagues. Moreover, the prestige attached to a position on the General Staff, made outwardly visible by the famous trousers with the distinctive red stripe, seemed to justify all this effort.

The conditions of work within the General Staff were surprisingly basic, given the image of this institution. Modern technology did not rate highly in the everyday working of the General Staff, according to Hermann von Santen's memoirs. The Railway Department owned only one typewriter, and in one of the corridors there was one phone-box to conduct urgent telephone calls. Santen could not recall it ever having been used. The General Staff did not even own a car, which, in Santen's opinion, was no disadvantage: work could be conducted more calmly and regularly, he argued, and orders were thought through more carefully than happened in later times when they could be changed with a telephone call. Despite the fact that working hours were long, '12, 14 and

---

[91] Bucholz, *Moltke*, pp. 223ff. provides extensive detail of the work undertaken in the various departments.

[92] Uhle-Wettler, *Ludendorff*, pp. 39ff; Stahl, 'Preußische Armee', p. 216. Samuels gives the number at 4–5: *Command and Control*, pp. 18ff. On promotions, see p. 27.

more hours tied to the office', as Santen recalls, there was no canteen (*Kasino*), and General Staff officers would bring sandwiches and thermos flasks to work.[93] In many ways, the General Staff must have resembled any other bureaucratic institution of the time, the only difference being that officers instead of civil servants conducted the daily routine business.

New recruits were issued with a large quantity of printed material, most of which outlined the various rules and regulations that a General Staff officer had to comply with. It was deemed important that a certain image of discipline and superiority be upheld outside of the General Staff. Thus, officers were issued with a list of the names of streets in which it was forbidden to smoke in the day-time, and a list of pubs which were out of bounds for soldiers, usually those which Socialists frequented. It was paramount that one adhered to the rules, for 'any punishment, even the slightest, resulted in immediate replacement and return to the troops'.[94] Considering the effort it had taken to get to this prized position, that must have been a terrifying prospect.

Much of General Staff work was paper work. Its schedule was regulated by the mobilization year, *Mobilmachungsjahr*. At the end of March of each year, mobilization plans would be completed, and a new mobilization year would begin on 1 April. During the summer, parts of the current strategic plan would be tested in the field. In the winter half, indoor war games and map exercises continued the testing process.[95] Work on the mobilization plans would not start until the beginning of October, following the autumn manoeuvres. New recruits to the General Staff also began their duties on 1 April, giving them time to be trained in the quiet period (Santen called it 'saure Gurkenzeit', the slack time). During the winter months, the preparation of the new mobilization plan kept the Railway Department in particular very busy. According to Hermann von Kuhl, it was 'an enormous task'.[96]

The Second Department compiled the annual mobilization plan, and a draft plan for the initial operations in the event of war. The head of the Second Department was designated to be the Chief of the General Staff's operations officer when war broke out. The department liaised with the Railway Department to compile the annual deployment plan, based on the potential of the German army, and on the news and intelligence which had been received on foreign armies in the 'Language

[93] Santen, 'Erinnerungen', vol. 10, p. 348.   [94] Ibid.   [95] Bucholz, *Moltke*, p. 196.
[96] Kuhl, *Der Deutsche Generalstab*, p. 3.

Sections'.[97] During the major annual army manoeuvres, which were based on current political situations, plans and strategies were tested, and 'the real thing' simulated as far as possible. Such exercises provided an opportunity to practise and experiment with different tactical ideas, and new strategies could be developed as a result of the evaluation of the manoeuvres. The annual *Kaisermanöver* were the largest of such exercises, and could involve as many as 100,000 men and 18,000 horses.[98]

In his memoirs, Santen outlines at length the secrecy that surrounded General Staff proceedings. For example, the railway deployment plans and secret handbooks for General Staff members and other official instructions were locked away in safes. Surviving correspondence between the Berlin-based General Staff and their Bavarian colleagues provides examples of the great secrecy surrounding the 'handbook of a General Staff officer' (*Taschenbuch des Generalstabsoffiziers*, called 'der rote Esel', the red donkey, on account of its red cover). Whatever information it may have contained, it was considered so secret that every one of the exactly numbered copies dispatched to Munich had to be accounted for and returned when new editions were issued. The password for access to the safe was changed frequently, and the handbook was only to be read in the vicinity of the safe, immediately to be locked away again.[99] Security was increased, for example in 1908 and 1911, when there was a rumour that foreign intelligence services had tried to acquire a copy of the *Taschenbuch*.

With the beginning of every new mobilization year all the previous year's mobilization plans were destroyed. They were burned, under the supervision of a General Staff officer, in the ovens of the *Reichsdruckerei*. The supervising officer was responsible for ensuring that no scrap of paper escaped.[100] Security was considered paramount everywhere. The two exits to the General Staff building were guarded by porters who would only allow access to officers whom they recognized. Potential leaks were avoided by not having secretaries or even soldiers who were solely responsible for secretarial duties,[101] although each department employed an older civil servant who registered and expedited the mail. Officers had to execute their own written work, all writing of files and

[97] Ibid.   [98] Bucholz, *Moltke*, p. 245.

[99] Santen, 'Erinnerungen', vol. 10, pp. 347–348; BayHSTA-KA, MKr 983 'Notizen für den Generalstabs-Offizier zum Taschenbuch für den Generalstabsoffizier'.

[100] Santen, 'Erinnerungen', vol. 10, p. 364. See also documents marked 'Geheim! Am 1.4.14 zu vernichten.' in BayHSTA-KA, Generalstab 644, Mobilmachungsvorbereitungen 1913/14. Interestingly, despite such tight security and strict instructions, some of the documents escaped destruction.   [101] See Kuhl, *Der Deutsche Generalstab*, p. 4.

correspondence, filing and other clerical duties. Santen made a point of emphasizing that the General Staff was an all-male domain. Women – early morning cleaners aside – were not allowed to enter the premises at all (with the exception of the family of a Chief of Staff; Eliza von Moltke lived in the Chief of Staff's apartment, which was located in the General Staff building, with Moltke and their children).

In order to ensure that the enemy did not learn about German military planning, only the relevant departments within the General Staff (the Operations Department and the Railway Department), knew about the deployment plan, and within these departments, only a very few officers knew details of intended operations. Personnel, even down to the printers, were chosen carefully, and the caution paid dividends, for Germany's enemies did not know the exact details of her intended operations.[102] Tappen's recollections of the pre-war years give an impressive account of what can only be termed spy-mania:

> Our neighbours in the East and West [tried] all possible means to learn about our preparations for war. It had become known in the General Staff that enemy agents would not flinch from using any means, break-ins, murder, robbery, in order to obtain our mobilization and deployment information.[103]

Tappen's suggestion of having a soldier posted outside the rooms of the Second Department and the Railway Department at night to guard the deployment details was implemented: a measure which, according to Tappen, paid off as the guards had twice noted 'signs of an attempted entry'. Deployment details were particularly at risk during staff journeys and manoeuvres, when it was apparently not unheard-of for briefcases believed to contain secret information to be stolen. Instances of attempted bribery were also known. Such incidents led to renewed vigour regarding discretion and secrecy.[104]

On the basis of the manoeuvres and exercises organized by the General Staff, the Chief of Staff updated and altered the annual deployment plan and recommended to the Minister of War the requirements

---

[102] BA-MA, W-10/51062, Harbou to Reichsarchiv, 4 April 1925. The same degree of secrecy was employed during the first operations in August and September 1914 – with detrimental results (see Chapter 5). Depite the pre-war secrecy, however, Germany's general strategy in 1914 had largely been anticipated by her enemies and came as no great surprise, although details had remained a secret. See e.g. Victor Chernavin, 'What the Allies knew of the German Military Plan before the Outbreak of the Great War', *The Army Quarterly*, 29, January 1935.

[103] Tappen, 'Kriegserinnerungen', BA-MA, W-10/50661, pp. 7–8.

[104] Ibid. See also Bucholz, *Moltke*, p. 238, who claims that Moltke was preoccupied with secrecy and that he had a 'pathological fear of spies'. Under his auspices, the General Staff even began to censor memoirs of former leading militaries before publication: Görlitz, *Generalstab*, p. 197.

for troop and equipment increases.[105] The conflict between the two institutions over the issue of army increases is a well-known factor in the military decision-making of the pre-war years. The envy (*Ressortneid*)
between them amounted almost to hatred, and stemmed from the time
when both institutions had to assert their authority.[106] Certainly, each
institution lacked a detailed understanding of the other's constraints and
problems. In addition, the fragmented structure in which military planning had to be conducted hindered effective decision-making, as
General Franke, for example, argued after the war:

> Many a mistake could have been avoided if we had worked together with more
> trust in peace-time, rather than each branch cutting itself off from the others.
> Not only were the General Staff and the Ministry of War not really in touch
> with each other, nor either with the navy offices, but the division between above
> and below was also exaggerated. . . . Not once was I asked before the war to
> attend a meeting that could have given me an idea for the task of supplying the
> army with ammunition in the coming war![107]

In such a climate of competition and lack of co-operation, being Chief
of Staff was no easy task, as Moltke, the surprise candidate for the position, would find out when his candidacy to this influential post was
announced.

---

[105] See e.g. Stahl, 'Preußische Armee', p. 213.

[106] Major van den Bergh recalled in January 1927 how he had 'almost hated the Ministry of War
before and was not happy when I was transferred to it'. He soon realized what an important job
the Ministry did and became 'a convinced fan'. BA-MA, W-10/50629, p. 4.

[107] BA-MA, W-10/50636, Erinnerungen des Generals der Infantrie a.D. Franke an seine
Dienstzeit, o.D., p. 11.

CHAPTER TWO

Alfred von Schlieffen and Helmuth von Moltke: 'military genius' and 'reluctant military leader'?

Central to the Schlieffen myth is the allegation that Schlieffen was replaced at the wrong time and by the wrong person. His supporters frequently maintain that Schlieffen should have remained in office, and that Moltke's appointment was a grave mistake that ultimately lost Germany the war. Any investigation into Moltke's succession of Schlieffen must therefore begin by asking why Schlieffen was replaced in 1906, and must compare his role as Chief of the General Staff with that of his successor.

Concerns about the possibility of war in the winter of 1904/1905 were one of the reasons for the decision to replace Count Alfred von Schlieffen, who had been Chief of the General Staff since 1891, although there had been talk about replacing him since 1903. Both Wilhelm II and Chancellor Bernhard von Bülow feared that the 72-year-old general would be too old to lead the troops effectively should war break out.[1] As a result of the Moroccan Crisis, war with France seemed likely by the end of 1905. After Delcassé's dismissal, the French were rearming with vigour. Although Schlieffen's supporters were later to deny this, after initial reluctance Schlieffen himself actually seems to have agreed that it was time for him to leave.[2] However, replacing such a long-serving Chief of Staff would not be easy.

Wilhelm von Hahnke, Schlieffen's son-in-law and one of his most ardent supporters, advanced a different version of events after the war,

---

[1] Ritter, *The Schlieffen Plan*, p. 111. At the end of 1904 Einem told Goltz that there had been talk of appointing him (Goltz) as Chief of Staff if the Moroccan Crisis were to result in war. Schlieffen was no longer considered 'fit for action'. Colmar Frhr. von der Goltz, *Denkwürdigkeiten*, ed. Friedrich Frhr. von der Goltz and Wolfgang Förster, Berlin 1929, p. 256. See also Eberhard Kessel (ed.), *Alfred von Schlieffen. Briefe*, Göttingen 1958, pp. 303–304, for a letter from the Kaiser dated 29 December 1903. Having heard from Hülsen that Schlieffen might consider resigning, he suggested the training of an '*Adlatus*' and put forward Moltke's name. 'He has the necessary leadership qualities, the necessary daring courage and does not fear responsibility; and [he has] a name with a good ring [to it] in army and country.'   [2] See Wallach, *Dogma*, p. 127, note 3.

blaming envious and ambitious men around Schlieffen for plotting against him. Part of the deliberate construction of the Schlieffen myth was to maintain that Schlieffen had been ousted from office, and that he could have continued to be an effective Chief of the General Staff if he had stayed on. Hahnke maintained that Schlieffen had been pushed out of office by disgruntled colleagues, such as Dietrich von Hülsen-Haeseler, the Kaiser's Chief of the Military Cabinet, who allegedly could not forget a sarcastic manoeuvre critique of Schlieffen's in 1900. In addition, Hans von Plessen was worried that Moltke might push him out of office and, according to Hahnke, favoured Moltke's candidacy on these grounds, while Moltke allegedly plotted against Schlieffen because he was upset that the latter ignored him following his promotion to *Generalquartiermeister* in February 1904.[3] This last statement, at least, makes little sense, for it was only with Moltke's advancement to *Generalquartiermeister* that he became the candidate to succeed Schlieffen. With the Kaiser in favour of his appointment, there would have been no need for him to plot against Schlieffen once he had been made his deputy. It is true, however, that Schlieffen reacted badly to Moltke after his promotion, and did indeed snub him, as Bruno von Mudra reported to Colmar von der Goltz: 'Schlieffen is said to be outraged about the choice of Count Moltke [*sic*] and is cutting him out completely. It is said that he withholds all information from him.'[4] Animosities existed, but they were not the reason for Schlieffen's replacement.

According to a further contemporary account it was neither Schlieffen's old age nor his bad health, nor any of his immediate colleagues' plotting, that led to his dismissal. The Austrian plenipotentiary reported to Friedrich Freiherr Beck-Rzikowsky, the Austrian Chief of Staff, in January 1904 that 'the reasons for the probable resignation lie rather in the fact that the Count is, in military questions, of a different

---

[3] BA-MA, NL Hahnke, N36/10, Hahnke to Freytag-Loringhoven, 5 March 1924.

[4] Mudra to Goltz, 8 March 1904, BA-MA, NL Goltz, N737/15. I am grateful to Prof. John Röhl for pointing out this and other documents in the Goltz papers pertaining to Moltke's controversial appointment. See also Mantey to Förster, 15 May 1931: 'But it is a tragedy for our German people that two men like Schlieffen and Moltke . . . stood so far apart from the beginning. . . . Moltke only came to an audience with Schlieffen 34 days after [having been made *Generalquartiermeister*]. Moltke's bitterness is understandable and unfortunately one cannot put it any other way than that Schlieffen literally treated him badly': BA-MA, RH61/v.68, pp. 59–60. Holger Herwig concludes from a positive manoeuvre critique that Schlieffen wrote about Moltke, which apparently mysteriously disappeared after the war, that Groener, Kuhl, Foerster and others were wrong to claim that Schlieffen opposed Moltke's appointment: *First World War*, pp. 43–44. The available evidence, however, leaves no doubt that Schlieffen, at least initially, disapproved of being replaced by Moltke.

opinion from the Allhighest Position'.[5] In other words, Schlieffen's views on military matters differed from those of the Kaiser. It would certainly not have been unusual for the Kaiser not to have tolerated opposing views among his closest advisers and to have replaced such a deviant with another candidate of his choice.

Whatever animosity existed between Schlieffen and his 'Supreme War Lord' was increased during the Moroccan Crisis, when the Kaiser objected to Schlieffen's demands for a preventive war. Although Schlieffen never stated this explicitly, it would seem from all accounts that he was willing to go to war in 1905. As Peter Rassow rightly points out, a lack of evidence does not preclude the possibility that Schlieffen and Friedrich von Holstein, senior councillor and *éminence grise* in the Foreign Office (Auswärtiges Amt), who had known each other since their youth, discussed political events during their frequent meetings at the time. Rassow is convinced 'that the military man would have proved to the politician that the military back-up to his daring policy [during the Moroccan Crisis] was assured'.[6] Holstein's policy at the time threatened war in order to intimidate the French – accepting a calculated risk of war resulting from the crisis.[7] This risk, however, was calculable only if the Chief of the General Staff agreed that it could be taken. Schlieffen certainly alerted Chancellor Bernhard von Bülow to the fact that the circumstances for war were favourable, as Hahnke confirmed after the war:

The fleet building was definitely decided upon and thus the future enmity of England assured. Therefore it was completely natural and understandable even to any layman that the Chief of the General Staff wanted to see the reckoning with France, which was equally unavoidable, before England had openly crossed over to Germany's enemies, especially at a point in time at which France's ally [Russia] was herself embroiled in a war in the Far East and France thus stood isolated. Count Schlieffen alerted Prince Bülow to this militarily favourable situation at the right time in a matter-of-fact and sober manner.[8]

In Hahnke's opinion, the 'pacifist' Bülow could not forgive Schlieffen for suggesting preventive war against France in 1904. According to Hahnke, this was another reason for Schlieffen's dismissal.[9] Both Bülow and the

[5] Austro-Hungarian military plenipotentiary to Beck, 12 January 1904, quoted by Regenauer in 'Materialsammlung zur "Darstellung der operativen Verhandlungen des Grafen Schlieffen mit Österreich-Ungarn"', BA-MA, w-10/50222, pp. 57ff.

[6] Peter Rassow, 'Schlieffen und Holstein', *HZ*, 173, 1952, p. 306.

[7] On Holstein's policy during the Morocco Crisis, see Norman Rich, *Friedrich von Holstein. Politics and Diplomacy in the Era of Bismarck and Wilhelm II*, 2 vols., Cambridge 1965, vol. 2, pp. 678ff.

[8] BA-MA, NL Hahnke, N36/12, pp. 4–5.

[9] BA-MA, NL Hahnke, N36/10, Hahnke to Freytag-Loringhoven, 5 March 1924.

Kaiser opposed war at the time, while Schlieffen regretted that such a favourable situation was allowed to pass. Groener, admitting hindsight, concluded after the war that Schlieffen was right to have demanded preventive war in 1905 and that he, too, had been in favour of it.[10]

Wilhelm von Dommes, first adjutant of the Chief of the General Staff from 1905–1910, considered 1905 an 'opportunity so favourable that it would probably never be expected again', due to Russia's preoccupation in the East. This would have allowed Germany to deploy almost her entire army against France, leaving only a containing force on her border with Russia. According to Dommes, the opportunity was passed up primarily because of the Kaiser's 'love of peace'. Dommes himself was an outspoken advocate of war on this and other occasions, especially as the preconditions for it were worsening with every passing year:

Therefore I repeatedly asked my Chiefs [Schlieffen and Moltke] – particularly during the crises of 1905, 1909, 1912 – whether it would not be far better to rebuff the impositions of our opponents and to let things develop into a conflict. Every time I received the reply that His Majesty would never be in favour of a preventive war.[11]

Despite the monarch's reluctance, Dommes and his Chiefs of Staff agreed in principle, and war 'the sooner the better' was to become a recurrent theme in Moltke's thinking and reasoning in the pre-war years, as he was faced with a situation in which conditions for war seemed to be steadily worsening for Germany.

The truth behind the decision to replace Schlieffen was probably a combination of the above theories. Schlieffen was old, the Kaiser was not on very close terms with him, and ambitious intriguers were always close at hand. However, those commentators who felt that Schlieffen should not have been replaced, indeed that he was irreplaceable, have shaped military history writing in subsequent decades, and their views

[10] Groener, *Lebenserinnerungen*, pp. 84–85. Despite such evidence, there is disagreement over the question of Schlieffen's intentions in 1905. Fritz Fischer supports Rassow's theory (*Krieg der Illusionen. Die deutsche Politik von 1911–1914*, paperback reprint of 2nd edn 1970 [1st edn 1969], Düsseldorf 1987, pp. 99ff.), whereas Ritter denies that Schlieffen wanted preventive war (*Schlieffen Plan*, pp. 97ff.), as does Albrecht Moritz, *Das Problem des Präventivkrieges in der deutschen Politik während der 1. Marokkokrise*, Bern and Frankfurt/M. 1974, pp. 107ff.

[11] BA-MA, NL Moltke N78/34, 'Gutachtliche Stellungnahme des Generalmajors von Dommes für die Friedensverhandlungen', February 1919. Wolfgang Förster is another contemporary who confirms Schlieffen's conviction that the situation of 1905 was favourable for war. He disagrees with Ritter on the point of Schlieffen's intentions in 1905. Ritter concluded in *Schlieffen Plan* that, whatever Schlieffen's shortcomings, he did not want war at that time; but according to Förster, Schlieffen considered 1905 a particularly favourable moment for Germany for war with France: 'Einige Bemerkungen', p. 44.

have produced the orthodox view of a reluctantly replaced Schlieffen who was succeeded by an equally reluctant, and much less gifted, Moltke. The available evidence suggests that Schlieffen was far less unwilling to leave than has previously been suggested. In September 1905, he wrote: 'I am nearly 75 years old, almost blind, half deaf and now have a broken leg, too. It is high time that I take my leave and I have good reason to believe that my repeated request for retirement will be granted this year.'[12] Unlike many of his defenders, who continued to argue that he should not have been replaced, Schlieffen had clearly accepted the inevitable.

HELMUTH VON MOLTKE: THE UNLIKELY SUCCESSOR

In the light of allegations of Moltke's inadequacy and reluctance to be a military leader, it is necessary to evaluate Moltke's suitability for the post, and to establish whether a different replacement candidate might have been a better choice. How unlikely a successor was Moltke, and how reluctant was he to accept this important position?

When his replacement was proposed, Schlieffen was particularly choosy about his successor. Dommes remembered that Schlieffen opposed Colmar von der Goltz, Karl von Bülow and Hans von Beseler: none seemed adequate to him. 'General von Moltke he also only considered unwillingly and hesitatingly.'[13] Schlieffen apparently revised his opinion regarding Moltke's suitability later, telling Dommes in 1909 or 1910 that Moltke had been the most suitable candidate to replace him – no doubt meaning the best available, not necessarily the best possible. Indeed, Schlieffen treated Moltke courteously when his candidacy was first considered, as Moltke reported back from a General Staff ride in June 1904: 'I get along very well with Schlieffen. He is polite and at times even charming towards me. Sometimes he even chats about something. I honestly admire his sprightliness.' Even when Moltke opposed Schlieffen's point of view, Moltke commented that 'he receives my opinions with courtesy and dignity'.[14]

Nonetheless, Schlieffen's followers were to make much mileage out of the fact that he had not condoned Moltke's appointment in 1905. It was

[12] Quoted in Wallach, *Dogma*, p. 127, note 3. Schlieffen's illness is attested to in the reports of the Saxon military plenipotentiary Salza und Lichtenau of 18 September 1905, Sächs. HSTA, Sächs. Milit. Bevollmächtigter in Berlin, 1426, pp. 47–48, and of the Bavarian military plenipotentiary Gebsattel of 2 November 1905, BayHSTA-KA, MKr 43, No. 2309.
[13] BA-MA, w-10/51061, Dommes to Reichsarchiv, 14 January 1926, p. 184.
[14] Moltke, *Erinnerungen*, 16/18 June 1904, pp. 291–292.

not only Schlieffen who disapproved of the successor that the Kaiser had chosen; within the General Staff and in the officer corps as a whole the reception was mixed. There was general surprise when the new candidate was announced in January 1904, especially as it had been assumed that the former *Generalquartiermeister* Karl von Bülow would be Schlieffen's natural successor.[15] Alfred von Waldersee recorded on 5 January: 'The most important event of the new year was the assignment of Generalleutnant v. Moltke to Schlieffen, with the definite intention of making him his successor.'[16] Some commentators were appalled at the choice, and Waldersee feared that 'the impression that this must make in the army upon anyone who has but the slightest judgement, is one of surprise and then deep concern'.[17] There was even widespread criticism in the press. The *Berliner Tageblatt* regretted that Moltke had allowed himself to be swayed into accepting the position, adding: 'The great name alone won't do the trick.'[18] Moltke's misfortune was having to succeed a man of Schlieffen's reputation, the General Staff's 'big chief', who left behind a whole school of ardent followers.[19] He was also unfortunate to inherit from his uncle a famous name, with the implicit expectation that he live up to it.[20] There were many voices that maintained his famous name was his only qualification for the position, claiming that his military career had not distinguished or equipped him for the important post.

Who was the candidate to whom there was such widespread objection? Helmuth Johannes Ludwig von Moltke was born on May 25, 1848, on the Gersdorf estate in Mecklenburg-Schwerin in East Prussia.[21] He

[15] BA-MA, w-10/50222, Austrian plenipotentiary to Beck, 12 January 1904.

[16] Waldersee, *Denkwürdigkeiten*, vol. 3, p. 225.

[17] See e.g. Waldersee's diary entry of 5 January 1904, following Moltke's appointment to the General Staff, with the intention of making him Schlieffen's successor. Prof. John Röhl kindly provided me with excerpts from the original diary, which differs significantly from Meisner's edited version. See also *Denkwürdigkeiten*, vol. 3, pp. 224ff.

[18] *Berliner Tageblatt*, 2 January 1906, BayHSTA-KA, MKr 42.

[19] Although much of this view was created after the war, Schlieffen had already come to personify the position of Chief of the General Staff in his lifetime. See e.g. Mudra to Goltz, suggesting that Goltz might 'become Schlieffen', i.e. Chief of Staff ('daß Euer Excellenz Schlieffen werden müssen'): BA-MA, N732/15.

[20] Something that, in his critics' eyes, he would never succeed in doing. See Fabeck, 'Charakteristik des General Oberst von Moltke' [*sic*], 15 February 1921, BA-MA, w-10/51061: 'As a military leader (*Feldherr*), Moltke cannot be compared to his great uncle.' But see also Goltz's view in January 1906: 'Many years ago he [Moltke] once worked under my direction, and I thought at the time that I recognized various character traits of his uncle in him.' Goltz, *Denkwürdigkeiten*, p. 279.

[21] See Karl Bosl *et al.* (eds.), *Biographisches Wörterbuch zur deutschen Geschichte*, vol. 2, Munich 1974. The younger Moltke is often falsely referred to as 'Graf von Moltke'. His branch of the Moltke family did not carry this title.

was a member of the famous Moltke family, and his father was the brother of the future *Generalfeldmarschall* Count Helmuth von Moltke, who would acquire fame on the battlefields of the German wars of unification. Moltke's army career began on 1 April 1869, when he entered the Füsilier-Regiment 86, moving to the Seventh Grenadier Regiment in Liegnitz, close to Kreisau, a year later (*Grenadier-Regiment König Wilhelm I (2. Westpreußisches) Nr. 7*). In 1870, at the age of 23, he distinguished himself in the Franco-Prussian war. The regimental history of the Seventh Grenadier-Regiment singles him out for his leadership skills and personal bravery during the battle of Weißenburg.[22] He also participated in the battles of Wörth and Sedan, as well as the siege of Paris, and was promoted to *Leutnant*[23] in September 1870. In 1872 he joined the First *Garde Regiment zu Fuß*, and was promoted to *Oberleutnant* in 1877. During the years 1875–1878 he attended the War Academy in Berlin for General Staff training. In 1880, he joined the General Staff and was promoted to the rank of *Hauptmann* a year later. Judging by his enthusiastic letters to his wife from the autumn manoeuvres at that time, he was a committed soldier, eager to further his career in the army; there is no hint in them of the reluctance to be a military leader or of the alleged peaceable attitude of which he was later accused.[24]

Moltke's army career had been far from unusual until 1882, when it took a turn that would distinguish him from his fellow soldiers. He was appointed to a position *à la Suite* on the General Staff as second adjutant to the Chief of the General Staff, replacing his cousin in this role. In other words, he became his uncle's personal adjutant. As such, he spent the next years accompanying the elder Moltke on his journeys and assisting him with his General Staff duties. While some would argue that this limited his experience and training in 'real' military matters, others emphasize that the time spent with the elder Moltke was training second to none, 'as only constant contact with an important man can provide'.[25]

---

[22] Hauptmann v. Lewinski and Premier-Lieutenant v. Brauchitsch, *Geschichte des Grenadier-Regiments König Wilhelm I (2. Westpreußisches) Nr. 7*, Glogau 1897, 2 vols., vol. 1, p. 281; Eugen von Schlopp, *Geschichte des Königs-Grenadier-Regiments (2. Westpr.) Nr. 7*, Berlin 1877, p. 87. When the First Company's commanders had been injured and killed, *Portepeefähnrich* von Moltke and *Feldwebel* Magnitz had led the company on and thus averted a defeat. On Moltke's early army career see also Turner, 'The Significance of the Schlieffen Plan', p. 59; Bucholz, *Moltke*, pp. 216–217; Konrad Leppa, *Moltke und Conrad. Die Heerführung des Generaloberst v. Moltke und des Generals der Infantrie Frhr. v. Conrad [sic] im Sommer 1914*, Stuttgart 1935, pp. 1–2; Heinrich Walle, 'Helmuth von Moltke', *NDB*, vol. 18, pp. 17–18.   [23] See Hierarchy of Ranks for Officers, p. xiii.

[24] See e.g. Moltke, *Erinnerungen*, 13 September 1881, p. 100.

[25] See e.g. Hermann von Stein, *Erlebnisse und Betrachtungen aus der Zeit des Weltkrieges*, Leipzig 1919, p. 37. Moltke was certainly unusually widely travelled as a result of his time as an adjutant, as the letters in his *Erinnerungen* prove.

The younger Moltke's adjutant, Friedrich von Mantey, recalled after the war that the uncle had discussed questions of operations and war history questions with his nephew.[26] In 1888 he rose to first adjutant and promoted to the rank of *Major* soon after. After the elder Moltke's death in April 1891, Wilhelm II made Moltke his personal aide-de-camp (*diensttuender Flügeladjutant*), a prestigious position at court. As the Kaiser's adjutant, he was from then on in almost daily contact with the monarch. Moltke's duties involved travelling to several European courts, as well as frequently accompanying Wilhelm II on his North Sea cruises.[27] In 1893, now promoted to *Oberstleutnant*, Moltke became the commander of the *Schloßgarde Companie* and in 1896, having advanced to *Oberst* the previous year, he went on to command the *Kaiser Alexander Garde Grenadier Regiment Nr. 1* in Berlin. At the same time, he became *Generaladjutant* to the Kaiser. Moltke further advanced to command the First Guard Infantry Brigade in 1899 (now as *Generalmajor*), with the additional position of Commander of Potsdam. He moved on to command the First Guard Infantry Division 1902 as *Generalleutnant*, while still remaining *Generaladjutant* to the Kaiser.[28]

Although he had occupied several prestigious commands by the time he was singled out as a possible successor to Schlieffen, as a long-time adjutant Moltke had not followed a usual General Staff career. At the time of his promotion to *Generalquartiermeister* in 1904, he occupied a fairly high-ranking position in the army, and had been steadily promoted, the last time in 1902 to *Generalleutnant*. He had, however, never occupied the position of chief of staff of an army corps.[29] When his name was mentioned as a possible future Chief of the General Staff, his suitability for this important position was seriously questioned, owing not least to his unusual army career. This was arguably the most important military post in the country, as even civilians were ready to admit. Chancellor von

---

[26] Friedrich von Mantey, 'Graf Schlieffen und der jüngere Moltke', *Militär-Wochenblatt*, 10, 1935, p. 396.

[27] BA-MA, W-10/50222, Austrian plenipotentiary to Beck, 12 January 1904. 'Because of his wide language skills (he speaks Danish and Swedish very well, among others), he would frequently take part in the North Sea Cruises.' Fig. 5 (p. 123) shows the royal party in civilian attire on a land excursion during one of these cruises.

[28] For Moltke's early army career see Lewinski and von Brauchitsch, *Geschichte des Grenadier-Regiments König Wilhelm I*, vol. 2, p. 64. See also Bucholz, *Moltke*, p. 217; Walle, 'Moltke', p. 17. It should be pointed out that Schlieffen's highest position had been as regimental commander before he became head of the Third Department of the General Staff. He was thus hardly more qualified in this respect than Moltke.

[29] Leppa, *Moltke und Conrad*, p. 3. Moltke clearly realized that placements as personal adjutant might jeopardize his career prospects. When he found out in 1896 that he was in line to become commander of the *Kaiser Alexander Gardegrenadier Regiment*, he welcomed this opportunity because he was concerned about having been removed from active service for too long.

Bülow expressed his views on the importance of the position in a conversation with Minister of War Karl von Einem in 1904, when he favoured Schlieffen's replacement by a younger candidate:

His Majesty can afford to have a bad Reich-Chancellor some time; that will be possible to offset. He can also have a bad Minister of War some time, because that would not put the army into disarray. But under all circumstances the Kaiser must always have the best man as Chief of the General Staff, because the outcome of a war, that we may face any day, depends on the choice of leader for the army.[30]

One of Moltke's former teachers at the War Academy, on hearing that he had become Schlieffen's deputy, feared that 'this man could be disastrous'.[31] Foreign observers were as surprised at the choice as were Moltke's colleagues in Germany. The Austrian plenipotentiary reported on Moltke's advancement to *Generalquartiermeister* in January 1904:

His military knowledge, his expertise do not exceed those of an average officer and are – according to my Russian colleague here – supposed to be so shallow that for that reason alone his suitability for this high, responsible post must be completely denied. He is a complete stranger to the activities within the great General Staff.[32]

It is often overlooked, however, that there were certain parallels to the reaction to the elder Moltke's appointment and even that of Schlieffen. The elder Moltke had been rejected as a theoretician, 'a man of the green [map] table'. Only after 1866 did the mistrust in him abate. Schlieffen encountered prejudice because he was a long-time commander of a Guard Cavalry Regiment, and was even less well known to the army at the time of his appointment than the younger Moltke was in 1906.[33] No appointment to the position of Chief of the General Staff had ever been without critics, and Moltke was no exception.

However, commentators also had positive views of Moltke: his character in particular seemed without fault. He was considered honest, dedicated and earnest, 'an exceedingly honourable personality', in Karl von Fabeck's words.[34] Baroness von Spitzemberg recorded that her brother, Axel Freiherr von Varnbüler, considered Moltke 'a highly cultured man, and of supremely decent, brave character, especially towards superi-

[30] Einem, *Erinnerungen*, p. 149. See also Bucholz, *Moltke*, p. 215.
[31] BA-MA, NL Goltz, N737/16, R. Wagner to Goltz, 19 January 1904.
[32] BA-MA, w-10/50222, Austrian plenipotentiary to Beck, 12 January 1904.
[33] BayHSTA-KA, MKr 43, No. 36, Gebsattel to Horn, 3 January 1914.
[34] Fabeck, 'Charakteristik', 15 February 1921, BA-MA, w-10/51061. Fabeck joined the Great General Staff in April 1905 and became Moltke's first adjutant in 1910.

ors'.[35] Colmar von der Goltz considered the negative accounts in the press to have been 'superficial', as Moltke had not yet had the opportunity to demonstrate his ability.[36]

Unfortunately, the negative opinions far outweighed such positive voices. Moltke was considered pessimistic and too 'philosophical'.[37] For a military officer at the time, he was indeed surprisingly 'cultured'. Goethe's *Faust* was his constant companion; he played the cello and even had his own painting studio at Kreisau.[38] In his letters he frequently shared with his wife his views about the latest books he had read and enjoyed, among them the *Deutsche Geschichte des 19. Jahrhunderts* by the nationalist historian Heinrich von Treitschke (which Moltke praised for its 'spirit of patriotism and love of the German fatherland'), Theodor Mommsen's *Römische Geschichte*, Thomas Carlyle's *History of the French Revolution* as well as Houston Stewart Chamberlain's notorious racist publication, *Die Grundlagen des neunzehnten Jahrhunderts (The Foundations of the Nineteenth Century)*.[39] He shared and displayed the typical attitudes of his military contemporaries, and his letters attest to his anti-Semitic, xenophobic, nationalistic and monarchist views and demonstrate clearly his bellicose designs from the 1880s onwards.[40]

In addition to his 'unmilitary' pursuits, there was Moltke's apparent inclination towards 'Occultism'[41] – by no means a secret to his

---

[35] Rudolf Vierhaus (ed.), *Das Tagebuch der Baronin Spitzemberg. Aufzeichnungen aus der Hofgesellschaft des Hohenzollernreiches*, Göttingen 1960 (cited as Spitzemberg, *Diary*). Diary entry, 10 November 1905, p. 450. Varnbüler was a member of Eulenburg's infamous Liebenberg Circle and as such perhaps inclined to be more positive about the Kaiser's favoured candidate than a military commentator might have been. However, his views were echoed by other positive opinions about Moltke's character, even from within military quarters.

[36] Goltz, *Denkwürdigkeiten*, vol. 3, letter dated 9 January 1906, p. 279.

[37] See e.g. Fabeck's 'Charakteristik', in which he calls Moltke a 'pronounced pessimist': BA-MA, w-10/51061. Moltke's wife also considered him a pessimist. See e.g. Moltke, *Erinnerungen*, 17 June 1907, p. 345.   [38] Ibid., 29 May 1888, p. 139.

[39] Ibid., 6 June 1880, 11 July 1880, 29 May 1988, 10 August 1898, 5 September 1904.

[40] He was, for example, sorely disappointed that the Kaiser denied him his wish to accompany the troops to China in 1900 following the Boxer Rising. 'How much I would have like to lead the black-white-red flag against the yellow scoundrels who killed our fellow countrymen.' Ibid., 11 July 1900.

[41] 'Occultism' is often used as a blanket term for a variety of beliefs that were particularly widespread at the turn of the century, including Theosophy, Spiritualism, Mysticism and Anthroposophy. See Robert C. Galbreath, 'Spiritual Science in an Age of Materialism. Rudolf Steiner and Occultism', Ph.D. Dissertation, University of Michigan 1970, who uses the term 'Occultism' to sum up these phenomena. It should, however, be noted that members of the Anthroposophical Society would not regard Occultism as part of Anthroposophy. Rather, Anthroposophy is a 'spiritual science' (the German term *Geisteswissenschaft* expresses this better), 'based on the premise that the human intellect has the ability to contact spiritual worlds'. See *The New Encyclopaedia Britannica*, vol. 1, *Micropaedia*, 15th edn 1991, p. 447. See also the definition of Theosophy as a 'religious philosophy with mystical concerns', ibid., vol. 11, p. 696.

confederates. In 1902, for example, the Kaiser's brother in law, Bernhard, Hereditary Prince von Sachsen Meiningen, commented in a letter to Goltz on the Moltke family's belief in that 'wretched faith-healing, this first-class nonsense that the Moltke family practises with a vigour worthy of better things'.[42] A man known for his pessimism and reputed to be under the influence of both his wife, Eliza Gräfin von Moltke-Huitfeld, and her spiritual mentor Rudolf Steiner,[43] was an outrageous choice as Chief of the General Staff in many people's minds.[44] Dietrich Graf von Hülsen-Haeseler, Chief of the Military Cabinet, was ready to offer his resignation over Moltke's appointment. He put his objections quite bluntly: 'Above all, he [Moltke] was a religious dreamer (*Phantast*), [who] believed in guardian angels, faith-healing, and similar nonsense.'[45] Yet although in theory at least it was the Military Cabinet that decided military appointments, Hülsen's protests did nothing to change the Kaiser's mind.

As Moltke has so frequently been accused of having been a Spiritualist, and therefore unsuitable for the position of Chief of the General Staff, this aspect of his life, as well as his involvement with the founder of Anthroposophy, Rudolf Steiner, deserves closer investigation.[46] His wife Eliza had become interested in Steiner's philosophy, and in 1904 she became one of the first pupils at Steiner's new Esoteric School.[47] It was at this time that Helmuth von Moltke first met Rudolf Steiner in person, and he was to remain in contact with him until Moltke's death in 1916.[48] Steiner confirmed this in a public speech in

---

[42] BA-MA, NL Goltz, N737, Zug. 228/95, Bernhard von Sachsen Meiningen to Goltz, 11 February 1902. Prof. John Röhl kindly made this document available to me.

[43] Eliza Gräfin von Moltke-Huitfeld was a descendent of the Swedish branch of the Moltke family. The Austrian Rudolf Steiner (1861–1925) was a key figure in the Theosophy Society, and founded the Anthroposophical Society in February 1912. His teachings combined eastern religion and philosophy with science. Today he is perhaps best known for his paedagogic theories as exercised in Waldorf (or Steiner) Schools world-wide. On Steiner see Rudi Lissau, *Rudolf Steiner. Life, Work, Inner Path and Social Initiatives*, Stroud 1987; Galbreath, 'Spiritual Science', p. 65; Christoph Lindenberg, *Rudolf Steiner*, Hamburg 1992; Rudolf Steiner, *Mein Lebensgang*, 8th edn, Dornach 1982.

[44] According to Meyer, *Helmuth von Moltke*, vol. 2, nine or ten séances were held in the Moltke house between 21 March 1904 and 25 May 1905. Post-war claims that Moltke also held séances after his appointment in his *Dienstwohnung* (official residence) in the General Staff building must be seen as attempts to discredit him, and are not based on any evidence. See Friedrich von Boetticher, *Schlieffen*, 2nd edn, Göttingen 1973, p. 99.

[45] Bogdan Graf von Hutten-Czapski, *Sechzig Jahre Politik und Gesellschaft*, 2 vols., Berlin 1936, vol 1, p. 410, relating a conversation he had with Hülsen at the end of 1905. Otto Friedrich points out that of all the charges against Moltke, spiritualism was 'the most damaging': *Blood and Iron. From Bismarck to Hitler. The von Moltke Family's Impact on German History*, New York 1995, p. 230.

[46] For a definition of Anthroposophy, see above, note 41.

[47] Johannes Tautz, *Walter Johannes Stein. Eine Biographie*, Philosophisch-Anthroposophischer Verlag am *Goetheanum*, Dornach 1989, p. 169.

[48] The first mention of Steiner in Moltke's edited letters is on 6 and 8 March 1904. His first meeting occurred in February or early March 1904. Tautz, *Walter Johannes Stein*, p. 169. See also Jens Heisterkamp, 'Helmuth von Moltke: eine Lebensskizze', in Meyer, *Helmuth von Moltke*, vol. 1.

May 1921, in which he denied that he and Moltke ever spoke about military or political matters before the outbreak of war, but affirmed that Moltke had been interested in getting to know Steiner's spiritual science.[49] Moltke admired Steiner's writings, for example on Nietzsche and Haeckel, and certainly felt equipped and inclined to explain Theosophy to a group of sceptics on board the royal yacht *Hohenzollern* in July 1904. He proudly wrote to his wife, 'because I was the only one who knew something about these matters I had to lead the conversation. At first some laughed, then they became more and more serious and in the end they listened to me as to the priest in church.'[50]

The Moltkes were not alone, of course, in their interest in Spiritualism and the supernatural. Their views were shared by many of their contemporaries, not least by influential people like Philipp Eulenburg and even the Kaiser himself. Eulenburg's Schloss Liebenberg was described by Maximilian Harden as a 'Spiritistennest'.[51] Such beliefs were a widespread European phenomenon, possibly as a reaction to the uncertainties of a rapidly changing world, as Robert Galbreath speculates:

The popularity of occultism during this time can be related to its fusion of scientific and religious postures, concern with inherent meaning, emphasis on spiritual wholeness in an age of fragmentation, and positive attitude toward the non-rational facets of man.[52]

Whatever the reason behind its popularity, and despite the fact that even the Kaiser was interested, Moltke's apparent belief in Spiritualism did not recommend him to be Chief of the General Staff, at least in his critics' eyes. Even the Kaiser realized this, and demanded of Moltke that he stop 'dabbling' in the supernatural once he became Chief of the General Staff.[53]

Eliza had always been the more committed follower of Steiner's Anthroposophy. Although Anthroposophy and Spiritualism are often mentioned together in accounts of Moltke's beliefs, they are in fact quite different. While Moltke's wife was also susceptible to general 'Occultism',

---

[49] I am grateful to Konrad Donat for supplying me with a summary of this unpublished speech, delivered on 25 May 1921 in Stuttgart, as well as other material relating to Rudolf Steiner and Moltke. [50] Moltke, *Erinnerungen*, 17 July 1904, p. 295.

[51] John C. G. Röhl, *Kaiser, Hof und Staat. Wilhelm II und die deutsche Politik*, Munich 1988, pp. 71ff.; idem (ed.), *Philipp Eulenburgs Politische Korrespondenz*, Boppard/Rhein 3 vols. (1976, 1979, 1983), vol. I, pp. 47ff. Other military men with an expressed interest in Spritualism included (for example) Erich Ludendorff, Friedrich von Bernhardi and, outside of Germany, Field Marshal Sir Douglas Haig. [52] Galbreath, 'Spiritual Science', thesis abstract, p. 2.

[53] See e.g. Einem, *Erinnerungen*, p. 151. The fact that Moltke was quite willing to give up this pursuit demonstrates that he was keen to accept the promotion, for it would have been easy to decline on the grounds of his beliefs; on the other hand, it shows that Moltke put his army career ahead of any 'occult' interests he may have had.

Moltke himself remained open-minded but sceptical.[54] His wife contin-ued her acquaintance with Steiner after Moltke's death. In fact, Steiner became important for Eliza, who believed him to be a link for communi-cating with her deceased husband. Steiner, as well as both the Moltkes, believed in reincarnation as part of his Anthroposophical philosophy, and Moltke's widow was convinced that her deceased husband was com-municating with her from the grave, via the medium Steiner.[55]

After the outbreak of war, Moltke and Steiner were to meet again, and his critics saw this as further proof of his 'supernatural' interests, which they considered irreconcilable with his position. However, it would seem as if Moltke had complied with the Kaiser's demand. In a letter to his wife in July 1907, he referred to the fact that he could not combine being Chief of the General Staff with what he called 'my own interests'. Considerations concerning his position were more important to him than Eliza's ambitions, he told his wife, and he explained that owing to his important position he could not lead the life that he would otherwise choose to live. 'If I do not accompany you on all your jour-neys then this is because I have a very real profession and have to remain with both feet firmly on the ground, as long as I want to do justice to that profession.'[56] Clearly, being Chief of the General Staff was more impor-tant to him than his interests in Anthroposophy.

A 'RELUCTANT MILITARY LEADER'? MOLTKE'S CONTROVERSIAL APPOINTMENT IN JANUARY 1906

Does Your Majesty really believe that you will win the first prize twice in the same lottery?[57]

Lieutenant-General von Moltke is in his 58th year. He is a relation of the great Moltke. . . . In person he is a big heavy man with a reserved manner, and he is believed to be capable of filling his new post with credit.[58]

---

[54] See Tautz, *Walter Johannes Stein*, p. 169; also Bucholz, *Moltke*, pp. 218ff. Rudolf Steiner's widow maintains that Moltke – like Steiner – was sceptical about Spiritualism, and that he had warned his wife about this, but respected her views and right to practise her beliefs. Marie Steiner, 'Helmuth von Moltke und Rudolf Steiner', *Das Goetheanum*, 5 March 1933.

[55] Thomas Meyer edited these alleged posthumous messages from Moltke to Steiner in the second volume of *Helmuth von Moltke 1848–1916*.

[56] Moltke, *Erinnerungen*, 19 May 1907, pp. 344–348; 18 July 1908.

[57] Franz Conrad von Hötzendorf, *Aus meiner Dienstzeit 1906–1918*, 5 vols., Vienna, Leipzig, Munich 1921–1925, vol. 1, p. 69, relaying a question Moltke allegedly asked the Kaiser before his appoint-ment.

[58] PRO, wo106/6182, Report on Changes in Foreign Armies During 1906, prepared by the General Staff, War Office, p. 39. My thanks to Dr Robert Foley for alerting me to this document.

The fact that Moltke himself had voiced doubts about accepting the promotion to Chief of the General Staff led to the coining of the phrase 'Feldherr wider Willen' (reluctant military leader). According to this view, Moltke had been a reluctant military leader who 'lacked the inner fire to enforce his will' and had been a bad choice for this important position.[59] Moltke's ultimate failure in leading the army in 1914 helped to lend credence to this interpretation. Yet, how much of this view is part of the myth-making of the Schlieffen school? How reluctant was Moltke to succeed Schlieffen?

It is certainly true that Moltke's attitude towards the sudden career prospect was ambiguous. Moreover, it seems clear that it was to a large extent the lack of a more suitable candidate, rather than Moltke's outstanding ability, that led to his appointment, as other candidates were either too old, or opposed Schlieffen's strategic views, or were not the Kaiser's choice. It goes almost without saying that only a man of whom the Kaiser approved could have been appointed. In that sense, at least, Moltke was an ideal candidate. Goltz commented in a letter of January 1906 that 'the supreme commander should only have a chief next to him whom he likes. This is the case with Moltke. Every thing else we have to wait and see.'[60] Moltke had been the Kaiser's friend as well as his long-term adjutant[61] (the Kaiser nick-named him 'Julius', and used the familiar 'Du' when speaking to him): in the Kaiser's mind, this made him a good candidate.[62] Wilhelm II believed that character, rather than genius, was tested in war, and Moltke's character seemed to commend him.[63] Moreover, he was a tall, dashing military figure, a fact that was important in securing the Kaiser's support; and his pleasant manners and varied cultural pursuits made him an appealing candidate to the monarch.[64] Critics of Moltke, however, alleged that the Kaiser was

---

[59] Groener, *Der Feldherr wider Willen*, p. xii. See Groener to Oberstleutnant von Strube, 7 January 1931, BA-MA, NL Groener, N46/39. Interestingly, Moltke's Austrian counterpart Franz Conrad von Hötzendorf had also initially turned down the offer of becoming Chief of the Austro-Hungarian General Staff in 1906, but he has not become known as a reluctant military leader. See e.g. Diether Degreif, 'Operative Planungen des K.u.K. Generalstabes für einen Krieg in der Zeit vor 1914 (1880–1914)', Ph.D. Dissertation, Mainz 1983, pp. 104–105; Herwig, *First World War*, p. 43. [60] Goltz, *Denkwürdigkeiten*, letter dated 9 January 1906, p. 279.

[61] On 14 September 1881, Moltke told his wife that Prince Wilhelm had been riding with him, and that the future Kaiser considered him 'an old acquaintance'. Moltke, *Erinnerungen*, p. 101.

[62] BA-MA, W-10/50222, Austrian plenipotentiary to Beck, 12 January 1904. 'The Kaiser is particularly inclined towards [Moltke] personally, and Herr von Moltke has this fact to thank for his current intended position.'

[63] See the account of Moltke's appointment, and critical evaluation of his abilities, in the Reichsarchiv manuscript 'Die Oberste Heeresleitung September 1914', BA-MA, W-10/51051, pp. 27ff. [64] Görlitz, *Generalstab*, p. 193.

primarily attracted to the famous name, and Moltke, too, suspected that the Kaiser wanted to win again in the same lottery by betting twice on the Moltke name.[65]

In January 1905, Wilhelm II informed Moltke that he considered him the only possible successor to Schlieffen. He told Moltke that 'General von der Goltz has also been recommended to me, whom I don't want, and also General von Beseler, whom I don't know. I know you and I trust you.'[66] The Kaiser had been impressed by Moltke's comments and 'his clear and healthy strategic views' during previous army manoeuvres.[67] His mind was made up.

When Wilhelm II asked Schlieffen about his views regarding Moltke's suitability, he apparently supported the monarch's choice. Schlieffen even told Moltke that 'he had observed you [Moltke] for a year now and he could suggest no better successor than you above all others'.[68] It should, however, be remembered that Schlieffen was unlikely to oppose the Kaiser on anything, even his chosen successor. Whatever Schlieffen might have told Moltke or the Kaiser, it is without doubt that he was not pleased with the monarch's choice.

Being Chief of the General Staff was a prestigious position, but it was no easy office. One of Moltke's tasks would be to expand and upgrade the German army in the face of opposition from the Minister of War, who was unwilling to support large army increases in the Reichstag. The conflict between the two military institutions, the debate over the quality and quantity of available soldiers, had hampered military planning for successive Chiefs of the General Staff.[69] The Military Cabinet and the commanding generals were further persons with potentially conflicting opinions, all of whom were in influential positions and able to oppose decisions made by the General Staff. And there were further difficulties. Since 1897, when Germany had embarked upon a naval policy designed to threaten and challenge British maritime supremacy, the army had received considerably less public exposure, and considerably less money, than previously. Instead, the navy had become

---

[65] Hülsen to Hutten-Czapski: 'Modern battles cannot be won with a great name alone.' Hutten-Czapski, *Sechzig Jahre Politik und Gesellschaft*, p. 410.

[66] Moltke, *Erinnerungen*, p. 306.

[67] BA-MA, w-10/51051, 'Die Oberste Heeresleitung September 1914', p. 28.

[68] Moltke, *Erinnerungen*, p. 306. Hermann von Santen's memoirs confirm that many had considered Beseler a better candidate. Santen, 'Erinnerungen', vol. 10, p. 362.

[69] See Stig Förster, *Der Doppelte Militarismus. Die deutsche Heeresrüstungspolitik zwischen Status-quo-Sicherung und Aggression, 1890–1913*, Stuttgart and Wiesbaden 1985. The wranglings over army increases in the last pre-war years will be examined in the next chapter.

Germany's pride and joy, not least because of the Kaiser's childish delight in having his very own navy constructed. *Weltpolitik* and ship-building meant that the army was no longer seen as synonymous with German power and prestige. Not until 1911 did it reclaim a position of importance resembling that of the navy, and only after that date was the General Staff able to push through some of the army increases that it had been advocating. In 1906, such a change of fortune could hardly be anticipated.

The position that Moltke took over was thus fraught with difficulty.[70] Waldersee recorded in January 1905: 'Moltke himself is clever enough to regret the decision of the Kaiser.'[71] It is not surprising that he initially refused the promotion, although it hardly helped increase his standing that his son-in-law apparently 'told everyone who wanted to hear it that his father-in-law was very unhappy' about the chance of promotion to Chief of the General Staff, that he 'did not consider himself suitable and that he was aiming for the command of an army corps'.[72] According to his son, it was modesty ('zurückhaltende Bescheidenheit') that motivated him to turn down the advancement. [73] It is more likely, however, that he himself had doubts whether he was a suitable candidate, and that he was worried that the Kaiser's personality might prove an insuperable obstacle to effective work.[74] The constant interference of a megalomaniac monarch, who considered himself able to intervene and determine military planning, war games and manoeuvres, added to the many difficulties the Chief of Staff had to face. In this light, Moltke's advancement in 1906 appears hardly to have been a golden opportunity.

Moltke's attitude towards these sudden career possibilities was thus ambiguous. Although he expressed doubts regarding his suitability for the position of Chief of the General Staff, he was, at the same time, an ambitious man who had prided himself on his previous military career. To have been considered suitable for the most important

[70] See also Goltz to Mudra, 28 December 1904: 'Whether I could seriously have changed things, if I had actually got the position, is very doubtful.' Goltz, *Denkwürdigkeiten*, p. 270.

[71] Waldersee, *Denkwürdigkeiten*, vol. 3, p. 224.

[72] BayHSTA-KA, MKr 43, No. 2309, Bavarian military plenipotentiary Gebsattel to Minister of War, 2 November 1905.

[73] BA-MA, NL Moltke, N78/37, Adam von Moltke, 'Eine Antwort an Herrn Walter Görlitz, das Kapitel "Der Krieg ohne Feldherr" in seinem Buch "Der Deutsche Generalstab"/betr. Gen. Obst Helmuth von Moltke', 1958, p. 3. But see Wallach, *Dogma*, p. 127, who does not believe that Moltke really turned down the position, and suspects that this 'cheeky lie' ('plumpe Lüge') was probably initiated by Groener.   [74] See also Heisterkamp, 'Lebensskizze', p. 32.

military position within Germany was simultaneously flattering and frightening. His letters to his wife reveal him as a man harbouring high aspirations for a military career. During the time he spent as his famous uncle's personal adjutant, he was both proud of his ancestor, and at the same time crippled by being in his shadow. He would constantly compare his own ability to that of his uncle, and did not always display the lack of self-confidence that his critics would later accredit to him. During a manoeuvre in 1879, for example, Moltke acted against the advice of his superior in the defence of his battalion. As he told his wife, he saw a chance to beat the opponent 'with the military sharp eye with which I was born', and after a successful defence he wrote: 'Indeed, the enemy's attack was rebuffed, and I was so proud that an ordinary strategist like uncle Helmuth seemed very small to me.'[75] It is likely that Moltke was harbouring secret ambitions and wanted to prove to himself and the world that he could live up to the grand name he had inherited. This would explain why it was relatively easy to talk him into accepting the position, despite the openly voiced criticisms and his own doubts.

Moltke's good relationship with the Kaiser proved to be to his advantage. Right from the start, he was able to make demands and lay down conditions. It is well known that he made his acceptance of the position dependent on the Kaiser's promise to stop interfering in army manoeuvres. Prior to Moltke's appointment, the Kaiser had enjoyed bringing about decisions in military manoeuvres by personally leading great cavalry attacks, despite the fact that this was nonsensical in the light of modern fire power. The Kaiser apparently knew that these attacks were of no practical benefit, but he enjoyed the impressive spectacle.[76] When Wilhelm decided in 1890 that he would personally take part in the annual big army manoeuvres, Alfred von Waldersee as Chief of Staff transformed the manoeuvres into 'a massive outdoor spectacle, a stage on which Wilhelm could perform'.[77] The so-called *Kaisermanöver* frequently resulted in blunders and misunderstandings, because the Kaiser failed to understand the manoeuvre plans. In front of foreign observers,

---

[75] Moltke, *Erinnerungen*, 11 September 1879, pp. 60–61.
[76] See Holger Afflerbach, *Falkenhayn. Politisches Denken und Handeln im Kaiserreich*, Munich 1994, p. 61.
[77] Bucholz, *Moltke*, p. 99. Interestingly, Waldersee was later to complain about the manoeuvres and war games, which had turned into ineffectual 'kids' games' in his opinion. Waldersee diary, 5 January 1904, unpublished original, courtesy of Professor John Röhl. Meisner's edition omits this quote, although some of Waldersee's criticisms of manoeuvres and war games remain in the published text: *Denkwürdigkeiten*, vol. 3, p. 226.

who were customarily present at war games, this must have been a great embarrassment. Moreover, these potential war-planning exercises became almost pointless, not only because the Kaiser insisted on taking part, but especially because his side had to win, for in Schlieffen's opinion, the Kaiser could not be treated 'like an ordinary mortal'.[78] The former Minister of War Karl von Einem first made the observation that the Kaiser seemed to be invincible in manoeuvres in 1898, and repeatedly after that date. In his opinion, the Kaiser was unjustly blamed for this. 'As a matter of fact it was Count Schlieffen himself who was responsible for the Kaiser's manoeuvre victories. This was a mistake of his – of a man <u>who perhaps made only this one mistake</u>.'[79]

Such interference resulted in a noticeable lack of discipline and commitment among the participants.[80] During the 1903 *Kaisermanöver* the leading generals were depressed and uninspired, because they were unable to make their own decisions and were dependent on instructions from the monarch's headquarters, as Zedlitz-Trützschler recalled in his memoirs. They were told where fights had to take place, what sort of attacks to launch ('mass attacks are preferred. . . . Battle has to take place right here, because the cavalry can only attack here'), and the result was a complete shambles.[81] In the following year things were no better, again largely due to the Kaiser's interference, whose enthusiasm led to unnecessary rushing around. He even rode right into the firing line to speed up the attack. Zedlitz-Trützschler summed up, 'as a matter of fact, these manoeuvres, as in previous years, were of no use either to the troops or the General Staff.'[82] For the work of the General Staff, *Kaisermanöver* were of particular importance, because they were the only time when the General Staff exerted direct control over troops.[83] Based on this experience, strategic planning would be conducted. It was thus all the more important that such exercises were based on realistic scenarios. As a result of the Kaiser's interference, officers were increasingly unwilling to pose as the opposing army to His Majesty's side – as Moltke was the first to explain to the astonished Kaiser, who had until this time naively assumed that both sides had been treated equally and that his victories

---

[78] Otto Graf zu Stolberg-Wernigerode, *Die Unentschiedene Generation. Deutschlands konservative Führungsschichten am Vorabend des Ersten Weltkrieges*, Munich 1968, p. 121.

[79] Einem, *Erinnerungen*, pp. 146–147. Emphasis in the original.

[80] See e.g. the description of the 1900 manoeuvres by Count L. von der Asseburg-Falkenstein, recorded by Baroness Spitzemberg, *Diary*, 3 November 1900, pp. 401–402.

[81] Zedlitz-Trützschler, *Zwölf Jahre am deutschen Kaiserhof*, p. 42.   [82] Ibid., pp. 83–84.

[83] Samuels, *Command or Control*, p. 30.

1 Scenes at the annual summer manoeuvres, 1899
a 'The Garde du Corps on Parade'

1b The Kaiser (on horseback) talks to Archduke Franz Ferdinand (in German uniform)

1c The Kaiser greets his staff officers. Moltke is on the right.

1d The Kaiser with Moltke (left). To the right of the Kaiser are his sister, Margarethe von Hessen, and General von Plessen

had been *bona fide*.[84] Schlieffen was too much of a monarchist to oppose the Kaiser, even on the issue of cavalry attacks, although he, too, was aware of their redundancy.[85]

In July 1904, the Kaiser's usual interference in army manoeuvres[86] led to Moltke's reflection on the position of the future Chief of the General Staff. 'More and more I realize what a difficult inheritance [Schlieffen's] successor will have to accept. That this is so is certainly to a large extent Schlieffen's fault.'[87] Moltke expected the Chief of Staff to exert his authority more strongly, and to curb the Kaiser's unwanted and unwarranted meddling with army manoeuvres. Moltke was able to speak openly with the Kaiser, more openly perhaps than most. In January 1905, he told his wife: 'Last night I was at His Majesty's. I had a conversation with him that lasted three quarters of an hour, and I told him everything that was on my mind. I think no man has ever spoken to him like that.'[88] In another frank conversation with the monarch in January 1905, Moltke raised this point, as he recalled in a letter to his wife: 'Count Schlieffen says that the Kaiser has to win if he participates; as Kaiser he cannot be beaten by one of his generals.' Moltke's conclusion was therefore that the Kaiser should not lead at all in manoeuvres. Rather, he would have to keep out of such exercises if they were to have any real benefit. 'The kind of war game in which the opponent is delivered to Your Majesty tied hand and foot at the start must conjure up completely false impressions, which will be detrimental when war really comes', he told the Kaiser.[89] In his frank discussions with the monarch, Moltke attempted to carve out a favourable position for himself as future Chief of Staff, and in March of the same year the Kaiser asked Moltke instead of Schlieffen to prepare the next manoeuvres.[90] Moltke's manoeuvre

---

[84]   Moltke, *Erinnerungen*, 29 January 1905, p. 309. Later, not everyone who remembered the manoeuvres as useless exercises was convinced of their damaging results. Former Minister of War Karl von Einem considered it an advantage that the Kaiser's interference had ceased after 1906, but felt that they should not have been taken quite so seriously. In the event of war, Einem was convinced, Schlieffen, not the Kaiser, would have led the troops, and that was more important than manoeuvres. The bias of these memoirs published in 1933, should, however, not be underestimated. Most commentators at the time agreed that the manoeuvres were a scandal. Einem, *Erinnerungen*, p. 147.

[85]   Walter Görlitz, *Kleine Geschichte des deutschen Generalstabes*, 2nd edn Berlin 1977, p. 128.

[86]   Falkenhayn regarded that year's manoeuvres as appalling ('zum Himmel schreiend'). However, in 1906, after Moltke had taken over from Schlieffen, Falkenhayn was happy with the new-style manoeuvres, in which leaders had for the first time enjoyed 'complete freedom of action': Afflerbach, *Falkenhayn*, pp. 59, 61.   [87]   Moltke, *Erinnerungen*, 23 July 1904, p. 296.

[88]   Ibid., 8 January 1905, p. 303.   [89]   Ibid., 29 January 1905, pp. 304ff.

[90]   Ibid., 7 March 1905, pp. 319–320. Schlieffen tried in vain to boycott this plan.

2 Army manoeuvres, 1904. Behind the Kaiser (1) is Moltke (2). The chief of the Military Cabinet, Count von Hülsen-Haeseler, is at the centre (3)

plan of that year was received favourably by the Kaiser, something that Moltke evidently felt strongly about, as he informed his wife:

I am very glad that everything has been initiated well and I have the daring hope that it will be possible for once to have a war-like manoeuvre without wilful interference and without unnatural cavalry battles etc. – If I succeed in this I have not lived in vain.[91]

Moltke was even prepared to resign if his plan failed, believing that his own fate was less important than achieving the desired goal of keeping the Kaiser from imposing 'unmilitary aberrations' on the manoeuvres. As a result of Moltke's insistence, during his time in office the value of *Kaisermanöver* for military planning greatly increased. They became a continuous exercise lasting several days without interruption, and a means to test different combat formations, envelopments and breakthroughs.[92] The manoeuvres of 1906 certainly made a good impression on foreign commentators, as a report prepared by the British General Staff noted:

This year great efforts were made to render the operations more warlike. . . . The manoeuvres were continuous throughout the four days, and the Emperor refrained from taking command of either side. . . . On the whole there seems little doubt that the new chief of the general staff has infused fresh life into these manoeuvres, and that a marked advance has been made on previous years.[93]

Moltke wanted the Kaiser to delay his appointment until after the autumn manoeuvres. He thought that if he were able to conduct them successfully and to the Kaiser's satisfaction, he would also make a successful Chief of Staff. But as early as July 1905, on board the royal yacht *Hohenzollern*, the Kaiser's mind was made up.[94] The manoeuvres were a success: 'they were much more war-like than usual, e.g. without the cavalry attacks', as Baroness von Spitzemberg noted,[95] and Moltke was rewarded with a high decoration ('the "Roter-Adler-Orden" First Class with oak leaves and the royal crown').[96] The Kaiser was pleased with the conduct of the manoeuvres, and Moltke was appointed to the position of Chief of the General Staff on 1 January 1906, while remaining the Kaiser's *Generaladjutant*.[97]

[91] Ibid., 10 July 1905, pp. 323–324.   [92] Samuels, *Command or Control*, p. 30.
[93] PRO, wo106/6171, 'Report on Foreign Manoeuvres 1906', p. 131. My thanks to Dr Robert Foley for alerting me to this document.   [94] Moltke, *Erinnerungen*, 21 July 1905, p. 325.
[95] Spitzemberg, *Diary*, 10 November 1905, p. 450.
[96] Moltke, *Erinnerungen*, Kabinettsorder 15 September 1905, p. 341.
[97] Ibid., Kabinettsorder 1 January 1906, pp. 343–344. According to the Bavarian military plenipotentiary Gebsattel, however, Moltke had not gained in esteem among his military colleagues as a result of the manoeuvres, which Gesattel described as 'not exactly a happy confirmation of Moltke'. BayHSTA-KA, MKr 43, No. 36, 3 January 1906; MKr 45, No. 1973, 23 September

As early as 1904, the Kaiser had brushed aside Moltke's objections to accepting the post, asserting that 'a Prussian officer must be confident in everything and be able to do anything'.[98] Apparently he believed that Moltke would be all right in peace-time, and that he himself would take over as leader of the army in times of war.[99] Waldersee recorded in his diary during the autumn manoeuvres of 1903 that 'the Kaiser had repeatedly talked about the General Staff in the most degrading way', even going as far as saying 'he did not need a General Staff, he would do everything alone, with his *Flügeladjutanten*'.[100] The Kaiser apparently wanted to be his own Chief of Staff, just as he was determined to be his own Chancellor and Supreme Commander of the Navy. In his desire to decide most matters personally, he regarded these lesser men as mere instruments of his will.[101] Hermann von Stein recorded that Wilhelm II told Moltke at the time of his appointment: 'You can do that little bit of peace work, and in times of war, I will be my own Chief of the General Staff.'[102] It is possible that the Kaiser's choice fell on Moltke precisely because he was evidently not the best possible candidate. He certainly ruled out those candidates who would have been difficult to control, in line with his desire to exercise ultimate personal control over his subordinates.

Rather than regretting the fact that Schlieffen was replaced and did not lead the German army into war in 1914, as Schlieffen's supporters do, it is more interesting to speculate what impact one of the other possible candidates for Schlieffen's replacement would have had on the General Staff. Contrary to the impression one might get from post-war military writings, not everyone in the General Staff shared Schlieffen's strategic views, and Moltke was not the only 'heretic' to disagree with certain aspects of them.[103] Another candidate would not necessarily

---

1905. For a critical view of the *Kaisermanöver* of 1905, see Oberst a.D. Gädke in *Berliner Tageblatt*, 2 January 1906. A British interpretation of the 1905 manoeuvres can be found in the report of the Special Correspondent of the *Standard*, *Journal of the Royal United Service Institute*, January–June 1906, pp. 181–199, who commented on the confusion caused by spectators who rushed on to the scene, and criticized the dominant role exercised by General Staff officers in directing the manoeuvres.   [98] BA-MA, NL Goltz, N732/15, Mudra to Goltz, 8 March 1904.

[99] See e.g. Groener: 'I don't know whether the saying that is attributed to the Kaiser, that he would be his own military leader (*Feldherr*) in times of war, is true, but I don't consider it unlikely.' BA-MA, N46/39, Groener to Oberstleutnant von Strube, 7 January 1931. Also Groener, *Testament*, p. 79.

[100] Waldersee diary, marginal note, 5 January 1904, not printed in published edition. Courtesy of Professor John Röhl.

[101] See also Schmidt-Bückeburg, *Militärkabinett*, p. 194.   [102] Stein, *Erlebnisse*, p. 36.

[103] Critics of Schlieffen's plan included Generals von Bülow and von Schlichting, and also, famously, the military writer Friedrich von Bernhardi. Ritter, *Schlieffen Plan*, pp. 51–52.

have conformed any more closely to Schlieffen's strategy. There were three other possible contenders for the position: Karl von Bülow (1846–1921), *Generalquartiermeister* in the General Staff from 1902 to 1903 and Commanding General of the Third Army Corps since 1903; Colmar von der Goltz (1843–1916), at the time Commanding General of the First Army Corps in East Prussia; and Hans Hartwig von Beseler (1850–1921), *Oberquartiermeister* in the General Staff since 1899.

Beseler was Schlieffen's preferred candidate. During his successful career he had been both Waldersee's and Schlieffen's protégé and had served as *Oberquartiermeister*. Schlieffen considered him his likely successor, and Hülsen-Haeseler suggested him as such to the Kaiser.[104] In 1904, Beseler was ennobled, a clear sign that he was destined for the post of Chief of Staff, as Minister of War Einem told him.[105] According to Groener, Beseler, reputed to have had great operational abilities, had not yet had an opportunity to make his mark, and his leadership qualities were uncertain.[106] Ultimately, however, the Kaiser was unlikely to agree to a candidate that Schlieffen favoured. Mudra rightly suspected that, as the Kaiser did not like Beseler, it was highly unlikely that he would be a serious candidate.[107]

Karl von Bülow was a further possible candidate. He was regarded by many as a natural successor to Schlieffen. From 1902, as *Generalquartiermeister*, he had a chance to prove his suitability, but his stubborn independence had made co-operation with Schlieffen impossible.[108] Bülow disapproved of Schlieffen's envelopment idea and was, according to Groener, 'an outspoken advocate of frontal attack (*Frontalstratege*)'.[109] His name is associated with the fateful defeat on the Marne. It is impossible to predict how Germany's strategic plan would have developed under his leadership. Perhaps he would have exchanged the rigid Schlieffen Plan for a more flexible strategy. One could even speculate that under his leadership Germany might have been spared the odium of beginning an

---

[104] Beseler and Huelsen had been school friends. See Bucholz, *Moltke*, p. 216; W. Conze, *Polnische Nation und Deutsche Politik im Ersten Weltkrieg*, Cologne and Graz 1958, p. 110. After his successes in conquering Antwerp and Modlin in 1914, Beseler was appointed Governor of Warsaw, being responsible for the administration of Poland. Conze's book on German policy in Poland in the First World War includes further biographical details on Beseler.   [105] Ibid., p. 110.

[106] Groener, *Feldherr wider Willen*, pp. xiv–xv.

[107] Mudra to Goltz, 8 March 1904, BA-MA, NL Goltz, N732/15. According to Mudra's account, the army favoured the current commanding general of the first army corps, August von Mackensen.

[108] BayHSTA-KA, MKr 43, No. 2309, Bavarian military plenipotentiary Gebsattel to Minister of War, 2 November 1905. That Bülow was a candidate seems to have been forgotten over time, and Heinz Kraft's entry in the *NDB* does not mention him as having been in line for promotion to Chief of Staff. *NDB*, vol. 2, Berlin 1955, pp. 736ff.   [109] Groener, *Lebenserinnerungen*, p. 90.

offensive war. Bülow was the most likely alternative candidate to Moltke, and even when Moltke became Schlieffen's deputy there was still a chance that Bülow would ultimately succeed Schlieffen, depending on Moltke's performance. However, Bülow's reputed 'Bismarck-like nature' did not work in his favour, for the Kaiser was unlikely to be keen on a candidate who would want to stand his own ground too much.[110]

Colmar von der Goltz was perhaps the most bellicose in the selection of possible candidates.[111] He was also the most senior and most experienced contender. He had already made a name for himself as a military writer, and was known as the 'father of the Turkish Army', owing to his endeavours to help modernize, train and advise the Turkish Army during his time as inspector of Ottoman military schools from 1883 to 1895.[112] Goltz was a passionate campaigner for reforms within the German army which were, in his opinion, a necessary prerequisite for Germany's future success in war – an event that he regarded as both unavoidable and necessary. He was a controversial, even unpopular figure, owing to his demands for army increases, and the reduction of military service from three to two years.[113] A further reason for controversy was his view on the state of Germany's fortification system, which Goltz regarded as inadequate. This did not increase his popularity in military circles.[114] A further disadvantage, probably the most serious one, was that he did not have a personal relationship with the Kaiser.[115] Goltz was a competent and experienced candidate, even 'one of the most interesting and versatile personalities of the Wilhelmine Era',[116] but not one under whose leadership Germany would have followed a more peaceful path. Goltz continually warned of the danger that Britain posed to Germany, and repeatedly advocated war against Britain. Bruno

---

[110] BA-MA, w-10/50222, Austrian plenipotentiary to Beck, 12 January 1904: 'It is, by the way, not out of the question that Herr von Bülow might become Chief after all, if the attempt with Moltke were not to create a definite solution (*ein Definitivum*). They say that Herr von Bülow is too much a kind of "Bismark-Natur" [*sic*] to become Chief of the General Staff under the current conditions.'

[111] See e.g. his sarcastic remark about the Peace Conference at the Hague: 'We truly don't need the Hague Peace Congress, we are peaceful enough without it.' *Denkwürdigkeiten*, letter to Mudra, 24 August 1907, p. 284. See also his bellicose statements during the Bosnian Crisis, in Chapter 3.

[112] F. A. K. Yasamee, 'Colmar Freiherr von der Goltz and the Rebirth of the Ottoman Empire', unpublished manuscript study, 1996, p. 2. Now in *Diplomacy & Statecraft*, 9, 2, 1998. My thanks to Dr Yasamee for making this paper available to me. See also Jehuda L. Wallach, *Anatomie einer Militärhilfe. Die preußisch-deutschen Militärmissionen in der Türkei 1835–1919*, Düsseldorf 1976, pp. 64ff.

[113] Herman Teske's entry on Colmar von der Goltz-Pascha, *NDB*, vol. 6, Berlin 1964, p. 630.

[114] Yasamee, 'Colmar Freiherr von der Goltz', p. 15.

[115] In 1910/1911, the Kaiser was much more favourably inclined towards Goltz, and his excellent performance in the *Kaisermanöver* earned him a promotion to *Generalfeldmarschall*, an unusual honour to receive in peace-time. *NDB*, vol. 6, p. 631.   [116] Ibid., p. 632.

3 Colmar Freiherr von der Goltz, postcard *c.* 1914

von Mudra, Goltz's Chief of Staff and friend, hoped in March 1904 that Goltz might still be considered as a candidate to succeed Schlieffen, and had high hopes that a military leader who believed in war as essential for Germany might make good use of the opportunity that the Moroccan Crisis offered:

The current times are, as it were, tailor-made for Your Excellency – Germany has got into a wonderful political and military situation, without her own doing. Now something can be done and prepared. But it requires a far-reaching view in the leading position, purified by an absolute belief in the war-like development of Germany and by real desire for war (*Kriegslust*).[117]

When Moltke's successful candidacy was confirmed, Goltz expressed relief at not having been appointed. Goltz thought that Moltke deserved a chance to prove himself and was quite impressed with his efforts.[118] If he was disappointed at having been turned down, or if he begrudged Moltke the position, he certainly did not show it, and the two men maintained friendly relations for the rest of their lives.

Two other possible candidates who, according to Groener, might have been suitable had already left the General Staff: General Georg von Alten and General Karl von Endres.[119] The army conventions regarding seniority prevented promotion of a suitable candidate if he was younger or had had fewer years in office than another. This restriction made it impossible to find other possible successors at the time. Thus, concluded Groener, 'the choice fell on a personality who was particularly close to the Monarch, the younger Helmuth von Moltke, the nephew and adjutant for many years of the *Generalfeldmarschall*'.[120]

It is important to realize that the Kaiser, even as late as 1905/1906, enjoyed unopposed authority to appoint candidates of his choice to important offices, purely at his own discretion and without ministerial counterchecks. If need be, he could even act contrary to the advice of his Chief of the Military Cabinet, as he did in the case of Moltke's appointment. The Kaiser was encouraged by his friend and confidant Philipp zu Eulenburg, who was possibly behind Moltke's appointment

---

[117] Mudra to Goltz, 8 March 1904, BA-MA, NL Golz, N732/15.

[118] Goltz, *Denkwürdigkeiten*, p. 279.

[119] Bucholz, *Moltke*, p. 215. Bucholz names further possible candidates: Gottlieb Graf von Haeseler, Moritz Frhr. von Bissing (both already retired), and Maximilian Graf Yorck von Wartenburg (who died during Waldersee's China expedition). According to Gebsattel, possible candidates, apart from Goltz, Bülow and Beseler, were General von Bock und Polach (too old) and Generalleutnant von Scheffer (too junior). BayHSTA-KA, MKr 43, No. 2309, Bavarian military plenipotentiary Gebsattel to Minister of War, 2 November 1905.

[120] Groener, *Feldherr wider Willen*, pp. XIV–XV.

as he was behind others.[121] Whether Eulenburg suggested Moltke as a candidate remains unclear, but he was a friend of Moltke, and it was he who advised him to make his acceptance of the post dependent on certain conditions, such as the issue of manoeuvres.[122] Mudra was quite correct in his assessment of the situation when he wrote in March 1904 that Moltke was 'a victim of the most direct *sic volo, sic jubeo*'.[123] In any other system, Moltke would almost certainly not have been appointed Chief of the General Staff, and he would not have ended up leading a million-strong army into war, given that many contemporary military observers considered him ill-equipped to do so.

Despite the fact that Moltke's appointment had not been without opposition, he occupied the position of Chief of the General Staff from January 1906 until September 1914 – crucially important years in which he was to have a great impact on strategic planning and military preparations of the German army. Armed with Schlieffen's legacy, the Schlieffen Plan, his task would be to prepare Germany for the war on two fronts that she would face in the not too distant future.

SCHLIEFFEN'S LEGACY: THE SCHLIEFFEN PLAN

A complete battle of annihilation had been fought, particularly admirable because, contrary to all theory, it had been won by a minority.

Alfred von Schlieffen, 'The Battle of Cannae'[124]

Those who do not share [Schlieffen's] faith in miracles must judge that in any case he overrated German strength enormously. But this is entirely in the tradition of the Wilhelminian epoch.

Gerhard Ritter, *The Schlieffen Plan*[125]

At the end of his time in office, Schlieffen composed a memorandum to his successor, outlining his envisaged future strategy. It is not known who termed this memorandum 'the Schlieffen Plan', but it has become

---

[121] In his accusations against Eulenburg in 1906–1907, Harden maintained that 'for years, no important post was filled without his [Eulenburg's] help', and that in doing so, Eulenburg 'took care of all his friends'. Quoted in Hull, 'Kaiser Wilhelm II and the "Liebenberg Circle"', p. 193.

[122] Johannes Haller, *Aus dem Leben des Fürsten Philipp zu Eulenburg-Hertefeld*, Berlin and Leipzig 1926, p. 333, note 2. Haller's biography of Eulenburg is now quite discredited. For a more accurate account see Röhl (ed.), *Eulenburgs Politische Korrespondenz*.

[123] Mudra to Goltz, 8 March 1904, BA-MA, N732/15.

[124] Alfred von Schlieffen, 'Die Schlacht bei Cannae', *Gesammelte Schriften*, vol. 1, Berlin 1913, p. 29.

[125] Ritter, *Schlieffen Plan*, p. 68. All quotes from the English edition.

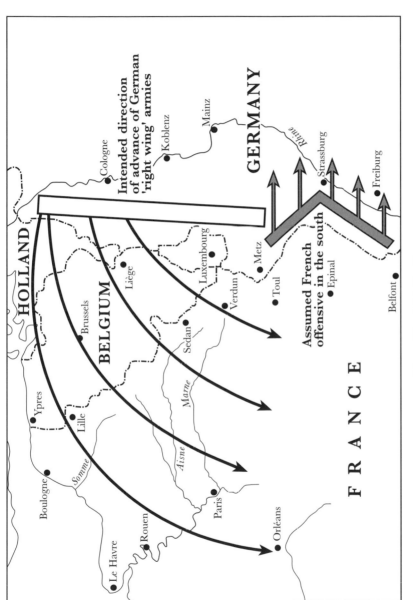

Map 2 The Schlieffen Plan

Labels within the map:

HOLLAND

BELGIUM

GERMANY

FRANCE

Intended direction of advance of German 'right wing' armies

Assumed French offensive in the south

Boulogne
Le Havre
Ypres
Lille
Rouen
Somme
Brussels
Liège
Cologne
Koblenz
Mainz
Paris
Sedan
Luxembourg
Verdun
Metz
Strassburg
Freiburg
Orléans
Aisne
Marne
Toul
Epinal
Belfont
Rhine

known as such.[126] The plan has acquired an almost mythical reputation. It came to be regarded by many commentators after the war as a recipe for certain victory, if only it had been implemented in the way its creator had intended. Schlieffen has been celebrated as the man who had the answer to Germany's military dilemma of facing enemies on two fronts,[127] a problem that German military strategists had faced even before Germany's neighbours in the East and West, Russia and France, had concluded their alliance in 1894. As the two opposing alliance systems became strengthened over time – the Entente between France, Britain and Russia on the one hand, and the Triple Alliance of Germany, Austria-Hungary and Italy on the other – the chances of a future war *not* being fought on two fronts diminished. Schlieffen's famous memorandum of December 1905 – the culmination of almost 15 years of strategic planning in the face of this predicament – has come to be regarded 'as a showpiece of German General Staff work'.[128]

The problem of a two-front war had occupied Schlieffen's famous predecessor, the elder Moltke, ever since Germany had defeated France in 1871. Following the experience of the Franco-Prussian war, Moltke was doubtful that a total victory against two opponents was possible at all. As far back as April 1871, he wrote: 'Germany cannot hope to rid herself of one enemy by a quick offensive victory in the West in order then to turn against the other. We have just seen how difficult it is to bring even the victorious war against France to a conclusion.'[129]

---

[126] Jäschke, '"Schlieffenplan" und "Marneschlacht"', p. 185. According to Kuhl, Schlieffen 'explicitly handed over the memorandum of 1905 to his successor when he took his leave'. BA-MA, N56/7, NL Tappen, Müller-Loebnitz to Tappen, 29 December 1920. Recently, Terence Zuber has advanced the argument that 'there never was a "Schlieffen Plan"'. Zuber's thesis seems to be confused by terminology, and concludes from 'massive inconsistencies' in the memorandum that it was no war plan at all. Unfortunately the article appeared too late to be incorporated in this study. It should by pointed out, however, that the 1905 memorandum was merely the culmination of several years of planning, that it was an outline of strategy, and was not intended to be 'a war plan' in itself. In many ways, the term 'Schlieffen Plan' is a mere short-hand for the overall strategy of turning the threatening two-front war into two one-front wars, and, of course, Schlieffen and his contemporaries did not consider the 1905 memorandum a 'war plan'. However, in 1914 and subsequently, the men in charge of military operations certainly felt they were implementing the 'Schlieffen Plan', and they would have objected strongly to Zuber's assertion that there was no such plan. See Terence Zuber, 'The Schlieffen Plan Reconsidered', *War in History*, 6, 3, 1999, pp. 262–305.

[127] He was particularly admired by younger General Staff officers who regarded him as a demigod: Wallach, *Kriegstheorien*, p. 94.   [128] Ritter, *Schlieffen Plan*, p. 48.

[129] Quoted in ibid., p. 18. For Moltke's reaction following the transition from the 1866 *Kabinettskrieg* to the *Volkskrieg* of 1870–1871, see Christian Müller, 'Anmerkungen zur Entwicklung von Kriegsbild und operativ-strategischem Szenario im preußisch-deutschen Heer vor dem Ersten Weltkrieg', *MGM*, 57, 1998, pp. 329ff.

According to Ritter's analysis, Moltke 'was content with a defensive which was to exploit any opportunity for offensive thrust'.[130] Moltke believed that the French fortifications along the Franco-German border would make an offensive attack in the West impossible. His plan was therefore to concentrate on an initial attack in the East, with a limited objective. He did not aim for a total annihilation of the opponent, merely to establish a front after overrunning Congress Poland.[131]

Alfred von Waldersee replaced Moltke in 1889, but during his short time in office he made few changes to his predecessor's plan.[132] He was replaced in 1891, having lost the Kaiser's favour following a harsh manoeuvre critique,[133] by the 58-year-old Generalleutnant Alfred von Schlieffen.[134] During his time as Chief of the General Staff from 1891 to 1905, Schlieffen altered the elder Moltke's strategic plan.[135] According to Ritter, that change went much deeper than a mere reversal of the initial direction of the attack, from the East (under Moltke) to the West (Schlieffen). While Moltke had intended to split the German army into two roughly equal parts, Schlieffen wanted to mass most of the army on one front, where a decisive battle of annihilation was to be fought. The division of forces that Schlieffen eventually aimed for was a ratio of 1:8.[136]

Schlieffen began to doubt whether an offensive against Russia would be possible, after the Russians, apparently due to their knowledge of Germany's strategic plan, started to concentrate their troops in their northern and western military districts and to fortify places along the Njemen and Narew rivers, thus increasing their defensive capabilities.[137] Unlike the elder Moltke, Schlieffen did not consider that the French fortifications would necessarily render an offensive in the West impossible. Instead, he saw Germany's best chance of victory in a swift offensive in the West, against France, while in the East, the German army

---

[130] Ritter, *Schlieffen Plan*, p. 21.   [131] See Turner, 'Significance', p. 47.

[132] See Graydon A. Tunstall, Jr., 'The Schlieffen Plan: the Diplomacy and Military Strategy of the Central Powers in the East, 1905–1914', Ph.D. Dissertation, Rutgers University 1974, p. 34 (now published as *Planning for War Against Russia and Serbia: Austro-Hungarian and German Military Strategies, 1871–1914*, New York 1993). Waldersee's importance lay in encouraging a closer contact with the Austrian General Staff, rather than in any changes to military planning.

[133] Stein, *Erlebnisse*, p. 26.

[134] Schlieffen was born in Berlin on 28 February 1833, and died 4 January 1913. For biographical details, see e.g. Gustav Frhr. von Freytag-Loringhoven, 'Generalfeldmarschall Graf von Schlieffen. Lebensgang und Lebenswerk', in Schlieffen, *Gesammelte Schriften*, Berlin 1913, pp. VII–XLIII.

[135] Dieckmann, 'Der Schlieffenplan', unpublished manuscript, no date, BA-MA, W10/50220, p. 8.

[136] Ritter, *Schlieffen Plan*, p. 21.   [137] Dieckmann, 'Schlieffenplan', p. 9.

was initially to be on the defensive.[138] Russia would be dealt with after France had been delivered a decisive blow. In effect, Schlieffen aimed to turn a two-front war into two one-front wars.[139] Germany would have to attack France in such a way as to avoid the heavy fortifications along the Franco-German border. Instead of a 'head-on' engagement, which would lead to position warfare of unpredictable length, the opponent should be enveloped.[140] Moving through Switzerland would have been impractical, whereas in the North, Luxembourg had no army at all, and the weak Belgian army was expected to retreat to its fortifications.[141] Schlieffen had decided to concentrate all German effort on the right wing, even if the French opted for offensive action along another part of the long common border[142] and even at the risk of allowing the French temporarily to reclaim Alsace-Lorraine. In his last manoeuvre critique, Schlieffen had outlined how it was possible for a smaller army to defeat a larger one. To avoid being swallowed up by the opponent in a frontal attack, it would have to advance on the most sensitive areas – the flanks and the rear, and aim to catch the opponent by surprise.[143] German troops would be concentrated on the right wing, and would have to envelop the French army, aiming to reach Paris. Once the French capital was taken and the French army annihilated, German troops would be moved to the eastern theatre of war.[144]

[138] In his diary, Waldersee recorded that the impetus for changing the direction of the offensive from the East to the West came from Wilhelm II, rather than Schlieffen himself: *Denkwürdigkeiten*, vol. 2, p. 318. According to Dieckmann, 'Schlieffenplan', pp. 47–48, there is no reason to doubt Waldersee's statement, although Waldersee was wrong to claim that the reason for the change was the Kaiser's naïvity ('unreife Ideen'). Rather, political considerations seem to have been behind the Kaiser's wish to alter the strategic plan: at the time (in 1894), Wilhelm was eager to improve relations with Russia. A change of military strategy was thus in keeping with current political aspirations.

[139] Peter Graf Kielmansegg, *Deutschland und der Erste Weltkrieg*, Frankfurt/M. 1980, p. 24.

[140] Schlieffen was inspired by the historic battle of Cannae of 216 BC, in which the Carthaginian military leader Hannibal defeated the numerically far superior Romans with one of the most famous envelopments in history. See e.g. David Eggenberger, *A Dictionary of Battles*, London 1967; *Cambridge Ancient History*, vol. 3, *Rome and the Mediterranean to 133 B.C.*, Cambridge 1989; Martin Samuels, 'The Reality of Cannae', *MGM*, 1/1990, pp. 7–31. However, Schlieffen failed to notice that although the Romans were defeated at Cannae, they won the war overall on account of their superior sea power. See Herwig, *First World War*, p. 49; Wolfgang von Groote, 'Historische Vorbilder des Feldzuges 1914 im Westen', *MGM* 1/1990, pp. 33–55; Wallach, *Kriegstheorien*, p. 106.

[141] Quoted in Dieckmann, 'Schlieffenplan', pp. 121–122.

[142] BA-MA, NL Tappen, N56/2, letter from Reichsarchiv to Tappen, December 1923, p. 255.

[143] BayHSTA-KA, Bestand Generalstab 1237, Schlussbesprechung 23 December 1905, p. 13.

[144] This strategic thinking sums up the Schlieffen Plan. However, not just Schlieffen's memorandum of 1905, but his entire strategic thinking from 1897, should be understood to amount to what is generally referred to as the Schlieffen Plan, and there can be no doubt of its general direction and intentions. For a different view, see Terence Zuber, 'The Schlieffen Plan Reconsidered', pp. 262ff.

The idea of enveloping the opponent and of violating Belgian neutrality was not new. Following the Boulanger crisis, Bismarck had asked Waldersee whether it would not be practicable to march through neutral Belgium.[145] Far from having been 'Schlieffen's ingenious idea',[146] a violation of neutral Belgium had been a frequently discussed topic, just as it was of serious concern to German strategists whether France herself might begin hostilities by marching through Belgium.[147] The first written record of Schlieffen's plan to violate Belgian neutrality dates from August 1897. As he put it bluntly: 'An offensive which aims to circumvent Verdun must not shy away from violating not only the neutrality of Luxembourg but also that of Belgium.'[148] However, British neutrality hinged on Belgian neutrality. To violate the latter meant risking a British involvement. Only when Anglo-German relations worsened, and when it was thought increasingly likely that Britain would be on the side of Germany's enemies regardless of the issue of Belgian neutrality, did the option of marching through Belgium gain feasibility.[149] The available evidence suggests that the military planners decided much earlier than the civilian government that British involvement in a future war would be unavoidable. Bethmann Hollweg in particular still pursued his desperate attempts at achieving reconciliation with Britain, hoping for British neutrality until the very last moment of the July Crisis, whereas the younger Moltke never shared his optimism.

In his planning, Schlieffen counted on two things – that German victory in the West would be quick (he estimated this would take about six weeks), and that Russian mobilization would be slow, so that a small German defensive force would suffice to hold back Russia until France was beaten. In 1905, when Schlieffen finalized his strategy, the recently defeated Russians posed no great threat, and would indeed have been slow to mobilize along their western front: not surprisingly, Russia was known as the 'clay-footed colossus'. After a swift victory in the West, the full force of the German army would be directed eastwards. Russia would be beaten in turn. This was the recipe for victory, the certain way out of Germany's encirclement.

The international background to the development of Schlieffen's plan

[145] Dieckmann, 'Schlieffenplan', p. 57.   [146] Ibid., pp. 60–63.

[147] Schlieffen's memorandum of 1905 did not yet express the intention of necessarily violating Dutch neutrality. In his later memorandum, he decided that Holland's neutrality could not be respected. German fears of a possible French violation of Belgium are discussed in Chapter 3.

[148] Quoted in Dieckmann, 'Schlieffenplan', p. 64.   [149] Ibid., pp. 60–63.

is significant to an analysis of its genesis. From the summer of 1904 onwards, when Schlieffen drafted his first version of his famous plan, the Russians were losing in the Russo-Japanese war. In January 1905, Russia suffered the domestic effects of the war – revolution. The *Entente Cordiale* between Britain and France was only just being shown to be effective during the First Moroccan Crisis, which began in March 1905. German attempts at splitting up the new alliance were failing, but clearly the Entente was not yet considered a serious threat. Schlieffen regarded Russia and France as Germany's main enemies. Until the autumn of 1905, at least, he expected a position of benevolent neutrality from Britain.[150] Nonetheless, he was prepared to face a hostile Britain, too, for he felt confident that the British expeditionary force would easily be defeated. Given such encouraging circumstances, Schlieffen appears to have been in favour of preventive war, and his plan, formulated against this background, was thus more than simply his 'military testament' to Moltke, as Christian Müller argues.[151]

Schlieffen's lack of respect for British fighting power was not unique; the German military attaché in London, Count von der Schulenburg, was apparently looking forward to 'giving them a reception they will remember for centuries'.[152] Even Bismarck had once joked that he would send the police to arrest the British army, were they to land on the German coast,[153] and the younger Moltke, as will be seen, was also quick to dismiss Britain as a serious opponent. Wilhelm von Hahnke summed up Schlieffen's attitude towards England in a similar way, although he overrated the significance that Schlieffen supposedly attached to the British navy 'if England is found on the side of Germany's enemies in the war that is certain to come'.[154]

Schlieffen opposed Tirpitz's naval policy, realizing that it was bound to lead to Anglo-German antagonism. Yet he conducted his planning to suit a political situation that he preferred, one in which Britain would remain neutral in the initial stages of war. 'England' is mentioned by Schlieffen for the first time in his last manoeuvre critique of 23 December 1905, eight days before he left office. The manoeuvre – the first one to be devised and directed by the younger Moltke – was conducted on the assumption of a two-front war. As well as Russia and

---

[150] Hahnke, 'Die militär-politische Einstellung Graf Schlieffen's [*sic*] zu England', 1931, BA-MA, NL Hahnke, N36/12, p. 7.   [151] Müller, 'Anmerkungen', p. 403.

[152] Quoted in Ritter, *Schlieffen Plan*, p. 71.

[153] John H. Maurer, *The Outbreak of the First World War. Strategic Planning, Crisis Decision Making and Deterrence Failure*, Westport, Connecticut, and London 1995, p. 36.

[154] BA-MA, NL Hahnke, N36/12, Hahnke, 'Die militär-politische Einstellung', 1931, p. 2.

France, England was a further assumed opponent. Schlieffen was still not convinced that Britain would pose a serious threat, and his rather dismissive manoeuvre critique was no doubt intended as a dig at his future successor, whom he had tried to stop from devising that year's manoeuvre plan.[155] In his opinion, 'not the most important, but the most interesting question is how England will participate in the war', rather than whether she would be involved.[156] And yet, although he posed the question, he did not attempt to answer it or to consider ways of avoiding Britain's involvement altogether.

The Anglo-Russian Entente of 1907, leading in effect to a Triple Entente between Britain, France and Russia, was still in the future when Schlieffen drafted his memorandum. It would become a political reality that his successor had to face. Schlieffen not only overlooked the danger that the powerful British navy posed, but also failed to consider the influence that Britain would have on the continuation of the war beyond the first encounters with France. In Jehuda Wallach's words, 'the belief that to win the battle [against France] would mean overall victory in the war was a typically military mistake'.[157]

During the First Moroccan Crisis Germany began to feel the full effects of her own expansionist foreign policy. British involvement in a future war was now almost certain, and as a consequence Italy, allied to Germany and Austria since 1882, became a less reliable ally, for she would be unable to defend her long coastlines from a hostile Britain and might therefore opt to stay neutral in a future war.[158] The international events of 1905–1906 marked the beginning of Germany's perceived 'encirclement' by alliances of possible future enemies against her. Between this time and the outbreak of war in 1914, the General Staff became more and more concerned about the increasing military strength of Germany's enemies, without ever realizing that these enemies were largely *reacting* to German provocation.

At the end of 1905, Russia emerged defeated from the Russo-Japanese war. When Schlieffen finalized his strategic plan, Germany's eastern neighbour was no longer a strong force to be reckoned with; on the

---

[155] See Moltke, *Erinnerungen*, 7 March 1905, pp. 319–320, where Moltke describes to his wife how Schlieffen tried to ignore the Kaiser's order for Moltke to devise a manoeuvre plan for the coming autumn.

[156] Schlieffen's manoeuvre critique, quoted from files of the Reichsarchiv in BA-MA, N36/12, Hahnke, 'Die militär-politische Einstellung', p. 7. Schlieffen's additional memorandum of February 1906 does, however, address the contingency of a British deployment of 100,000 men to Antwerp. See Ritter, *Schlieffen Plan*, pp. 161–164.   [157] Wallach, *Kriegstheorien*, p. 101.

[158] See Reichsarchiv, *Weltkrieg*, vol. 1, p. 10. This thinking was accurate, as the events of August 1914 were to prove. Worse still, of course, Italy eventually opted to join the Allies' side in May 1915.

contrary, Russia was no serious opponent after her recent defeat. That she would eventually recover was not a possibility that Schlieffen's memorandum of 1905 foresaw. It is perhaps unfair to expect Schlieffen to have calculated with such foresight. However, while Moltke attempted to adapt the plan to changing circumstances, and was to be savagely criticized for this, we must note that Schlieffen failed to do so. Even following the Balkan crises of 1908–1909 and 1912, Schlieffen refused to recognize that Russia had recovered from the lost war and had built up an army that was superior to that of the Austrians. 'With staggering one-sidedness the octogenarian [kept] his spellbound gaze on the Western front', Ritter concludes.[159] In his final memorandum, written shortly before his death in January 1913, Schlieffen even went as far as to suggest keeping no reserve of troops for deployment against Russia, hoping that German victories in France would deter the Russians from entering the war – a plan that Moltke rejected out of hand.[160] In the light of this one must doubt whether Germany really would have fared better with Schlieffen running the General Staff, as was so frequently maintained after the war.[161] However, the tales that make up the Schlieffen myth conveniently overlook episodes which cast doubt on his image. Despite such serious shortcomings – admittedly formulated at a time when he was nearing death – the popular image of Schlieffen has largely remained that of an infallible genius.

SCHLIEFFEN'S IMPACT ON THE GENERAL STAFF

In 1906, Schlieffen left a wider legacy than his operational plan for a future war. He had also changed the General Staff. Under his leadership, members of the General Staff had been allowed to become military specialists at the expense of more general, non-military knowledge. Non-military problems were consciously excluded from General Staff thinking.[162] Military decision-makers were thus allowed to conduct their planning in a 'military vacuum', with scant regard for the political situation around them. The consequences of this one-sided and narrow-minded approach were all too apparent.

In contrast with his predecessors Moltke and Waldersee, Schlieffen had been extremely secretive in his dealings with the Austrian ally.

---

[159] Ritter, *Schlieffen Plan*, p. 74.   [160] Ibid., p. 76. See also Wallach, *Dogma*, p. 92, note 111.
[161] See e.g. Hermann von Kuhl: 'If Schlieffen had been alive and leading the army in 1914, the battle of the Marne would not have been lost': quoted in Eibicht, *Schlieffen*, p. 5.
[162] See Görlitz, *Kleine Geschichte des deutschen Generalstabes*, p. 122.

Whereas both Moltke and Waldersee had fostered close relations with their Austrian counterpart, Friedrich Freiherr Beck-Rzikowsky, this liaison stopped under Schlieffen.[163] When he took over from Waldersee, Schlieffen had assured the Austrian military plenipotentiary Oberst Steininger that he intended to continue as Waldersee had done. However, Steininger remarked in his report to Vienna that co-operation was bound to be more difficult, for Schlieffen was 'the most taciturn man one could ever meet'.[164] It did not take long for the relationship to deteriorate. In 1893, it seemed to Beck that the German General Staff had become mistrustful of its ally: 'On the German side they had suddenly grown suspicious of us and doubted whether we would, in case of war, actually proceed offensively against Russia.'[165] Beck's diary entries of 1893–1894 show a steady worsening of the relationship between the Austrian and German General Staffs. After 1896, in an atmosphere of secrecy, the two allies developed their plans for a possible war in the East independently of one another: Germany for East Prussia, and Austria for Galicia. Co-operation was no longer discussed.[166] While Schlieffen wanted to find out details of the Austrian deployment plan, he gave orders to avoid mentioning details of German intentions to the Austrian ally.[167]

---

[163] Maurer, *Outbreak*, p. 32; Scott W. Lackey, *The Rebirth of the Habsburg Army*, Westport, Connecticut 1995, p. 152. After 1882, the co-operation between the two allies had been closer than even during the First World War itself. On the changing relationship between the German and Austro-Hungarian General Staffs, see also Gerhard Ritter, 'Die Zusammenarbeit der Generalstäbe Deutschlands und Österreich-Ungarns vor dem ersten Weltkrieg', in Wilhelm Berges and Carl Hinrichs (eds.), *Zur Geschichte der Demokratie: Festgabe für Hans Herzfeld*, Berlin 1958, pp. 523–549; Holger Herwig, 'Disjointed Allies: Coalition Warfare in Berlin and Vienna, 1914', *Journal of Military History*, 54, July 1990, pp. 265–280. Lothar Höbelt's analysis of the breakdown of communication between Berlin and Vienna aims to redress the balance by not regarding the events as solely initiated and directed by Berlin, arguing instead that Austria was not a helpless victim in the events: 'Schlieffen, Beck, Potiorek und das Ende der gemeinsamen deutsch-österreich-ungarischen Aufmarschpläne im Osten', *MGM*, 2/1984, pp. 7–30. For a recent analysis of the relationship between the allies see Günther Kronenbitter, 'Bundesgenossen? Zur militärpolitischen Kooperation zwischen Berlin und Wien 1912–1914', in W. Bernecker and V. Dotterweich (eds.), *Deutschland in den internationalen Beziehungen des 19. und 20. Jahrhunderts. Festschrift für Josef Becker*, Munich 1996.

[164] Beck, diary excerpts, BA-MA, w-10/50222. Materialsammlung von Regenauer zur 'Darstellung der operativen Verhandlungen des Grafen Schlieffen mit Österreich-Ungarn', no date, p. 16.

[165] Beck diary, BA-MA, w-10/50222. The Austrian Chief of Staff also received interesting insights from Steininger regarding the day-to-day running of affairs in Berlin. He commented early in 1893 on the limited dealings the Kaiser had with his Chief of Staff, 'not the latter's fault, but all other ministers complain, too, that the Kaiser had only rarely time for them'. See also Herwig, 'Disjointed Allies', p. 272, who quotes Beck to Steininger, 5 February 1894, expressing similar views. [166] See also Ritter, *Schlieffen Plan*, p. 30.

[167] BA-MA, w-10/50221. No doubt this secrecy was due to the fact that he was aware that Germany's revised plans would ultimately leave Austria out on a limb in the East. On Schlieffen's attitude towards the Austrian ally, see also Lackey, *Rebirth of the Habsburg Army*, pp. 151ff.

The German General Staff under Schlieffen's leadership displayed a damaging contempt for the Austrian ally, and he seemed convinced that Germany could discount its help: 'Those characters will only desert or run to the enemy', he alleged.[168] Ritter suspects that something more than feelings of military superiority played a part in this development, detecting 'a kind of political dyed-in-the-wool Prussianism of which the elder Moltke had been so completely free'.[169] Schlieffen apparently regarded the Dual Alliance between Germany and Austria as a mistake; he did not trust the ally and he was not prepared to commit German troops to the defence of the Austro-Russian border. Famously he declared that Austria's fate would be decided on the Seine, not on the Bug (a statement that was repeated by Moltke vis-à-vis Conrad in 1913).[170] After 1896, the contact between the two General Staffs was virtually reduced to the exchange of New Year greetings.[171]

The antagonism that developed between the German and the Austrian Chiefs of the General Staff was not reduced until 1908, when Moltke and his Austrian counterpart Franz Conrad von Hötzendorf began a correspondence that lasted until the outbreak of war. However, even Moltke never discussed with Conrad the important issue of establishing a unified allied military command, despite the fact that the next war would have to be an alliance war. Although relations improved during Moltke's time in office, 'there nevertheless remained an incredible lack of concrete planning as to how the two allies would co-ordinate their wartime strategies'.[172] While the same could perhaps also be said of the Entente's war planning, it was Germany's strategic plan that crucially depended on an Austrian deployment against Russia in the early weeks of a war. And yet no attempt at co-ordinated strategic planning was made.

Secrecy regarding military planning also existed vis-à-vis the other military and civilian institutions in the Reich. The Ministry of War was not informed about the demands of the strategic plan, and as a result did not support the General Staff in its requests for army increases.[173] Co-operation with civilian decision-makers was out of the question because, like most of his military contemporaries and indeed the Kaiser, Schlieffen had nothing but contempt for civilians. His concern was to

---

[168] Quoted in Herwig, 'Disjointed Allies', p. 272.   [169] Ritter, *Schlieffen Plan*, pp. 31–32.

[170] Ibid., p. 32; Herwig, 'Disjointed Allies', p. 273, note 18.

[171] Holger H. Herwig, 'From Tirpitz Plan to Schlieffen Plan: Some Observations on German Military Planning', *Journal of Strategic Studies*, 9, 1986, p. 56; Höbelt, 'Schlieffen, Beck . . .'.

[172] Herwig, 'Tirpitz Plan to Schlieffen Plan', p. 56; Conrad, *Dienstzeit*, vol. 4, p. 259. Details of this relationship are discussed in Chapter 3.   [173] Reichsarchiv, *Kriegsrüstung*, vol. 1, p. 65.

plan the conduct of the future war. What the diplomats arranged in turn was irrelevant to him. Despite the fact that a violation of neutral neighbours was obviously a matter for the diplomats to handle, Schlieffen had not informed outsiders about the nature of the General Staff's strategic planning. Not until December 1912 were the Ministry of War, the Chancellor and the Auswärtiges Amt finally told of the General Staff's strategic intentions.[174] The General Staff cultivated the secrecy that Schlieffen had initiated, and even the outbreak of war did not tempt it to trust the Minister of War with details of operations.[175]

A further shortcoming in Schlieffen's planning was his disregard for the German navy. Germany had increased her fleet to the second most powerful in the world, surpassed only by Britain. Despite this, Schlieffen had no intention of using the fleet in his planning, for example to obstruct British deployment through the Channel.[176] Nor did he plan to use the fleet in the Baltic, where it could have been an effective and superior weapon.[177] From the General Staff's point of view, the huge funds being spent on the navy must therefore have appeared doubly wasted, for the military did not envisage a decisive role for the navy in the future war. Schlieffen was adamant that Germany's fate would not be decided at sea. Furthermore, Schlieffen did not hold the leading admirals in high esteem; while he thought them accomplished technicians, he did not believe them capable of operational thinking.[178] With both the Admiralty Staff and the General Staff being secretive about their planning, co-operation between them hardly existed.

However, Schlieffen did not complain about the naval policy, even though it increased the likelihood of Britain becoming an extra opponent in a future war and led to funds being 'squandered' on the navy that would, in his opinion, have been better spent on the army. Again, Ritter's critique is apt:

But the Navy was not the province of the Chief of the General Staff (perhaps it was even beyond his military horizon); and as he estimated the danger from England so lightly, he saw no reason to utter a word of warning against the

---

[174] For details see Chapter 3.
[175] See BA-MA, w-10/50629, Aufzeichnungen des Generalmajors van den Bergh, pp. 5–6. See also Chapter 5.
[176] Herwig, 'Tirpitz Plan to Schlieffen Plan', p. 57. On the German navy, see also Jonathan Steinberg, *Yesterday's Deterrent. Tirpitz and the Birth of the German Battle Fleet*, London 1965; Volker R. Berghahn, *Der Tirpitz-Plan. Genesis und Verfall einer innenpolitischen Krisenstrategie unter Wilhelm II*, Düsseldorf 1971; Holger Herwig, *'Luxury' Fleet. The Imperial German Navy, 1888–1918*, London 1991.   [177] See Ritter, *Schlieffen Plan*, p. 72.
[178] BA-MA, N36/12. Hahnke, 'Die militär-politische Einstellung', p. 6.

extravagant policy of the Naval Board and its imminent political consequences.[179]

It is unclear why he chose not to speak up. He may well have considered Tirpitz too powerful an opponent, and he was, of course, aware
that the navy was the Kaiser's favourite toy. Wilhelm von Hahnke maintained his silence was due to the fact that he was never allowed to see the
Kaiser on a one-to-one basis. The Minister of War and Chief of the
Military Cabinet attended his audiences, and he may not have wanted
to utter his concerns in their presence, especially because, according to
Hahnke, he suspected from 1903 onwards that the generals Einem,
Hülsen-Haeseler and Plessen were working towards his dismissal.
Furthermore, in Schlieffen's opinion it was not the Chief of Staff's job
to get involved in politics, and to have protested against the fleet-building
programme would in any case have been completely pointless. For the
same reasons, Hahnke suspected, Schlieffen refrained from seeking a
personal audience with the Chancellor in order to discuss the direction
of German foreign policy, even though he considered it to be 'fateful'.[180]

When Schlieffen drafted his plan, there were not sufficient numbers
of soldiers to carry it out, nor would it have been possible to transport
them to the theatre of war in the necessary short space of time. His planning relied on army corps that were 'nothing but dreams' and, moreover,
the vast numbers of troops required were impossible to obtain in the
near future, considering that seven army corps would have been necessary for the envisaged siege of Paris alone.[181] Given the difficulties that
the German military faced in getting further army increases approved
in the Reichstag, Schlieffen himself was not confident that the necessary
numbers of recruits for his strategic plan would ever be obtained, at least
not during his time in office. Rather, he considered his memorandum a
plan of action for his successor. Liddell Hart's critique is cutting.
Schlieffen, he writes,

seems to have taken the technician's view that his duty was fulfilled if he did the
utmost with the means available, and 'made the best of a bad job' in compli-
ance with the customs and rules of his profession. He did not consider that he
had the higher responsibility of warning the Emperor and the Chancellor that
the chances of success were small compared with the risks, and that German
policy ought to be adjusted to that grave reality.[182]

[179] Ritter, *Schlieffen Plan*, p. 72.
[180] BA-MA, N36/12, Hahnke, 'Die militär-politische Einstellung', pp. 3/4.
[181] Wallach, *Dogma*, pp. 94–95; idem, *Kriegstheorien*, p. 129.
[182] Liddell Hart, Foreword to English edition of Ritter, *Schlieffen Plan*, p. 7.

This was a serious failing indeed, and both Schlieffen and his successor, the younger Moltke, were guilty of it. The consequences were grave, for, as we will see, their insistence on German superiority, their conjuring up of an image of near invincibility, led the political decision-makers to believe that they *could* conduct an aggressive foreign policy, backed up by the conviction that Germany would emerge victorious from any possible conflict.

According to ardent Schlieffen supporters, he should not be blamed for failing to secure adequate army increases in time. Rather, those who decided to dismiss Schlieffen were responsible for the inadequate increases and lack of troops – by dismissing him at a time when his planning was just being completed. Hahnke maintained that it was precisely at the time that Schlieffen would have proceeded to make demands on the Ministry of War that he was 'torn from his work . . . and, like Bismarck, brutally removed from office'.[183] It is doubtful whether this idealized picture represents the truth. As we have seen, Schlieffen failed to stand up for General Staff demands throughout his time in office, and, in the words of one of his critics, was someone 'who timidly shied away from any conflict with other institutions and with the Kaiser'.[184] It is unlikely that he would have changed his attitude in later years.

Schlieffen's strategy clearly was 'born out of despair'. Holger Herwig raises doubts as to whether the daring plan was 'in line with German capabilities'.[185] The fact that Germany was unable to fulfil the demand for army numbers required by the Schlieffen Plan was largely due to the existence of differing visions of military policy, with the General Staff demanding more manpower, while the Ministry of War was intent on increasing *matériel*. Furthermore, while Schlieffen's plan 'demanded utmost mobility and mechanization', a belief in 'traditional' advances on foot and horse, and in nineteenth-century practices of operations and tactics, prevailed.[186] Herwig outlines an '"ostrich-like refusal" to tackle the "technical side" of the military plan, [which] guaranteed exhaustion rather than victory'.[187] Other commentators tend to agree. The Schlieffen Plan did not allow for 'frictions' – essential according to Clausewitz, on whose work Schlieffen apparently believed he had based

---

[183] Hahnke to Freytag-Loringhoven, 5 March 1924, BA-MA, NL Hahnke, N36/10. For a similar view that both Schlieffen and Bismarck were dismissed too early, see Groener, *Testament*, p. 78.

[184] BA-MA, W-10/50629. Aufzeichnungen des Generalmajors van den Bergh, p. 5.

[185] Herwig, 'From Tirpitz Plan to Schlieffen Plan', p. 53. See also Wallach, *Kriegstheorien*, p. 129, who wonders if the plan had not been 'too extravagant for the available means'.

[186] Herwig, 'Tirpitz Plan to Schlieffen Plan', p. 58.   [187] Ibid.

his own.[188] Instead, everything had to conform to a rigid, preconceived pattern. Chance was to be eliminated.[189] Contrary to the claims of the Schlieffen school, such planning was ultimately no more than a desperate gamble.

According to the Reichsarchiv, Schlieffen's plan had been 'at the same time a programme for the further enlargement of the army and for its mobilization'.[190] The task of Schlieffen's successor would have been to instigate the army increases necessary to ensure that the Schlieffen Plan could go ahead as envisaged. Initially, however, Moltke seems to have been as inactive as Schlieffen had been. If the Schlieffen Plan was intended as a blueprint of action for Moltke, he seemed unaware of it. Russia continued to be a negligible opponent, the navy continued to be favoured in terms of funding. Only the Agadir Crisis of 1911 achieved a change in attitude, and it was from then on that the General Staff, under his leadership, began to prepare for war in earnest.[191]

FROM SCHLIEFFEN TO MOLTKE: CONTINUITIES AND CHANGES

The transition from Schlieffen to Moltke involved no immediate changes to the day-to-day work and war planning of the General Staff, which had become so specialized and technical that experts were needed for the various tasks. Initially, work thus went ahead under the new chief as it had under his predecessor.[192]

When Moltke took over from Schlieffen, there was no immediate possibility of increasing the strength of the army. Schlieffen, throughout his time in office, had preferred to plan a future war, and to point out the requirements for it, while resigning himself to the fact that Tirpitz had been more skilled in lobbying for the navy's needs than he could be for the army. In his first years as Chief of the General Staff, Moltke followed the same path.[193] This, according to Theobald von Schäfer of the Reichsarchiv, was due to the fact that Russia had not yet recovered from her recent defeat, as well as to the great attention that was still at this

---

[188] See e.g. Wallach, *Kriegstheorien*, p. 128; also idem, 'Feldmarschall von Schlieffens Interpretation der Kriegslehre Moltkes d.Ä.', in Roland G. Foerster (ed.), *Generalfeldmarschall von Moltke. Bedeutung und Wirkung*, Munich 1991, p. 53 (NB: Like the elder Moltke, Schlieffen was actually *Generalfeldmarschall*).

[189] See e.g. Hew Strachan, *European Armies and the Conduct of War*, London 1983, p. 132; Wallach, *Dogma*, pp. 93–94; idem, 'Feldmarschall von Schlieffens Interpretation', p. 54.

[190] Quoted in Ritter, *Schlieffen Plan*, p. 66.

[191] See e.g. Schäfer manuscript, 'Der Kriegsplan für den Zweifrontenkrieg', 1924, BA-MA, w-10/50223. For the Agadir Crisis, see Chapter 3.   [192] Groener, *Testament*, p. 79.

[193] See e.g. Reichsarchiv, *Weltkrieg*, vol. 1, p. 11.

point given to the navy. Both the Chief of Staff and the Minister of War, General von Einem, were reluctant to press for military increases at that time.[194]

At the end of his period in office, Schlieffen had been concerned about the fact that, while Germany had 'invented general conscription and a people at arms', as he put it in his December 1905 memorandum, she was not training future soldiers to the extent that France, for example, was:

> But having brought our sworn enemies to the point of increasing their armies out of all measure, we have relaxed our own efforts. We continue to boast of the density of our population, of the great manpower at our disposal; but these masses are not trained or armed to the full number of able-bodied men they could yield. The fact that France with a population of 39 million provides 995 battalions for the field army, while Germany with 56 million produces only 971, speaks for itself.[195]

This word of warning for his successor was at first ignored by Moltke.[196] Rather than demand army increases, Moltke even supported the Ministry of War's view that the army's inner strength needed attention. In April 1907 he assured the Minister that by that time

> the three main arms had been developed so far that the framework of the army could be regarded as stable for a while, and that what was required was primarily inner development and further improvement of the auxiliary weapons and up-to-date weapons (*Kriegsmittel*).[197]

One can only speculate as to his motivation; the dominant role of Tirpitz and the navy, the fact that he was still new in his position, the relatively stable international situation and Russia's weakness all may have played their part. He also seems to have wanted to establish a good relationship with the Minister of War.[198] Only in 1910, when Minister of War Josias von Heeringen himself felt that the planned small increases

---

[194] Schäfer Manuscript, 'Der Kriegsplan für den Zweifrontenkrieg', 1924, BA-MA, w-10/50223, p. 6.

[195] Ritter, *Schlieffen Plan*, p. 143. Also BA-MA, w-10/50276: 'Die Militärpolitische Lage Deutschlands', p. 41.   [196] On this and the following see ibid.

[197] Ibid., p. 42; Reichsarchiv, *Kriegsrüstung, Anlagen*, doc. 33.

[198] According to Theobald von Schäfer, Stein, Moltke's confidant, was also keen to be on good terms with the Minister of War. Schäfer considered Ludendorff, the new arrival on the scene, the decisive figure behind demands for army increases. Once Stein had left office in October 1912, Ludendorff was able to put into action his own plans for army increases. Schäfer's account is, however, marred by its hidden agenda. It is an example of unashamed hero-worship of Ludendorff as 'Vorkämpfer für Deutschlands Rüstung' (champion of the arming of Germany), and as such is not a very reliable account. Schäfer, *Ludendorff. Der Feldherr der Deutschen im Weltkriege*, Berlin 1935, pp. 9,13.

for the *Quinquennat* (five-year army law) of 1911–1915 should be larger, did Moltke agree. It was the Chancellor who vetoed these plans. The Army Bill of 27 March 1911, the result of these wranglings, was a disappointment for Moltke, increasing the peace-time army by fewer than 10,000 men.[199]

No significant change in Moltke's attitude occurred until the end of 1911, when the political situation and army increases of Germany's opponents suggested to him that Germany's future position was looking increasingly endangered. The popular support for the army, fuelled by the propaganda of the German Army League, encouraged him to become more demanding on the issue of army increases.[200] Erich Ludendorff's support further helped the Chief of Staff to stand firm against the General Staff's opponents.[201]

When taking over from Schlieffen, Moltke did have some immediate impact by improving manoeuvres as part of war-planning, leading to increased esteem with his colleagues.[202] The Kaiser no longer insisted on leading 'his' troops, and as a result the large manoeuvres of 1909 and 1912, for example, could be 'as war-like as possible', as Ludendorff recalled.[203] On the whole, however, manoeuvres continued to be relatively chaotic events. Hermann von Santen's descriptions of the 1908 summer manoeuvres give a vivid insight into the proceedings. The participating soldiers were at the point of sheer exhaustion, falling asleep on their similarly exhausted horses, often having to lead them home on foot. The exaggerated emphasis on horses particularly struck Santen: 'For the reasonable among us it was clear that such images, as they were displayed during the various exercise days, would never ever come about in reality, at least not on a modern battlefield.'[204] And while the Kaiser did indeed refrain from leading one of the opposing sides, he was none-

---

[199] See BA-MA, w-10/50276, 'Die Militärpolitische Lage Deutschlands', p. 42.

[200] See Chapter 3 for details.

[201] Erich Ludendorff, *Meine Kriegserinnerungen 1914–1918*, Berlin 1919, p. 20

[202] Groener, *Testament*, p. 79: 'By way of the *Kaisermanöver* his military esteem also increased.' Einem, *Erinnerungen*, p. 151: 'His manoeuvre plans were good, and he also understood how to push the Kaiser into the role of a spectator during the great autumn manoeuvres.'

[203] Ludendorff, *Militärischer Werdegang*, p. 123. In 1910 only small manoeuvres were held, in which the troops were wearing field-grey uniforms for the first time. Ludendorff's verdict on the post-1906 *Kaisermanöver* was favourable: 'The *Kaisermanöver*, like the other manoeuvres, had become a good exercise (*waren ... zu einer guten Schule geworden*)', pp. 123–124.

[204] Santen, 'Erinnerungen', vol. 10, pp. 303–304. But compare Dennis E. Showalter, 'The Eastern Front and German Military Planning, 1871–1914 – Some Observations', *East European Quarterly*, 15, 1981 p. 172, who argues that it has been 'militarily and academically fashionable to deride the cult of the horse. Yet critics overlook the fact that before World War I, cavalry was the only strategically and operationally mobile arm in existence.'

4 The Kaiser with Moltke, 1911

theless the cause of major disturbances. He visited the 1908 manoeuvres for two days, prior to which asbestos barracks had to be erected especially for him, and large numbers of soldiers had to scan the terrain in search of rabbit holes and ditches which needed to be filled in to prevent the danger of falls during riding expeditions. As Santen remembered, 'the exercises on the two *Kaisertage* were nothing but a wild chase (*eine wilde Raserei*). Most of the time, one was surrounded by a thick cloud of dust that obstructed sight at even the shortest distance. Four deaths from unfortunate falls were the result of the two days.'[205] But the Kaiser, at least, seemed happy with the annual manoeuvres. In his manoeuvre critique of 1912, he wrote proudly: 'I am convinced that such manoeuvres will not be copied by any other army in the world. They would not dare ask this of their people.'[206]

An important change in the staging of manoeuvres was, however, noted by foreign observers. Under Moltke's auspices, war games became classified information, even ranked as top secret documents with restricted access, for fear of allowing the enemy insight into Germany's

[205] Santen, 'Erinnerungen', vol. 10, p. 204.
[206] BA-MA, NL Moltke, N78/23, Kaisermanöver 1912, pp. 6 19.

war planning. It was becoming increasingly difficult for officers from foreign armies to be present at manoeuvres and observe the proceedings. The British military attaché, Colonel Frederick Trench, commented on the increasing secrecy surrounding the manoeuvres, and the new measures which aimed at preventing observers from acquiring any real information about the training of the German army. In Trench's words, their attendance was now 'a waste of time', and he was certain who was responsible for this development:

That General v[on] Moltke, Chief of the General Staff, is responsible for [the policy] seems undoubted. Not only did its adoption synchronize with his appointment to the present post, but he referred to the subject with some warmth on most of the occasions when he has conversed with me.[207]

Other traditional tasks of General Staff work continued under Moltke as they had under Schlieffen. Part of a General Staff officer's task was to work on a solution for the so-called 'Schlieffen or Moltke question'. This was a strategic problem posed by the Chief of the General Staff to all General Staff officers, including the Troop General Staff. It would end in a large-scale discussion, during which the Chief of the General Staff would comment on the various solutions that had been advanced and would then present and explain his own solution.[208]

Moltke adopted Schlieffen's 'testament', the strategic plan that was to be the answer to the task of having to fight a war on two fronts. Initially no changes were made to the plan, but from 1909, Moltke began to make his mark on General Staff planning, as he and his aides Erich Ludendorff and Hermann von Stein began to devise important changes to Schlieffen's original concept of 1905.[209] Moltke was able to stick to the plan of his predecessor because, contrary to the claims of the Schlieffen school, he essentially agreed with the basic principle behind it, as a memorandum of December 1911 confirms:

[207] Cited in Matthew Seligmann, 'A View from Berlin: Colonel Frederick Trench and the Development of British Perceptions of German Aggressive Intent, 1906–1910', *Journal of Strategic Studies*, 23/2, 2000, pp. 114–147. I am grateful to Dr Seligmann for making excerpts from his forthcoming article available to me. For the secrecy under Moltke's leadership, see also Bucholz, *Moltke*, p. 242.

[208] Santen's memoirs comment on these exercises and their popularity in the entire army, under both Schlieffen and Moltke: 'Erinnerungen', vol. 10, pp. 354, 361–362.

[209] It was in 1909, too, that Moltke offered to resign over the Kaiser's criticisms regarding the practice of asking new General Staff officers to solve exam questions pertaining to a war on two fronts. The Kaiser feared that this could betray military secrets and wanted it stopped. Moltke considered this a criticism of his leadership, and offered to resign. Upon the Kaiser's insistence, he withdrew his resignation, 'due to the critical political situation'. Moltke, *Erinnerungen*, pp. 350–351.

On the fight against France depends the outcome of the war.* The Republic is our most dangerous opponent, but we can hope to achieve a decision here quickly. Once France is defeated in the first big battles, then this country, which does not have great reserves of people (*Menschenmaterial* [!]), will hardly be able to continue a long war**, while Russia can divert the war after a lost battle towards the interior of her vast terrain and can drag it out for an unforeseeable length of time. However, Germany's entire ambition must be to end the war on at least one side with a few big strokes as soon as possible.[210]

However, unlike Schlieffen he was not convinced that the French would necessarily be on the defensive in a future war. Already in 1906, the annual big General Staff exercise was based on the assumption of a French offensive in the South.[211] Were that to happen, the German right wing, advancing through Belgium, would be unable to bring about the desired decisive speedy victory, as the majority of French troops would be engaged elsewhere, Moltke explained in his critique.[212] Moltke's operational planning in the years to come would reflect his view of likely French intentions in a forthcoming war. He expected that the French decision of offensive or defensive war would depend on the *casus belli*.[213] From 1908 onwards, he started to change details regarding the ratio of strength and the deployment area in the West, because he considered a French offensive in Alsace or Lorraine a possibility. He commented in the margin of Schlieffen's 1905 memorandum:

If the war is wanted and initiated by France, then she will in all likelihood lead it offensively. If France wants to re-conquer the lost provinces, she must march into them, that is act offensively. I do not consider it certain that France will be defensive in all circumstances. The border fortifications, built soon after the war of 1870/1871, do, however, express a defensive attitude. Yet this does not correspond with the offensive spirit that has always been inherent in the nation, nor with the currently predominant teachings and views in the French Army.[214]

---

[210] BA-MA, w-10/50279, p. 19. The memorandum was sent to the Chancellor and Minister of War on 2 December 1911. Heeringen made the following marginal notes in his copy: '*) 'richtig', **) '70/71?', thus indicating that the French had already demonstrated their ability to continue fighting longer than anticipated once before. Moltke's adjutant Mantey also confirms that Moltke's views on operational matters were no different from Schlieffen's: 'Graf Schlieffen und der jüngere Moltke', p. 396.

[211] 'Aus der Schlussbesprechung der grossen Generalstabsreise 1906', quoted in BA-MA, w-10/50897, 'Aeusserungen des Generals von Moltke über die Möglichkeit einer schnellen Feldzugsentscheidung im Westen', p. 138. See also H. Gackenholz's defence of Moltke's strategic planning in *Entscheidung in Lothringen 1914. Der Operationsplan des jüngeren Moltke und seine Durchführung auf dem linken deutschen Heeresflügel*, Berlin 1933, pp. 14ff.

[212] BA-MA, w-10/50897, p. 138.   [213] Ritter, *Schlieffen Plan*, Moltke's marginal note, p. 135.

[214] See Reichsarchiv, *Weltkrieg*, vol. 1, pp. 62–63; Ritter, *Schlieffen Plan*, p. 135.

The deployment plan for 1908/1909 considered for the first time the deployment of an army corps to defend Upper Alsace.[215] From that date, it was intended to keep the Seventh Army, with three army corps and one reserve corps, on the Rhine to defend Alsace, in addition to the Sixth Army (four corps) in southern Lorraine. Initially, the Seventh Army was to remain on the Rhine, ready either to come to the help of the Sixth, or to be transported to another theatre of war. In the mobilization year 1910/1911, there was no longer any intention to transport the troops of the Seventh Army elsewhere.[216] The last pre-war deployment plan envisaged the deployment of both armies in Lorraine; thus a total of eight army corps were to be deployed on the left wing, away from the 'crucial' right wing of Schlieffen's plan.[217] Schlieffen's supporters, informed by hindsight, have argued that by strengthening the left wing Moltke weakened the all-important right wing, and by changing the ratio that Schlieffen had aimed for, jeopardized the 'guaranteed' victory that Schlieffen's plan would otherwise have ensured. Critics maintain that while Schlieffen wanted to impose his will on the enemy, Moltke allowed the enemy to dictate the action by subordinating his measures to those of the opponent. However, if Moltke's plan is understood as a plan in its own right, developed against a different political background, and allowing for changed international circumstances, one might arrive at a fairer appraisal. It was a plan that accepted that the march through neutral Belgium might be necessary, but that allowed for flexibility if the French attacked in Alsace-Lorraine.[218] Moreover, the numbers of troops that Schlieffen had wanted to deploy could not have been transported, owing to the insufficient capacity of the available rail network. In 1914, the successful deployment was possible only because the numerical requirements were less than in Schlieffen's 'unadulterated' plan.[219] As Friedrich von Mantey sums up quite correctly: 'Moltke did not dilute the Schlieffen Plan, he gave it up. That there was nonetheless a similarity was natural: it was not possible any other way, given the available room to manoeuvre.'[220] Unlike Schlieffen, Moltke was unwilling to relinquish any territory to the enemy, either along Germany's southern border with

---

[215] Reichsarchiv, *Weltkrieg 1914–1918*, vol. 1, p. 61.   [216] BA-MA, w-10/50730, p. 56.

[217] Ibid., p. 62.

[218] Gackenholz outlines a fundamental difference between Moltke's and Schlieffen's planning, rather than agreeing with the 'traditional' view that Moltke simply did not understand his predecessor's plan, or that he was unable to live up to Schlieffen's standard: *Entscheidung in Lothringen*, pp. 18ff.

[219] Michael Salewski, 'Moltke, Schlieffen und die Eisenbahn', in R. G. Foerster (ed.), *Generalfeldmarschall von Moltke. Bedeutung und Wirkung*, Munich 1991, p. 99.

[220] Mantey, 'Graf Schlieffen und der jüngere Moltke', p. 398.

France or in the East, where Schlieffen had been willing to allow a Russian advance into East Prussia if necessary. Under Moltke's leadership it became increasingly important to defend all territory and not to allow the enemy onto German soil.

In these early years as Chief of the General Staff, Moltke co-operated closely with Erich Ludendorff,[221] who had become Head of the Second (Deployment) Department in the General Staff in 1908. With Ludendorff's appointment, things began to change within the General Staff.[222] He was a driving force in trying to push through much-needed army increases, and a key figure on the General Staff, much valued by Moltke for his abilities and dedication.[223] One of the important changes that Moltke, together with Ludendorff and Tappen,[224] made to Schlieffen's original concept was to think of a way of avoiding a violation of neutral Holland. It has been argued that Moltke had 'more political sense and scruples than his predecessor' regarding the violation of neutrality.[225] This is perhaps an overestimation of Moltke's political concerns. Primarily, he wanted to avoid marching through the Dutch province of Limburg because he did not consider such a violation of Holland's neutrality a *military* necessity.[226] In a marginal note to Schlieffen's memorandum, Moltke had commented as early as 1905 on Schlieffen's speculation that it might be possible to come to an agreement with the Netherlands: 'If our diplomacy manages this, it will be a great advantage. We need the Dutch railways. The value of Holland as an ally would be incalculable.'[227] However, as Moltke explained in a

---

[221] Ludendorff had joined the General Staff in 1904, at the age of 39, and, after a period spent as a teacher at the war academy, had become head of the Second Department of the General Staff, responsible for the deployment of troops. Wolfgang Venohr, *Ludendorff. Legende und Wirklichkeit*, Berlin 1993, p. 12. The author of this recent study of Ludendorff cannot hide his fascination with his subject and echoes other uncritical accounts, such as Karl Tschuppik, *Ludendorff. Die Tragödie des Fachmanns*, Vienna and Leipzig 1931; Schäfer, *Ludendorff*. For the latest Ludendorff biography, see Uhle-Wettler, *Ludendorff*.

[222] And not all for the better. See e.g. Kuhl's complaint to Müller-Loebnitz: 'There used to be a continuous exchange of ideas on all questions of the war in the West between the 2nd and 3rd Departments. This only stopped when Ludendorff became Chief of the 2nd Department.' BA-MA, N56/2, NL Tappen, Müller-Loebnitz to Tappen, 29 December 1920.

[223] See BA-MA, N78/37, Adam von Moltke, 'Eine Antwort an Herrn Walter Görlitz, das Kapitel "Der Krieg ohne Feldherr" in seinem Buch "Der Deutsche Generalstab" betreffend Gen. Oberst Helmuth von Moltke', 1958. Also Heisterkamp, 'Lebensskizze', p. 33.

[224] See Harbou to Reichsarchiv, 4 April 1925, who blamed Ludendorff and Tappen for the changes to the deployment plan which included a 'significant strengthening of the right wing and an extention of the deployment direction further towards the North'. BA-MA, W-10/51062.

[225] Liddell Hart, 'Foreword' to Ritter, *Schlieffen Plan*, p. 8. Another sensible change was not leaving East Prussia unprotected, in contrast with Schlieffen's planning. Kielmansegg, *Deutschland*, p. 26.

[226] BA-MA, W-10/50276, 'Die Militärpolitische Lage Deutschlands', pp. 71–72.

[227] Quoted in Ritter, *Schlieffen Plan*, p. 137.

revealing letter to General von Freytag-Loringhoven in 1915, he had never shared Schlieffen's optimistic view that Holland would merely protest but stay neutral in case of a German invasion: 'I, on the other hand, predicted that the German army wing would lose so much strength as a result of a hostile Holland that it would lose the necessary offensive power against the West.'[228] Tappen recalled after the war that 'Moltke wanted to avoid under all circumstances any contact with Dutch territory, even the enclave around Maastricht.'[229] In November 1914, when the difficult manoeuvre of squeezing the German troops into Belgium while avoiding Holland had been executed successfully, Moltke prided himself on having instigated this significant change to the Schlieffen Plan:

Count Schlieffen even wanted to march the right wing of the German army through Southern Holland. I changed this in order to avoid forcing the Netherlands also on to the side of our enemies, and preferred to take on the great technical difficulties which were caused by the fact that the right wing of our army had to squeeze through the narrow space between Aachen and the southern border of the province of Limburg.[230]

Moltke's decision to spare Holland may appear 'honourable'; indeed, after the war much was made of this by Moltke's supporters. However, the alteration of the plan was not done out of concern for the Dutch, but primarily for military reasons, and to allow Germany access to outside markets during the war. Moltke summed up his motives in an important memorandum of 1911, in which he expressed his view that the planned envelopment did not necessarily require a violation of Dutch as well as Belgian neutrality.

A hostile Holland at our back could have disastrous consequences for the advance of the German army to the west, particularly if England should use the violation of Belgian neutrality as a pretext for entering the war against us. A neutral Holland secures our rear, because if England declares war on us for violating Belgian neutrality she cannot herself violate Dutch neutrality. She cannot break the very law for whose sake she goes to war. Furthermore it will be very important to have in Holland a country whose neutrality allows us to have imports and supplies. She must be the windpipe that enables us to breathe.[231]

---

[228] BA-MA, w-10/51063, Moltke to Freytag-Loringhoven, 26 July 1915.

[229] Tappen, 'Kriegserinnerungen', BA-MA, w-10/50661, p. 6.

[230] Moltke, *Erinnerungen*, p. 17.

[231] Ritter, *Schlieffen Plan*, 'General Observations on the Schlieffen Plan by H. von Moltke (apparently dated 1911)', pp. 165ff. This memorandum is also quoted in the Reichsarchiv files. It includes the following addition, not printed in Ritter's *Schlieffen Plan*: 'Moreover in a war of the

Moltke's desire to use Holland as a 'windpipe' suggests that he did not share Schlieffen's dogmatic insistence that a future war must be short. It is a common misconception that Schlieffen believed a future war could not actually be long. Rather, he insisted that Germany could only hope to win a short war, given her geographical position and the strength of her enemies, and therefore refused to consider a strategy that would result in a long war. Schlieffen wanted to avoid a long war at all costs, and the Schlieffen Plan was the logical outcome of this intention. Groener confirmed after the war that Schlieffen's biggest fear was that the fighting would drag on without an actual decision: 'It is not true that he considered only a short war possible. The truth is that his goal was as short a war as possible.'[232]

Moltke, on the other hand, wanted to be ready for a worst-case scenario too. He expected the coming war to be long, certainly in terms of Lothar Burchardt's definition of a 'long' war as one that lasted about two years.[233] Stig Förster, too, argues that Moltke was not convinced that the next war would necessarily be short, or indeed that the idea that a future war would be short was generally shared by influential military men. Wanting to use Holland as a 'windpipe' certainly indicates such concerns in Moltke's thinking.[234]

The change of plan led to further complications. If Dutch neutrality had to be respected, the German army would have to advance through a narrow corridor into Belgium, and then on towards the French border. The deployment of the right wing would be seriously disupted and

Triple Entente against the Triple Alliance, not only the German coastlines, but also most of the Austrian and Italian coasts, will be blockaded, [and] food imports will be exceedingly difficult, particularly for Germany. As long as Holland remained neutral, imports would be possible via that country under the American flag. It is hardly to be expected that England would not respect that flag. If we turn Holland into our enemy, then we block our last windpipe through which we are able to breathe.' Quoted in BA-MA, w-10/50276: 'Die Militärpolitische Lage Deutschlands', pp. 72–73.

[232] BA-MA, NL Hahnke, N36/11, Groener, 'Über den Schlieffenplan'. See also Lothar Burchardt, *Friedenswirtschaft und Kriegsvorsorge. Deutschlands wirtschaftliche Rüstungsbestrebungen vor 1914*, Boppard/Rhein 1968, pp. 24–27, 43. See e.g. Schlieffen's 'Der Krieg der Gegenwart': 'Such [long] wars are however impossible at a time when the existence of the nation depends on an uninterrupted continuation of trade and industry, and the wheels which have been brought to a standstill have to be restarted by means of a speedy decision. A strategy of attrition cannot be employed when the support of millions requires the expenditure of billions.' *Gesammelte Schriften*, vol. 1, Berlin 1913, p. 17. In his 1905 manoeuvre critique, Schlieffen expressed a similar point of view: BayHSTA-KA, Bestand Generalstab, 1237, 23 December 1905.

[233] Burchardt, *Friedenswirtschaft*, p. 26.

[234] Stig Förster, 'Der deutsche Generalstab und die Illusion des kurzen Krieges, 1871–1914. Metakritik eines Mythos', first published in *MGM*, 1995, here cited from Joseph Becker et al. (eds.), *Lange und Kurze Wege in den Ersten Weltkrieg*. Augsburger Beiträge zur Kriegsursachenforschung, Munich 1996, pp. 61–98 (cited as 'Metakritik'); Herwig, *First World War*, p. 50.

slowed down by this change of plan, for without a violation of Dutch territory there was little room for German troop manoeuvring. A solution seemed to offer itself in a lighting strike on Liège: this strategically important fortress town had to be taken even before actual mobilization began. Since 1908 the General Staff had worked on the idea of this *coup de main*.[235] In 1915, Moltke recalled his motivation: 'The fortress had to be in our hands if the advance of the First Army was to be at all possible. This realization led me to the decision to take Liège by a *coup de main*.'[236]

The *coup de main* on Liège, and Moltke's adamant refusal to violate Dutch neutrality, were significant differences between the Schlieffen and the Moltke Plan.[237] While Moltke's critics have accused him of 'diluting' the Schlieffen Plan and of putting too much emphasis on the left wing, his plan was actually very distinct in anticipating a French offensive, as opposed to Schlieffen's rather dogmatic belief in a French defensive attitude. Moltke felt he had to react to the fact that French war planning had indeed changed in its emphasis. Since 1911 Joffre had been reshaping French strategy, both in terms of preparations for offensive action and by increasing the effectiveness of the support from her allies.[238] Unusually for German military planning at the time, some political and economic considerations had also entered into Moltke's calculation, although it should not be overlooked that the primary motivation behind his changes to the deployment plan was military. The fact that a move such as the *coup de main* on Liège would need diplomatic preparation was, however, overlooked by the General Staff. The planned *coup de main* was one of the General Staff's best-guarded secrets, and even the Kaiser, whose inability to keep secrets was notorious, did not know about its details. Of course, it was obvious to contemporaries that Liège would have to be taken by German troops in a scenario such as the German

---

[235] For Ritter the *coup de main* on Liège was 'a plan bordering on the adventurous': *Staatskunst und Kriegshandwerk. Das Problem des 'Militarismus' in Deutschland*, 4 vols., Munich 1954–1968, vol. 2, p. 332. Ritter claims that the plan was not finalized and formally laid down until 1 April 1913. Perhaps he is referring here to the final version of the plan which envisaged taking Liège by the fifth mobilization day, a significant reduction from the previously planned eleven-day scenario.

[236] BA-MA, w-10/51063, Moltke to Freytag-Loringhoven, 26 July 1915.

[237] Helmuth von Moltke's son Adam coined the phrase 'Moltkeplan': BA-MA, N78/37, Adam von Moltke, 'Eine Antwort an Herrn Walter Görlitz'. Another difference was the intended use of reserves. Schlieffen did not want to use them on the front, but primarily as back-up, while Moltke had decided by 1912 to mix reserve corps with regular troops at the front. See Bucholz, *Moltke*, pp. 267–268. Moltke also wanted to pay more attention to the East in his military planning, and advocated the need for more troops and better fortifications there. See Moltke's memorandum, 21 December 1912, Reichsarchiv, *Weltkrieg, Anlagen*, pp. 158–164.

[238] Samuel R. Williamson, Jr., 'Joffre Reshapes French Strategy', in Paul M. Kennedy (ed.), *The War Plans of the Great Powers, 1880–1914*, London 1979, p. 135.

deployment plan envisaged, but the secret was the tight timing of the strike – before hostilities were even officially declared. The Chancellor did not find out about the intended attack on Liège until 31 July 1914.[239] However, there was a serious disadvantage that Moltke was prepared to accept: the urgent need to take the fortification of Liège effectively precluded any last-minute options for peace – as was indeed the case in 1914.[240] There were military shortcomings resulting from this plan, too. The First and Second Armies – almost 600,000 men, plus horses and equipment – had to pass through a narrow twelve-mile corridor. By forcing the advancing German armies through such a tight 'bottleneck', Moltke's change of plan resulted in serious logistical complications.[241]

Interestingly, the men who assisted Moltke in this, in particular Ludendorff, Groener and Stein, became Moltke's most outspoken post-war critics. This is not surprising in the light of the criticisms directed against Moltke and his aides after the war. The fact that the plan had been altered came to be regarded as an unforgivable sin, and Moltke was blamed for all the shortcomings that the plan had displayed in practice. However, some General Staff officers regarded Ludendorff, rather than Moltke, as the 'father of the "dilution"' of the Schlieffen Plan,[242] and

---

[239] See Turner, 'Significance', p. 62; Ritter, *Staatskunst*, vol. 2, p. 332. The fateful consequences of this restrictive plan in the last days of peace will be examined in Chapter 5.

[240] According to an unsubstantiated thesis it was German knowledge of Dutch intentions to blow up strategically important railway bridges across the River Meuse that may have been behind the change of plan. As the German advance depended on the Dutch and Belgian railways, this could certainly have been another reason for Moltke to alter the deployment plan. However, nowhere in the literature is this mentioned as a reason for the change of deployment plan; it is thus very unlikely that Moltke's strategy was influenced by a knowledge of Dutch intentions. See J. Buijs, 'De spoorbrug bij Roermond. Oorzaak van Nederlands neutraliteit in 1914?', *Militaire Spectator*, 161, 1992, p. 9.

[241] Turner, 'Significance', p. 61; Bucholz, *Moltke*, p. 266.

[242] BA-MA, NL Tappen, N56/3, letter from Dr H. Zatschek to Tappen, 7 April 1925, p. 101. Zatschek believed that Moltke had been solely responsible for the changes, that as early as 1905 his views differed from those of Schlieffen, and that he had never endorsed Schlieffen's strategy. Theobald von Schäfer admitted that Ludendorff had also been party to the alteration of the Schlieffen Plan, 'but only after Moltke and Stein', and that this was the reason why he had been blamed for the Plan's adulteration (Schäfer, *Ludendorff*, p. 19). Ludendorff himself, however, tried to deny his own responsibility in the face of allegations after the war. Moltke had conferred with him and had discussed operations, Ludendorff had given his point of view, but Moltke alone had had the final say regarding the deployment plan: 'I, too, have been affected [by criticism], although General v. Moltke himself in the last instance decided on the deployment' (Ludendorff, *Mein Militärischer Werdegang*, p. 128). As with all such justificatory accounts, it is almost impossible to tell truth from fiction. See also Tschuppik, *Ludendorff*, pp. 48, 41ff., who shows Ludendorff as a defender of Moltke's changes to the ratio of troops deployed, blames not these changes, but inadequate leadership for the failure of 1914, and argues that *Oberquartiermeister* von Stein, rather than Ludendorff, had been Moltke's strategic adviser. Tschuppik alleges – quite wrongly – that Ludendorff had been merely an 'anonymous head of department'.

General von Stein was also held responsible. After the war, Moltke's critics conveniently overlooked the fact that they, too, had been involved in changing Schlieffen's fool-proof plan, instead accusing Moltke of never really understanding Schlieffen's strategic concept, and of never fully endorsing it.[243] Moltke became a convenient scapegoat.[244] It became a recurrent theme in military history writing after the First World War to blame changes made to Schlieffen's plan for the catastrophe that followed. Rather unfairly, Moltke's critics maintained that he should not have tampered with the plan, ignoring the fact that it was Moltke's right, even his duty, to adapt the war plan to changing circumstances.[245]

The degree of involvement of Moltke or Ludendorff, or indeed any other member of the General Staff, in the development of the idea of the coup against Liège is difficult to gauge.[246] Tappen revealed after the war that he did not know who the 'inventor of the attack on Liège' was. He remembered that the plan was already in existence when he joined the Second Department in the autumn of 1910, although the *coup de main* was then still envisaged to take place at a later date, around the eleventh mobilization day. In 1914, it was scheduled for the fifth day.[247] In 1915 Moltke claimed the coup had been his idea. He boasted: 'I had had the terrain around Liège reconnoitred precisely, [and] had all paths planned on which columns could march on the inner city without coming into the field of vision of the outer forts.'[248]

After 1906, when Schlieffen had lost his influence over military decision-making, he had to stand by and watch Moltke make alterations to his strategic plan. The former Chief of the General Staff was no longer consulted. If he wanted to state his views, he had to do so in military journals – which he did frequently, producing a number of popular arti-

---

[243] An argument that is echoed by Bucholz, who maintains that Moltke 'lacked a detailed understanding of the war plan and the confidence that it would work': *Moltke*, p. 214. The latter is certainly true.   [244] Wallach, *Dogma*, p. 126.

[245] See e.g. Gackenholz, *Entscheidung in Lothringen*, p. 3.

[246] Theobald von Schäfer is certain that Liège had been Ludendorff's suggestion and that the preparations had gone ahead under his leadership: *Ludendorff*, p. 20.

[247] Tappen to Mantey, 20 March 1933, BA-MA, N56/5, NL Tappen, p. 222.

[248] A marginal note written by Kluck next to this passage in Moltke's letter reads: 'But this cannot possibly be published! K[luck].' BA-MA, W-10/51063, Moltke to Freytag-Loringhoven, 26 July 1915. Ludendorff was sent to Liège, ostensibly as a tourist, in order to assess the location. See Uhle-Wettler, *Ludendorff*, p. 85, who found a postcard of a 'vue panoramique' of Liège sent to Ludendorff's mother in 1908 and asserts in Ludendorff's defence that – while Ludendorff was no holiday man – he was certainly not a spy, but merely walked through the town 'with his eyes open'.

cles.[249] That Schlieffen was completely shut out of military planning after his replacement was much bemoaned by his supporters. Groener accused Moltke of deliberately missing a vital chance that could have been of 'immeasurable benefit' to him, by not remaining in close contact with Schlieffen from the time he took over his position until the latter's death in January 1913. This was due to what Groener described as a 'deep mental rift' between the two men.[250] Even as late as 1977, Gotthard Jäschke lamented this non-consultation: 'How valuable a "Conscil supérieur de la défense nationale" could have been for Germany, especially in those years [1906–1912]!'[251] Yet, disregarding the fact that such critics are wise after the event, one might ask how effective this 'Conseil' in France had been in any case?[252] In Wilhelmine Germany, there was no tradition of consulting previous Chiefs of Staff: Waldersee had not consulted Moltke, nor Schlieffen Waldersee. Why should Moltke have considered it necessary to consult his predecessor, after having spent several months with him in preparation for the position? It was only after he failed to conduct the war successfully that it seemed to commentators that one of his biggest mistakes had been not to consult the older, wiser Schlieffen.

Curiously, Groener seems to have had no problems with the changes Moltke implemented at the time, for he was the person who, as Chief of the Railway Department, adapted the strategic railway plans annually to suit the deployment plan. Before 1914, Groener's views echoed those of Moltke.[253] Yet, after the war, Groener was of the opinion that the deployment plan that had been put into practice in August 1914, based on Schlieffen's plan but including substantial alterations by Moltke, Stein and Ludendorff, would never have gained Schlieffen's approval. In Groener's eyes, critics of the Schlieffen Plan based their judgements on the 1914 plan, and they were thus wrong to blame Schlieffen for short-comings that were, in his opinion, clearly due to Moltke's decision to

---

[249] See also Ritter, *Schlieffen Plan*, p. 72, on Schlieffen's 'fluent pen'. In at least one case (1908), he sent drafts of his essay 'Der Krieg der Gegenwart' to Moltke and to the Minister of War, as well as the Kaiser, who ordered the article to be read out to the Commanding Generals at a New Year's reception. Wallach, *Kriegstheorien*, p. 98.

[250] Groener, *Feldherr wider Willen*, p. XIII. But see also idem, *Testament*, p. 80, where he admits that it was not usual for 'the epigones' to consult their predecessors.

[251] Jäschke, '"Schlieffenplan" und "Marneschlacht"', p. 189. For a similar view, see Boetticher, *Schlieffen*, p. 89.

[252] See Williamson, 'Joffre Reshapes French Strategy', p. 136 for a critical evaluation of the 'lack-lustre French equivalent of the Committee of Imperial Defence'.

[253] Wallach, *Dogma*, p. 133 also notes this striking fact. Burchardt, *Friedenswirtschaft*, p. 46, points to the similiarities of Groener's and Moltke's views *before* 1914. Only after the defeat did Groener decide to highlight his differing opinion.

weaken the right wing in favour of protecting Alsace-Lorraine and Baden in the South.[254] Jäschke argues similarly that the lost battle of the Marne cannot be equated with a defeat of the Schlieffen Plan itself, for it was not actually Schlieffen's plan that had been put into action in 1914. According to Jäschke, it is thus wrong to claim that the Schlieffen Plan failed.[255]

In Groener's opinion, Moltke, Stein and Ludendorff had been too cowardly to implement the Schlieffen Plan properly; yet, instead of dropping it altogether and developing an alternative, they turned it into something half-baked (*eine "Halbheit"*).[256] Unfortunately, Groener contends, most observers did not actually realize that the plan implemented in 1914 bore little resemblance to Schlieffen's original intentions: 'Because the original Schlieffen Plan was only known to a few General Staff officers there was a general impression in 1914 that the operations were being conducted according to Schlieffen's thinking.'[257] To Groener and fellow members of the Schlieffen school, the case was simple: Moltke had diluted and adulterated the Schlieffen Plan, and had thus gambled away Germany's chance of certain victory. It is surprising how widely accepted their views would become in standard accounts of German military history written in the inter-war period. According to this view, the appointment of Moltke was a grave mistake that ultimately cost Germany the war. And yet, not only were the critics themselves involved in the changes made to the Schlieffen Plan, but it is also difficult to see how Moltke could have fulfilled his role as Chief of the General Staff had he not adapted and updated Germany's strategic plan on an annual basis.

Another important aspect of strategic planning in which Moltke's influence was decisive was the scrapping of the Eastern Deployment Plan. Until 1913, an alternative had existed to Schlieffen's plan of an offensive in the West with an initial defensive operation in the East: the scenario of an eastern deployment only, the so-called *Grosser Ostaufmarschplan*. It had been worked out concurrently with the Schlieffen Plan, although the Franco-Russian alliance of 1892 had made its success unlikely. The plan envisaged a scenario in which Russia acted as the

---

[254] Groener, 'Über den Schlieffenplan', copy in NL Hahnke, BA-MA, N36/11.
[255] Jäschke, '"Schlieffenplan" und "Marneschlacht"', *passim*.
[256] Groener to Kuhl, 22 September 1935, copy in NL Hahnke, BA-MA, N36/10.
[257] Groener, 'Über den Schlieffenplan', BA-MA, N35/11. But compare this with General von Kuhl's recollection that 'the underlying concept behind the Schlieffen Plan had been more or less common knowledge within the army or at least the General Staff': BA-MA, N56/2, NL Tappen, Müller-Loebnitz to Tappen, 29 December 1920, quoting Kuhl.

aggressor and France initially stood back, perhaps even declaring herself neutral. In such a case, a major offensive across the River Narew was planned, with four armies, totalling nearly the whole of Germany's armed forces (sixteen army corps, seven reserve divisions and six cavalry divisions), on the attack.

Moltke doubted the plan's chances of success, just as Schlieffen had before him. The biggest worry was that the Russians would retreat and move their deployment area back as far as Brest-Litovsk, making a quick decision impossible. The other concern was that French neutrality, if declared, would be unreliable. With the German armies deployed deep in Russian territory, the French would be free to attack Germany and meet very little resistance.[258] Moreover, as Moltke noted in his comments on Schlieffen's amended plan (which the latter dictated to Hahnke shortly before his death), his predecessor had not taken the strength of the Franco-Russian Alliance sufficiently into account. Any future war would involve Germany on two fronts: 'As matters stand now, it is impossible for a situation to arise where either France or Russia initially stands by as a passive spectator. Rather, both will simultaneously mobilize and enter as enemies of Germany', he wrote.[259] Given that this was Moltke's conviction, it made sense to abandon the *Ostaufmarschplan*, at least if war were to occur in the near future. Only if a different diplomatic constellation developed would this plan be a practical solution.

Major Christian von Harbou recalled in 1925 that two deployment plans had existed until the mobilization year of 1913/1914. 'Deployment Plan I' was the Schlieffen/Moltke Plan, while Plan II was intended for a defensive operation in the West and an offensive in the East, north of the Vistula. Harbou recalled why it was decided that the *Ostaufmarschplan* should be scrapped:

For the mobilization year [19]14/15 only Deployment I was prepared, [firstly] because the General Staff considered a war against Russia without France's involvement out of the question, and, secondly, because it considered a quick offensive against France in case of a two-front war to be unavoidable. The Russians would probably indeed have retreated into the centre of their country in case of a German offensive. Thus the possibility of a decisive success was lacking.[260]

Interestingly, Harbou knew of another reason why it seemed imperative to direct an initial offensive to the West, arguing that the iron-ore

[258] Ritter, *Schlieffen Plan*, pp. 34–37.
[259] Cited in David G. Herrmann, *The Arming of Europe and the Making of the First World War*, paperback edn, Princeton 1997, p. 208.
[260] Major a.D. von Harbou, letter to Reichsarchiv, 4 April 1925, BA-MA, W-10/51062.

deposits in Lorraine, which were essential to Germany's war economy, necessitated an advance of the army into France. Such economic considerations may indeed have helped with the decision to abandon the *Ostaufmarschplan*, but they would have been of only secondary concern to the military planners.

In April 1913, it was decided to discontinue the annual updating of the Eastern Deployment Plan. At the end of the July Crisis such a plan might have provided Germany with a feasible alternative when, for a short while, it looked as if French neutrality, contrary to all expectations, was a possibility. In the event, this turned out to be merely wishful thinking, but the fact remains that no alternative plan existed: if France had decided to remain neutral, Germany would still have had to attack her, despite the fact that the trigger for war was a Balkan issue. No matter what the political situation, military planning dictated the events. As Waldersee recalled in September 1914: 'When war became unavoidable in the last days of July, the political situation was not yet completely certain. There was certainty within the supreme army command, however, that the strike would have to be conducted with all force (*mit aller Wucht*) against France through Belgium.'[261]

In September 1914 Waldersee claimed responsibility for the idea of scrapping the plan. 'My suggestion was accepted by the Chief [Moltke] and was gladly welcomed by the two relevant heads of department (II and Railway), Oberstleutnant Tappen and Groener.'[262] In a secret memorandum he spelt out his reasons for suggesting that the General Staff concentrate on one plan only: 'From a strictly technical point of view I had reached the conclusion that two big deployments could not be worked on simultaneously with the necessary precision and safety for a speedy implementation.' It is unlikely that this was the real reason for abandoning the second deployment plan. Dropping the plan only made sense if its viability was seriously in question. As it was becoming increasingly unlikely that a deployment in the East only would provide Germany with a chance to defeat her enemies, the preparation of two deployment plans would indeed have appeared too costly and work-intensive.

Those who regarded Britain, rather than Russia, as the real enemy were certainly in favour of dropping the plan, for that would allow

[261] Waldersee, 'Meine Erlebnisse', BA-MA, w-10/51032, p. 4. See Chapter 4 for details on the possibility of French neutrality in 1914.
[262] Ibid., p. 1 and Waldersee's letter to the Reichsarchiv (marked 'very confidential'), BA-MA, w-10/51032.

Germany to concentrate her forces on the front that really mattered. Waldersee recalled: 'A further reason to stick to the one deployment plan was to rule out half measures right from the start. We can only be strong and superior in one place; the defeat of France and her western allies is the most important.'[263] On a more sinister note, abandoning any alternative plan to a deployment in the West was regarded as a way to ensure that the politicians did not end up interfering at the last moment, for fear of escalating a localized conflict. Military planning thus became a way of influencing political decision-making. Waldersee prided himself that the narrowness of Germany's deployment plan prevented last-minute attempts to limit the extent of hostilities: 'The politicians could have worked towards the initial idea of fighting only against Russia. Indeed, as I know, attempts were made to proceed in this manner. That idea failed because of our preparations for war. I believe I can say today already: thank God.'[264] It is possible that the suggestion to scrap the plan really did stem from Waldersee, but responsibility for it lay with Moltke, who sanctioned the idea. Germany's military strategy was now reduced to one single plan of action in the event of a future war, arguably a grave shortcoming. Although it may have appeared to Moltke and his colleagues that an eastern front deployment plan was not feasible, it must be regarded as a serious failing that no alternatives were sought.

The Swiss historian Adolf Gasser regards the decision to abandon the only existing alternative to the Schlieffen Plan as a very grave step. In his opinion, a Germany that desired peace would necessarily have required a deployment plan that led her main forces East.[265] As Gasser explains, the plan for a deployment in the East was scrapped at the very moment when it became foreseeable that it would become an essential alternative to the Schlieffen Plan. Germany's new army bills had resulted in Russian army increases, and the German military were aware that by 1916/1917, Russia would have completed her railway lines, thus allowing her troops to reach the German border much more quickly. The Schlieffen Plan would become redundant in such a scenario, relying as it did on Russian initial slowness. There was thus, Gasser argues, more need than ever for an alternative plan of action – yet the only alternative was scrapped. Gasser comes to a disturbing conclusion. With no other plan of action, and in the certain knowledge that the Schlieffen Plan would eventually 'expire', Germany's military planners must have

---

[263] Waldersee, 'Meine Erlebnisse', BA-MA, w-10/51032, p. 4.   [264] Ibid., p. 3.
[265] Adolf Gasser, *Preußischer Militärgeist und Kriegsentfesselung 1914. Drei Studien zum Ausbruch des Ersten Weltkrieges*, Basel and Frankfurt/M. 1985, p. 5.

decided on a war in the near future, when they decided to scrap any alternatives to the Schlieffen plan. This was proof, in Gasser's view, that in December 1912 Moltke had decided on a 'preventive' war in the near future.[266]

The scrapping of the plan for an attack in the East was almost certainly partly a result of the war council meeting of December 1912, held in response to the bad news from London which shattered the illusion that Britain might remain neutral, at least in the initial stages of a war arising from a Balkan conflict.[267] Unlike the Chancellor, who continued to hope for British neutrality, and whose policy was geared towards achieving this aim until the last days of the July Crisis, the military decision-makers believed in neither French nor British neutrality after the clear warning from Lichnowsky in December 1912. If there was no chance of such neutrality, the *Ostaufmarschplan* was indeed redundant. April 1913, the beginning of the new mobilization year, was the first opportunity following the meeting when the deployment plan could be changed.[268]

The insufficient army increases of the previous year, by which the General Staff's demands were effectively halved, may have been a further contributing factor.[269] Moltke also had to consider technical problems in his decision regarding the *Ostaufmarschplan*. The railway tracks and road networks leading east were insufficient to allow for the quick deployment and major offensive required by the plan. This was a further reason why the General Staff abandoned the *Ostaufmarschplan* in 1913.[270] Even if the deployment plan had been carried out, logistical problems would have impeded Germany's advance on the other side of her border. Poor rail and road networks and the different railway gauge would have created supply problems for the German troops (a problem actually encountered during the 1915 summer offensive). Furthermore, Moltke knew that Russia was planning to deploy her troops further east, a fact that would put increasing pressure on German and Austrian

---

[266] Ibid., pp. 5–7. See also Förster, *Militarismus*, p. 255, who is not convinced by Gasser's conclusion that the government as a whole had decided on preventive war at that time.

[267] See Röhl, *Kaiser, Hof und Staat*, p. 185, on the illusion regarding British neutrality. The war council is examined in detail in Chapter 3.

[268] For a similar argument see Imanuel Geiss, who regards the scrapping of the *Ostaufmarschplan* and the big army increases of 1913 as 'practical consequences of the programme of 8 December 1912': *Der Lange Weg in die Katastrophe. Die Vorgeschichte des Ersten Weltkrieges, 1815–1914*, Munich 1990, p. 269.

[269] Dieter Groh, '"Je eher desto besser!" Imenpolitische Faktoren für die Präventivkriegsbereitschaft des Deutschen Reiches 1913/14', *Politische Vierteljahresschriften*, 13, 1972.

[270] See Salewski, 'Moltke, Schlieffen und die Eisenbahn', pp. 98–99.

troops in an *Ostaufmarsch* scenario.[271] Immediately prior to his decision to scrap the plan, a major map exercise had confirmed to Moltke that an offensive in the East would not offer the same chance of a decisive initial victory as he hoped for in France.[272]

The decision of April 1913 marks an important juncture, and is certainly damning evidence that Germany's military decision-makers were unwilling or unable to develop military strategies for all political contingencies. The lack of any alternative to an all-out war scenario suggests that within the General Staff there was certainly no desire to avoid a war on two fronts – perhaps even, as Gasser suspects, an explicit desire to ensure that only such a war could occur, and that it would break out before this single war plan would become redundant. It can certainly not be denied that a military leadership that was determined to keep peace would have struggled to develop alternative plans, no matter how slim the chance that they could ultimately be implemented.

[271] BayHSTA-KA, Bestand Generalstab, 925, Denkschrift, Grosser Generalstab, 1. Abtl., February 1914.　　[272] Herrmann, *Arming*, p. 209.

CHAPTER THREE

From crisis to crisis: the international background to military planning in the pre-war years

The years 1908 to 1914 confronted German decision-makers, both military and political, with a succession of crises, culminating in the events of July 1914 and the resulting war. Every major pre-war crisis threatened to escalate into armed conflict, and when war was averted on many occasions before 1914, not everyone approved. During these years, Moltke became convinced that war was unavoidable, even that it was a necessity for Germany, and he continually advocated it.

However, Moltke's hands were tied as long as a number of necessary preconditions for war were lacking. These were, first of all, the much-needed army increases. The Chief of the General Staff knew that Germany's deployment plan required huge numbers of troops. His aim was a numerical superiority to, or at least parity with, the enemies in the West and East. However, before 1911, the General Staff did not exert any real pressure to push for army increases. Only after the humiliation at Agadir did the General Staff manage to gain support for its demands. The 'dual militarism'[1] of the time is only one explanation of why Moltke remained passive on the important issue of army increases until 1912. The General Staff and the Ministry of War differed in their opinions about the kind of increases Germany's army required: while the General Staff wanted numerical increases on the highest scale possible, the Ministry of War was more concerned with the quality than the quantity of available soldiers. Other restraints were financial: there was simply not enough money to fund the huge naval increases of Tirpitz's programme as well as General Staff demands. It has also been suggested that Germany felt reasonably secure on the continent until about 1912, and that there was a general confidence within the army that Germany was still superior to her prospective opponents.[2] Ultimately the argu-

---

[1] A term coined by Stig Förster, *Der Doppelte Militarismus*.
[2] See Jack R. Dukes, 'Militarism and Arms Policy revisited: the Origins of the German Army Law of 1913', in Jack R. Dukes and Joachim Remak (eds.), *Another Germany: A Reconsideration of the Imperial Era*, Boulder and London 1988, p. 25.

ments over army increases highlight the Chief of the General Staff's main problem: his position was not one of absolute authority in military matters. Different military bodies vied with each other for influence, and far from being the most influential military institution, the General Staff had to accommodate other points of view.

Aside from army increases, other conditions had to be met if a successful war were to be engaged in. The *casus belli* had to result from circumstances that would definitely involve Germany's main ally, Austria-Hungary. Germany's decision-makers knew that the perfect set-up would be a Balkan crisis, with Austria relying on German support rather than vice versa. The events of the First Moroccan Crisis had proved that Austria could not necessarily be counted on. One of Moltke's tasks would be to renew the once cordial relations between the German and Austrian General Staffs and to assure the alliance partner of German military support in a future war between Austria and Russia. In addition, Germany's relationships with other European countries had to be reassessed, in order to determine who could be counted on as an ally and who would be an enemy. Public opinion was a further important factor. Moltke did not underestimate the potential damage of popular discontent, or the benefit of wide-ranging public support. There was no doubt in the decision-makers' minds that great efforts would have to be made to make Germany appear innocent in a future war, and that the *casus belli* had to be chosen carefully. In August 1914, Crown Prince Rupprecht of Bavaria put this notion quite bluntly: 'Everyone knows what this war, which is forced upon us, is all about; it is a true people's war (*Volkskrieg*), whereas if war had resulted from the Moroccan matter, this would not have been understood among the people.'[3]

A further prerequisite for war was the Kaiser's approval. That this might be difficult to obtain might seem surprising, given the Kaiser's well-known bellicose outbursts and threats of war. Due to Moltke's close relationship with the Kaiser, he was able to impress his sense of urgency on the Kaiser, who was easily convinced that war would have to be fought in the near future. However, the Kaiser lacked the courage to act upon his threats, and more than once retreated when things began to look serious.[4]

As early as May 1907, Heinrich von Tschirschky of the Auswärtiges

[3] BA-MA, w-10/50659, Crown Prince Rupprecht, diary entry, 24 August 1914, p. 23. Also published as *Mein Kriegstagebuch*, ed. Eugen Frauenholz, 3 vols., Berlin 1929, vol. 1, p. 42.
[4] See e.g. his frequent assertions during July 1914 of 'this time I won't fall over', quoted in Fritz Fischer, 'Kaiser Wilhelm und die Gestaltung der deutschen Politik vor 1914', in John C. G. Röhl (ed.), *Der Ort Kaiser Wilhelms II in der deutschen Geschichte*, Munich 1991, p. 280.

Amt also realized the importance of ensuring that these conditions were met. He informed the Prussian general and military writer Friedrich von Bernhardi that he was quite willing to go to war:

But he [Tschirschky] would be in a difficult position, with Bülow as well as the Kaiser. Also, the war would have to be brought about in such a way that one would have public opinion in Germany in one's favour. That would not be easy. Moreover, Russia would have to be paralysed by Austria, because Russia would be forced to proceed against us as well. If the Tsar opposed this, he would be removed. Austria's participation was therefore necessary, because Moltke had said that we would need our entire army against France and England and would therefore need to have our backs covered.[5]

Moltke was well aware of the need to achieve these favourable conditions, but very little progress was made until the diplomatic events of the Agadir Crisis once again put the German army in the limelight. With increasing public support following the disastrous Moroccan adventure, major steps were taken on the road towards war.

Following the army bill of 1 October 1913, the idea of waging a 'preventive war' took shape in Moltke's mind.[6] France and Russia had reacted to German armaments programmes with their own initiatives, which, once completed in the near future, would all but remove the marginal advantage that Germany was gaining as a result of her own expansion. Thus, the temporary advantage following the October 1913 army increases would, by 1916/1917 at the latest, have turned into a disadvantage for Germany. From a military point of view, this spelt disaster. A quick victory over France, as necessitated by the Schlieffen/Moltke Plan, was possible only as long as Russia's army increases were not completed and her railway network not extended to the Russo-German border. By 1916/1917, the Schlieffen Plan would become redundant. Once Russia's increases were completed, her troops would be in Berlin as quickly as the Germans hoped to be in Paris.[7]

A picture thus emerges in these crucial years of Moltke as an advocate of war as soon as possible, before it became impossible to wage a

---

[5] Michael Behnen (ed.), *Quellen zur deutschen Außenpolitik im Zeitalter des Imperialismus, 1890–1911*, Darmstadt 1977, No. 197, p. 384. It is interesting to note that as early as 1907, Tschirschky was reasonably well informed about the Chief of Staff's views, and even had an idea of the ramifications of the Schlieffen Plan.

[6] 'Preventive' war is here to be understood not in the sense of pre-empting an attack from one of Germany's possible future enemies, but of preventing a situation in which Germany would no longer herself be able to launch an attack successfully. On preventive war, see also Adolf Gasser, *Deutschlands Entschluß zum Präventivkrieg 1913/14*, offprint from *Discordia concors, Festschrift für Edgar Bonjour*, Basel 1968; Bernd-Felix Schulte, *Die Deutsche Armee 1900–1914. Zwischen Beharren und Verändern*, Düsseldorf 1977, pp. XXII ff.   [7] See Groh, "Je eher desto besser!", pp. 515–517.

war successfully. At the same time, however, the longer 'the great fight' was postponed, the less certain the Chief of the General Staff became that victory could be assured. Moltke never shared Bethmann Hollweg's belief in the possibility of British neutrality; rather, he emphasized repeatedly that Britain would come to her allies' support.[8] While the full implications of the disastrous international developments for military capability must have been apparent to him, he never informed the relevant political decision-makers of the extent of the danger. As time ran out for the Schlieffen/Moltke Plan, rather than develop alternative plans, Moltke began to push for war while he still felt reasonably confident of the recipe for victory. His sense of urgency was only heightened by the fact that the Ministry of War was unwilling to grant him the army increases he deemed necessary to safeguard Germany in future.

In examining Moltke's reactions to the international events of the pre-war years, this chapter addresses a further important point. It aims to redress the balance in favour of an assessment of Moltke as a Chief of Staff whose decision-making was much more important than most historians are willing to acknowledge. Arden Bucholz argues, for example, that

there is little evidence that [Moltke] had a consistent impact on war planning. Except at two points, when he altered the west front attack plan and changed the Austrian alliance, his main day-to-day influence was in his dealing with the Kaiser, chancellor and war minister, the world outside the G[reat] G[eneral] S[taff].[9]

From this observation Bucholz concludes that Moltke's role has justifiably been marginalized. But this argument is misleading. The 'two points' of influence that Bucholz credits Moltke with, i.e. the changes to the Schlieffen Plan in the West, including the crucial decision not to violate Dutch neutrality, and the assurance to Conrad in 1909 that Germany would support her ally, regardless of whether Austria was the attacked or the attacker,[10] are of crucial significance. In both cases Moltke made decisions based on political considerations which were more important than the minutiae of the day-to-day work within the General Staff that Schlieffen had apparently excelled at. Moreover, other considerations have to be added to Bucholz's two points. Moltke was also responsible for the scrapping of the eastern deployment plan, which, as we have seen, was a decisive step towards reducing Germany's

---

[8] For examples in September 1911, and after February 1913, see below, p. 124 and pp. 159–160.
[9] Bucholz, *Moltke*, p. 223. Bucholz's account reflects the arguments of 'Schlieffen-school' writers such as Staabs and Groener.   [10] See below, p. 111.

options in times of international crises. The fact that Moltke so frequently and vociferously demanded war must also not be overlooked.
Bucholz contends that Moltke 'smoothed over the differences between
the G[reat] G[eneral] S[taff], the War Ministry and the Military
Cabinet that had existed during Schlieffen's time' – no mean achievement, one might add, given the volatile situation between the different
military institutions.[11] To assume that this liaising role was inferior to
that of a technical expert who made decisions behind the scenes is to
evaluate military decision-making through the eyes of the 'Schlieffen
school'. The decisions that Moltke took in the years from 1908 to 1914
resulted in crucial changes to Germany's military planning, and led to
Germany's military defeat in the First World War. While it is true to say
that Moltke played no decisive part in developing military doctrine, and
that as Chief of the General Staff his scope for commanding troops and
imparting his strategic ideas at ground level were rather limited, his
importance lay particularly in the political sphere. Here he actually
wielded much more power than Schlieffen had ever done, expanding the
traditional role of a Chief of the General Staff due to his close personal
relationship with the Kaiser. Moltke's influence cannot, therefore, be
described as negligible.

THE BOSNIAN ANNEXATION CRISIS: A MISSED OPPORTUNITY
FOR WAR

Following the Young Turk revolution in the Ottoman Empire, the Austro-
Hungarian Foreign Minister, Aehrenthal, decided formally to annex the
provinces of Bosnia and Herzegovina on 6 October 1908. Allocated to
Austro-Hungarian administrative rule at the Congress of Berlin in 1878,
the provinces were still nominally under Turkish suzerainty in 1908.
Although Austria initially struck a deal with Russia, whose interests in the
area had to be considered, the two countries eventually fell out over the
annexation, and Russia objected to Austrian moves in the Balkans.[12]
Serbia also reacted indignantly. War between Austria-Hungary and

---

[11] Bucholz, *Moltke*, p. 224.

[12] For details on the Bosnian Annexation Crisis, see Samuel R. Williamson, Jr., *Austria-Hungary and
the Origins of the First World War*, paperback edn, London 1991, pp. 58ff.; Jost Dülffer, M. Kröger
and R.-H. Wippich, 'Ein gerade noch berechenbares Risiko. Die bosnische Annexionskrise
1908/09' in idem, *Vermiedene Kriege. Deeskalation von Konflikten der Grossmächte zwischen Krimkrieg und
Erstem Weltkrieg (1856–1914)*, Munich 1997, pp. 603–614. See also Herrmann, *The Arming of Europe*,
pp. 115ff. Brigitte Hamann, *Hitlers Wien*, Munich 1996, pp. 150ff., provides a detailed description
of the motivation of Austria's politicians and shows that the annexation during the Kaiser's 60-
year jubilee was intended as a 'jubilee gift' to the monarch.

Serbia, and possibly even Russia, seemed increasingly likely, and with the uncertainty of how the various Alliance and Entente partners would react, it was possible that the conflict might escalate into a European war.[13]

In the ensuing crisis Germany and Austria forged a stronger bond, as Germany pledged unconditional support to her ally. Aehrenthal and Bülow co-operated to arrange an exchange of views between Conrad and Moltke.[14] In January 1909, with Bülow's approval, Moltke assured Conrad that Germany would honour the 1879 agreement, if the *casus foederis* arose from a Russian attack on Austria-Hungary, even one that was provoked by an Austrian attack on Serbia – a significant departure from the defensive stance of the original Dual Alliance agreement of 1879. In effect, Moltke and Bülow changed the Alliance from a defensive to an offensive one.[15] By 1909, Germany's decision-makers feared that not to support Austria would lead to the latter becoming a second-rate power.[16] This was a decisive step, and one that Moltke's predecessor might not have taken, due to his pronouncedly low opinion of the Austrian ally. In March 1909, when Austria and Russia began to mobilize, Germany backed Austria's ultimatum to Russia, and even issued a warning to the latter. Germany's decision-makers were confident that Russia was at that time still weakened by the effects of war and revolution, and uncertain of her own allies.[17] There were striking parallels between this crisis and the events of July 1914.[18] Yet peace prevailed in 1909, because the current political situation in Germany was not suited to a bellicose foreign policy. Public opinion would probably not have supported a war over a Balkan issue. Moreover, the Kaiser objected to war at that time – a major contributing factor in avoiding a conflict. In a conversation with Count Zedlitz-Trützschler in March 1909, General von Lyncker said he considered that the chances of success in a war against

[13] Bucholz, *Moltke*, p. 256.

[14] PA Bonn, R2408, 'Militärische Besprechungen mit Italien, Österreich-Ungarn, Rumänien, 1908–1914', Tschirschky (Vienna) to Bülow, 17 December 1908. On Austria's initiative for an exchange of thoughts between Conrad and Moltke see also *Der Weltkrieg*, vol. 2, pp. 4ff.

[15] Conrad von Hötzendorf, *Dienstzeit*, vol. 2, *Die Zeit der Annexionskrise*, p. 380, Moltke to Conrad, 21 January 1909. See Bucholz, *Moltke*, pp. 257–258; Gordon A. Craig, *Germany 1866–1945*, Oxford, paperback edn 1981, p. 323; Ralf Forsbach, *Alfred von Kiderlen-Wächter (1852–1912). Ein Diplomatenleben im Kaiserreich*, 2 vols., Göttingen 1997, vol. 2, pp. 292ff.

[16] See e.g. Wolfgang J. Mommsen, *Großmachtstellung und Weltpolitik 1870–1914. Die Außenpolitik des Deutschen Reiches*, Frankfurt/M. and Berlin 1993, p. 203; Bülow to Wilhelm II, 5 October 1908, *GP* xxvi, (1), pp. 50ff.; Herrmann, *The Arming of Europe*, p. 121, who argues that Bülow was motivated by a desire to do everything 'to stiffen Vienna's resolve'. [17] Fischer, *Illusionen*, p. 105.

[18] See also Mommsen, *Großmachtstellung*, p. 202; Ralph R. Menning, 'The Collapse of "Global Diplomacy": Germany's Descent into Isolation, 1906–1909', Ph.D. Dissertation, Brown University 1986, p. 173; Imanuel Geiss, *German Foreign Policy 1871–1914*, London and Boston 1976, p. 117.

both France and Russia resulting from the Bosnian Crisis were good, and he thought it desirable to bring about a war straight away, in order to solve domestic and international problems. Zedlitz-Trützschler pointed out the major flaw in this thinking, namely 'that the Kaiser's nerves were bad, and that one had to take very careful account of his difficult personality', to which Lyncker agreed, adding: 'Moltke does not fear the French and the Russians, but the Kaiser.'[19] In the following years, military and political decision-makers worked towards achieving the right conditions that would allow a more decisive stand in the future.

Both Moltke and Conrad regretted missing out on what they regarded a good opportunity. In September 1909, Moltke wrote to Conrad 'that I, together with Your Excellency, very much regret that an opportunity has passed unused that might not present itself again under such favourable conditions in the near future'.[20] Arden Bucholz wonders how Moltke could come to this conclusion, considering that international circumstances had actually worsened seriously for Germany since 1905/1906.[21] However, Moltke's statement makes sense considering his prediction that conditions could only get worse, and that for the present at least, Germany had a marginal advantage over her opponent. In 1909, he cannot have harboured high hopes for substantial army increases in the near future. What he did know was that at that point in time, the situation was still favourable. Although he regarded the French army 'all in all . . . as capable (*tüchtig*)', he believed that most of its confidence stemmed from the expected support from France's allies. Moltke did not doubt Germany's chances of victory: 'We can take on the fight against [the French army] with a prospect of complete success', he claimed. Regarding Russia, Moltke's asserted that 'the army had still not overcome the repercussions of the years of war and revolution.'[22] Only one month later, however, Moltke was concerned about Russia's hostile attitude, and considered it diplomacy's task to establish whether or not Russia was bluffing. A report of 23 February 1909 declared: 'The Chief of the General Staff regards the situation, which has been changed by Russia's newest position, as serious.'[23]

[19] Zedlitz-Trützschler, *Zwölf Jahre*, 26 March 1909, p. 226.
[20] Conrad, *Dienstzeit*, vol. I, p. 165.   [21] Bucholz, *Moltke*, p. 259.
[22] PA Bonn, R995, 'Mitteilungen des Generalstabes der Armee und des Admiralstabes der Marine über die militärische Leistungsfähigkeit anderer Staaten', Moltke's memorandum, 29 January 1909: 'Die militärische Leistungsfähigkeit der wichtigsten Staaten Europa's [sic] zu Beginn des Jahres 1909'.
[23] PA Bonn, R2408, 'Militärische Besprechungen mit Italien, Österreich-Ungarn, Rumänien, 3. 1908–8.1914', 23 March 1909: 'Der Generalstabschef über die Lage'.

Moltke was not the only leading general to fear that Germany's super-iority over her enemies would deteriorate in time. Colmar von der Goltz wrote to General von Kluck in April 1909, after the crisis had been resolved peacefully:

What a good opportunity we missed of bringing the great European question to a decision! I was honestly upset about that. . . . This time Austria was com-pletely united and firmly dependent upon us, while we, with our enormous strength, were positioned behind them and could choose our opponent. The question is whether the same situation will ever occur again. . . . In my opinion, the army is just now at a high level of training and tension that can be neither significantly increased nor kept up permanently. This [factor] should be made use of.[24]

During the Bosnian Annexation Crisis of 1908/1909, relations between the General Staffs of Germany and Austria-Hungary finally improved, after the long period of secrecy under Schlieffen which had led to a complete breakdown of communications. Even before the crisis, however, there had been tentative attempts at renewing and strengthen-ing the links between the two military allies, as in May 1907, following Conrad's attendance at the German manoeuvres. Conrad was invited to Moltke's house, 'where I had the honour also to make the acquaintance of his witty wife (*geistreiche Gattin*)', as he recalled in his memoirs. 'General von Moltke's open and honest personality soon brought us personally close together, and thanks to his calm, clear judgement we found our-selves similarly close during the discussion of the many military and political questions.'[25] It was the Austrian Chief of Staff who initiated talks at the end of 1908, as he was keen to establish what kind of support the ally was willing to grant during the latest crisis.[26] In 1909, the per-sonal relationship between Moltke and Conrad helped improve the mil-itary alliance.[27] The correspondence between Moltke and Conrad is one of the most important sources on Moltke available to us. Like most edited memoirs, Conrad's multi-volume *Aus meiner Dienstzeit* is not

---

[24] BA-MA, NL Goltz, N737/12, Goltz to Kluck, 24 April 1909.

[25] Conrad, *Dienstzeit*, vol. 1, p. 68. Conrad and Moltke discovered that they had things in common when Conrad explained that he had been forced to accept the position of Chief of Staff against his will. Moltke alleged this had also been the case with his own appointment, although, as we have seen, this was not the whole story. See also Norman Stone, 'Moltke and Conrad: Relations between the Austro-Hungarian and German General Staffs, 1909–1914', in Paul M. Kennedy (ed.), *The War Plans of the Great Powers, 1880–1914*, London 1979.

[26] Fischer claims that the monarchs of Austria-Hungary and Germany had given orders for talks between the Chiefs of Staff to begin: *Illusionen*, p. 105. Moltke and Conrad make no mention of this. They attended each other's manoeuvres in 1909, and met the respective monarchs. As a result of Conrad's approach in 1909, they began corresponding about military matters. See Moltke to Conrad, 21 January 1909, in Conrad, *Dienstzeit*, vol. 1, pp. 379ff.   [27] Ibid., p. 202.

without shortcomings and distortions, but the inclusion of official and private letters makes it invaluable. Notwithstanding the fact that Moltke's letters did not always accurately portray his true intentions, because the demands of the Schlieffen Plan were not in accordance with those of the Austrian ally, his bellicose statements, designed both to impress and to encourage the 'junior partner', should be taken seriously. Moltke's attitudes to Austria-Hungary, and to likely future enemies and possible allies, are highlighted in these documents. They also show that both Chiefs of Staff were unwilling to reveal their true intentions to the other. As the Reichsarchiv concluded, Conrad never abandoned his desire to fight a war in the Balkans, even if this meant weakening the forces available against Russia, while Moltke only ever considered Austria's future role from the German point of view that everything depended on a decision against France.[28] On this basis, honesty between the allies was scarcely possible. Conrad even had secret documents marked with a specially created stamp, 'Not to be Relayed to the German General Staff'.[29] The crucial issue of joint military planning and a joint command in war-time was never discussed, an oversight that was to have serious consequences once war had broken out.[30]

That war was not only inescapable, but also desirable was a notion that Moltke shared with most of his military contemporaries, and even some civilians. Friedrich von Bernhardi recalled a conversation he had with Tschirschky in May 1907: 'War was . . . unavoidable', he told Bernhardi, 'and he, Tschirschky, was completely prepared to wage it. Therefore, he always worked hand in hand with the Chief of the General Staff v. Moltke.'[31] Moltke encouraged Conrad to use the Bosnian Annexation Crisis as a trigger for war, because the Alliance would then have a better chance of winning against Russia than it would have in the rather uncertain future. This fear of what the future held became a recurrent theme in Moltke's reasoning until the outbreak of war. He envisaged that Germany would be in an increasingly weak position, and this concern was one of the major factors in shaping his decision-making. In 1909, it seemed to Moltke at least a possibility that Russia might not become involved in a confrontation between Austria and Serbia, 'considering Russia's currently still prevailing military weakness, as well as the suppressed, but not extinguished revolutionary movement in that country and the urgent need of money of the [Russian]

---

[28] *Der Weltkrieg*, vol. 2, p. 13.   [29] Herwig, *First World War*, p. 51.
[30] See also Herwig, 'Disjointed Allies', pp. 265–280; Ritter, 'Die Zusammenarbeit', p. 538.
[31] Behnen, *Quellen zur deutschen Außenpolitik*, No. 197, p. 383–384.

empire', as he put it in a letter to Conrad. He anticipated that the time would come when Austria could no longer put up with Serbian provocation and would have no choice but to march into Serbia.[32] Conrad, however, hardly needed Moltke's encouragement – he was himself an outspoken warmonger. Eager to wage war on the troublesome Serbian neighbour, he was frequently disappointed by the political leaders of the Dual Monarchy, who repeatedly curbed his bellicose designs.[33]

In his letter of January 1909, Moltke went on to speculate about the attitudes of other major players in the current crisis. Italy, despite the fact that she belonged to the Triple Alliance, having joined Germany and Austria-Hungary in 1881, was still an uncertain factor. Unlike Conrad, however, Moltke did not expect Italy to turn against her allies at that time. 'I would like to think that Austria can calmly conduct her business in the Balkans without being disturbed by Italy', he wrote to Conrad. In his opinion, the state of Italy's army was dubious, and seemed to him 'unlikely to make a war desirable for Italy, or even possible'. He promised Conrad that Germany would 'consider covering the rear of her ally as a natural duty', should Austria be attacked by Italy.[34]

Moltke's attitude towards the likely French reaction to war resulting from a Balkan quarrel between Austria and Serbia is particularly interesting because it was to be echoed in 1914. In 1909, he thought that France did not want war. However, he was aware that a German mobilization against Russia would also result in a war with France, because France could not allow Germany to mobilize without doing so herself, and in Moltke's opinion two massive armies could not be mobilized next to each other without war resulting from this. As soon as one of the great European powers 'drew the sword', the obligation to attack each other ('einer über den anderen herzufallen') would be created. However, at the same time it was his view that the existence of the alliance systems guaranteed to a certain extent that each power would try to avoid a major conflagration resulting from a Balkan conflict. As he wrote on 21 January 1909,

The circumstances alluded to here are well known to the entire European diplomacy, and perhaps this fact contains the assurance that none of the great states

---

[32] Conrad, *Dienstzeit*, vol. 1, p. 380.

[33] On Conrad see e.g. Ritter, *Staatskunst*, vol. 2, pp. 282ff.; Herwig, *First World War*, pp. 52ff.; Tunstall, *Planning for War Against Russia and Serbia*; Ritter, 'Die Zusammenarbeit', p. 523, points out that Conrad's constant demands for war must have influenced Austrian politicians in their decision-making.

[34] Conrad, *Dienstzeit*, vol. 1, p. 381, Moltke to Conrad, 21 January 1909. Conrad did not share Moltke's optimistic view of Italy's reliability as an alliance partner (ibid., pp. 202–203).

will, because of Serbian ambitions, light the torch of war that could set alight the roof of all Europe. That Russia, motivated by such considerations, will stay quiet in a warlike conflict between the Austro-Hungarian monarchy and Serbia does not seem at all unlikely to me.[35]

Although Moltke was clearly aware of the serious repercussions that any aggressive act by Austria might have on the international system, he never considered it Austria's or Germany's duty to ensure that the fragile balance remained undisturbed, never felt deterred by the increasing likelihood that war could result from any localized European conflict, or tempted to urge caution. Instead he merely hoped that the threat of escalation would deter other nations from attempting to curb Austrian and German ambitions. The Alliance partners were not, in this view, constrained in their ability to start a localized conflict by the threat of an escalation into a European war. This attitude continued in German thinking and would be displayed prominently during the July Crisis.

In his letter to Conrad, Moltke did not speculate on the likelihood that the envisaged war would include England. In any case, he shared the general convinction of the superiority of the German army over the British one. After the war, Bülow recalled a conversation with Moltke in 1908 or 1909, when he had pointed out to the latter that he might be underestimating 'England and the English', to which Moltke replied that 'he would prefer to see the English as an open enemy rather than a malevolent onlooker'. Bülow remembered that this was a point of view that was common to a wide range of people within the army.[36] The General Staff was, however, aware that Britain was increasing her military potential, as a positive assessment of the British army in 1909 exemplifies. This report noted a marked increase in the interest of the British population in army matters, due to a heightened fear of invasion. It was noted that the idea of a conscript army was being discussed, although this seemed unlikely to be put into effect in the immediate future. The General Staff's opinion of the British troops was a very favourable one:

The troops are well trained and practically equipped throughout. They made an excellent impression on the German officers present, during deployment as

---

[35] Moltke to Conrad, 21 January 1909, ibid., p. 382. The fact that Germany and France had come to an agreement over their Moroccan interests on 9 February 1909 was an important factor in German policy-making during the Bosnian Crisis, leading to the view that an Austro-Russian conflict might be localized. See Menning, 'Collapse', p. 174.

[36] BA-MA, NL Tirpitz, N253/173, Bülow to Tirpitz, 11 June 1922.

well as during combat. . . . All in all, the English army has made significant advances over the last years. The regular army is gradually becoming quite a considerable opponent.[37]

It is difficult to reconcile this knowledge with the pronounced underestimation of the British army that was expressed not only by Moltke throughout his time in office, but also by his predecessor. Moltke was under no illusion as regards Britain's naval power, as he expressed in a meeting at the Reichskanzlerpalais in June 1909 with leading naval officers and the Chancellor, who wanted to discuss the possibilities of reaching a détente with England. Moltke had little faith in the German navy's chances – not surprisingly, since at that time not even Tirpitz could guarantee a naval victory. The minutes of the meeting recorded that 'General von Moltke is of the opinion that we have no chance whatsoever of fighting successfully in a [naval] conflict with England. An honourable agreement, for example on the basis of a reduction in the speed of building, thus seemed desirable to him, too.'[38] Moltke agreed in this point with the Chancellor, hoping that a reduction in naval increases would work in the army's favour by freeing up some of the tight budget. The General Staff refused to acknowledge that Britain was becoming a serious opponent, not only at sea, where her superiority was not really questioned, but also on land, where German strategy depended on the assumption that England would dispatch only a weak force. Instead the General Staff, with typical wishful thinking, continued to base its planning on the assumption that a British force would be weak, if they did not discount it altogether.

In 1908/1909, Moltke was concerned that war over a Balkan issue might not prove popular with the German people. He was aware that popular support was an indispensable prerequisite for war in the age of 'people's wars', especially if Germany might appear as the aggressor. Zedlitz-Trützschler's diary records a conversation with Moltke, after the latter had discussed the political situation with the German Crown Prince in November 1908. Apparently, the Crown Prince had expressed the opinion that only a war could help Germany out of the tangled situation in which she found herself, but Moltke had pointed out to him the importance of public support, which would have been difficult to obtain in the current crisis:

[37] BA-MA, PH3 654. Berichte über fremde Heere, 1907–1911, esp. 'Jahresbericht über England', 1909, pp. 187–192.
[38] *GP*, vol. 28, Nr. 10306, 3 June 1909: 'Protokoll einer Besprechung im Reichskanzlerpalais am 3. Juni 1909 über die Frage einer Verständigung mit England'.

General v. Moltke told me that he had advised the Crown Prince that the time of cabinet wars was over and that a war that the German people did not want or did not understand, and would therefore not greet with sympathy, would be a very dangerous affair. If, however, the people thought that the war had been conjured up in a frivolous fashion and was only intended to help the governing classes out of an embarrassment, then it would have to start with us having to fire on our own subjects.[39]

To secure public support for international hostilities was therefore of the utmost importance. However, if a favourable situation arose, Moltke was not opposed to war, even if public opinion was not particularly bellicose. The Bosnian Crisis fulfilled the important condition of being a Balkan crisis, thus guaranteeing Austria's involvement. Colmar von der Goltz shared Moltke's views, as he told Mudra:

I have encountered disbelief wherever I have pointed out the possibility of an outbreak of war during the last few days. Only today with Moltke did I find a similar point of view [to mine] and also a grave mood. By the way, I cannot put it any other way than that I like this man more every time and that I have come to the conviction that, contrary to such widespread expectation, he has proved to be the right choice.[40]

The crisis of 1908/1909 was resolved without war. Although a diplomatic victory had been attained, Conrad considered it worthless, and what was more, only 'an apparent victory (*Scheinerfolg*)'.[41] Moltke regretted that an opportunity for a localized war between Austria and Serbia had been missed, at a time when the risk of an escalation of the conflict could still have been taken quite confidently. In September 1909, he declared in a private letter to Conrad:

I am firmly convinced that it would have been possible to localize the war between Austria-Hungary and Serbia, and the monarchy would have been stabilized within and strengthened without as a result of the war's victorious completion and could have won a preponderance in the Balkans that would no longer be rocked so easily. Even if Russia had become active and a European war had developed, the conditions for Austria and Germany could now have been better than they will probably be in a few years' time.[42]

The Bosnian Crisis and the renewed link with the Austrian ally were an important juncture, for they mark one of the significant changes

---

[39] Zedlitz-Trützschler, *Zwölf Jahre*, 29 November 1908, p. 195. There is an obvious and interesting contradiction between this thinking and the strategy behind the Schlieffen Plan which assumed that only a short war, a *Kabinettskrieg*, was possible for Germany. Moltke did not believe that the next war would be a short war, yet was willing to implement a strategic plan based on the premise that Germany's only chance of victory lay in a short, decisive initial campaign.

[40] Goltz to Mudra, 8 March 1909, Goltz, *Denkwürdigkeiten*, pp. 332–333.

[41] Conrad, *Dienstzeit*, vol. 1, p. 166.   [42] Moltke to Conrad, 14 September 1909, in ibid., p. 165.

between Schlieffen's and Moltke's planning. Moltke's two-front war was to be an alliance war, although not in the true sense of the word. In his correspondence with Conrad, Moltke adopted a false optimism to convince the ally of Germany's good intentions and her reliability (Ritter aptly called this 'Zweckoptimismus' – calculated optimism). Moltke had to disguise the fact that Germany's main focus and first area of deployment was on her western front. The knowledge that Germany would only deploy the most minimal forces in the East might have resulted in Austria deciding not to attack Russia, perhaps only adopting a defensive stance in the Carpathian Mountains, thus seriously endangering Germany's strategic position in the East. Thus, while Conrad wanted to make detailed arrangements with Moltke regarding an operational plan, Moltke attempted to avoid any real commitment.[43] Yet, while he was never completely honest with his partners and never trusted their abilities wholeheartedly, he knew that Germany's success depended on Austria's involvement. Unlike Schlieffen, who had all but discounted the idea of counting on the ally, Moltke relied on an alliance war motivated by 'Nibelungentreue' (undying loyalty to the German spirit).[44]

Moltke's war planning required certainty regarding the political situation in which Germany would have to fight a war; therefore he was keen for the political leaders to clarify as early as possible who would be friend and who would be foe.[45] As he informed Conrad in January 1910, he had suggested

that, if war between the allies and Russia had to be regarded as unavoidable and immediately imminent, the German government must demand an immediate and completely clear declaration from the French government as to how the latter intended to behave if a war broke out. Such a declaration would have to occur immediately, because the decision whether the main German forces should be deployed in the West or the East cannot allow for any delays.[46]

It is interesting that Moltke at this point still considered the possibility of an offensive in the East, if a French assurance of neutrality could be obtained – something that he was no longer willing to consider in 1914, because he felt that French assurances could not be trusted. Indeed, as

[43] Ritter, *Staatskunst*, vol. 2, pp. 300ff.

[44] Max von Szcepanski, 'Stellungnahme zu Wolfgang Förster; Die deutsche Westoffensive und die Marneschlacht, 1921', in BA-MA, w-10/50220, pp. 14–20, p. 16. The term 'Nibelungentreue' was first applied to German–Austrian relations during the Bosnian Crisis: Hamann, *Hitlers Wien*, p. 155.   [45] BA-MA, w-10/50276: 'Die Militärpolitische Lage Deutschlands', p. 11.

[46] Ibid., pp. 12–13.

we have seen, the plan for an attack in the East was scrapped in 1913.[47] It is, of course, entirely possible that even in 1910 he felt uncertain whether he could rely on a French promise, if one could be secured by the German government, and that his statement was merely intended to reassure the Austrian Chief of Staff that there was a possibility of a German offensive in the East. To Conrad, any involvement of the German army in the West was damaging to the Austrian cause; he wanted the German ally to tackle the Russians while Austria defeated the Serbs.

During the Bosnian Crisis, German military planners also speculated about possible future allies. Turkey, with whom the General Staff had established a close link due to Germany's connection with the latter, was an obvious choice. Colmar von der Goltz, known as the 'father of the Turkish Army', had been involved in attempts to modernize the latter. Goltz and Moltke were on friendly terms, and Goltz's views on Turkey would have informed Moltke's thinking. In a report about his time in Turkey, written in October and November 1910, Goltz highlighted in particular the important role that an allied Turkey could play in a future war. While Turkish help could be employed against Russia, Goltz explained that Turkey's real value lay elsewhere: 'However, we do not strictly need them on that side, for there we can get to the opponent ourselves. But against England, which is not directly accessible to us, [Turkey's] alliance may be of the highest value for us. She can attack British power in two very sensitive places.'[48] As a consequence, Goltz advocated not only observing Turkish military development favourably, but even supporting and encouraging it as much as possible.

Relations between Germany and Russia became more cordial once the Bosnian crisis had been resolved peacefully. The newly appointed Russian Foreign Minister, Sazonov, travelled to Potsdam in September 1910 and met with Chancellor Bethmann Hollweg. Better relations resulted from the German promise not to support aggressive moves by Austria in the Balkans. In turn, Russia dropped her opposition to the Baghdad railway project, a move that shocked Russia's allies Britain and France.[49] In early November 1910, the Kaiser and the Tsar met in Potsdam to confirm the cordial mood between the two countries.[50] In fact, until the outbreak of the Balkan Wars in October 1912, relations

---

[47] See Chapter 2, pp. 100ff. for the scrapping of the Eastern Deployment Plan, and Chapter 4, pp. 219ff. for the possibility of an offer of French neutrality during the July Crisis.

[48] BA-MA, NL Goltz, N737/5, 'Berichte aus der Türkei, 1909 und 1910', 18 December 1910.

[49] Dominic Lieven, *Russia and the Origins of the First World War*, New York 1983, p. 38.

[50] Dukes, 'Militarism', p. 23.

remained quite amicable, especially as Russia displayed restraint during the Agadir Crisis. These cordial relations may have influenced the military to feel more confident about possible future military engagements, despite the fact that numerical superiority against the Triple Entente could not be achieved. Until the Balkan Wars, the cordial relations with Russia offered at least a possibility that she would keep out of a conflict between Germany and France.

FROM THE AGADIR CRISIS TO THE 1912 ARMY BILL

The dispatch of the German gun-boat *Panther* to the Moroccan port of Agadir on 1 July 1911 marked the beginning of the second Moroccan Crisis. German foreign policy at the time was 'master-minded' by the State Secretary for Foreign Affairs, Alfred von Kiderlen-Wächter. In fact, German policy was conducted by him to such a degree that even the Chancellor was not informed about his intentions.[51] Germany felt provoked by French military intervention in Morocco in the spring of 1911 (the 'dash for Fez'), which amounted in effect to the establishment of a French protectorate in Morocco. This was a move that ran counter to the Algeciras Agreement of 1906 and to the 1909 Franco-German agreement on Morocco.

Germany's reaction is perhaps understandable in the light of the rules of imperialism that applied at the time. Germany's pretext for getting involved was the protection of German citizens and German business interests in Morocco. The issue was, however, much more about European concerns.[52] As in the previous Moroccan conflict, Germany was intent on asserting her status as a great power, and on ensuring adequate compensation for any gains that another power might make in the colonial sphere, with an eye to weakening the Entente in the process. The public response to Kiderlen-Wächter's forceful foreign policy was

[51] The Chancellor had to resort to trying to get Kiderlen drunk to find out what his intentions were. Karl Dietrich Erdmann (ed.), *Kurt Riezler. Tagebücher, Aufsätze, Dokumente*, Göttingen 1972, Riezler's diary entry of 29 July 1911, p. 178 (hereafter as Riezler, *Tagebücher*). On Kiderlen's handling of the crisis see also David Stevenson, *Armaments and the Coming of War. Europe 1904–1914*, Oxford 1996, pp. 180ff.; Thomas Meyer, *"Endlich eine Tat, eine befreiende Tat...". Alfred von Kiderlen-Wächters "Panthersprung nach Agadir" unter dem Druck der öffentlichen Meinung*, Husum 1996; Forsbach, *Kiderlen-Wächter*, vol. 2, pp. 41ff.

[52] Geoffrey Barraclough's account of the Agadir Crisis is perhaps too sympathetic to German intentions, although he is accurate in his description of German action as 'hastily put together without troubling to plan its execution in detail, and from the start it moved from expedient to expedient': *From Agadir to Armageddon. Anatomy of a Crisis*, London 1982, p. 107. See also Gerd Fesser, *Der Traum vom Platz an der Sonne. Deutsche 'Weltpolitik' 1897–1914*, Bremen 1996, pp. 140–145.

largely positive, even enthusiastic; and, not surprisingly, the mood among Germany's leading military men was far from peaceable. They advocated unleashing a war (*losschlagen*) over the Moroccan issue, especially in view of the relatively favourable military situation at the time.[53] Ludwig von Gebsattel, the Bavarian military attaché, reported that 'in military circles, particularly here in Berlin, the mood is more war-like than a little while ago, more war-like than I myself thought a few days ago. On our side – even among the higher ranks – it is emphasized that we should use the situation, which is relatively favourable for us, to strike.'[54] At the same time, Admiral von Müller told the Kaiser, who was worried about the possibility of escalation, that 'war is not the worst of all evils'.[55] Russia's attitude towards Germany was reasonably positive, and it seemed possible that she might choose to stay out of a conflict over Morocco.[56] At the back of Kiderlen's mind was information about the current state of the Russian army, as conveyed to him in a memorandum of August 1910, in which the General Staff speculated on the likely results of the current Russian army reorganization. In the long run this reorganization meant that Russia's striking power would improve. 'Currently this is, of course, quite doubtful. . . . The Russian army urgently requires a rest for at least one to two years.'[57] Looking back on the events of October 1911, Otto Hamman, Press Secretary at the Auswärtiges Amt at the time, recalled: 'Just as we didn't seek the war, we didn't fear it either.'[58]

At the height of the crisis, Moltke's mood was pronouncedly bellicose. Milan Ulmansky, of the Austrian General Staff, recalled a conversation with him on 7 August, shortly after the German Chief of Staff had returned from the annual North Sea cruise with the Kaiser. Moltke gave his complete support to Kiderlen-Wächter and considered the current Moroccan Crisis the most favourable time for a 'reckoning with England'.[59] Moltke expressed his discontent over the renewed diplomatic wranglings in a letter to his wife on 19 August 1911:

[53] See e.g. Förster, *Militarismus*, pp. 209f.; John C. G. Röhl, 'Admiral von Müller and the Approach of War, 1911–1914', *HJ*, 12, 4, 1969, pp. 653ff; Afflerbach, *Falkenhayn*, pp. 78–79.

[54] BayHSTA-KA, MKr 41, No. 1731, 3 September 1911. See also Förster, *Militarismus*, p. 210; I. Lambi, *The Navy and German Power Politics 1862–1914*, Boston 1984, p. 321.

[55] W. Görlitz (ed.), *Der Kaiser . . . Aufzeichnungen des Chefs des Marinekabinetts Admiral Georg Alexander von Müller über die Ära Wilhelms II*, Göttingen 1965, p. 88.   [56] Lieven, *Russia*, p. 38.

[57] PA Bonn, R 10450, 'Russische Militär- und Marine-Angelegenheiten', memorandum 'Die Reorganisation der russischen Armee', beginning of August 1910.

[58] BA Abteilung Potsdam, NL Otto Hamman, 90Ha6/56, p. 23.

[59] Ulmansky's report of 7 August 1911, Vienna Kriegsarchiv, quoted in Ritter, 'Zusammenarbeit', p. 544, note 44.

5 North Sea cruise, 1912. In this rare shot in civilian clothes, the Kaiser is third from the left and Moltke third from the right.

The wretched Morocco story is beginning to get on my nerves. It is certainly a sign of laudable stamina to be eternally sitting on [hot] coals, but it is not pleasant. If we once again emerge from this affair with our tail between our legs, if we cannot bring ourselves to make energetic demands which we would be ready to force through with the sword, then I despair of the future of the German Reich. In that case I will leave. But before that I will make a request to get rid of the army, and to have us placed under a Japanese protectorate; then we can make money without being disturbed and we can turn completely simple-minded.[60]

These were Moltke's feelings in the light of disturbing news from Detlev von Winterfeldt, the German military attaché in Paris. He was convinced 'that a fight with the French army could not be conducted without severe sacrifices, but that it could nonetheless be embarked on with a cheery prospect of success (*mit freudiger Aussicht auf Erfolg*)'. On 19 August he advised that the French Foreign Ministry and the Ministry of War were preparing for the possibility of war against Germany. On 24 August, Winterfeldt confirmed suspicions that the French army manoeuvres had been cancelled, which caused concern in Germany, particularly when it transpired that the British manoeuvres had also been called off.[61] By 7 September, Moltke believed that while it was uncertain whether France was actually ready for war, the British army and navy certainly were not. Nonetheless, he did expect Britain to get involved in support of France.[62]

Moltke's concern during the Agadir Crisis also extended to the military repercussions of French predominance in Africa, for the General Staff feared the potential danger that the French might build up their army by recruiting Moroccan soldiers. From Moltke's point of view, this was a much more serious threat to Germany than the economic consequences French predominance might have.[63]

Some historians have been tempted to dismiss Moltke's aggressive 'tail between the legs' statement, implying that he was 'all talk' and did not actually mean what he said. L. C. F. Turner, for example, maintains that 'like many weak men, he frequently indulged in extravagant and bellicose talk', and that 'too much importance should not be attached to such outbursts' because Germany's dangerous mood at the time was, accord-

---

[60] Moltke, *Erinnerungen*, letter to his wife, 19 August 1911, p. 362.
[61] Winterfeldt sent reports to the Ministry of War; copies were sent to the AA. See PA Bonn, R 6916. See also Bucholz, *Moltke*, pp. 260–261; Lambi, *The Navy*, p. 320; Emily Oncken, *Panthersprung nach Agadir. Die deutsche Politik während der 2. Marokkokrise 1911*, Düsseldorf 1981, pp. 214–215.
[62] Moltke's assessment of the current situation, 7 September 1911, in Bucholz, *Moltke*, p. 261.
[63] Forsbach, *Kiderlen-Wächter*, vol. 2, p. 45.

ing to Turner, due less to 'a craving for *Weltpolitik*' than to 'injured pride and uneasy feeling'.[64] However, the evidence of Moltke's desire for war suggests quite the opposite. His 'extravagant and bellicose talk' was aimed at achieving war before too long, and 'injured pride and uneasy feeling' do not exclude a desire for *Weltpolitik*. What was at work in Germany was a dangerous combination of the two sentiments, which were in no way mutually exclusive.

When the crisis was resolved peacefully, and in effect resulted in a diplomatic defeat for Germany,[65] her military leaders saw their suspicions confirmed that in future only a war would hold any guarantee of changing the status quo in Germany's favour. They also became more convinced that their *Weltbild*, a Germany encircled by hostile powers, was indeed based on reality.[66] The consequences of the crisis were detrimental, both internationally and within Germany. 'From Agadir to Armageddon'[67] suggests a causality of events that can indeed be demonstrated. Arguably the most significant result was that Germany had clearly identified herself as an aggressor and troublemaker. The list of direct and indirect results was, however, seemingly endless.

In the light of the fact that both Britain and Germany were being compensated for the French gains in Morocco, Italy, too, claimed recompense. She opted for Libya, and the Italian attack on Tripoli has to be seen as a 'direct sequel to the French march on Fez'.[68] Turkey, weakened by the conflict, became an easy target for the Serbian-led Balkan League. Indirectly, the Moroccan affair thus led to the Balkan Wars of 1912/1913. Italy moved further away from the Alliance, and became a more unreliable partner for Germany and Austria.[69] The strengthened Serbia and Montenegro posed a threat to Austria, who would in future have to deploy a sizeable number of troops against them, troops which

---

[64] Turner, *Origins*, p. 21; idem, 'Significance', p. 59

[65] Germany gained 263,000 square kilometres of the French Congo, but only in exchange for a part of the Cameroons. This was considered an insufficient gain by all the German parties, and led to resentment of both the other European powers and the Chancellor (Michael Fröhlich, *Imperialismus. Deutsche Kolonial- und Weltpolitik, 1880–1914*, Munich 1994, p. 118). Tirpitz called the result another Olmütz, as Müller recalled (Görlitz, *Der Kaiser*, p. 89). Following the Agadir Crisis, the Prussian Crown Prince began publicly to advocate war, applauding the bellicose Reichstag speech of the leader of the Conservatives, Ernst von Heydebrand, on 9 November. The *Kreuzzeitung* reported: 'One had the impression that the Crown Prince, like a number of nationalists, and certainly many officers, would probably have preferred a different solution to the Morocco conflict.' Quoted in Fischer, *Illusionen*, p. 142.

[66] Holger H. Herwig, 'Imperial Germany', in Ernest R. May (ed.), *Knowing One's Enemies: Intelligence Assessment before the Two World Wars*, Princeton 1984, p. 81; Afflerbach, *Falkenhayn*, p. 77.

[67] As Barraclough's study of the Agadir Crisis is aptly entitled.   [68] Barraclough, *Agadir*, p. 142.

[69] See also Förster, *Militarismus*, p. 209.

would be lacking on the Russian front. In France, Germany's aggressive and provocative behaviour led to a revival of the revanche idea. If the mood in France had already been hostile towards Germany before Agadir,[70] it was now distinctly anti-German. The annexed provinces on the Franco-German border became a focal point once again. As *La France Militaire* put it in November 1911: 'Beside the lost provinces of Alsace and Lorraine, no colony, be it Tongking, Madagascar or Morocco, is worth anything. "Alsace", "Lorraine", these two words cry out what the policy of France ought to be.'[71]

While Britain was now more wary of Germany, the latter, in turn, developed a hostile, anti-British mood. Following Lloyd George's Mansion House speech on 21 July 1911, when the British Chancellor of the Exchequer warned Germany against any acts of aggression towards France, Britain became an antagonist in the eyes of the German public.[72] Ludendorff commented after the war on the effects of Lloyd George's speech: 'all doubts regarding the military agreement between France and England against Germany also disappeared. But Russia was not yet completely ready for war! Germany retreated once again.'[73]

A long-term consequence of German provocation was the Anglo-French naval agreement, discussed during 1912 and signed in February 1913. The Entente emerged strengthened in its resolve to oppose Germany, who by now had shown herself clearly as an aggressor. As Kiderlen told Bethmann Hollweg in July 1911: 'Our reputation abroad has deteriorated (*ist heruntergewirtschaftet*), we must fight',[74] an astonishing statement by the man who was responsible – almost single-handedly – for the disastrous Moroccan policy in the first place. Falkenhayn sarcastically remarked in the aftermath of the Agadir Crisis that 'a war between Germany and England had become unavoidable', because of the disgrace that Britain ('our dear blood-relatives') had inflicted upon

[70] According to the accounts of the German military attaché in Paris Winterfeldt. See Dukes, 'Militarism', p. 26.   [71] Quoted in Turner, *Origins*, p. 20.

[72] Fischer, *Illusionen*, p. 126. Sir Edward Goschen, Britain's ambassador in Berlin, reported on 12 January 1912 to Nicholson: 'I wish I could give a better report of Anglo-German relations, but my few England-loving German friends tell me that they have never known the feeling of irritation against England so strong and so widespread as it is at present.' Quoted in Terence F. Cole, 'German Decision-Making on the Eve of the First World War. The Records of the Swiss Embassy in Berlin', in Röhl (ed.), *Der Ort Kaiser Wilhelm II*, p. 57. On the Mansion House speech, see also Keith Wilson, 'The Agadir Crisis, the Mansion House Speech, and the Double-Edgedness of Agreements', *Historical Journal*, 15, 3, 1972, pp. 513–532.

[73] Ludendorff, *Mein militärischer Werdegang*, p. 115.

[74] Kiderlen to Bethmann, as recorded by Hamman, 30 July 1911, quoted in Fischer, *Illusionen*, p. 129. See also Riezler's diary entry during July 1914: 'Kiderlen always said that we must fight' (Riezler, *Tagebücher*, 14 July 1914, p. 185).

Germany in that year: 'Neither the great Kaiser of peace . . . nor the followers of Bertha [von Suttner] will be able to change this in any way.'[75]

Schlieffen, too, regarded Britain as Germany's main enemy in the aftermath of Agadir. In a letter to the editor of the journal *Deutsche Revue* of December 1911, he explained that the only reason why war had not resulted from the Agadir Crisis, although England had probably wanted it, was that the British army and navy were not quite prepared yet. He painted a gloomy picture of Germany's chances in a future war, if she did not utilize her military potential:

Because 65 million Germans do not deploy more trained soldiers than 41 million French, Germany will be in a minority even vis-à-vis France alone, quite apart from the English and perhaps also Belgian troops that will come to her aid. Whether the English fleet and army as well as the French fleet have gained in spirit of enterprise for the possible war is unclear, but the self-confidence and desire for war of the French army and the whole nation have in any case increased substantially over the last summer.[76]

Germany's political decision-makers, however, and foremost among them Kiderlen-Wächter, did not actually want war in 1911, although they were willing to threaten it in order to achieve foreign policy gains. Both military and civilian decision-makers were well aware that Austria was unlikely to support Germany in a war with France over Morocco, as Aehrenthal had clearly warned.[77] Although the mood in Germany was favourable and many would have agreed with the statement 'war rather than give in' ('Lieber Krieg als nachgeben'), as printed in a Protestant church newspaper,[78] the circumstances were not yet right for a war.

The Moroccan incident aroused bellicose public expectations, leading to heated debates in the Reichstag and to 'a wave of national outrage' at the end of 1911.[79] Public interest in the army and in Germany's military preparedness vis-à-vis her opponents became more pronounced, especially due to the propaganda work of the German Army League

---

[75] Falkenhayn's letter to Hanneken, 3 December 1911, quoted in Afflerbach, *Falkenhayn*, pp. 78–79.

[76] PA Bonn, R 788, copy of Schlieffen's letter of 13 December 1911.

[77] Fischer, *Illusionen*, p. 135.

[78] *Allgemeine Evangelisch-Lutherische Kirchenzeitung*, 8 September 1911, quoted in Fischer, *Illusionen*, p. 135.

[79] Volker Berghahn and Wilhelm Deist (eds.), *Rüstung im Zeichen wilhelminischer Weltpolitik. Grundlegende Dokumente 1890–1914*, Düsseldorf 1988, p. 371. Friedrich von Bernhardi's book *Deutschland und der nächste Krieg* was also a product of the aftermath of the Moroccan adventure, published in 1912. Selling many thousands of copies, the book had a huge influence on public opinion, and helped re-emphasize the notion that war was unavoidable in the future.

(*Deutscher Wehrverein*), which was officially founded on 28 January 1912.[80] It was an off-shoot of the German Navy League and made use of the latter's already successful propaganda methods.[81] August Keim, the former leader of the Navy League, who had been forced out of office because his demands for naval increases exceeded even Tirpitz's, found a new purpose in the quest for expanding the army, and his time spent with the Navy League proved useful training for this new task. August Keim echoed Ludendorff in his vociferous demands for army increases; both men were *bürgerlich*, bourgeois rather than gentry, an important similarity, because it meant they both advocated army increases without worrying about the reputedly bad influence that lower-class input might have on the army and the officer corps.[82] As we shall see, in Ludendorff's case this persistence led to his dismissal from the General Staff in January 1913.

The Army League exerted pressure on the government to increase the size of the army, and argued that for a land power like Germany any future war would be decided on the continent, not on the sea. Enough attention and money had been lavished on the navy – it was time to substitute the primacy of the army for that of the navy. The League 'wanted to explain to the nation the importance of army increases, just as the Navy League had done previously with the Navy'.[83] Its activities would play a significant part in the events leading to the army bills of 1912 and 1913. While the newly founded Army League was perhaps the most vociferous pressure group following Agadir, other, more established nationalist groups, notably the Pan-German League (*Alldeutscher Verband*) also advocated war during and after the crisis. The Pan-Germans, encouraged by Kiderlen to advocate an uncompromising foreign policy, were disappointed at the outcome of the Moroccan affair.[84] The League's propaganda had aroused public expectations,

---

[80] On the Army League, see Marily S. Coetzee, *The German Army League. Popular Nationalism in Wilhelmine Germany*, Oxford 1990; Roger Chickering, 'Der "Deutsche Wehrverein" und die Reform der deutschen Armee 1912–1914', *MGM*, 25, 1/1979, pp. 7–34.

[81] See Fischer, *Illusionen*, p. 162 on the popularity of the DWV. Coetzee refers to a whole 'propaganda machine' – publications, pamphlets, songs, postcards and other memorabilia (*Army League*, pp. 59ff).   [82] Fischer, *Illusionen*, p. 160.   [83] Berghahn and Deist, *Rüstung*, p. 233.

[84] Kiderlen had arranged meetings with some of the League's leaders, in which he suggested that the League could help in mobilizing public opinion in favour of Germany's foreign policy escapades. He did not realize that the patriotic societies were forces that, once unleashed, would prove extremely difficult to control, and that while Kiderlen was willing to *threaten* war in 1911, the Pan-German League was prepared to go all the way. The various patriotic societies of Wilhelmine Germany were thus indeed 'potentially sorcerer's apprentices', and proved to be impossible to control: Roger Chickering, 'Patriotic Societies and German Foreign Policy', *International History Review*, 1, October 1979, pp. 482–483, 489; idem, 'Der "Deutsche Wehrverein"', p. 8; Michael Peters, *Der Alldeutsche Verband am Vorabend des Ersten Weltkrieges (1908–1914)*, Frankfurt/M. 1992, pp. 111ff.

which in turn resulted in severe disappointment at the perceived international humiliation. The leaders of the Pan-German League shared Moltke's concern over the mobilization of public opinion as a necessary condition for war. In June 1913, Konstantin von Gebsattel, the League's deputy leader, regretted that the government had not attempted to manipulate public opinion towards accepting the inevitability of war in 1911:

I am the last person to reproach the League for pushing for a war during the Morocco time – again, it is a question of tactics: our people would hardly have understood if we had begun a war for existence (*Existenzkrieg*) because of Morocco, but a popular pretext could indeed have been found.[85]

It was easy for the nationalist pressure groups to create feelings of fear, even panic, among certain parts of the population, and to make the populace believe that Germany's evil and envious neighbours, to both the West and the East, were only waiting for a chance to 'pounce'. For some, this situation of permanent danger – whether real or imagined – was even regarded as an essential prerequisite for ensuring that the nation did not 'soften', in both 'body and spirit'. This is a view that is expressed, for example, by Gebsattel in a letter in May 1913 to one of the founders of the Pan-German League, Heinrich Class:

You [i.e. Class] want a future victory to reduce France to a state of eternal impotence. But how can you reconcile this with the view, which I fully share, that it is fortunate for the German people that it must constantly defend itself against opponents from the East and the West, and that the awareness of this compels it to keep itself physically and mentally fit?[86]

There were striking parallels in the views of the Pan-Germans and the military decision-makers who, by nature of their professional convictions, believed in war as a necessity.

The Agadir Crisis had frightened Moltke sufficiently for him to recommend in January 1912 that the German army be prepared for war at

[85] BA Abteilung Potsdam, NL Konstantin v. Gebsattel, 90 Ge 4/1, pp. 15ff., Gebsattel to Class (ADV), 10 June 1913. On the correspondence between Class, Gebsattel and the ADV cf. Hartmut Pogge-von Strandmann, 'Staatsstreichpläne, Alldeutsche und Bethmann Hollweg', in Hartmut Pogge-von Strandmann and Imanuel Geiss (eds.), *Die Erforderlichkeit des Unmöglichen. Deutschland am Vorabend des ersten Weltkrieges*, Frankfurt/M. 1965.

[86] BA Abteilung Potsdam, NL Konstantin v. Gebsattel, 90 Ge 4/1, p. 6. Other Pan-Germans echoed similar feelings, e.g. Ernst Hasse, who had preceded Class as head of the ADV. In 1907, he wrote: 'Enemies all around us: that has always been our position. And we suffered from this like no other people. Enemies all around us, that will continue to be our position for the entire future. And this is our fortune.' Quoted in Roger Chickering, 'Die Alldeutschen erwarten den Krieg', in Jost Dülffer and Karl Holl (eds.), *Bereit zum Krieg*, Göttingen 1986, p. 24.

all times. The proceedings at the 1912 annual mobilization conference (every January Moltke assembled his corps chiefs of staff and other officials to discuss mobilization procedures)[87] were conducted in the shadow of the recent Moroccan Crisis, as Moltke emphasized: 'The preparations for mobilization are still influenced by the after-effect of the political developments of last summer.' In his after-dinner speech on 30 January he left no doubt that the situation had been serious and that German troops were not to be caught off guard again in a future crisis:

The seriousness of the situation has left us in no doubt that it is necessary to keep ourselves prepared at all times, among other things to prepare precisely the transport of deployed troops back from the training grounds and manoeuvre areas to their mobilization places.[88]

The crisis showed in no uncertain terms that the Entente was no longer fragile, and that Germany was unable to break it, as she had been attempting to do virtually ever since France and Britain had signed their agreement in 1904. Russia, France and Britain were now regarded in Germany as encircling powers, and it seemed almost certain that they would stick together in the future. Following the Crisis, German foreign policy became less concerned with colonialism. Much more emphasis was now placed on continental policy, because, as the Chancellor outlined in the Reichstag, only if Germany managed to retain a strong position on the continent would *Weltpolitik* be possible.[89] The events of 1911 made it appear vital to increase Germany's armed power.[90] The decision to concentrate on army increases, after the long period of naval dominance, was a direct result of Germany's Moroccan adventure. At the same time, other factors helped to create a mood that was favourable towards at last enlarging the army. Friedrich von Bernhardi's publication *Germany and the Next War* reached a huge readership, while the electoral success of the Social Democrats in January 1912 led to a growing sense of insecurity in conservative sections of society. The Haldane mission of February 1912, which failed to establish more cordial relations between Britain and Germany, led to further disappointment and made war appear increasingly likely, thus further helping Moltke and the General

[87] Bucholz, *Moltke*, p. 235.

[88] Minutes of the meeting of 29/30 January 1912, and of dinner speech notes, in BA-MA, NL Moltke, N78/25. See also Bucholz, *Moltke*, p. 235.

[89] Bethmann Hollweg's speech in the Reichstag, 9 November 1911, Sten. Berichte, Bd. 268, S.7712. See also Hartmut Pogge von Strandmann, 'Nationale Verbände zwischen Weltpolitik und Kolonialpolitik' in Herbert Schottelius and Wilhelm Deist (eds.), *Marine und Marinepolitik im kaiserlichen Deutschland*, Düsseldorf 1972, p. 311.

[90] See e.g. Reichsarchiv, *Weltkrieg*, vol. 1, p. 11; Stevenson, *Armaments*, p. 181.

Staff to achieve a change to an attitude that was supportive of army increases.[91]

This, at last, was the change of fortune that the General Staff had been waiting for, and their chance finally to press ahead with the army increases that were necessary to ensure that their strategic plan could be successfully implemented. In November 1911, Moltke argued that further increases were 'a requirement of self-preservation'.[92] The General Staff was able to tap into the mood that was created by the Army League's propaganda and by the shock of the Agadir Crisis. Over the last decade, the General Staff had got used to its demands for army increases going unheeded. Neither Schlieffen nor Moltke had been in a strong enough position to be unopposed by critics from within the military, the navy and civilian institutions until this point. How far the General Staff might have informed the Army League leadership secretly of its requirements is no longer possible to say, but they seem at least to have been in touch with the General Staff.[93] The similarities between Keim's and Ludendorff's demands for increases suggest some co-operation. For the General Staff, this was an opportunity brought about by a combination of favourable circumstances: bellicose public opinion (aided by Army League propaganda), and the resulting widespread support for the army, as well as skilful advocates of army increases within the Staff, in particular Erich Ludendorff, whose name more than any other is linked with the 1912/1913 army increases.

There was, however, another advocate of army increases at that time, and from a surprising quarter. In October 1911, Bethmann Hollweg proposed a new army bill to Minister of War Josias von Heeringen, which the latter ruled out on financial and political grounds.[94] The Chancellor, who had opposed Heeringen's modest demands for increases for the *Quinquennat* 1911–1916 only the previous year, began to support army increases following the Agadir Crisis, partly because of his wish to curb the naval increases that had proved detrimental to his policy towards

[91] Herwig, 'Imperial Germany', p. 83. On the Haldane Mission, see Paul M. Kennedy, *The Rise of Anglo-German Antagonism*, London 1980, pp. 451–452; Jonathan Steinberg, 'Diplomatie als Wille und Vorstellung: Die Berliner Mission Lord Haldanes im Februar 1912', in Schottelius and Deist (eds.), *Marine und Marinepolitik*, pp. 263ff.; Forsbach, *Kiderlen-Wächter*, pp. 579ff. The Kaiser was particularly disappointed that the meeting failed, as Müller noted in his diary. 'His Majesty was full of hope. He already saw himself as the leader of the policy of the United States of Europe, and for Germany a colonial empire right through central Africa. Tirpitz and I added much water to the Imperial wine' (Görlitz, *Der Kaiser*, p. 112).

[92] BA-MA, w-10/50276, 'Die militär-politische Lage', p. 35.

[93] Fischer, *Illusionen*, p. 163; Berghahn and Deist, *Rüstung*, p. 372.   [94] Bucholz, *Moltke*, p. 263.

Britain.[95] Bethmann saw an opportunity to join forces with the General Staff against the Navy, in the hope of curbing Tirpitz's power. Bethmann's support was not, however, solely motivated by anti-navy feelings. Against the background of the recent international humiliation, he was also susceptible to Moltke's arguments that there was an urgent need for army increases.[96]

Although the initiative was thus not Moltke's, he recognized and seized the opportunity for making General Staff demands. On 2 December 1911, shortly after the Moroccan Crisis had been resolved, and against the background of the Italian war, Moltke sent a memorandum to the Chancellor.[97] With the imminent army bill in mind, Moltke speculated as to who the likely opponents in a future war might be. France, he thought, probably did not want to provoke a war against Germany at that time, but there existed in France a chauvinistic mood that could provoke a war. England would actively support France. Italy's support could not be relied upon by Germany, despite her contractual obligations, as Italy's coasts were exposed to a British attack, and Italy lacked a desire to fight against France. Similarly, Austria-Hungary was under no obligation to support Germany against France and England. Germany, Moltke thought, should prepare herself to face such a contingency on her own. If, however, it turned out that Russia had undertaken to assist France, this would be the *casus foederis* for Austria-Hungary. Turkey's role should also not be underestimated, were she to participate on the Alliance's side. Turkey, Moltke argued (echoing Goltz's views), was the only power that could threaten England on land (Suez Canal, Egypt, Aden), an argument that he was still advocating in 1914. Moreover, in case of Turkish intervention, Russia would be forced to deploy troops in the Caucasus which could otherwise be used on the German-Austrian front.

The only certain factor in this calculation was that Germany and Austria faced a coalition of France, England and Russia, whose military power had increased over the last few years, to the detriment of the Alliance. Russia had reorganized her army, equipped it with better *matériel*, increased her armed forces, simplified mobilization procedures, extended the strategic railway system and provided for a younger officer

---

[95] See e.g. Berghahn and Deist, *Rüstung*, p. 371; Volker Berghahn, *Germany and the Approach of War in 1914*, paperback edn London 1973, pp. 104ff.; Förster, *Doppelter Militarismus*, pp. 211ff.; BA-MA, w-10/50276, p. 34; Herrmann, *The Arming of Europe*, p. 162.   [96] Dukes, 'Militarism', p. 25.

[97] This memorandum was excluded from the official publication of documents in *Der Weltkrieg*, but was paraphrased in the text, vol. 1, p. 11ff., and cited in the unpublished Reichsarchiv study 'Die Militärpolitische Lage Deutschlands', BA-MA, w-10/50276.

corps. Moltke warned that it was no longer true to say that Russia would not be able to wage a European war, as it had been in 1905/1906. Fear of Russia's increasing military potential now became a recurrent theme in Moltke's reasoning, but it was not the only threat Germany faced. Britain would wage war primarily at sea, but would also send a well-equipped army of 150,000 men to the continent. And France, the memorandum concluded fatalistically, enlisted her entire population in a way that left Germany far behind:

> The equipping, perfecting and strengthening of her military power in all areas are making France an ever more powerful and dangerous opponent. All are preparing themselves for the big war that is widely expected sooner or later. Only Germany and her ally Austria are not participating in these preparations.[98]

It is, of course, important to realize that the purpose of this memorandum was to convince the many sceptics that further, and extensive, army increases were indeed necessary. However, these themes were echoed by Moltke constantly in the years leading to the outbreak of war. At the end of his memorandum, Moltke demanded an increase in both the army and the navy, realizing that the army's bargaining power had not yet increased sufficiently to exclude the navy altogether. He argued that both a further extension of the fleet and an increase of the army's peacetime strength were 'a prerequisite for self-preservation. Both have to go hand in hand.'[99]

Following the Agadir Crisis, voices from within the Ministry of War also began to advocate substantial army increases. A memorandum from Minister of War Josias von Heeringen of 19 November 1911 is a first indication of this change of attitude. Clearly, Agadir had unsettled him: 'In view of the experiences of 1911 it must be asked whether the military-political conditions can now still be judged to be as favourable [as in 1910].' Heeringen demanded army increases because Germany's position vis-à-vis her potential enemies was worsening.[100] Similar arguments can be found in a memorandum by the Chief of the General War Department, Franz von Wandel, of 29 November 1911. He acknowledged that the recent political developments had demonstrated that in a future war France, as well as Russia and Britain, would be Germany's opponent, and that such a prospect had serious implications. In

---

[98] Ibid., pp. 14–17; Reichsarchiv, *Weltkrieg*, vol. 1, pp. 12–13. For a discussion of Moltke's memorandum, see also Stevenson, *Armaments*, pp. 202–203 and Herrmann, *The Arming of Europe*, pp. 169ff.

[99] Quoted in BA-MA, w-10/50276: 'Die Militärpolitische Lage Deutschlands', p. 43.

[100] BA-MA, w-10/50279, Heeringen to Bethmann, 19 November 1911. This memorandum was not included in Reichsarchiv, *Kriegsrüstung, Anlagen*. See also Förster, *Militarismus*, pp. 222–223.

6 Helmuth von Moltke, postcard *c.* 1912, captioned 'Excellenz von Moltke, Chief of the General Staff of the German Army'

Wandel's words, this news 'makes Germany's military situation appear in quite a different light than when the last peace-time army law was passed.'[101] For the first time, the Chief of Staff had found allies in the Ministry. The Kaiser was clearly convinced by the arguments from both the General Staff and the Ministry of War. On 30 November 1911, he sent a telegram to the Chancellor: 'Strengthening at sea and on land absolutely essential', a demand which Bethmann underlined.[102] However, the State Secretary of the Reich Treasury, Adolf Wermuth, had the last say in this matter. He warned of the financial constraints and advocated delaying further measures to increase the army.[103]

The army increases of 1912, the result of these negotiations, amounted to an increase of just under 30,000 men, and the creation of two new army corps.[104] The General Staff had not had a significant

---

[101] *Kriegsrüstung, Anlagen*, No. 41, pp. 132ff.

[102] PA Bonn, R 852, Angelegenheiten der deutschen Armee, Wilhelm II to Bethmann Hollweg, telegram, 30 November 1911, and Bethmann Hollweg to Wilhelm II, 30 November 1911.

[103] Reichsarchiv, *Weltkrieg*, vol. 1, p. 13; idem, *Kriegsrüstung, Anlagen*, No. 42, Wermuth to Bethmann Hollweg, 8 December 1911. On Wermuth's opposition to further spending on either navy or army, see Peter-Christian Witt, *Die Finanzpolitik der Deutschen Reiches von 1903 bis 1913. Eine Studie zur Innenpolitik des Wilhelminischen Deutschland*, Lübeck and Hamburg 1970, pp. 337ff.

[104] BA-MA, W-10/50276: 'Die Militärpolitische Lage Deutschlands', p. 44. Details also in Herrmann, *Arming*, p. 171.

influence on this army bill,[105] which fell short of its requirements. Nonetheless, 1912 was a significant juncture. Previously, the General Staff had lacked self-confidence vis-à-vis the predominant navy and had received no support from other military or civilian bodies. Most importantly, the Kaiser was now behind the army, thus leading crucial support to the cause.[106] The navy's pre-eminence was finally broken, and the road was clear for the General Staff's main protagonists, Moltke and Ludendorff, to push for an increase in the size and capability of the German army.

THE BALKAN WARS AND THE WAR COUNCIL OF 1912

If war is coming, I hope it will come soon before I am too old to cope with things satisfactorily.

Helmuth von Moltke, 22 October 1912[107]

Gen. v. Moltke: 'I consider a war unavoidable, and the sooner the better.'

Admiral von Müller's diary, 8 December 1912[108]

Germany's military decision-makers considered the Balkan Wars, which broke out between the Russian-sponsored Balkan League and Turkey in October 1912, another opportunity for war. Much to their surprise, the Kaiser was initially on the side of the Balkan states; in fact, he displayed an 'unusually peaceable attitude'.[109] On 2 October 1912, he wrote to the Chancellor: 'As regards the Balkans, my order of this summer remains that we are not getting involved there in any way, but will let matters take their course.'[110] On 9 November, he asked Tirpitz and Moltke whether Germany was ready for war, which both confirmed to be the case.[111] The Chancellor and Kiderlen-Wächter

[105] Berghahn and Deist, *Rüstung*, p. 371.   [106] Stevenson, *Armaments*, p. 204.
[107] Moltke in conversation with his niece, Dorothy von Moltke: *Ein Leben in Deutschland. Briefe aus Kreisau und Berlin 1907–1934*, ed. Beate Ruhm von Oppen, Munich 1999, letter of 22 October 1912, p. 36.
[108] Admiral von Müller's diary entry, 8 December 1912, quoted in John C. G. Röhl, 'An der Schwelle zum Weltkrieg: Eine Dokumentation über den "Kriegsrat" vom 8. Dezember 1912', *MGM*, 21, 1/1977, doc. 4, p. 100 (cited as Röhl, 'Schwelle').
[109] Röhl, 'Schwelle', pp. 78ff., here p. 79; idem, 'Admiral von Müller', p. 659. Details of the Balkan Wars in the context of worsening European relations in Stevenson, *Armaments*, pp. 231ff.
[110] PA Bonn, R 1358, Reichskanzler Bethmann Hollweg, Oct. 1912–Dec. 1914.
[111] Ibid., 9 November 1912, p. 552. See Walter Görlitz (ed.), *Regierte der Kaiser? Kriegstagebücher, Aufzeichnungen und Briefe des Chefs des Marinekabinetts Admiral Georg Alexander von Müller 1914–1918*, Göttingen, Berlin, Frankfurt/M., 2nd edn 1959, p. 121ff. (cited as Müller, *Kriegstagebücher*); Röhl, 'Admiral von Müller', p. 659.

tried hard to change the Kaiser's mind during those days, as they feared losing Austria as an ally if Germany refused to support her. Wilhelm was, however, reluctant to accept their position. In a memorandum in his own handwriting, dating from 11 November 1912, the Kaiser summarized the talks he had had with Bethmann and Kiderlen on 9 November, when the two had tried to change his mind. Then, he was still adamant that Germany should not be forced to go to war by Austria-Hungary, who had provoked the Serbs. Germany would not enter into a major war (*Existenzkampf*) against three major powers just because Austria did not want the Serbs in Albania or Durazzo. The Triple Alliance agreement had not been intended for such eventualities, he maintained.[112] Wilhelm only changed his mind over the course of the next two weeks on account of the change of attitude in the press and public opinion, which now regarded Austria as the injured party in the dispute.[113]

On hearing the news of the outbreak of war in the Balkans, the Kaiser assembled some of his political and military advisers at his hunting lodge at Hubertusstock on 13 October 1912. At the meeting the worried Kaiser suggested that another army increase might be necessary in the face of international threats, but this was opposed by his military advisers. He was reassured by both Heeringen and Moltke that the German army was prepared for all eventualities, should the Balkan War escalate. One day later, however, Moltke had changed his mind about this and demanded a substantial army increase, contradicting all his earlier statements.[114] It is possible that Moltke realized that the current crisis would be useful in providing a pretext for requesting more extensive army increases and, moreover, that the crisis actually confirmed the need for a stronger German army. It has been suggested that this change of heart was due to Ludendorff's influence, and he certainly would have encouraged Moltke's demands at that time.[115] This was the first attempt by the General Staff to go further than simply pointing out the need for further increases as a precondition for its strategic planning, and to push decisively for its demands. In the light of the fighting in the Balkans, Moltke, Heeringen and Bethmann would eventually agree that there was a need to increase Germany's army.[116] The seriousness of the Balkan situation led Moltke to fear in October that 'there may be war

[112] *GP*, 33, 12349, 11 November 1912.   [113] Röhl, 'Schwelle', p. 81.

[114] Moltke's memorandum to the Minister of War, 14 October 1912, in Bucholz, *Moltke*, p. 263.

[115] On the meeting at Hubertusstock and Ludendorff's alleged influence, see Dukes, 'Militarism', p. 29; Berghahn and Deist, *Rüstung*, p. 372.   [116] Herrmann, *Arming*, p. 181.

for the simple reason that everyone has prepared for it for so long and such tremendous armaments are always a danger', as he told his niece. She recorded in a letter that

> he too thinks there is absolutely no reason for going to war and he said 'If only England and Germany would go together they would lead the world; this whole "Spannung" [*sic* (tension)] is the work of King Edward.' He thinks the feeling in England against Germany is manufactured by politicians, the press and the diplomats.[117]

In November 1912, Moltke travelled to Vienna, where he had an audience with Emperor Franz Joseph and was able to meet with General Blasius Schemua, who had replaced Conrad as Chief of Staff in November 1911.[118] A few days before this meeting, the military attaché Kageneck had reported back to Berlin his impression following a conversation with Schemua:

> as if he had arrived at the opinion that one would hardly be able to avoid a call to arms. . . . Today, after a conversation with a number of General Staff officers I, too, had the impression that the chances for war or peace stood at 50:50 as Poincaré remarked recently.[119]

The meeting between the two Chiefs of Staff had gone well, according to Kageneck, who informed Berlin on 23 November 1912 that 'General Schemua expressed to me his complete satisfaction at the discussion that had taken place.'[120] Moltke, who had known about Austria's bellicose intentions, had obviously not travelled to Vienna hoping to restrain his Austrian colleague, but had found himself rather in agreement with the ally.

The Balkan Crisis triggered an increasing fear of Russia, as it spelt the end of the period of cordial relations between Germany and her eastern neighbour.[121] Turkey was weakened, if not lost as a potential ally, and Britain's attitude was regarded with some apprehension. At the end of

---

[117] Dorothy von Moltke, *Ein Leben in Deutschland*, letter of 22 October 1912, p. 35. My thanks to Frau von Oppen for making the original English letter available to me.

[118] Conrad's bellicose anti-Italian policy ran counter to Aehrenthal's moderate views, and Conrad was dismissed in November 1911 when he advocated war against Italy while the latter was fighting Libya. During the Balkan Crisis in December 1912 Archduke Franz Ferdinand demanded his reinstatement because Schemua was not considered experienced enough to deal with this crisis. Williamson, *Austria-Hungary and the Origins of the First World War*, p. 49; John Leslie, 'The Antecedents of Austria-Hungary's War Aims', *Wiener Beiträge zur Geschichte der Neuzeit*, 20, 1993, pp. 313–314.

[119] PA Bonn, R8627, Militär- und Marineangelegenheiten Oesterreichs, report by military attaché Kageneck, 18 November 1912.

[120] PA Bonn, R2408, report by Kageneck, 23 November 1912.

[121] Dukes, 'Militarism', p. 28; Lieven, *Russia*, p. 38.

November and beginning of December 1912, Britain had given the impression of being 'friendly'. All the greater was the shock created by the news from London in the first week of December that Britain would not keep out of a war on the continent, but would come to France's aid.[122] As a result, the Kaiser's previously peaceful attitude changed completely. At a meeting of 8 December 1912, the so-called war council which he called in response to this news, the Kaiser was at his most bellicose. His violent reaction is partly explained by the personal disappointment that the news represented to him, only days after he had been led to believe by Lichnowsky that British neutrality was an option. He considered the news from London a 'moral declaration of war'.[123]

The notorious war council meeting has divided historians into those who feel that war was more or less decided upon at this meeting, although the decision to go to war was postponed for approximately eighteen months, and those who deny that any real importance can be attached to the events in the Berlin *Schloss* on one Sunday in December 1912.[124] Between these two extremes exist a variety of positions and variations on the theme.[125] The infamous meeting must be seen in the context of the international crisis, and of the wrangling over army increases. Barely two months previously, at Hubertusstock, the Kaiser had demanded army increases, but had been unable to convince his military advisers. Thus, when he described the news from Britain as a welcome clarification of her intentions, this was directed both against his

---

[122] Groh, 'Je eher, desto besser!', pp. 504–505. See also Röhl, 'Admiral von Müller', p. 660, who argues that one reason why Germany had supported Austria in this crisis was because there seemed reason to expect that Britain would remain neutral in a conflict triggered by an East European crisis. The disappointment over Britain's clarification of her position was thus even greater. The diplomatic background to the meeting is analyzed in Stevenson, *Armaments*, pp. 251ff.

[123] Wilhelm II to Karl von Eisendecher, 12 December 1912, quoted in Röhl, 'Schwelle', p. 106.

[124] Due to the controversy surrounding the war council, the literature on this topic is extensive. Most of the relevant documents and a detailed analysis of the events can be found in Röhl, 'Schwelle'. See also idem, 'Admiral von Müller'; idem, 'Die Generalprobe. Zur Geschichte und Bedeutung des "Kriegsrates" vom 8. Dezember 1912', in Dirk Stegmann, Bernd-Jürgen Wendt and Peter-Christian Witt (eds.), *Industrielle Gesellschaft und politisches System. Beiträge zur politischen Sozialgeschichte. Festschrift für Fritz Fischer zum siebzigsten Geburtstag*, Bonn 1978; idem, *Kaiser, Hof und Staat*, pp. 175ff; Fischer, *Illusionen*, pp. 231ff; Gasser, *Preußischer Militärgeist und Kriegsentfesselung 1914*. Historians who have denied the importance of the famous meeting include Wolfgang J. Mommsen, 'Der Topos vom unvermeidlichen Krieg: Außenpolitik und öffentliche Meinung im Deutschen Reich im letzten Jahrzehnt vor 1914', in idem, *Der autoritäre Nationalstaat*, Frankfurt/M. 1990, pp. 380ff.; Egmont Zechlin, 'Die Adriakrise und der "Kriegsrat" vom 8. Dezember 1912', in idem, *Krieg und Kriegsrisiko. Zur Deutschen Politik im Ersten Weltkrieg*, Düsseldorf 1979; Turner, *Origins*. For a detailed bibliography on the war council, see Röhl, *The Kaiser and his Court*, London 1995, pp. 255–256.

[125] John Röhl outlines as many as seven in 'Die Generalprobe', p. 358.

civilian and military advisers who had so recently opposed his views. In the events leading to the 1913 army increases, the meeting of December 1912 is crucial. While the decision for further increases did not stem solely from the meeting, since army increases were already being discussed before it, attitudes were confirmed and the opposition of sceptics was overcome.

The Kaiser invited three admirals, Alfred von Tirpitz (Chief of the Reich Navy Office), August von Heeringen (Chief of the Admiralty Staff), and Georg Alexander von Müller (Chief of the Naval Cabinet), as well as Moltke, the only representative of the army, to his *Schloss*.[126] This overemphasis on naval advisers was probably due to the fact that the subject of discussion was Britain, and that Wilhelm considered the fleet the appropriate weapon against this enemy. The meeting's topic was, after all, that day's discovery that Britain would not stand aside in a dispute involving Germany and France. That no politicians were invited to the meeting is not surprising considering the Kaiser's insistence that military matters were to be decided by the military only. In a letter to his brother on 12 December 1912, the Kaiser outlined both the events of the meeting and the news from England, emphasizing a clear distinction between the civilian and military reactions. He made it quite apparent, too, that he considered himself in the latter camp: 'My diplomats are very concerned. But not us military [men]. We have always reckoned on the English as our probable enemies.'[127] In fact, however, the truth seems to have been the exact opposite, for Bethmann Hollweg wrote quite calmly to the Prussian envoy in Karlsruhe, Karl von Eisendecher, that the Kaiser had overreacted to the news: 'Haldane's revelation to Lichnowsky was not actually that serious. It only revealed what we have known for a long time: that England still advocates the policy of balance of power and that she will therefore support France.'[128]

---

[126] One of the key documents on the war council, the diary of Captain Albert Hopman, also mentions the Chief of the Military Cabinet, Moriz Freiherr von Lyncker, as a participant at the meeting. Admiral von Müller's account, the most reliable because he was himself present at the meeting, does not mention Lyncker. We cannot rule out the possibility that Müller made a mistake in his diary entry; but it is more likely that Hopman, basing his account on second-hand information about the meeting that he received from the masseur Schulz, was mistaken when he recorded that Lyncker and the Prussian Minister of War Josias von Heeringen were also present. For Hopman's diary entry, see Röhl, 'Der militärpolitische Entscheidungsprozeß', in idem, *Kaiser, Hof und Staat*, p. 178.

[127] Wilhelm II to Prince Heinrich of Prussia, 12 December 1912, quoted in Röhl, 'Schwelle', p. 105.

[128] Bethmann Hollweg to Eisendecher, 20 December 1912, quoted in Röhl, 'Schwelle', p. 124. See also Kiderlen-Wächter to Eisendecher, 19 December 1912: 'I do not attach any special importance to the utterances of the minister but regard them rather as a well-intentioned attempt to warn us to be cautious' (ibid., p. 124).

At the meeting, the Kaiser, Moltke and Müller were keen for war to
result from the current crisis, while Tirpitz expressed concern that the
fleet was not yet ready, and asked for a postponement of 'the great fight'
for about one and a half years.[129] He argued that at the very least the
Kiel Canal, linking the Baltic and the North Sea, and the submarine
base at Heligoland should be ready before a war was entered into.[130] On
this occasion, Moltke was a clear advocate of war now rather than later,
as Admiral von Müller recorded in his diary: 'Gen.v. Moltke: "I consider
a war unavoidable, and the sooner the better."'[131] The Bavarian military
plenipotentiary Wenninger had received similar information about the
meeting: 'Moltke was in favour of an immediate strike (*sofortiges
Losschlagen*); since the Triple Alliance had been formed the opportunity
had never been more favourable.'[132] The army's position was quite clear:
Germany could only lose her slight advantage over her enemies as time
went on, because German army increases had led in turn to army
increases in France and Russia. Moltke's bellicose words should be taken
quite literally. He was not in favour of the delay of one and a half years
that Tirpitz had demanded, as Müller remembered: 'Moltke says that
the navy would then not be ready either, and that the army would be
getting into an increasingly disadvantageous position, because the
enemies are increasing their armies more than us, since we are
financially very restricted.'[133]

At the meeting, Moltke also underlined one of his main concerns,
public opinion, leading even him to suggest that a postponement of the

---

[129] Wenninger recorded: 'Tirpitz demanded postponement for 1 year', and Albert Hopman had
heard that Tirpitz requested them 'to delay war, if possible, for 1–2 years'. Röhl, *Kaiser, Hof und
Staat*, pp. 177ff.

[130] Interestingly, a similar argument had been used previously by Müller during the Agadir Crisis,
when he had advised the Kaiser and the Chancellor 'to postpone this war, which was probably
unavoidable in the long run, until the completion of the Canal'. Quoted in Fischer, *Illusionen*, p.
133. This was not the first occasion on which Tirpitz speculated on the earliest possible date at
which the fleet might be ready. At a meeting with the Kaiser and Moltke in June 1909, a similar
argument had already been presented. 'Admiral von Tirpitz assures us that, in 5 to 6 years, when
the widening of the Kaiser-Wilhelm-Canal and the position on Heligoland were completed, the
danger posed by England would be removed. Even in two years' time it would be considerably
less.' *GP*, 28, No. 10306, p. 176, 3 June 1909. Moltke never really shared Tirpitz's confidence in
the navy's ability to engage the British fleet successfully. Ritter is probably correct in explaining
Moltke's flippant attitude on that occasion, when he turned down Tirpitz's suggestion of dis-
rupting the landing of the BEF, as motivated by his certainty that the navy would be unable to
help anyway. (Ritter, *Staatskunst*, vol. 2, p. 197). See also Geiss, *Der Lange Weg in die Katastrophe*, pp.
256–257. In December 1911, Falkenhayn wrote dismissively to his friend Hanneken that 'by 1914
the navy (†††) [sic] also wants to be ready': Afflerbach, *Falkenhayn*, p. 79.

[131] Müller diary entry, 8 December 1912, quoted in Röhl, 'Schwelle', doc. 4, p. 100.

[132] General von Wenninger to Bavarian Minister of War, 15 December 1912, printed in Röhl,
'Schwelle', doc. 22, p. 113.   [133] Ibid., doc. 4, p. 100.

war might be necessary. The German people would need to know why they were being expected to fight. He suggested starting a campaign in the press to prepare the public to accept the necessity of a war against Russia.[134] Articles to such effect in the press were one of the immediate outcomes of the meeting, which those who wanted an actual decision to go to war at that time considered disappointing (Müller felt that regarding this aspect the outcome had been 'pretty much zero'). Moltke and the General Staff were, however, unhappy with the extent of the press campaign, which did not seem wide-ranging enough to them. According to the Austrian military attaché Karl Freiherr von Bienerth, in the General Staff's view, the press was not given enough information by the press bureau of the Auswärtiges Amt. As Bienerth reported back to Vienna, 'in the General Staff they want to aim at an improvement that is already considered certain in case of war, but that should, if possible, take effect straight away.'[135]

Moltke's other main concern, the fact that time was running out for a successful application of the Schlieffen Plan, was also expressed at the meeting. The basic idea behind Germany's deployment plan was common knowledge. Even Britain expected that Germany would begin a war in the West. Lichnowsky had reported 'that England, if we [i.e. Germany] attacked France, would in any case support France.'[136] Although the current crisis was centred around the Balkans, the danger that a German involvement would shift the theatre of war from the East to the West was apparent to everyone concerned. The Kaiser was certainly aware of the intended direction of deployment, if not of all the details, should a war result from the current crisis. On 9 November he had telegraphed to Kiderlen his decision 'that I [sic!] will not be marching against Paris and Moscow because of Albania and Durazzo', at a time when it could not have been regarded as certain that France would become involved.[137] On 11 November he revealed even more fully that he was aware of the implications of an escalation of the crisis. He expressed resentment at the harsh attitude that Austria had displayed towards Russia, thus risking an escalation of the crisis, which would invoke the *casus foederis* for Germany. The Kaiser knew what this would mean for Germany: 'It demands mobilization and war on two fronts for

[134] Ibid., doc. 4, p. 100.
[135] Quoted ibid., p. 90. According to Forsbach, however, the article 'Um Durazzo?' in the *Deutsche Tageszeitung* of 9 December 1912, probably written by Kiderlen, or at least requested by him, was hardly encouraging war '(kriegsanstachelnd)'. *Kiderlen-Wächter*, p. 740, note 403.
[136] Müller diary entry, 8 December 1912, quoted in Röhl, 'Schwelle', doc. 4, p. 100.
[137] *GP*, 33, No. 12348. See also Röhl, *Kaiser, Hof und Staat*, p. 181.

Germany, i.e. [for us] to march against Moscow, Paris must first be conquered.'[138]

The Chancellor was also in no doubt of the implications of a war with Russia. On 18 December he wrote to the Kaiser: 'It is certain that a war with Russia also means a war with France for us.'[139] Bethmann still refused to believe that Britain would definitely get involved, despite Lichnowsky's clear warning of 3 December. If Russia and France could be made to appear to be the provoking powers, British involvement seemed at least doubtful to him. This was in line with his previous policy of trying to establish closer ties with Britain, an aim that he would pursue until the very last days of the July Crisis.

The often-posed question of whether or not war was really decided upon in December 1912 cannot be resolved on the basis of the evidence available. However, the war council is important in highlighting military decision-making in Imperial Germany with all its particularities:[140] the exclusion of political decision-makers; even the Chancellor, the tense relationship between the army and the navy, which typically did not agree on a strategy or even share a common point of view regarding the situation, and the Kaiser's influence and attitude – bellicose in the company of his close advisers, but later again as timid as before. At various points of crisis, the Kaiser assembled key advisers who influenced his decisions, for example at the meeting at Hubertusstock, or during the July Crisis of 1914. This influence waned, however, almost as soon as the Kaiser received someone else's advice. Moreover, as John Röhl observes,

the 'war council' itself must be regarded as one of the most obvious signs that the Army had regained its traditional position of pre-eminence in Prussia-Germany after the collapse of Tirpitz's originally grandiose naval plans and the fiasco of the Agadir Crisis of 1911.[141]

In addition, the meeting emphasizes the repeatedly and increasingly forcefully expressed disposition of the military to provoke a war at an opportune moment and a readiness for war that would only increase during the coming months.[142]

It is no doubt significant that no civilians were present at the infamous meeting, although it is not true that the Chancellor was not officially

---

[138] GP, 33, No. 12349.   [139] Röhl, 'Schwelle', doc. 31, pp. 122–123.
[140] See also Röhl, *Kaiser, Hof und Staat*, p. 180.
[141] Röhl, *1914: Delusion or Design?*, p. 31.
[142] See Volker Ullrich, *Die nervöse Grossmacht 1871–1918. Aufstieg und Untergang des deutschen Kaiserreiches*, Frankfurt/M. 1997, p. 234.

informed about the meeting by any of the military men present, as historians keen to dismiss the importance of the meeting have maintained.[143] Rather, Bethmann Hollweg was informed by Müller on the same day and given the Kaiser's order to arrange for the public to be informed via the press of the German interests that would be at stake in an Austro-Serbian conflict.[144] It is not convincing to interpret the fact that no civilians were present as proof of the insignificance of the event, as has been suggested.[145] Rather, it was precisely because the Kaiser attached importance to the meeting that he did not ask civilians to attend.[146] In a situation that required military decision-making, the Kaiser wanted his military advisers to encourage his sudden desire for action. And while there is no direct evidence to prove that military decision-makers understood December 1912 as a decisive moment at which a future war had been agreed upon, it is striking how often Moltke echoed the arguments that he advanced at the infamous meeting in the months to come. Moltke's request for war 'the sooner the better' was a serious demand, and one that he would repeat with increasing conviction.

As on previous occasions, however, the crisis was resolved without the war that the military had hoped for, and again the Kaiser turned out to be more peaceable than his aggressive rhetoric had suggested. The result was renewed disappointment with the 'Supreme War-Lord', and regret over another missed opportunity. Falkenhayn was not the only general to feel disappointed. In January 1913 he wrote:

If Kiderlen had still been alive, he and Moltke would probably have pushed for the matter to have been brought to a decision now. Both were of the very sensible opinion that we cannot gain anything but only lose by continuing to wait. . . . Now Moltke is on his own, a fact that gives cause for concern as regards the struggle with H.M.[147]

---

[143] E.g. Wolfgang J. Mommsen, who argues that the Chancellor had only been informed about the meeting eight days after the event: Mommsen, 'Innenpolitische Bestimmungsfaktoren der deutschen Außenpolitik' in his *Der autoritäre Nationalstaat*, p. 326.

[144] Röhl, *Kaiser, Hof und Staat*, p. 176.

[145] See e.g. Wolfgang J. Mommsen, 'Der Topos vom unvermeidlichen Krieg', in his *Der autoritäre Nationalstaat*, pp. 392ff.; idem, 'Domestic Factors in German Foreign Policy before 1914', *Central European History*, 6, 1973, pp. 3–43; Turner, *Origins*, p. 49.

[146] A view expressed e.g. by Cole, 'German Decision-Making', p. 62.

[147] Falkenhayn to Hanneken, 29 January 1913, quoted in Afflerbach, *Falkenhayn*, p. 102. Kiderlen died of a heart-attack on 30 December 1912. Falkenhayn may have overestimated the Foreign Secretary's desire for war, for according to his biographer Forsbach, he was not among those 'political powers around Helmuth von Moltke who . . . considered a preventive war': *Kiderlen-Wächter*, p. 774.

Baroness von Lyncker, the wife of the Chief of the Military Cabinet, was conveying her husband's opinion when she told Baroness von Spitzemberg of the military's disapproval of the Kaiser's 'great love of peace' (by now a recurrent theme), and that it was believed that Germany had missed her chance, as she could have defeated France while the Russians were preoccupied in the Balkans.[148] Konstantin von Gebsattel, the Pan-German leader, later regretted that Germany had not supported Austria better in 'the Balkan matter', particularly with reference to the favourable opportunity that the crisis had offered in terms of public opinion. Gebsattel felt that the Austrians should have been encouraged. 'I deeply regretted that we did not support Austria in the Balkan matter – apparently we even appeased! If this had been the trigger, everyone would have understood it and approved of it.'[149]

The Balkan Wars of 1912/1913 resulted in a complete upheaval of the previous European balance of power.[150] Turkey was defeated (regrettable from the German point of view, due to the General Staff's vague hopes of forming a military alliance), and Bulgaria also suffered a severe defeat, while the other Balkan states, notably Serbia and Montenegro, were strengthened and now constituted a dangerous Slavic front against Austria in the Balkans. Rumania had clearly shown herself to be unreliable as an alliance partner. It became obvious that Austria would have to deploy a number of troops against Rumania to protect herself when attacking Serbia and Montenegro, troops which could then not be used against Russia. The future, from a military point of view, began to look even more daunting, both for Moltke and for his Austrian counterpart. An active involvement of Italy on Germany's side against France continued to be unlikely. In the winter of 1912/1913, the Italian General Staff informed Moltke that, while Italy was still willing to do her duty to help defend Germany against her western neighbours in a defensive war, the army that had been intended for use on the upper Rhine could no longer be sent.[151] This information, and the knowledge that necessary

---

[148] Spitzemberg, *Diary*, 19 November 1913, p. 563. The Austrian military attaché Bienerth suspected in February 1913 that the Kaiser's cautious attitude was partly motivated by his desire to celebrate his 25-year jubilee in peace. Bienerth further mentioned as reasons behind the Kaiser's desire for peace the Kaiser's fear of England, the fact that the Kiel Canal and the harbour of Heligoland were not yet ready and his concern that the German people would not understand why Germany should go to war over Durazzo. Bienerth to Conrad, 20 February 1913, quoted in Röhl, 'Germany', p. 42.

[149] BA Abteilung Potsdam, NL Konstantin v. Gebsattel, 90 Ge 4/1, 10 June 1913, pp. 15ff.

[150] See BA-MA, w-10/50276, 'Die Militärpolitische Lage Deutschlands', pp. 18ff.

[151] Ibid., pp. 18–19.

army increases would not be forthcoming in the near future, added to Moltke's increasing pessimism.[152]

On 21 December 1912, Moltke sent a memorandum to the Chancellor in which he argued for another extensive army increase. Dated just a few days after the war council, it picked up on some of the themes that he had emphasized during that meeting, and that he was to reiterate until July 1914. Moltke forecast a loss of prestige for Austria, and consequently for the Triple Alliance and for Germany herself, if Austria were unable to achieve a full political and military victory against her strengthened Balkan opponents. He stressed the importance of public support for any future military involvement, especially as the alliance agreements – essentially defensive – might require a nation to go to war over an issue that would appear unrelated to its interests:

The Triple Alliance was concluded as a *defensive* alliance. It incorporates all the weaknesses of such an alliance. If one of the allied states is being attacked, the other two must support it – that is, without being themselves attacked, enter a war for which there might not be any inclination or understanding within the nation. However, only if the entire people is fully aware that harming to the ally also endangers its own vital interests will it develop *the kind of* will to make sacrifices that every state requires in our time, [a time] that no longer wants, no longer needs cabinet wars in order to conduct a war energetically.[153]

Moltke depicted the enemy nations, i.e. France, England and Russia, as having offensive aims in a future war, and therefore being able to rally public support much more easily than Germany, whose aims he describes as defensive, as merely trying to preserve the status quo. In the event of war, however, it was actually the assertion that one was being attacked that rallied the populace and conjured up a fighting spirit, as Moltke must have suspected, and as was demonstrated by the events of July and August 1914.

If war came in the very near future the Chief of Staff was still quite confident of victory, especially if the nation could be inspired to fight, but in the longer term, success could only be guaranteed if the army was increased as necessary:

If war occurs, there can be no doubt that the main weight of responsibility will be on Germany's shoulders which will be gripped on three sides by her opponents. Nonetheless we can, *under the current conditions*, still face even the most difficult tasks with confidence, if we manage to formulate the *casus belli* in such a way that the nation will take up arms unitedly and enthusiastically.[154]

---

[152] The role of the Italian ally in German war planning is explored below, pp. 167ff.
[153] Moltke to Bethmann, 21 December 1912, *Kriegsrüstung, Anlagen*, pp. 158ff.   [154] Ibid., p. 163.

Because he was aware that the longer she waited before provoking a war, the more Germany would lose her edge over her future opponents, Moltke's attitude was war sooner rather than later, much in keeping with the views he had expressed at the war council meeting. In the long run, however, Moltke warned that the numerical strength of the German army was insufficient for her to face the trials of the future. In the aftermath of the Balkan Wars, he advocated the introduction of universal military conscription, which in Germany had only ever existed on paper. He wanted to match the percentage that France recruited, which would have amounted to an increase of about 300,000 men, equalling at least three new army corps.[155] However, it was a demand that would be difficult to push through in the Reichstag. In the aftermath of the war council, and against the background of the Balkan Wars, the General Staff made further demands for army increases. Franz von Wandel recorded in his diary on 9 January 1913: 'A thorough discussion with deputies of the Chief of the General Staff demonstrated today that, due to the military-political situation, he is demanding a huge army increase, to be achieved in a few years, numbering at least 100,000 men in peacetime.'[156] As we have seen, the Chief of the General Staff was not overly concerned about Britain's involvement. However, in terms of propaganda, the news from London could serve a useful purpose in trying to get army increases approved. Wandel's diary entry is proof that this argument was used by Moltke and the General Staff in discussions with the Ministry of War.

The army increases agreed in May 1912 had been far from satisfactory – on this, Moltke and Ludendorff agreed with the Army League, whose propaganda echoed the demands of the General Staff. The year 1912 marked an important juncture, because it saw the first attempts by the General Staff to push through increases, rather than merely to warn of the strategic necessity of providing sufficient armaments.[157] Moreover, Moltke and Ludendorff now demanded vociferously what they (like Schlieffen before them) had considered essential for Germany's

[155] Reichsarchiv, *Weltkrieg*, vol. 1, pp. 14–15.

[156] Wandel's diary in Granier, 'Deutsche Rüstungspolitik', p. 142. The military-political situation referred to is the recent discovery that Britain would definitely be found on the side of Germany's enemies, i.e. the topic of the war council meeting.

[157] Berghahn and Deist, *Rüstung*, p. 372. Direct links between Ludendorff and the League cannot be proved, although some authors feel able to assert that close connections did exist. See Friedrich, *Blood and Iron*, p. 259: 'When even gripping Moltke like a vice failed to bring him what he wanted, Ludendorff joined forces with the former general August Keim and other warriors of the Pan-German League.' The author cites no evidence to substantiate this claim.

strategic plan: the introduction of universal military service, rather than having only a fraction of the population serve in peace-time.[158]

Ludendorff's influence over Moltke and his role in the debate on army increases is a much-discussed subject. Critics of Moltke tend to credit Ludendorff with bringing about the army increase of 1913, and suspect him as the author behind every official memorandum. According to Carl Mühlmann of the Reichsarchiv, Ludendorff was 'the driving force of the General Staff, who wanted to make Germany as strong as possible for the unavoidable war'.[159] However, authorship of General Staff memoranda is often difficult to ascertain. In the case of the famous memorandum by Moltke of 21 December 1912, the Reichsarchiv concluded in its official publication that, while Moltke's demands were actively supported by Ludendorff, they were not actually Ludendorff's demands.[160] Nonetheless, it is without doubt that his influence over the Chief of Staff was pronounced, and it is likely that Wandel of the Ministry of War was referring to him when he noted in his diary on 26 November 1912:

I am under the impression that the Chief of the General Staff of the army is in the hands of some restless and ambitious people – an impression that has been being registered in other places for some time, too – that he has no will of his own (that he is perhaps paralysed in his energy by a physical ailment), and that he is thus losing the clear aims that are urgently necessary, particularly now.[161]

Erich Ludendorff has been described as a typical example of a new type of General Staff officer, a non-aristocratic technocrat who was allegedly preoccupied with external enemies rather than internal ones.[162] If this was true before the war, Ludendorff's attitude certainly changed once the war was lost, when he developed astonishing conspiracy theories in trying to lay the blame for the loss of the war on enemies

---

[158] See Herrmann, *Arming*, p. 184.

[159] BA-MA, W-10/50721, 'Der Feldherr Ludendorff', by Carl Mühlmann, p. 1.

[160] Reichsarchiv, *Weltkrieg*, vol. I, pp. 14–15. But cf. e.g. Niall Ferguson, who speaks of 'Ludendorff's "great memorandum" of December 1912' in his essay 'Germany and the Origins of the First World War: New Perspectives', *Historical Journal*, 35, 3, 1992, p. 744. C. H. Hermann also asserts Ludendorff's central position regarding the army increases, and credits him with authorship of the General Staff memoranda of 1911–1912, claiming that the army increase of 117,000 men was Ludendorff's achievement (*Deutsche Militärgeschichte*, Frankfurt/M. 1966, pp. 263–264). Similarly, David Herrmann considers Ludendorff 'the driving force' behind General Staff demands (*Arming*, p. 184). Ludendorff's latest biographer, Franz Uhle-Wettler, also regards him as the real author of the memorandum, quoting his letter to his wife that 'he had to keep Moltke on the case "with iron tongs"' (Uhle-Wettler, *Ludendorff*, p. 71).

[161] Wandel's diary in Granier, 'Deutsche Rüstungspolitik', p. 142. Wandel probably refers to Moltke's demands for complete conscription of 25 November 1912.

[162] Ferguson, 'Germany and the Origins', p. 743.

within.[163] When he was appointed head of the Second Department of the General Staff in 1908, placing him in line for a future promotion to chief of the operations department and a position of influence in wartime,[164] army increases were not even on the horizon in the near future. Moltke had even agreed with the Minister of War's suggestion to extend the current army law until 1911. Only when Ludendorff's superior, General von Stein, left the General Staff on 1 October 1912 was he in a position to convince Moltke that the time was right to push for army increases.[165] Ludendorff was increasingly vociferous in his demands. Thus he wrote on 25 November 1912 of the need to use the full potential of Germany's manpower:

We must adopt measures that will keep the country free from attacks in breach of international law and that will make us independent of the measures adopted by our opponents. We must go further than this and give our entire army the strength that alone can guarantee ultimate success in the next war, a war that we will have to wage with [our] allies, but on the whole with our own strength for [the purposes of] Germany's grandeur. We must make the decision to utilize our human resources (*Menschenbestand*). We must again become the people in arms that great men made of us in the great days of the past.[166]

Conservatives within the military objected to Ludendorff's candour. Moriz von Lyncker, the Chief of the Military Cabinet, disagreed with him over the matter of army increases, and used his influence with the Kaiser to effect his demotion. Ludendorff was put in charge of a regiment in Düsseldorf on 27 January 1913, a decision that seemed to spell the end of his General Staff career.[167] Ludendorff himself maintained that his dismissal was due to his demands for army increases when he recalled after the war 'that I was removed from the General Staff as an inconvenient warning voice'. He apparently expected to be recalled in due course as *Oberquartiermeister*.[168] Perhaps Ludendorff's account of his role as a martyr for the cause of German army increases was all too easily accepted by historians. Uhle-Wettler argues that Ludendorff in fact needed to be moved to a corps command if he was to advance further within the General Staff in the near future. In order to be promoted to the rank of general in future, he needed to be placed with the

---

[163] See Chapter 5.   [164] Zechlin, 'Ludendorff', p. 316.   [165] Schäfer, *Ludendorff*, pp. 9ff.
[166] Memorandum quoted in BA-MA, W-10/50721, 'Der Feldherr Ludendorff', by Carl Mühlmann.
[167] Schäfer, *Ludendorff*, p. 17. Lyncker apparently advised the commanding general there to teach Ludendorff some discipline. At the same time, rumours appeared in the press that Moltke was being replaced, e.g. in *Berliner Tageblatt*, 14 January 1913. That these were unfounded is confirmed by Wenninger, BayHSTA-KA, MKr42, No. 191, 14 January 1913.
[168] Ludendorff, *Mein militärischer Werdegang*, pp. 131, 157.

troops again. The death of Oberst von Blumenstein, commander of *Niederrheinisches Füsilierregiment* 39 in Düsseldorf, provided such an opportunity.[169] At the same time, Wenninger reported to Munich on the pronounced wish in the General Staff and in parliamentary circles for the Minister of War to resign. Wenninger speculated that this was possibly connected with the desire to delay military budget decisions until Heeringen was replaced, thus increasing the chances of their acceptance in the Reichstag.[170]

It is important to note that, while Moltke apparently could not prevent Ludendorff's dismissal, he continued the quest for army increases without him.[171] Only three days after Ludendorff had been moved to Düsseldorf, Moltke wrote to Bethmann Hollweg re-emphasizing the need for the next army bill to provide considerable troop increases.[172] A few months after his dismissal, Moltke suggested Ludendorff for the position of Chief of the General War Department in the Ministry of War – a move that, if successful, would have established a voice in favour of army increases in the Ministry. Moltke gave Ludendorff credit for having initiated the moves that finally led to a new army bill in June 1913. He wrote to Stein: 'It is Ludendorff first of all who started the whole thing off; he deserves the Pour le Mérite'.[173] The Military Cabinet, however, did not share Moltke's enthusiasm.

Ludendorff's demotion led to significant changes in the personnel structure of the General Staff at this crucial moment. Moltke had lost a colleague whose work he had valued. In June 1910, for example, he had written to Dommes: 'Ludendorff [is] an excellent help, clear and understanding with [a] good overview who applies himself with great enthusiasm.'[174] Ludendorff was replaced by his former deputy, Oberstleutnant Gerhard Tappen. Apparently Tappen had been recommended by Ludendorff although he was, according to Krafft von Dellmensingen,

---

[169] Uhle-Wettler, *Ludendorff*, pp. 72–73 and pp. 425–426, note 53, referring to Stülpnagel, (BA-MA, N5/13, pp. 64–69) who claims that the decisive reason behind the dismissal was the custom of making General Staff officers serve with the troops, but that it was a welcome side-effect that this uncomfortable advocate of army increases was removed.

[170] BayHSTA-KA, MKr42, No. 191, 14 January 1913.

[171] Zechlin, 'Ludendorff', p. 316 argues that Moltke did not try to keep 'the importunate subordinate', while Jens Heisterkamp maintains that Ludendorff's dismissal and the fact that Moltke had tried to save him led to further animosity between Lyncker and Moltke: 'Helmuth von Moltke – eine Lebensskizze', in Meyer, *Helmuth von Moltke*, vol. 1, p. 33. The fact that the Military Cabinet's decisions regarding even the highest appointments frequently caused discontent within the General Staff suggests that at this time, too, the Chief of Staff may have resented the Cabinet's interference. He was, however, powerless against Lyncker's decision.

[172] Coetzee, *Army League*, pp. 38–39.   [173] Quoted in Schäfer, *Ludendorff*, p. 18.

[174] BA-MA, NL Dommes, N512/4, Moltke to Dommes, 16 June 1910.

not the obvious choice. 'This man, known hardly more than by name to General Moltke, now became the first adviser of the Chief in all operational matters', Krafft complained. Tappen did not strike Krafft as an outstanding figure. He tried to copy his predecessor, but imitated only Ludendorff's weaknesses, 'the stubborn and domineering side'.[175] According to Tappen's own memoirs, however, his appointment hardly came as a surprise, for he had been informed as early as December 1908 that he was to replace Ludendorff at some point in the future. His position as first General Staff officer in the Second Department made him an obvious successor, as he had worked under Ludendorff since September 1910.[176]

The other men in Moltke's immediate entourage at that time included the Chief of the Central Department, Max von Fabeck; Moltke's First Adjutant, Hans Tieschowitz von Tischowa; and the Chief of the Third Department, Oberstleutnant Richard Hentsch; as well as Tappen. Wilhelm Groener, Chief of the Railway Department, was a somewhat marginal figure. Also important was Oberstleutnant Wilhelm von Dommes, a former First Adjutant of Moltke, who had become commander of the *Potsdamer Garde Husaren* and then *Flügeladjutant* of the Kaiser. His exact position was unclear, but according to Krafft he was seconded for special tasks, possibly because Moltke wanted him. Dommes knew Moltke well and therefore had the most influence within this group.[177] General von Stein was also in an influential position on the General Staff. He later replaced Waldersee as *Generalquartiermeister* in August 1914, when Waldersee joined the Eighth Army. As Waldersee recalled, Stein 'always exerted great influence over General Moltke'.[178]

In trying to prepare and advocate the large army bills of 1912 and 1913 it became evident that a press department would be beneficial. Tirpitz had successfully utilized the press in his campaigns for naval increases, yet, until 1912, no press department existed to promote the army in a similar way.[179] Minister of War Falkenhayn decided to establish a press department resembling that of the Navy. 'The purpose of this body was primarily the continual and emphatic education of the public in military

---

[175] BA-MA, w-10/50594, Krafft von Dellmensingen, 'Aufzeichnungen', pp. 78–79.

[176] BA-MA, w-10/50661, Tappen, 'Kriegserinnerungen', p. 1.

[177] BA-MA, w-10/50594, Krafft von Dellmensingen, p. 79. Letters from Moltke to Dommes survive in the Dommes Nachlaß in Freiburg which demonstrate the friendly relations between the two (BA-MA, N512/5).

[178] BA-MA, Waldersee, 'Meine Erlebnisse zu Beginn des Krieges 1914', September 1914, w-10/51032, p. 10.

[179] On Tirpitz's use of the press, see Wilhelm Deist, *Flottenpolitik und Flottenpropaganda. Das Nachrichtenbüro des Reichsmarineamtes, 1897–1914*, Stuttgart 1976.

matters.'[180] The General Staff already had some experience of dealing with the press in giving out information to the public regarding the annual *Kaisermanöver*, a job that rested with the Third Department (*Spionage- und Abwehrabteilung*). However, the new press department aimed at more than such minimal dealings with the press. It sought to achieve some necessary prerequisites for war, such as preparing the public to accept new army increases by convincing them of the imminent threat that Germany's neighbours posed. The Reichsarchiv noted the positive and almost immediate results of using the press: the army bill of 1913 went through with much less difficulty than that of 1912.[181]

In February 1913, Moltke wrote to Conrad about his thoughts on the current political situation in the Balkans and on 'the waging of a great war of the Triple Alliance against the Triple Entente'.[182] He felt the need to explain to Conrad not only how he viewed the current situation, but also why he considered it necessary to comment on *political* considerations at all:

> Your Excellency will read these comments with some surprise. They do not really belong in the correspondence between two purely military bodies. I am also no politician, but the friendly relationship between Your Excellency and myself encourages me to speak confidentially and privately with Your Excellency about such matters, too. After all, politics and warfare (*Kriegsführung*) are in close interrelation.[183]

In this letter, Moltke again outlined the need for public support for any aggressive action taken by Austria or Germany, and the need for the public to understand why war might break out: 'Your Excellency knows that a war for the very existence of the state requires willing self-sacrifice and enthusiasm from the people.' Moltke was certain that the German people would support Austria if she were attacked by Russia. However, if Austria were to provoke a conflict, it would be difficult to find support for this among the German people. It had been different when tensions between Serbia and Austria first arose, because 'the monarchy, due to Serbia's provocative behaviour, doubtless had the sympathy of all the main powers – with the exception of Russia – on her side.' In 1913, this was no longer the case and it was important, in Moltke's view, to

---

[180] BA-MA, w-10/50300, 'Mitteilungen des Ministerialdirektors Deutelmoser über seine Tätigkeit als Leiter des Kriegspresseamts und als Chefs der Pressestelle der Reichsregierung im Weltkrieg 1914–1918'.   [181] Ibid.

[182] Moltke to Conrad, 10 February 1913, in Conrad, *Dienstzeit*, vol. 3, p. 146. The draft of this memorandum was sent 'for information' to Gottlieb v. Jagow, State Secretary in the AA, according to the author of 'Die Militärpolitische Lage', BA-MA, w-10/50276, p. 23.

[183] BA-MA, w-10/50276, 'Die Militärpolitische Lage Deutschlands', pp. 24–27.

re-create such feelings of sympathy before embarking on an armed conflict. 'It would, however, be difficult to find an effective [rallying] slogan, if at the present moment a war were demanded by Austria for which there were no understanding among the German people', he told Conrad.[184] Just like the Chancellor, Moltke had understood the importance of beginning a war under the most favourable circumstances. In February 1913, Bethmann Hollweg warned the Austrian Foreign Minister, Berchtold, not to strike against Serbia while the circumstances were unfavourable, stressing that 'I should regard it as an error of incalculable magnitude to bring about a solution involving force at a moment when there is a possibility – if only a remote one – that we may be able to wage the conflict under conditions more favourable to us.'[185] This is a notion that Moltke would have endorsed wholeheartedly.

Moltke's view of the political situation, as it was unfolding as a result of the Balkan Crisis, was reasonably optimistic. He forecast that the Balkan states, currently allied against Turkey, would themselves fall out once Turkey had been defeated (an accurate prediction). This might provide an opportunity for Austria to come to more cordial relations with Bulgaria, which, in Moltke's opinion, was quite eager to loosen her ties with Russia. In a situation in which Bulgaria and Serbia became opponents, Austria would have freedom of action against Russia. Because of this potential opportunity, the German Chief of Staff doubted the usefulness of any Austrian action against Serbia 'while the Balkan League still stands firmly united'.[186]

More than ever, Moltke was convinced that war would come. As he explained to Conrad, he envisaged a racial struggle between Germanic and Slavic races. The attack would have to come from the Slav side, but he considered it 'the duty of all states that carry the standard of Germanic culture (*Geisteskultur*) to prepare themselves for this'.[187] Again, Moltke emphasized the importance of public opinion. Rather insensitively, however, he had overlooked in his memorandum to Conrad the fact that the Austrian Chief of Staff had to take the multitude of different races in the Austro-Hungarian empire into account in his war-planning. Not surprisingly, Conrad was unimpressed by the idea of having to wage a racial war in the near future, as he explained in his

---

[184] Conrad, *Dienstzeit*, vol. 3, p. 146.
[185] Quoted in Fritz Fischer, *Germany's Aims in the First World War*, London 1967, p. 34.
[186] Ibid.
[187] Conrad, *Dienstzeit*, vol. 3, pp. 146ff., also BA-MA, w-10/50276; 'Die Militärpolitische Lage Deutschlands', p. 27.

reply of 15 February 1913, when he acidly pointed out that he doubted whether the Slavs in the Dual Monarchy – a substantial 47 per cent of the population – would rally enthusiastically behind the state if it declared a racial war against fellow Slavs.[188]

There were parallels between Moltke's and Bethmann's thinking, for the latter, too, envisaged a racial war between Germans and Slavs. On 7 April 1913, for example, the Chancellor highlighted racial differences (*Rassengegensätze*) between Slavonic and Teutonic peoples in a speech in the Reichstag.[189] Admiral von Müller, too, emphasized typically Social Darwinist views when he spoke of 'upholding the German race in opposition to Slavs and Romans'.[190] Notions of a forthcoming racial war were shared by the highest military and political decision-makers, as was the fear of what the future would hold once the Russian Empire had become too strong to be defeated by Germany. Given that Germany's potential future enemies responded to the army bill of 1913 with their own large army increases, that war seemed not only ever closer, but also increasingly difficult to fight successfully.[191]

THE QUESTION OF BELGIAN AND BRITISH NEUTRALITY

It is very much in the interest of the small states to be with us, because the consequences of the war will be grave for those who go against us.

Moltke to the Belgian King, 6 November 1913[192]

After the war, Germany was not allowed to forget the violation of her neutral neighbours Luxembourg and Belgium, despite attempts to justify this act of aggression as a necessary evil, 'ein Gebot der Not'.[193] In the early months of the war, nothing provided Germany's enemies with better propaganda material than German atrocities (both real and invented) against Belgian and French civilians, and nothing provided a better rallying force for the recruitment of volunteers and for Britain's entry into the war than Germany's violation of Belgian neutrality.[194]

[188] Conrad, *Dienstzeit*, vol. 3, pp. 149/150.
[189] *Verhandlungen des Reichstags*, XIII. Legislaturperiode, I. Session, vol. 289, Berlin 1913, pp. 4512ff.
[190] Cited in Niall Ferguson, *The Pity of War*, London 1998, p. 19.
[191] For the reactions of the Entente powers, see Herrmann, *The Arming of Europe*, pp. 191ff.
[192] Quoted in Jean Stengers, 'Guillaume II et le Roi Albert à Potsdam en novembre 1913', *Bulletin de la Classe des Lettres et des Sciences Morales et Politiques*, 7–12, 1993, pp. 227–253.
[193] Hermann von Kuhl, *Der Weltkrieg 1914–1918*, 2 vols., Berlin 1929, vol. 1, p. 7.
[194] On the subject of atrocities, see Alan Kramer, '"Greueltaten". Zum Problem der deutschen Kriegsverbrechen in Belgien und Frankreich 1914' in Gerhard Hirschfeld et al. (eds.), *Keiner fühlt sich hier mehr als Mensch. Erlebnis und Wirkung des Ersten Weltkriegs*, Essen 1993, pp. 85ff.

Important questions about military and political decision-making arise in this context. Did General Staff officers realize what the consequences of the intended violation of Belgium would be, and did they insist on this aspect of the Schlieffen Plan despite such knowledge? How much information did the civilian decision-makers have, not only about the intended violation of a neighbour's neutrality, but also about details of the Schlieffen Plan? After the war, politicians were keen to underline their ignorance of these fateful plans, but the evidence suggests not only that the military informed them, but that they relied on politicians to prepare this strategy diplomatically. The question of Belgian neutrality was one of the most striking examples of how military considerations dictated political decision-making in Imperial Germany.

Moltke was clearly aware of the need for military and civilian co-operation regarding a violation of Belgian neutrality. For a proper evaluation of international relations, he argued in November 1911, political and military concerns could not be separated; one without the other could easily lead to the wrong conclusions. In a letter to Bethmann Hollweg he pleaded for more co-operation between the military and political spheres, and for a discussion of military planning in a political context, which he assumed the Chancellor would also favour. Moltke clearly had the march through Belgium and the secret *coup de main* on Liège in mind, as well as the crucial timing of Germany's advance in the West. He realized that political preparations were needed to initiate this, particularly attempts by Germany's diplomats to try to preserve Belgian neutrality if German troops marched through Belgian territory. He continued his plea for support for military action by the political leadership:

Political relations change according to the aims and strengths of states. Thus Germany's aims, too, are more far-reaching today than in the past, while other states are able to summon and juxtapose equal sources of power, even superior ones when combined. The leader of the military operations thus faces a task that can only be solved fruitfully if his preliminary work is in accordance with the political guidelines of the state.[195]

The Chief of the General Staff seized the opportunity for possible co-operation that offered itself when the Chancellor suddenly came out in favour of army demands for military increases in late 1911. However, if Moltke's aim in sending the memorandum was indeed to bring about an improvement in the relations between civilians and the military, he failed

---

[195] BA-MA, w-10/50279, Moltke to Bethmann Hollweg, 2 December 1911.

to achieve his goal. Despite his initiative, the lack of co-operation continued.[196] The Reichsarchiv blamed the Chancellor, who, in their opinion, had wanted to avoid an arms race. For whatever reason, Bethmann Hollweg had apparently not been keen to co-operate with Moltke, as Karl von Einem also asserts in his memoirs:

Bethmann Hollweg had no relationship at all with the army. He never socialized with the Chief of the General Staff, which was of course a mistake, especially considering Germany's situation at the time. General von Moltke complained about this often and bitterly.[197]

If that was indeed the case, they still shared surprisingly similar views, as we have seen. It is possible that these military commentators simply wanted to blame the Chancellor for the apparent missed opportunity of better co-operation, and to exonerate the military decision-makers by emphasizing civilian shortcomings.

After 1918, when Germany tried to deny responsibility for the war, the violation of Belgian neutrality was a particularly sore point. The Reichsarchiv was anxious to prove the military necessity of this action, and attempted to show that the General Staff had tried to develop alternative strategies. In a letter to Tappen of 26 October 1918, the archive explained its motivation: 'The Belgian question will probably play a large part at the peace negotiations. We will perhaps be in a position where we have to justify and explain our march into Belgium.'[198] The Reichsarchiv found that although Moltke had wrestled with the idea of an invasion of Belgium and had asked himself often whether it could be avoided, he had come to the conclusion that it was essential. There had been no dispute within the General Staff over the necessity to invade Belgium. By 1913, Moltke did not doubt that England would 'get actively involved in the war on our opponents' side, whether we march through Belgium or not'.[199] This certainty was based on the information from Lichnowsky in December 1912 that Britain would not allow Germany to defeat France, and on the subsequent discussions during the war council meeting. Even when Moltke did worry about invading Belgium, his concern was not motivated by qualms about violating the neutral

---

[196] BA-MA, W-10/50276, 'Die Militärpolitische Lage Deutschlands', pp. 58–59.
[197] Einem, *Erinnerungen*, p. 161.
[198] BA-MA, NL Tappen, N56/2, Korrespondenz 1918–1923.
[199] Moltke's memorandum of 1913 (exact date unknown, but written after February 1913): 'Verhalten Deutschlands in einem Dreibundkriege: Ost- oder Westaufmarsch, Belgiendurchmarsch und England', in Erwin Hölzle (ed.), *Quellen zur Entstehung des Ersten Weltkrieges. Internationale Dokumente 1901–1914*, Darmstadt 1978, No. 69, pp. 153ff. Also quoted in Schäfer, 'Der Kriegsplan für den Zweifrontenkrieg', BA-MA, W-10/50223 pp. 25–26.

neighbour's territory, but rather by Britain's likely reaction to such a violation. Once British involvement seemed inevitable, Belgian neutrality was viewed only in terms of military parameters, and the necessity of an invasion was no longer doubted. Theobald von Schäfer confirms this view:

> There was no difference of opinion over the fact that the only possible way out was a German attack through Belgium. Even the Chancellor and the Auswärtiges Amt, who knew about the plan, subordinated their concerns to an appreciation of the compelling military reasons.[200]

Schäfer's account raises two significant points: that the civilians knew about the General Staff's plan to march through Belgium, and that they objected to it, at least initially. Their concerns were, however, regarded as secondary to military arguments, which the civilians could not counter.

However, there were not only civilian critics. Some generals, like Oberst Max Bauer, had also expressed unease about the invasion of Belgium in case of an armed conflict, as the Reichsarchiv discovered during its investigations.[201] In his papers, Bauer outlined how the invasion of Belgium had been planned because it had been considered impossible to develop artillery powerful enough to break through the strong, permanent French fortifications on the front between Verdun and Toul. He explained that he had harboured concerns about such a violation of neutrality, especially at the beginning of the war, and that in his opinion, in order to avoid Belgium, heavy artillery would have been necessary to break through directly on the Verdun–Toul front.[202] The Reichsarchiv, more than willing to believe that an alternative to the odious invasion of Belgium had been considered by the General Staff before the war, hoped that Tappen might be able to confirm Bauer's statements. While the archive had been unable to trace any references to such plans in the files, it speculated whether the negotiations between the General Staff and the Ministry of War of 1912/1913 regarding heavy

---

[200] Ibid., p. 26.

[201] Bauer's career in the General Staff had been exceptional. He was appointed to it in 1905 without having been to the war academy. After some years in the Seventh Department (*Festungsabteilung*) he had joined the Second (Deployment) Department in 1909. Throughout his General Staff career he worked at improving existing artillery to a standard that would make it possible to destroy even heavily reinforced fortifications. He was substantially involved in the development of the '42 *Mörser*' (howitzers). Adolf Vogt, *Oberst Max Bauer. Generalstabsoffizier im Zwielicht, 1869–1929*, Osnabrück 1974.

[202] Bauer's views were quoted in a letter from Haeften to Tappen, 16 October 1930, BA-MA, NL Tappen, N56/4, pp. 292 ff.

and heaviest artillery ('schwere und schwerste Geschütze') might suggest that a breakthrough on the French border had indeed been considered. According to Bauer's papers, it had been merely a matter of time before the march through Belgium would have become redundant: 'War, in the end, came before it was possible to create that artillery. Thus the march through Belgium was executed in 1914', Bauer claimed.[203]

Tappen's answer was disappointing, for he was certain that no decisive amendment of the German war plan had been intended for the years 1912/1913 and 1913/1914. Nonetheless, he confirms that Moltke was unhappy about the planned invasion of Belgium, and that he tried on several occasions to envisage a scenario of a war against France without a violation of Belgian neutrality. Tappen remembered that the winter war games of 1913/1914, and possibly those of 1912/1913, had been based on such a scenario. The negotiations with the Ministry of War had, according to Tappen, been preventive, in case the Belgian eastern front were to be fortified in the same way as the French already had been. The only alternative to a frontal breakthrough in such a scenario would have been a violation of Dutch neutrality, something that Moltke had always opposed very strongly.[204] Fear of future improved Belgian fortifications was thus another underlying reason to want 'war now rather than later', another potential worry in the not-too-distant future that influenced the General Staff's decision-making in the months preceding the outbreak of war.

In his memorandum of 21 December 1912, Moltke explained to the Chancellor that, owing to Germany's central geographic position, she would always have to fight on several fronts, and would therefore have to be defensive on one side and offensive on the other. The offensive side could only ever be France, because a quick decision could be hoped for on this front, while an offensive against Russia would harbour the risk of a long drawn-out struggle. In this memorandum, Moltke spelt out detailed strategic considerations to the Chancellor. In effect, he revealed the Schlieffen/Moltke Plan. He did so because he knew that the issue of Belgian neutrality would require the co-operation of the diplomats in the Wilhelmstrasse. Moltke outlined that in order to be on the offensive against France, it would be necessary to violate Belgian neutrality, asserting that only a deployment via Belgian territory would give German troops the opportunity to attack and defeat France. Although this meant that German troops would face the BEF and Belgium, too, 'if we do not

[203] Ibid., p. 292.
[204] Tappen to Reichsarchiv, 20 October 1930, BA-MA, NL Tappen, N56/4, p. 295.

manage to come to an agreement with Belgium', this operation was 'nonetheless more likely to succeed than a frontal attack against the fortified French eastern front'. He explained how a frontal attack would turn the war into something 'resembling siege warfare, it would take a lot of time and would rob the army of drive and initiative, which we require all the more the larger the number of enemies we have scores to settle with'.[205]

From this date onwards, at the very latest, we can be certain that the civilian decision-makers were aware of the planned invasion of Belgium, although the most secret details of the plan, such as the intended attack on Liège, were not revealed to them. With this memorandum the General Staff also informed the Ministry of War of its strategic intention to strike at France through Belgium. It is interesting to note that it did so as part of its attempt to secure further army increases, and not because it felt that the other military institution should know about the General Staff's military strategy. In his memorandum to Bethmann Hollweg, which was copied to Heeringen, Moltke explained how the numerical strength of the German army was insufficient for an offensive war on several fronts. 'We will therefore be forced to be defensive with weak forces on one side, in order to be offensive on the other side. That side can only be France. There it is possible to hope for a quick decision, while an offensive war into Russia would have no foreseeable end.'[206]

This was the first time the General Staff stated officially and in writing its strategic intentions in a future war. The civilian government, as well as the Ministry of War, was now aware of the General Staff's plan to attack France, and of the implications this had: the violation of the neutrality of Luxembourg and Belgium and the danger to East Prussia, where only very minor forces would have the task of defending the Reich's eastern border against the Russians during the initial weeks of war. From this date onwards, then, there was no excuse for the failure of the civilian decision-makers to intervene, or at least to query the General Staff's view that there could be no alternative to such a plan.

Some military commentators after the war felt that the political leadership should have endeavoured to prepare diplomatic measures for the eventuality of war, but failed to do so. Thus, General van den Bergh claims that the international outrage at the violation of Belgian neutral-

[205] Reichsarchiv, *Kriegsrüstung, Anlagen*, p. 164.
[206] Ibid., Memorandum, Moltke to Bethmann Hollweg, 21 December 1912, also sent to Minister of War Heeringen, pp. 156ff., quote pp. 163–164.

ity could have been avoided if this measure had been prepared diplomatically, and that as a consequence there would have been no need for Bethmann's controversial and damaging Reichstag speech on 4 August 1914, when the Chancellor admitted that Germany was in the wrong for violating the neutrality of her neighbours.[207] Similarly Tappen complained in 1936: 'It had been sufficiently established that passing through Belgian territory was necessary. What political considerations led the Reich Chancellor not to support this fully at the outbreak of war?'[208] Moreover, according to the Reichsarchiv, the civilians should have acted even earlier, not just when war was about to break out.[209] These are ill-disguised attempts at passing the responsibility for the violation of Belgian neutrality to the civilian decision-makers, by turning the issue into one of failure to make the necessary diplomatic arrangements.

The memorandum of December 1912 was not the only communication about military plans that the political leaders received. Tappen also remembered that the Chief of the General Staff had been in close contact with the Chancellor and the Auswärtiges Amt before the war, especially via Count Waldersee.[210] There were occasions during such exchanges when the political leaders did try to intervene, but their objections were all too easily overturned by military considerations. Shortly after replacing the deceased Kiderlen-Wächter as Secretary of State in the Foreign Office at the beginning of 1913, Gottlieb von Jagow arranged to meet Moltke in order to 'orientate myself about our military situation and to get in touch with the Chief of the General Staff'.[211] During this conversation in late January or the beginning of February 1913, Jagow enquired whether it was not possible to avoid marching through Belgium, as he told the Reichsarchiv in 1920. 'My suggestion was looked into by the military without, however, arriving at the result that I had wished for in order to keep England out [of the war]. I stuck to my point of view.'[212] Jagow remembered expressing concern about the violation of Belgian neutrality: 'I warned Moltke seriously about the violation of Belgian neutrality which, to my mind, was bound to bring England into the equation against us. Moltke became contemplative, but

---

[207] BA-MA w-10/50629, 'Aufzeichnungen des Generalmajors van den Bergh', p. 5.

[208] BA-MA, NL Tappen, N56/5, Tappen to RA, 30 September 1936.

[209] BA-MA, w-10/50276: 'Die Militärpolitische Lage Deutschlands', p. 70.

[210] BA-MA, NL Tappen, N56/5, Tappen to RA, 30 September 1936.

[211] PA Bonn, NL Gottlieb von Jagow, vol. 8, part 1, Politische Aufsätze, 'Der Durchmarsch durch Belgien', pp. 48ff.

[212] Quoted in a Reichsarchiv letter to former Secretary of State Wahnschaffe, 8 December 1930, BA-MA, w-10/50688. It is advisable to treat Jagow's post-war protestations with some caution, as it was obviously in his interest to portray his own role in these events in a favourable light.

then he said: "Well, I think if need be we would be able to deal with those 150,000 Englishmen, too."' Moltke was prepared to concentrate solely on military reasoning in justifying this important step. It is interesting to compare this to Joffre's attitude, shortly after the French Chief of Staff assumed command over the French army. Regarding Belgium, he was, of course, faced with very similar problems to Moltke. Yet he considered the question of Belgium as not simply a military, but also a diplomatic one. 'If we violate Belgian neutrality first, we will become *provocateurs*. England will not join us. Italy will be able to declare against us. We will consequently be stopped by political considerations. If only military considerations count, we should have, on the contrary, the greatest interest in taking the offensive through Belgium.'[213] In stark contrast to the situation in Germany, where only military considerations were allowed to count, in France Joffre demanded discussions with civilians on this important issue.

Jagow claims he stuck to his concerns, and asked Moltke whether it was not possible to redraft the plan so that Belgian neutrality could be observed. Moltke pointed out France's strong defences on the Franco-German border, which made a march through Belgium necessary, but he agreed 'to consider a change of plan to allow for the protection of Belgium'. The new Secretary of State for Foreign Affairs was so concerned about the Belgian question that he also talked to the Kaiser about it. According to their conversation, Moltke had clearly done the same, for the Kaiser told Jagow: 'Yes, yes, I have already discussed with Moltke that the operational plan should be changed.' In the aftermath of the meeting, Moltke had sought advice from other officers, as Jagow found out from General von Watter in Münster. The majority had been against a change of plan, since they considered the march through Belgium a necessity. As Jagow remembered after the war: 'Moltke himself told me in 1914, with reference to our earlier conversation, that he had checked the matter thoroughly.' Jagow was told that the march through Belgium was 'unfortunately unavoidable'.[214] Moreover, as Jagow informed the Reichsarchiv, he had known about the General Staff's strategic intentions even *before* his appointment in 1913: 'The General Staff's deployment plan was generally known to me long before my appointment as Secretary of State in the Auswärtiges Amt.'[215]

[213] Cited in Williamson, 'Joffre Reshapes French Strategy', p. 137.
[214] PA Bonn, NL Gottlieb von Jagow, vol. 8, part 1, Politische Aufsätze, 'Der Durchmarsch durch Belgien', pp. 48ff.
[215] BA-MA, W-10/50688, Bethmann Hollweg to Reichsarchiv.

In May 1920, Bethmann Hollweg informed the Reichsarchiv that he, too, had known about the General Staff's 'deployment plan for a war on two fronts long before the war. An oral discussion took place on several occasions. During those, I always pointed to the great political concerns, while General von Moltke kept emphasizing the military constraints (*die militärische Zwangslage*).'[216] While Bethmann's and Jagow's post-war protestations that they tried to avert the invasion of Belgium must perhaps be viewed with a degree of scepticism, the fact remains that they had been informed about the General Staff's plan. Only the *coup de main* on Liège had been kept a secret. Moltke had not mentioned it to Jagow in their talks of 1913, and not even the Kaiser knew about it. Haeften defended this secrecy after the war on the grounds that it was perfectly understandable because it was only a military detail of the overall plan, arguing that the decisive fact was that 'Moltke demanded of the political leadership an immediate march into Belgium in case of war.'[217] As the events of 31 July were to prove, however, the *coup de main* on Liège was much more than a mere detail within the overall strategy: it would burden Germany with the odium of starting hostilities before any official declaration of war.[218] It was no doubt very politic of Moltke not to mention this 'military detail' in his discussions with the political decision-makers. That Moltke's civilian colleagues had been convinced by his arguments can also be concluded from a discussion between former Chancellor Bülow and the journalist Theodor Wolff on 12 August 1914. Against Wolff's objections, Bülow declared 'that he considered the march through Belgium and the violation of neutrality to be right. . . . He assured me that he had the greatest confidence in the Chief of the General Staff, von Moltke, whom he knew well.'[219]

Moltke was under no illusions as to the possible ramifications of the intended march through Belgium. In a memorandum of 1913, he wrote:

One must not overlook the great difficulties that attach to a march through Belgium. It is not pleasant [!] (*angenehm*) to begin the war by violating the territory of a neutral neighbouring state. However, where the existence of our own state is at stake, all consideration for others must take second place.[220]

---

[216] Ibid., 27 May 1920.
[217] PA Bonn, NL Jagow, vol. 8, part II, Haeften to Jagow, 3 January 1931, pp. 237–238.
[218] See Chapter 4.
[219] Bernd Sösemann (ed.), *Theodor Wolff. Der Chronist. Krieg, Revolution und Frieden im Tagebuch 1914–1919*, Düsseldorf and Munich 1997, p. 33.
[220] Memorandum of 1913 (no exact date given), quoted in BA-MA, W-10/50276: 'Die Militärpolitische Lage Deutschlands', pp. 65–67.

It is important to remember that the General Staff's thinking regarding Belgium was motivated by the very real dangers either that Belgium might become actively involved on the Entente's side in case of war, or that France would herself not shy away from violating Belgian neutrality. This suspicion seemed to be confirmed by information from the German military attaché Detlev von Winterfeldt in Paris. On 29 August 1913, Winterfeldt reported back to Berlin about a conversation with his Belgian colleague Major Collon, who told him that the Belgians did not believe French assurances that they would enter Belgian territory only if it had already been violated by another power (i.e. Germany). Rather, Collon thought that French troops might march into Belgium as soon as a Franco-German war broke out. Indicative of this intention seemed to him the French General Staff's journey into Belgian territory the previous autumn.[221] The German General Staff could be under no illusions about Belgium's determination to defend her neutrality against any aggressor. The King of the Belgians had informed the Kaiser of his country's decision to increase her army in order to be able to meet a challenge from either France, Britain or Germany. On 21 December 1912, the Kaiser advised Bethmann and Moltke of his conversation with the King two days earlier. Bethmann recorded:

H.M. assured the King that in case of war his wish was merely to have a secure right flank. General von Moltke remarked to H.M. that he would have to think the situation over first. As is well known, our deployment against France was based on us advancing through Belgium. This deployment could not be altered, at least not before 1 April 1913.[222]

Belgium intended to increase her army in 1913, adding an extra 150,000 soldiers to the war-time strength, plus reserves. Such news would have repercussions for Germany's strategic plans. However, Moltke was not too concerned for the immediate future. In the aftermath of the war council meeting, he stated: 'The Belgian army increases would first of all actually have to be implemented. Before that, Belgium would probably be too weak to defend her neutrality with arms.'[223] In the longer term, however, the news of Belgian army increases provided another reason for Moltke to advocate a war 'the sooner the better', because a much stronger Belgium would jeopardize the execution of the German deployment plan. For the moment, however, he did not rate Belgian's

---

[221] BA-MA, NL Tappen, N56/2,Winterfeldt to General Staff, 29 August 1913, pp. 15–16. On Joffre's intentions regarding an offensive through Belgium, see also Williamson, 'Joffre Reshapes French Strategy', pp. 137ff.

[222] PA Bonn, R4463, Aufzeichnung Bethmann Hollweg, 22 December 1912.   [223] Ibid.

military power highly. To him neither Belgium nor Britain represented a significant threat. Despite the lessons of the Franco-Prussian war, which had demonstrated the dangers of a *Volkskrieg*, Moltke seriously underestimated the resolve that a small country, defending itself from an aggressor, could muster.

In 1913, Moltke advocated trying to come to an agreement with the Belgians, to arrange either that they would ally themselves to Germany, in which case they could be assured of territorial gains in the West, or, at least, that they would refrain from hostilities towards the German troops. In the latter case, Germany should guarantee that Belgium would keep all her territory once the war was over. Belgium should be made to understand that Germany did not want to annex any part of her, that Germany did not even want to wage war against Belgium, but that Belgian territory was merely needed to march the German troops to France.[224] Realistically, however, Moltke did not have much hope that such an agreement would be achievable:

> However, I consider it out of the question that our diplomacy might succeed in arranging such an agreement with Belgium; rather we will have to reckon with the fact that Belgium would consider a German advance through her territory as a *casus belli* and would immediately place herself on the side of our opponents.[225]

Not only would Germany have to fight the Belgian army, Moltke continued, but a violation of Belgian neutrality would turn Britain into an opponent, too. No matter how convincingly Germany argued that she was not seeking territorial gains on the Belgian coast, Britain would not believe her, and would not allow Germany to overrun Belgium and establish herself on the coast. Interestingly, it did not occur to Moltke that Britain might come to Belgium's aid because of her guaranteed neutrality. Would it therefore be worth considering *not* marching through Belgium, if this made English neutrality possible? This would indeed be the case, Moltke argued, if Britain had not made it absolutely clear that she would be actively involved on the side of Germany's opponents, whether or not Germany marched through Belgium. Even if an assurance of neutrality could be obtained, the risks for Germany were too grave:

---

[224] This was perhaps true for military decision-makers. It is well known, however, that extensive annexationist plans existed. On the so-called 'September-Programme' see Fischer, *Griff nach der Weltmacht. Die Kriegszielpolitik des kaiserlichen Deutschlands, 1914/18*, Nachdruck der Sonderausgabe 1967, Düsseldorf 1984, pp. 90ff.

[225] BA-MA, w-10/50276, 'Die Militärpolitische Lage Deutschlands', pp. 65–67.

I would consider it extraordinarily dangerous if, prompted by vague assurances from England, we were to give up our only chance provided by a quick deployment against France. We would impose on ourselves the difficulty of a frontal attack on the strong French eastern front and would have no guarantee that England would not intervene at a given moment after all.

Moltke argued that owing to Britain's close connection with the Franco-Russian Alliance there could be no security for Germany. Only an active involvement of Britain on the side of the Triple Alliance would provide such security, and Moltke was of course right to predict that one could not count on that in the foreseeable future. He was under no illusions regarding Britain's intentions and motivations in a war on the continent:

England considers Germany to be stronger than France. She fears a defeat of the latter and a German hegemony and, true to her politics which are aimed at preserving the European balance of power, she will do everything to hinder an expansion of power on Germany's side. Therefore, we will have to count England among our opponents.[226]

Given this accurate assessment of the situation, Britain's declaration of war on 4 August 1914 cannot have come as a surprise to Moltke. Within the General Staff, it had become an accepted assumption that the French and the English would march into Belgium when war came, and that Belgium would join their side, no matter what the Germans were to do. In early 1913, Moltke anticipated British strength, apart from the 'fleet which is far superior to ours' to be a 'well-equipped expeditionary army of six infantry and one cavalry division with a fighting power of 132,000 men'.[227]

The scrapping of the *Ostaufmarschplan* had put more emphasis than ever on the future Western Front, and highlighted the problem that the small neutral states in the West posed for Germany's military planners. They had come to accept that an attack in the West was the assured formula for victory that the *Ostaufmarschplan* had not been. They were willing, in Gerhard Ritter's words, to 'stake everything on this single card and leave the Austrians temporarily to their fate; [to] accept the political consequences of a breach of neutrality and a precipitate declaration of war'.[228] The only alternative to this all-out-war scenario would have been to remain on the defensive. Ritter complained that 'the idea of

---

[226] Ibid. Here Moltke is again refering to the discussion of the war council meeting of December 1912.   [227] Moltke memorandum, 1913, in Hölzle, *Dokumente*, No. 69, p. 157.
[228] Ritter, *Schlieffen Plan*, p. 37.

waging a war against France in a purely defensive fashion never occurred to Schlieffen'.[229] It would seem, however, as if Schlieffen did consider such an alternative, albeit only briefly. His last war games had been based on a defensive scenario, but he concluded from them that Germany's offensive war plan could not be abandoned.[230] His successor and his advisors also did not consider seriously developing a defensive strategy. Given their conviction of the enmity of Germany's neighbours, the country's strategic situation led them to assume that Germany could only hope to win a war in which she took the initiative in an offensive strike. Moreover, a defensive war plan was incompatible with the current views on offensive warfare, as well as with German war aims.[231] Indeed, war might never have happened if Germany had relied on a defensive strategy. With an offensive strategy like the Schlieffen Plan in place, the General Staff needed only to be concerned with *appearing* to have been attacked. Another strategy would actually have *required* such an attack. Moltke explained why he considered an offensive strategy necessary for Germany, and why that offensive had to be launched against the West first: 'If Germany does . . . not want to put herself into the sad position of doing without any initiative and offensive action in a war that decides whether she will survive or collapse, and to limit herself to a defensive war on both fronts, then the old idea of an offensive war against Russia and a defensive war against France must be dropped.'[232] Once Moltke had established that he saw no way of avoiding a violation of Belgian neutrality, both he and the Kaiser attempted to win over the Belgians. If they were not to be allies, then at least they should not resist the German march through their territory. According to Mantey's recollections, in 1905 Moltke had drawn attention to his uncle's views that there should be an attempt to influence Belgian politics to join Germany against France, given the likelihood of a French advance into Belgium.[233] At the very least, Moltke wanted to achieve a promise of non-intervention. An opportunity for negotiations offered itself in November 1913, when the Belgian King Albert travelled to Germany and visited Wilhelm II in Potsdam.[234] The Kaiser and his wife welcomed him pleasantly, but the

[229] Ibid., p. 47.
[230] See Robert T. Foley, 'Schlieffen's last Kriegsspiel', *War Studies Journal*, 4, 1, 1999, pp. 97ff.
[231] On the cult of the offensive, see Michael Howard, 'Men against Fire: The Doctrine of the Offensive in 1914', in Peter Paret (ed.), *Makers of Modern Strategy from Machiavelli to the Nuclear Age*, Oxford 1986 (reprint 1994), pp. 510–526; Jack Snyder, *The Ideology of the Offensive. Military Decision-Making and the Disasters of 1914*, Ithaca, New York, London 1984.
[232] Moltke memorandum, quoted in Hölzle, *Dokumente*, No. 69, p. 153.
[233] Mantey, 'Graf Schlieffen und der jüngere Moltke', p. 396.
[234] For details of this visit, see Stengers, 'Guillaume II et le Roi Albert'.

Kaiser's attitude soon changed when the topic of conversation became the important issue of Belgium's position between Germany and France. Wilhelm warned the King that he considered a war with France 'inevitable and near'.[235] Moltke, too, had a chance to talk with the King, and he was very outspoken on the subject of a future war. Indeed, when meeting with the Belgian military attaché de Melotte and the King he was quite candid ('déboutonné'). He told King Albert that he, like the Kaiser, believed war to be imminent, and that 'this time, it needed to be finished'. He felt certain of victory, and certain that the German people would enthusiastically support a war effort. Moltke did not stop short of trying to intimidate the Belgians, warning that it would be to the advantage of the smaller states to be on Germany's side, because the consequences would be grave for those who opposed her. To the Belgian military attaché he was, if anything, even more revealing and blunt:

The war with France is inevitable and much closer than you might think. We do not want it. We have nothing to gain from it. But we have had enough of the continuous alerts which hinder our development. It is absolutely essential that France stop obstructing and provoking us, otherwise we will have to confront them. The sooner, the better.

It is hardly a coincidence that Moltke repeated the bellicose words of the war council meeting on this occasion. We do not know if his next words were merely intended to intimidate and impress, or whether he really was convinced that 'we will win. We are certain of victory.' Not surprisingly, King Albert was 'profoundly alarmed' by these discussions, and while he was also worried about the potential threat that France might pose to his small country if war broke out, the meeting only increased his determination to defend Belgium against any invasion, whether from Germany or France.[236] If Moltke and the Kaiser had hoped to win over the King of the Belgians by intimidating him, their plan failed. The Belgian envoy Beyens summed up his impressions after the talks of November 1913:

What we must keep in mind from Moltke's suggestions is that the military leadership considers a war against France unavoidable or rather that it desires it to be so, contrary to the allegations of the General [Moltke]. As the Kaiser is surrounded solely by generals who have no doubt been ordered to speak the same

---

[235] The Belgian envoy Beyens, who recorded these conversations based on information from his King, noted that the Kaiser spoke French perfectly, much better than the King spoke German, and the conversation was therefore held in French. For all quotes relating to the meeting between the Kaiser, Moltke and the Belgian King, see Stengers, 'Guillaume II et le Roi Albert', pp. 234ff.   [236] Ibid., pp. 242, 246.

language as the Chief of the General Staff, they want to change H.M. [the Kaiser's] peace-loving attitude and to convince him of the necessity of this war.[237]

THE SEARCH FOR POSSIBLE FUTURE ALLIES

Once the *Ostaufmarschplan* had been abandoned, it became more pressing than ever for Moltke to ascertain the attitude of Germany's allies. Relations with Austria were well established, and there was no doubt that, given the right *casus belli*, Austria and Germany would fight together. Italy was another matter. After 1908, Italy was no longer regarded as a reliable ally, and the German General Staff was concerned whether the country could actually be counted upon to fulfil her alliance obligations.[238] In 1912 the Italian Chief of the General Staff, General Alberto Pollio, told Moltke that Italian armies would no longer be deployed on the upper Rhine, due to the Italian losses in Libya.[239] At the same time, however, Italy was keen to renew the alliance treaty with Germany and Austria, because she felt weakened by the Tripoli War.[240] In the years 1913/1914 Moltke attempted to ensure Italian support in the event of a future war.

In January 1913 Waldersee was sent to Rome 'on [a] very confidential mission' to establish the degree of support that Italy was willing to give.[241] Waldersee and Pollio discussed matters relating to naval warfare, but also to a land war. Pollio intended to deploy across the Alps such troops as he could spare from a deployment against France and a defence of Italy's coasts. At that time he could only promise to send a few cavalry divisions, but he hoped to be able to send a whole army soon. Moltke and Waldersee were grateful for even the most minimal amount of support. In fact, they were more concerned with the moral support of an Italian involvement than with actual troop numbers, as Waldersee

---

[237] Quoted in Fischer, *Illusionen*, p. 320.

[238] BA-MA, w-10/50279, Moltke's memorandum 'Die Militärpolitische Lage Deutschlands', pp. 13ff. (not published in *Weltkrieg, Anlagen*). Moltke expected that Italy's fear of a British attack on her exposed coasts might lead her to let her alliance partners down. He also pointed out the worrying fact that Italy and France had overcome the tensions that had previously existed between them, while Italy and Austria had not. See also Risto Ropponen, *Italien als Verbündeter. Die Einstellung der politischen und militärischen Führung Deutschlands und Österreich-Ungarns zu Italien von der Niederlage von Adua 1896 bis zum Ausbruch des Weltkrieges 1914*, Helsinki 1986.

[239] James Joll, *The Origins of the First World War*, 2nd edn, London 1992, p. 87.

[240] The Triple Alliance was renewed for the fourth time on 5 December 1912. Wolfgang Förster, 'Die deutsch-italienische Militärkonvention', *Berliner Monatshefte*, 5, 1927, p. 397.

[241] For the following, see Waldersee's account of his visit in 'Von Deutschlands militär-politischer Beziehung zu Italien', *Berliner Monatshefte*, 7, 1929, pp. 641ff.

recalled: 'We gladly agreed that Italy should initially only send us cavalry. It was not the increase in troops that was of value here, but solely the fact that Italian troops should become engaged on our side at all.'[242] In September 1913, Waldersee had the opportunity to talk with Pollio and Conrad during the German autumn manoeuvres in Schleswig. He arranged initially to get a general assurance from Pollio to renew the old agreement regarding the dispatch of an Italian army to the upper Rhine.[243] Alexander von Kluck, who was Pollio's host at the *Generalkommando* in Königsberg, was under the impression that Pollio was confident that the two countries' armies would co-operate in a future war. In his memoirs, Kluck recalled Pollio declaring that he hoped that German and Italian troops would march shoulder to shoulder in the next war.[244]

Waldersee succeeded in Rome later that year to revive the stale military relations with Italy. In December 1913 negotiations were held that concluded that in case of war, two cavalry and five infantry divisions were to be transported through Austria to Alsace.[245] In March 1914, General Zuccari came to Berlin, and assured the allied General Staff that an army consisting of three army corps and two cavalry divisions would be dispatched over the Alps to support Germany, and that their transport would be by Austrian railways. Moltke was, however, not sufficiently convinced by these assurances to rely on Italian help as a definite factor in his planning. Conrad could not persuade him to send men to the East in support of Austria, on the assumption that German troops could be spared if Italian troops were dispatched. Moltke explained his doubts to Conrad on 13 March 1914: 'At present we have to take the given circumstances into consideration, and we must begin the war as if the Italians were not to be expected at all. Therefore, we cannot now allow for any changes to the dispositions already agreed on.'[246] Despite Italian assurances in March 1914, and although Germany, Italy and Austria had concluded a naval agreement in the summer 1913, serious doubts remained regarding Italy's reliability, as Waldersee also emphasized in a memorandum of May 1914:

The excellent Chief of the General Staff, Pollio, is an intelligent and competent man. How long will his influence last? The King is dependent on his par-

---

[242] Ibid., p. 647.
[243] BA-MA, w-10/50276, 'Die Militärpolitische Lage Deutschlands', p. 33.
[244] Alexander von Kluck, *Wanderjahre–Kriege–Gestalten*, Berlin 1929, p. 161.
[245] BA-MA, NL Tappen, N56/5, Tappen to Reichsarchiv, 30 September 1936.
[246] Conrad, *Dienstzeit*, vol. 3, p. 610.

liamentary government. France has many influential friends, Pittoni, Luzzati, and many others. Add to this the strange circumstances on the Adriatic, [the] latent opposition to Austria. The new Italy has so far always done its business through the victories of others.[247]

While Pollio was held in high esteem by the German military, the Italian army was not regarded very favourably. In April 1914, Major von Kleist's estimation of the alliance partner's military power was dismissive:

In my opinion one can hardly expect more loyal views towards the Triple Alliance, or more initiative, from Pollio. He really is a clever man and a soldier. However, what his troops will achieve on the day is a different question, because, in my opinion and according to our views, and to stress it once more at the end of my stay here, the Italian army can do 'nothing'.[248]

In May 1914 members of the Italian General Staff visited Berlin, and an agreement was reached that Italy would provide two army corps and three cavalry divisions to support Germany in Alsace. Although the mobilization plan of spring 1914 no longer reckoned with Italian help and Moltke had told Conrad that Germany and Austria-Hungary must begin war without relying on the Italian ally, following the meeting in May 1914 the General Staff began again to hope that it could count on Italy's support.[249] The Kaiser and Bethmann Hollweg also believed that Italy could be relied upon.[250] That Moltke had at least hoped for Italian support is confirmed by his bitter words of November 1914 when he outlined that the Triple Alliance had failed because Italy had not honoured her agreement. Referring to the talks of 1914, he recalled:

these arrangements had been made so clearly and bindingly that there could hardly be any doubt regarding Italy's fidelity to the alliance. . . . Despite this Italy broke her word. She declared her neutrality and indifferently broke all

[247] BA-MA, w-10/50276, Waldersee's memorandum, May 1914, 'Die Militärpolitische Lage Deutschlands', pp. 35–36. See also Waldersee, 'Deutschlands militär-politische Beziehungen', p. 646. Kluck shared this positive assessment of both Pollio and his successor Cadorna. In his opinion the Italian General Staff had always been true to its alliance obligations, but the Italian Government had let Germany down: *Wanderjahre*, pp. 163–164.

[248] BA-MA, PH3/528, 'Denkschriften über England, das englische Expeditionskorps, Belgien und Italien, Denkschrift über Italien', 15 April 1914.

[249] BA-MA, w-10/51063, Post-war memorandum, Mewes. For a different view, see Tappen's letter to the Reichsarchiv of 31 March 1925: 'In my opinion one should not estimate the intended use of Italians on the left army wing very highly. For a start there was very little confidence that the Italians would actually arrive. Our deployment preparations did not count on this at all, so as to not experience any disappointment' (BA-MA, NL Tappen, N56/3).

[250] Statement issued to Berchtold by Wilhelm II and Bethmann, quoted in Leo Valiani, 'Verhandlungen zwischen Italien und Österreich-Ungarn, 1914–1915', in Wolfgang Schieder (ed.), *Erster Weltkrieg. Ursachen, Entstehung und Kriegsziele*, Cologne and Berlin 1969.

contracts. A more miserable breaking of a promise is perhaps not to be found in history.[251]

Pollio's influence was regarded as crucial, but there was awareness in Berlin that his influence had limitations. Pollio and Moltke had developed a more trusting relationship as a result of their private correspondence, during which the former had complained to his German counterpart that his government did not co-operate with him and left him in the dark about its policies. Ironically, he added that he was certain that Moltke did not have to contend with such adversities, speculating 'that that is much better in your wonderfully militarily organized country'. Moltke commented dryly in the margin: 'Unfortunately not!'[252]

The sense of urgency among the military decision-makers must have been greatly increased when the pro-German Pollio died on 28 June 1914, the very day of the assassination at Sarajevo.[253] His successor, General Luigi Cadorna, did not take office until 27 July. During the crucial weeks of July 1914, Italy was without a Chief of the General Staff. It was also at this crucial time that the trusted and experienced attaché Kleist was replaced. Moltke unsuccessfully protested against this decision by the Military Cabinet. Kleist was very well respected in Rome and was sorely missed during the July Crisis.[254] There was no telling what the future would bring in terms of the alliance with Italy. The feeling of 'now or never' was certainly increased by the news of Pollio's death, as it was feared that the Italian military under a new Chief of Staff might, in the long run, prove increasingly unreliable. In the event, Cadorna wanted to dispatch troops to Germany on 31 July, but was prevented by the King's order and Italy's declaration of neutrality.[255] On 2 August, Wenninger reported from Berlin on Italy's 'treachery'. Within the General Staff Pollio's death was widely regretted, as it was thought he would have opposed Italy's decision to stay neutral 'with full force'. The general feeling of betrayal led Wenninger to conclude: 'This much is certain: whether Italy now participates or not, the current war will be followed by an Austro-Italian war.'[256]

Rumania, too, had become a dubious ally by 1914, not least because

[251] Moltke, 'Betrachtungen und Erinnerungen', November 1914, in *Erinnerungen*, p. 9.

[252] Förster, 'Deutsch-italienische Militärkonvention', pp. 402ff.

[253] Ropponen, *Italien als Verbündeter*, p. 138, gives Pollio's death as 1 July. Waldersee mistakenly claims that Pollio died one week after the assassination ('Deutschlands militär-politische Beziehungen', p. 661).   [254] Ibid., p. 662.   [255] Joll, *Origins*, pp. 87–88.

[256] BayHSTA-KA, MKr 1765, No. 2720, Report No. 9, 2 August 1914.

Austria had preferred to establish more friendly relations with Bulgaria instead, as Moltke complained to Conrad on 13 March 1914:

I regret again and again that Austria swapped this reliable and valuable ally for a doubtful and weakened Bulgaria. I can assure Your Excellency that everything is being done from here to keep Rumania with the Triple Alliance. I neglect no opportunity to point out the importance of this matter to our Auswärtiges Amt, which also clearly recognizes it.[257]

In his memorandum of May 1914, Waldersee addressed the problematic relations with Rumania. He feared that there were a number of indications that Rumania was no longer a certain ally. He blamed Austria's policy for this, as well as the lure of the rouble and the franc. At the moment, the King was still professing his friendship to Germany, but Waldersee wondered how long he would be able to get support for his views. His vision of the future regarding Rumania was pessimistic: 'For the time being this country, which knows how to lie in wait, will in the best case be neutral. Whether [this will be the case] for much longer? It is very much to be doubted.'[258]

With Turkey relations had been amicable, and Germany's military decision-makers expected that she would side with them in a future war, especially as Turkey had trusted them with the reorganization of her army after 1913. Any hope that Turkey might prove an effective military alliance partner in a future war had, however, been shattered by that country's defeat in the Balkan War. Moltke summed up the current military thinking in March 1914:

Militarily, Turkey is nothing! The reports of our military mission sound positively hopeless. The army is in a condition that beggars description. If in the past one talked about Turkey as a sick man, then one now has to talk of a dying one. He no longer has any strength to live and is in a state of agony from which he cannot be saved. Our military mission equals that of a team of doctors who stand around the dying bed of an incurably sick man.[259]

In April 1914, General Liman von Sanders reported from Turkey that the army was in an abysmal state, 'one that would with absolute certainty lead to a quick military collapse in the event of war'. Based on these reports from the Chief of the German Military Mission, Moltke wrote

---

[257] Conrad, *Dienstzeit*, vol. 3, pp. 611–612. Only a year earlier he had recommended that Austria should try to cultivate relations with Bulgaria – obviously he did not intend this to be to the detriment of Austro-Rumanian relations. Note also the mention of co-operation between the General Staff and the Auswärtiges Amt in this document.

[258] Quoted in BA-MA, w-10/50276, 'Die Militärpolitische Lage Deutschlands', p. 38.

[259] Moltke to Conrad, 13 March 1914, *Dienstzeit*, vol. 3, p. 612. On the estimates of Turkish fighting power, see also Wallach, *Anatomie einer Militärhilfe*, p. 150.

in a memorandum of 18 May 1914: 'To count on Turkey in the near future as of benefit to the Triple Alliance or Germany must be regarded as completely mistaken.'[260] Turkey's importance would be primarily strategic, rather than in terms of her military abilities, especially if Britain became involved in the war.

In 1914, it must have seemed to Moltke as if time was running out for Germany's ability to rely on her 'lesser' alliance partners, adding yet further pressure to the General Staff's desire for a war 'the sooner the better'. At the same time, it seemed certain that Britain would be a future enemy. France, and in particular Russia, were increasing their armies to an alarming degree. Russia's 'Great Programme' of rearmament passed the Duma in June 1914; it would have expanded the standing army by 400,000 men by 1917, an increase equivalent to half of Germany's total 1913 strength, in addition to extensive technical improvements.[261] Even tiny Belgium would soon be a force to reckon with, following her planned army increases. Germany's own allies were becoming increasingly unreliable and might leave Germany isolated. This knowledge influenced Moltke's increasingly vociferous advocating of war. In May or June 1914, Moltke had a revealing conversation with the Foreign Secretary, Gottlieb von Jagow, in which he outlined his fears, particularly of Russia, who would complete her armaments programme in the next two to three years:

> The military superiority of our enemies would then be so great that he [Moltke] did not know how we could overcome them. Today we were still a match for them. In his opinion there was no alternative to making preventive war in order to defeat the enemy while we still stand a chance of victory. The Chief of the General Staff therefore proposed that I should conduct a policy with the aim of provoking a war in the near future.[262]

Already in the spring of 1914, Moltke had a discussion with the Bavarian military plenipotentiary in Berlin, Wenninger, in which he explained that 'the military situation is from the military point of view favourable to a degree which cannot occur again in the foreseeable future'.[263] Similarly, Hugo Count von Lerchenfeld-Koefering, the Bavarian envoy in Berlin, recalled a discussion with Bethmann in early June 1914:

---

[260] Both Moltke and Liman von Sanders quoted in Carl Mühlmann, 'Das deutsch-türkische Bündnis im Weltkriege', 1940, BA-MA, w-10/50/323, pp. 4–5. See also Wallach, *Anatomie einer Militärhilfe*, p. 151.   [261] Herrmann, *Arming*, p. 205.

[262] Quoted in Egmont Zechlin, 'Motive und Taktik der Reichsleitung 1914', *Der Monat*, 209, February 1966. English Translation in John C. G. Röhl (ed.), *From Bismarck to Hitler, The Problem of Continuity in German History*, London 1970, p. 70.

[263] Quote from Luigi Albertini, *The Origins of the War of 1914*, 3 vols., London 1952–1957, vol. 2, p. 487.

The discussion then moved on to the preventive war that many military men are demanding. I expressed the point of view that the right moment for it had already been missed. The Chancellor confirmed this by identifying the military situation in the year 1905 as the one that would have offered us the greatest chances. But the Kaiser had not waged a preventive war [then] and will not wage one [in the future].[264]

From a military point of view, the assassination of the Austrian Archduke on 28 June 1914 and the ensuing international diplomatic crisis could not have come at a better time. It was not only the military that were concerned about the future development of Germany's potential enemies, and of Russia in particular. In June 1914, Bethmann Hollweg did not think that France wanted a war, but he feared the eastern neighbour: 'Russia was more dangerous. There, the Slav non-sense (*Slawentaumel*) could corrupt heads in such a way that Russia might one day commit a foolish act.'[265] That both the Chancellor and Zimmermann were afraid of the future in terms of Russian military increases was noted by Karl Max von Lichnowsky, who spoke with both men at the end of June 1914. Bethmann 'complained about the Russian armaments' and did not share Lichnowsky's optimism about what the future might bring, and Zimmermann expressed his discontent with Russia when he told the ambassador that Russia was about to increase her army by 900,000 men.[266] According to Waldersee's recollections of the pre-war months, there had been a heightened sense of tension, suggesting, again, that the Sarajevo incident happened at just the right time. In September 1914, Waldersee recalled: 'Since the beginning of the year I had been in [a state of] intense activity and in constant touch with the Auswärtiges Amt. During . . . Moltke's stay in Karlsbad in April/May and in July I was his deputy and I corresponded with him constantly.'[267]

Not surprisingly, given the increasing tension that was building up in

[264] Lechenfeld to Hertling, 4 June 1914, in Ernst Deuerlein (ed.), *Briefwechsel Hertling–Lerchenfeld 1912–1917. Dienstliche Privatkorrespondenz zwischen dem bayerischen Ministerpräsidenten Georg Graf v. Hertling und dem bayerischen Gesandten in Berlin Hugo Graf von und zu Lerchenfeld*, 2 vols., Boppard/Rhein 1973, doc. 97, p. 295.   [265] Ibid.

[266] Karl Marx Fürst von Lichnowsky, *Meine Londoner Mission 1912–1914*, Berlin 1919, p. 27.

[267] BA-MA, w-10/51032, p. 9. In April 1914 Moltke was showing signs of the illness that was seriously to impair his work once war had broken out. He went to Carlsbad for four weeks on 15 April 1914, apparently suffering from bronchitis. See Moltke's letter to his niece Marie, 5 April 1914, BA-MA, N78/41; letter to Conrad, 20 April 1914, in Conrad, *Dienstzeit*, vol. 3, p. 667. Conrad visited Moltke in Carlsbad on 12 May; it was their last ever meeting. On this occasion, Moltke famously replied to Conrad's anxious enquiry as to what would happen if success in the West could not be achieved quickly: 'Yes, I will do what I can. We are not superior to the French.' Ibid., pp. 669ff.

Europe, Colonel Edward House, the American special envoy to London, reported on 29 May 1914 from Berlin: 'The situation is extraordinary. It is militarism run stark mad. Unless someone acting for you [i.e. the American President] can bring about a different understanding, there is some day to be an awful cataclysm.'[268]

The assassination of Franz Ferdinand at Sarajevo just a few weeks later provided the trigger for that cataclysm. In the last weeks of peace, military concerns increasingly began to dominate and finally to dictate political decision-making to ensure that the July Crisis would be the final pre-war crisis.

THE CONTINUING DEBATE ON ARMY INCREASES IN THE LAST MONTHS OF PEACE

Moltke continued to advocate army increases after Ludendorff's dismissal, and the debate on army increases continued right into July 1914. He does not seem to have feared suffering the same fate as Ludendorff – or Conrad, for that matter, who had also been dismissed in December 1911 for advocating army increases (although he was reinstated in December 1912). In view of probable French plans to return to a three-year term of military service, Moltke urged the Chancellor on 1 March 1913 to reconsider whether it was not possible to create at least one new army corps. On 5 March, he extended his demand, upon the news that Russia planned the creation of three or four new army corps, asking 'whether it were not essential to proceed to an *immediate* execution of his programme, which, in addition to a further increase in the peace-time budget, should achieve three further new army corps'.[269] Moltke considered this a minimum demand, but his pleas went unheeded. The army bill of 3 July 1913, the last peace-time *Wehrvorlage*, was the largest in German history, coming on the back of the 1911 *Quinquennat* and the modest increases of 1912. Financed with the help of substantial new taxes (especially the introduction of direct Reich taxes), it amounted to a militarization of the Reich's finance policy.[270] It legislated for an

[268] Edward House, *The Intimate Papers of Colonel House*, 2 vols., London 1926, vol. I, *Behind the Political Curtain, 1912–1915*, pp. 254ff.

[269] BA-MA, W-10/50276, 'Die Militärpolitische Lage Deutschlands', pp. 44–45. For the debates on army increases see also Förster, *Der Doppelte Militarismus*, passim.

[270] Herrmann, *Arming*, p. 190; Förster, *Der doppelte Militarismus*, p. 272. The problem of finance is discussed in Witt, *Die Finanzpolitik*, pp. 356ff. See also Volker Hentschel, *Deutsche Wirtschafts- und Sozialpolitik 1815–1945*, Düsseldorf 1980, pp. 29ff. Before the introduction of direct Reich taxes any direct taxes had gone to the federal states, while indirect taxes and duties went to the Reich. See Dieter Hertz-Eichenrode, *Deutsche Geschichte 1890–1918. Das Kaiserreich in der Wilhelminischen Zeit*, Stuttgart, 1996.

increase to the peace-time army of 117,000 soldiers, 15,000 NCOs and 5000 officers. Half of these were to be recruited by 1 October of that year. As this did not meet General Staff demand for more than 300,000 troops, Moltke continued to exert pressure over the next months. He advocated calling the same percentage of men to arms as neighbouring France, which would have resulted in an increase of approximately 300,000 men. However, the Minister of War still feared for the inner unity of the army if it were suddenly increased by such large numbers, and the Kaiser agreed with him.[271]

According to Tappen, Moltke discussed with him his options in the face of the denial of his demands. It was Tappen's opinion that Moltke could not remain in his position, now that his requests, which he had clearly justified as being essential for the conduct of a successful war, had been denied. However, according to Tappen, Moltke did not offer to resign over the issue of army increases. He remarked with scarcely hidden criticism that Moltke 'wanted to serve his country in his responsible position as long as this was possible for him'.[272] The issue of Moltke's resignation had been raised on at least one earlier occasion, when the *Berliner Tageblatt* of 14 January 1913 referred to Moltke's forthcoming resignation, which it claimed had been announced in the previous autumn. According to the paper, he was to be replaced by Generalleutnant von Gündell, commander of the Twentieth Division in Hanover. In a report of the same day, Wenninger explained to his superior in Munich that there was no truth behind this news: 'Excellency von Moltke is not contemplating resignation . . . in any way. Generalleutnant v. Gündell is said to be retiring soon.'[273] Whatever the circumstances behind this, the evidence suggests that there was talk of a resignation of the Chief of the General Staff at the end of 1912. If Moltke actually contemplated and then discounted a resignation over the important issue of army increases, he must have felt that he would still be able to carry out his duties under the given circumstances. Rather than resign, he continued to push for army increases.

In May 1914 Moltke had an audience with the Kaiser in which he attempted to convince the monarch of the need to introduce actual universal conscription. In his memorandum written for this meeting, he summarized the military developments that had recently occurred in France and Russia, painting a gloomy picture:

[271] Reichsarchiv, *Der Weltkrieg 1914–1918*, vol. 1, p. 15.
[272] Tappen, 'Kriegserinnerungen', BA-MA, w-10/50661, p. 2.
[273] *Berliner Tageblatt*, 14 January 1913; Wenninger to the Bavarian Minister of War, 14 January 1913, BayHSTA-KA, MKr 42.

France has introduced the three-year term of service and deployed a new army corps, Russia 3½ and 4½ years' service under deployment of four to five new army corps. At the same time Russia is in the process of improving her entire army from the bottom up, to an incredible extent.

Added worries were the changing circumstances in the Balkans. Moltke argued that Rumania was no longer a reliable ally. It was likely that she would be found in the ranks of Germany's opponents in a future war. This would have grave consequences, as it would tie up Austrian forces in the Balkans that would otherwise have been available for deployment against Russia. Austria would then not be able to launch an offensive against Russia, thus seriously jeopardizing Germany's strategy:

> Therefore we must be aware that the offensive of almost the entire Russian army will be directed against our forces which remain in the East – to be precise, a Russian army which will, from about 1917 onwards, probably already be fully fitted out and equipped in everything in a modern way, and which will be able to cross the border in the shortest time, under certain circumstances even without a previous declaration of war, thanks to its 3½ and 4½ years' service. We must not close our eyes to these facts which are so unfavourable for us!

This nightmare scenario would, of course, threaten the success of the German deployment plan. Moltke urged that the potential threats of French and Russian army increases should not be underestimated, and advocated a properly implemented full conscription of all Germans as a way of tackling the problem. His vision of what was at stake in a future war was made plain: 'There cannot be any more serious doubt about the fact that a future war will be about the existence (*Sein oder Nichtsein*) of the German people.'[274]

Not only Moltke's strong Social Darwinist convictions, but also his fear of Russia's future potential, are impressively highlighted in this memorandum. His only answer to the changing circumstances were repeated demands for more troops, never a change of strategy. More and more German troops were to oppose increasing numbers of enemy troops, while time was quickly running out for the Schlieffen/Moltke Plan. The fact that time would be needed to train and equip the new recruits made Moltke's demands all the more urgent. If Germany were to be ready by 1916/1917 to counter a numerically superior army, then the new recruits were needed straight away. Immediately after an army increase, the German army would effectively be weaker than before;

---

[274] BA-MA, w-10/50279, doc. 95, 'Entwurf eines Schreibens des Chefs des Generalstabs an den Reichskanzler'.

only in time, after training and new equipment, would an army increase actually spell an extension in fighting power.

Waldersee reiterated Moltke's points in a memorandum written in May 1914.[275] Despite the fact that Germany had only recently enjoyed considerable army increases, she should be under no illusions about her precarious situation. Waldersee urged that Germany needed to employ all her potential,

> unless she wants to buy peace whatever the cost. The main burden in a future war will rest on her, on her alone. Our opponents are intelligent enough to realize that only the defeat of Germany will clear a free path for them. Our geographic position is conducive to a simultaneous attack in the front and the rear.
>
> It will be historically indefensible if [the German army] does not attempt everything in order to prevent such a situation. We cannot therefore avoid the necessity of implementing general conscription.

Waldersee pointed out that France had already achieved this by introducing three-year military service, and that Russia would soon achieve a peace-time strength of one and a half million men. Waldersee feared that future generations might accuse those responsible for not having attempted everything in their power to prevent Germany's decline, and he also hinted that war might cease to be a policy-making option if Germany failed to upgrade her army in line with her enemies:

> German diplomats should realize that the successful continuation of their policy by the army can be possible only if the latter is put in a position where it can defend itself to some extent against an enormous, superior power. Otherwise it would be adviseable to revise the policy. What the result of that might be for the German Reich at the present moment is, however, doubtful.

Waldersee was clearly under the impression that the politicians ultimately wanted to do just that: to continue their policy with the help of the army. He was not suggesting, of course, that the politicians should be alerted to the flimsy basis for their bellicose foreign policy.

The memorandum is interesting not just because it confirms that the General Staff believed a war would come in the near future, and for its insistence on further army increases to ensure that Germany would be strong enough to fight successfully, but also because of Waldersee's

---

[275] 'Denkschrift über Deutschlands militärische Lage, Mai 1914'. Although this memorandum can be found in the files of the Reichsarchiv, BA-MA, w-10/50279, doc. No 94, it was not published in the *Anlagen* volume and has therefore only recently come to light. See also John Röhl's essay 'Germany', pp. 44ff. Excerpts from Waldersee's memorandum also in 'Urkunden des deutschen Generalstabs über die militärpolitische Lage vor dem Kriege', BA-MA, RM5 2651, Microfiche 7, pp. 370ff., 'Drucksache Nr. 32 der Geschäftsstelle für die Friedensverhandlungen des Auswärtigen Amtes'; and in BA-MA, w-10/50276, 'Die Militärpolitische Lage Deutschlands'.

forecast of the situation in the summer of 1914. At that point in time, he felt, Germany's opponents would not want to begin hostilities. 'On the contrary', he asserted, 'at the moment none of the main participants could gain anything from bringing about a war.' France was still coming to terms with the recent intake of two years of young recruits to the army; Russia had still not completed her armaments programme; Britain was preoccupied with the Irish question; the Balkans were unstable; Rumania's attitude was still unclear (but Waldersee felt certain that in future Germany's enemies would win her over); Italy was still a reasonably reliable ally, although one could not be certain for how long. Waldersee came to a logical conclusion – the time was right for Germany to engage in armed conflict feeling reasonably confident of victory:

> From these considerations it can be deduced that Germany will not have to endure an attack in the immediate future in the normal course of events; on the other hand, she not only has no reason to avoid a conflict whatever the situation, rather, the prospects for coming out of a great European war quickly and victoriously are today still very favourable for Germany and also for the Triple Alliance. Soon this will no longer be the case.

The international crisis caused by the assassination of the Austrian Archduke Franz Ferdinand occurred at a perfect point in time, as far as the military decision-makers were concerned. In the light of the recent revelations about secret Anglo-Russian negotiations on a naval agreement, Germany's complete 'encirclement' seemed unavoidable in future.[276]

Despite the concerns voiced by Moltke, the Minister of War still opposed further General Staff demands. On 8 July 1914, Falkenhayn expressed his view on the increased demands in a letter to Bethmann Hollweg (of which the General Staff received a copy). Actual general conscription he envisaged no earlier than 1916. Falkenhayn felt 'that the army absolutely needed a period of quiet in order to come to terms with the big army bill of 1913'.[277] Because the Russians could always exceed any increase in manpower that Germany might make, it was important that the quality of the available troops was upheld, Falkenhayn argued. New troops would have to be absorbed, new equipment and weapons were needed for the new recruits. He advocated postponing further increases until 1916.

---

[276] For details see Manfred Rauh, 'Die britisch-russische Marinekonvention von 1914 und der Ausbruch des Ersten Weltkriegs', *MGM*, 41, 1987.

[277] BA-MA, w-10/50279, doc. 96, 'Der Kriegsminister an den Reichskanzler'.

Moltke responded with a letter to the Chancellor of 18 July 1914, in which he commented on Falkenhayn's objections. He was unconvinced that the army really needed time to recover from the previous increase, which had in any case been insufficient and had not fulfilled his demands. He was not prepared to accept that financial limitations should restrict further increases:

The ceaseless attempts of our opponents to complete their armaments, [and] their more or less hidden and hinted at warlike intentions for the year 1916 do not allow us, in my opinion, just to make do with the results of 'the big army bill of 1913'. . . . And how times have changed to our misfortune since that time! The army bills of our neighbours are <u>considerably</u> larger. . . . What is possible in Russia and France will not be difficult for us. In duty bound, I must insist that a postponement of such an important and decisive measure until the autumn of 1916 is not permissible.

By 1916 it would indeed be too late, if further time were then needed for the quantitative increase to become a qualitative improvement. By then, Russia and France would have a dangerous head start, and Germany's position would be precarious vis-à-vis her enemies. Convinced of the urgency of the situation, and with the knowledge that his strategic plan depended on deploying as many troops as possible, Moltke conjured up images of the detrimental effects of a lost war. In the light of this future scenario, he was convinced that it would be possible to secure popular support for army increases. His emotional plea continued:

According to the address of the Minister of War in the Reichstag on 5 May of this year, 38,000 completely fit men who could not be trained were left over in the year 1913. In 1914 it will probably be more than 40,000 men who will again not be trained. <u>That is more than the strength of the fighting troops of an army corps being lost uselessly to us *annually*</u>. It will not be difficult to make plain even to the widest classes of the German people that we cannot afford to do without our military capacity (*Wehrfähigkeit*) under the current circumstances. The necessary financial means which are – as far as I am informed – available in abundance in the country and must be found. I need only point here to the incredible sums which are being spent by the German people every year on luxuries such as drink and tobacco. In any case the question of money must in my opinion not hinder us from executing immediately a measure that is considered essential for the security of the Reich. The burden that would fall on the people after a lost war cannot be imagined.[278]

[278] BA-MA, w-10/50279, doc. 97, 'Der Chef des Generalstabes der Armee an den Reichskanzler' (Entwurf von der Hand des Oberstleutnants Tappen)'. Michael Geyer, *Deutsche Rüstungspolitik 1860–1980*, Frankfurt/M. 1984, p. 92, shows that by 1914 the General Staff had finally asserted itself vis-à-vis the Ministry of War. Peter-Christian Witt even refers to a 'militarization' of the Reich's financial policy (*Die Finanzpolitik*, p. 356), although of course the amount spent on army increases

It was Falkenhayn's turn to reply to Moltke. He considered it out of the question that the Reichstag, or for that matter the Bundesrat, would grant the necessary finance for a further army bill at the present moment. Falkenhayn thought a break in the army increases advisable not only for reasons relating to the inner strength of the army, but also to safeguard the army's credibility among the people. After all, he argued, they had been told that the last army law would guarantee Germany's needs for the foreseeable future. If a new one were to be advocated straight away, the German population might lose faith in the army leadership. Falkenhayn did not consider a further increase of approximately one army corps to be essential, or even beneficial for Germany's army:

Such a small increase (of our peace-time strength by 30–40,000 men) will not deter our opponents from striking in the spring of 1916 if, as Your Excellency's hints suggest, they are determined to do so, and would give us only a small advantage in case of war compared to the disadvantages described above.

Falkenhayn's sarcastic tone suggests that he did not perhaps share Moltke's vision of an attack by Russia in the future; indeed, Falkenhayn saw Germany's real enemy not in the East, but in Britain, a fact that would be reflected by his actions as Chief of the General Staff during the war. If the situation were really as precarious as Moltke believed, then Falkenhayn did not consider the additional recruitment of 35,000 men in the autumn of 1915 sufficient preparation. Rather, he went as far as to recommend preventive war. 'It is not my place to express, without being requested to do so, my opinion on the question whether in such a case an immediate action from our side would not be preferable to awaiting the threatened attack.'[279]

Thus, both within the Ministry of War and the General Staff, the top military leaders shared the belief that the time was right for war in the summer of 1914. Yet, even while the July Crisis was unfolding, military planners still kept an eye to the future, quarrelling over army increases

---

footnote 278 (*cont.*)
    was never sufficient as far as the General Staff was concerned. Niall Ferguson argues that economically Germany would have been able to increase her military expenditure (an argument that echoes Moltke's desperate demands in this memorandum), but that it was impossible for political reasons. In Ferguson's opinion, this indicates that the strength of militarism in Germany has been overestimated. He further argues that increased spending on armaments, 'far from causing the First World War, might have averted it', by allaying the Germans' fears over their perceived encirclement. The evidence cited in this study, however, reveals such a pronounced desire for war on the part of Germany's military leaders that increased spending would only have made them more confident and bellicose, and hence precipitated war even sooner. See *Pity of War*, pp. 141–142.
[279] Falkenhayn's letter of July 1914 (no exact date, but written in response to Moltke's letter of 18 July), quoted in BA-MA, w-10/50276, 'Die Militärpolitische Lage Deutschlands', pp. 54–56.

that would only take effect in 1915 or even 1916. How can this apparent contradiction be explained? Given the real fear that Moltke felt about Russia's future potential, and given the many occasions in the past when the military had considered the opportunity for a strike to be present, but the civilians had preferred to pursue a more peaceful policy, there could be no certainty that a war could be provoked before Germany's enemies were ready. Until the very last days of the crisis, the military decision-makers did not trust the civilian decision-makers and the Kaiser to see things through to the end, and they had no reason to believe that this crisis would not like all previous ones, be resolved peacefully.[280] Falkenhayn's suggestion of 'immediate action' must, however, be taken seriously in the context of the current crisis, which offered an opportunity that might not present itself again in the foreseeable future. The importance of the debate on further army increases, so soon before the outbreak of war, lies in the way it confirms Moltke's concerns about what the future would hold – worries that no doubt influenced Wilhelm II and the Chancellor, too, in their decision-making during the July Crisis.

It was becoming painfully obvious to Moltke that his demands for army increases would not be complied with in the immediate future. Falkenhayn was deferring decisions until as late as 1916. To Moltke, who was convinced of the increasing invincibility of Russia, the years 1916/1917 appeared to be the turning point after which Germany would no longer be able to defeat Russia, especially if Germany were to delay her next army increases until 1916. Moltke's attitude in the July Crisis was thus not only a logical continuation of his previous demands for war 'sooner rather than later', but must also be seen against the background of the continuing arguments over army increases. Moltke could be relatively certain that no further army increases would be possible in the immediate future. Against this background, July 1914 was probably the last chance of engaging Germany's future opponents in a war under still relatively favourable circumstances. Another Balkan crisis, providing a suitable *casus belli*, might not occur before 1916. Moltke's resolve in the crucial days of July stemmed at least partly from his growing awareness of the future limitations of Germany's military power, and was a direct result of the arguments between the Minister of War and the Chief of the General Staff. The debate over army increases is thus crucial background to understanding Moltke's decision-making during the July Crisis.[281]

---

[280] See Chapter 4.
[281] Granier, 'Deutsche Rüstungspolitik', pp. 129 130. argues that Moltke's pessimism may have influenced the Kaiser and Bethmann, but that the arguments over general conscription between Moltke and Falkenhayn had no practical results.

CHAPTER FOUR

The July Crisis and the outbreak of war: the German perspective

[Germany] not only has <u>no</u> reason to avoid a conflict whatever the situation but <u>rather</u>, the prospects for coming through a great European war quickly and victoriously are <u>today</u> still very favourable for Germany and also for the Triple Alliance. Soon this will no longer be the case.

Georg von Waldersee, May 1914[1]

If only things would finally boil over – we are ready; the sooner, the better for us.

Helmuth von Moltke, June 1914[2]

The assassination of the Austrian Archduke Franz Ferdinand and his wife Sophie on 28 June 1914 provided a perfect pretext for provoking the war that so many German decision-makers had eagerly awaited. The Balkan crisis that resulted from it would ensure Austria's involvement on Germany's side if a major conflict ensued. Research into the July Crisis has established that the decision to use the assassination of the Archduke, supposedly by Serbian-controlled terrorists, as an opportunity for settling Austria's Balkan problems was arrived at as much in Berlin as in Vienna. What is more, Germany encouraged Austrian resolve to punish the Serbs, who were held responsible for the assassination, and put extensive pressure on her ally to provoke a conflict with Serbia. The risk of such a conflict escalating into a European war, if Russia decided to back Serbia and alliance obligations then forced France (and Britain) to become involved, was willingly taken in Berlin and Vienna.[3] By the end of July, however, their interests differed. While

---

[1] BA-MA, w-10/50279, May 1914, 'Denkschrift über Deutschlands militärische Lage', doc. no. 94.

[2] Moltke to Hermann von Eckardstein, conversation on 1 June 1914, in Hermann Frhr. von Eckardstein, *Lebenserinnerungen und politische Denkwürdigkeiten*, Leipzig 1921, vol. 3, p. 184.

[3] The events of the July Crisis have, of course, been the subject of numerous investigations. For further information on the diplomatic events see in particular Imanuel Geiss (ed.), *Julikrise und Kriegsausbruch*, 2 vols., Hanover 1963/1964, also the abridged English edition *July 1914. The*

Erzherzog Franz Ferdinand v. Oesterreich nebst Gemahlin
† 28. Juni 1914.

7 Archduke Franz Ferdinand and his wife Sophie, assassinated at Sarajevo on 28 June
1914; postcard *c.* 1914

Austria-Hungary still wanted to punish the Serbs, Germany, by virtue of
her military plans, wanted to begin hostilities against France and Russia.
Serbia was considered of secondary importance.

Most studies of German decision-making during July 1914 emphasize
the activities of the Chancellor and his diplomatic aides in the
Auswärtiges Amt, rather than military decision-making.[4] The military

Outbreak of the First World War. Selected Documents, London 1967; Fischer, *Illusionen*; Albertini, *Origins*;
Fritz Klein (ed.), *Deutschland im Ersten Weltkrieg*, vol. 1, *Vorbereitung, Entfesselung und Verlauf des Krieges
bis Ende 1914*, (East) Berlin, 1968, pp. 209ff; Joll, *Origins*; Wilson (ed.), *Decisions for War 1914*;
Stevenson, *Armaments*, pp. 366ff. John W. Langdon, *July 1914. The Long Debate 1918–1990*, New
York and Oxford 1991, provides an overview of the debate on July 1914. For a recent summary
see David Stevenson, *The Outbreak of the First World War, 1914 in Perspective*, London 1997. On
Austria-Hungary's desire for war in 1914, see Günther Kronenbitter, '"Nur los lassen!" Öster-
reich-Ungarn und der Wille zum Krieg', in J. Burkhardt *et al.* (eds.), *Lange und kurze Wege in den
Ersten Weltkrieg*, Munich 1996, pp. 159–187.

[4] There are some exceptions, e.g. Ritter's account of the July Crisis, *Staatskunst*, vol. 2, pp. 282ff.
His study is, however, too much motivated by his desire to exonerate Bethmann Hollweg in the
light of the first of Fritz Fischer's war-guilt allegations, by portraying the Chancellor as trying to
resist military pressure. Moreover, Ritter's study of 1960 is now very much out of date. L. C. F.
Turner, 'The Role of the General Staffs in July 1914', *The Australian Journal of Politics and History*,
11, 3 (1965), pp. 305–323 underestimates the involvement of the General Staff in the events of
July 1914, and Moltke's role in particular. Ulrich Trumpener's 'War Premeditated?' (*Central
European History*, 9, 1976) concentrates on the military during the July Crisis; Holger Afflerbach's
examination of the July Crisis highlights the actions of Falkenhayn and Moltke, and offers a re-
evaluation of the more common emphasis on the Wilhelmstrasse. Afflerbach's study is also
exceptional in demonstrating a much higher degree of involvement of the military in the decision-making of July 1914 than previously suspected: Afflerbach, *Falkenhayn*, pp. 147ff. See also

von Bethmann-Hollweg

8 Chancellor Theobald von Bethmann Hollweg, in military uniform, postcard *c.* 1916

leaders are often absent from such accounts, and indeed they were so quite literally, because most were away on holiday, keeping a deliberately low profile. Moltke, for example, spent four weeks in Karlsbad – his second stay at the spa that year. He arrived there on 28 June. The following chapter will show, however, that despite their absence, the military were both aware of the seriousness of the diplomatic crisis that was developing throughout July, and informed of events and of the decisions that were being taken in Berlin and Vienna. Until the Austrian ultimatum to Serbia was delivered, the key military decision-makers could afford to be absent from Berlin, and their return to the centre of decision-making was carefully timed to ensure that they had their say when it really mattered – once the ultimatum was delivered and it looked increasingly likely that the General Staff's hope for a war now, rather than later or never, would finally become reality.

To emphasize the military's role in the events of the July Crisis is not to suggest, however, that the civilian decision-makers were innocent victims of a military conspiracy. Some historians have too easily exonerated Bethmann Hollweg and the Auswärtiges Amt by stressing the General Staff's belligerence.[5] Blaming the military decision-makers in this way can easily serve as an alibi for the rest of the German government. Rather, the evidence suggests that, at different times in the crisis, decisions were predominantly made either by the civilians or the military. In early July, the Kaiser and Bethmann Hollweg opted to take the risk that a localized conflict between Austria and Serbia might escalate into a European war, basing their decision on the (largely military) fear that Germany's chances of victory would decrease as time went on, and on the assumption that Germany was still militarily superior at that point in time. In these early days, the military, while realizing the potential of the crisis, considered it to be no different from previous ones, and doubted both Austria's resolve and that of the Auswärtiges Amt in Berlin. Once events were developing, however, they did not want to miss the opportunity that the crisis offered. In the last days of July, when first the Kaiser and later Bethmann got 'cold feet', the military began to dominate decision-making as they pushed for mobilization as soon as possible, fearing that yet another change of heart might jeopardize their plans at the last minute.

footnote 4 (*cont.*)
Snyder, *The Ideology of the Offensive*; Ritter, 'Der Anteil der Militärs an der Kriegskatastrophe von 1914', *HZ*, 193, 1961, pp. 72–91; Marc Trachtenberg, 'The Coming of the First World War', in idem, *History and Strategy*, Princeton 1991; Annika Mombauer, 'A Reluctant Military Leader? Helmuth von Moltke and the July Crisis of 1914', *War in History*, 6, 4, 1999, pp. 417–446.
[5] See e.g. Ritter, *Staatskunst*, vol. 2.

This analysis of the July Crisis aims to identify the degree of influence of military decision-makers in the crisis management of 1914. A detailed study of the available evidence demonstrates a much higher degree of involvement of key military men than has previously been suspected. An examination of the July Crisis from the military point of view highlights quite strikingly the extent to which military concerns and arguments had become common currency, accepted by civilians and determining their decision-making. The tragic effects of the short-sighted and inadequate military planning of the pre-war years become apparent on the outbreak of war, as does the extent to which the dogmatic belief in the Schlieffen/Moltke Plan significantly reduced political and military options at the end of July.

There is a further important objective to this investigation – to address the apparent discrepancies between Moltke's continuous advocacy of war, 'the sooner the better', and his last-minute qualms when war was finally on the cards. Moltke's role in July 1914, and especially in the crucial last days of July, requires close examination. Holger Herwig maintains, in his recent study of the First World War, that the almost complete destruction of Moltke's papers 'precludes formal connection between Moltke's mind-set and the push for war in 1914'.[6] However, it is now possible to draw on a variety of materials, including many eye-witness accounts, that help shed light on his intentions, and to explain his actions in July and August 1914. Given the almost complete lack of personal papers, such accounts, many of which have only recently come to light in the records of the Reichsarchiv, help to fill some of the gaps in the primary material.[7]

MILITARY REACTIONS TO THE ASSASSINATION AT SARAJEVO

In the immediate aftermath of the assassination, Austria's readiness to take military action against Serbia and consciously to accept of the risk of war, and German willingness to support her in such a venture, were of major importance in determining the outcome of the ensuing crisis. In the early days of July, military commentators in Berlin emphasized what a good opportunity the current crisis represented, pointing in particular to Russia's relative unpreparedness. Thus the Saxon envoy in Berlin, Salza Lichtenau, reported back to Dresden: 'There is renewed pressure from the military for allowing things to drift towards war while

---

[6] Herwig, *First World War*, p. 45.
[7] The lack of primary source material is discussed in detail in the Introduction, pp. 6ff.

Russia is still unprepared, but I do not think that His Majesty the Kaiser will allow himself to be induced to do this.'[8]

The Saxon military attaché, Leuckart von Weissdorf, had further military insights to report to his Minister of War, Carlowitz. At the Archduke's memorial service he had discussed the current situation with Waldersee, Moltke's official deputy while the Chief of Staff was at Karlsbad. His impression was that Waldersee was conveying Moltke's views, too, and that both considered the current situation a good opportunity. 'In competent circles here [in Berlin]', Leuckart reported on 3 July,

the political situation is regarded as very serious – for us too. He [Waldersee] gave it as his opinion that we might become involved in a war from one day to another. Everything, he thinks, depends on what attitude Russia takes in the Austro-Serbian business. In any case the course of events is being closely watched by the Great General Staff. I had the impression that they would be pleased if war were to come about now. Conditions and prospects would never be better for us.[9]

The fact that the Kaiser-Wilhelm-Canal was finally ready for Dreadnoughts to pass through – one of the conditions that Tirpitz raised in December 1912 – was another reason why the crisis of July 1914 provided such a good opportunity. Admiral Hopman informed Tirpitz on 24 July that the attempt was being made to have S.M.S. *Kaiserin* pass through it. The Canal was not yet ready for fully loaded ships, but safe up to a draught of 8.5 metres.[10]

Moltke and Waldersee were aware of the potential dangers that the current crisis posed, although to them it seemed to present an opportunity, rather than a threat. There was nothing as yet to distinguish this crisis from earlier ones; just as on previous occasions, the General Staff was quick to point out the apparent advantages that the crisis offered,

---

[8] Salza Lichtenau to Vitzthum, 2 July 1914, Geiss, *Julikrise 1914*, doc. 12.   [9] Ibid., doc. 15.
[10] Berghahn and Deist, 'Kaiserliche Marine', doc.13, p. 57; Röhl, 'Germany', pp. 5iff., note 51. The Kaiser passed through the Kiel Canal on *Hohenzollern* and declared the newly widened canal officially open on 24 June 1914. Müller, *Diary*, p. 29. See also a secret document entitled 'Maßnahmen die auf Grund verschiedener Besprechungen zwischen Vertretern des Reichs-Marine-Amts und Admiralstabes in den Tagen vom 6.-22. Juli 1914 vereinbart worden sind' (Measures taken following several discussions between 6 and 22 July 1914 between the Reich Navy Office and the Admiralty Staff), which charted as one measure to be undertaken 'ascertaining whether Kaiser-Wilhelm-Canal is now useable for big ships. Attempt to pass through it to be undertaken immediately,' and listed on 25 July: 'Attempt can take place. High Sea Fleet was telegraphically notified about this on 22/7 by the Reich Naval Office, with the addition that the attempt has to be undertaken straight away in view of the situation.' BA-MA, RM5/1615, p. 191.

while doubting that the Kaiser would ultimately see things through to the end. Another factor of uncertainty was Austria's resolve. Germany's military decision-makers were unaware of the determination in Vienna for a reckoning with Serbia.[11] That time was running out, and that the opportunity for war under favourable circumstances for Germany was better now than it was likely to be in an increasingly uncertain future was a much-emphasized argument of the General Staff during the July Crisis, as on previous occasions. It was a fear that Conrad also shared, telling Berchtold in March 1914 'that the reciprocal power-relation was slowly worsening for us, the longer the decision was being delayed'.[12]

With their constant worrying about Germany's future chances the military leaders exerted a direct influence on political decision-making. The General Staff's Cassandra cries had obviously not fallen entirely on deaf ears, for there were also subscribers among the political decision-makers to its increasingly desperate views regarding Germany's best future options. The German journalist Victor Naumann informed the Austrian diplomat Count Hoyos during a meeting on 1 July, that

there was great uneasiness in Berlin over Russian armaments and the test mobilization of considerable Russian forces, recently fixed for the autumn. He himself had observed that not only in army and navy circles, but also in the Foreign Ministry, the idea of a preventive war against Russia was regarded with less disapproval than a year ago.[13]

The Chancellor in particular seems to have been convinced by Moltke's argument that Russia posed a potential future threat and that Germany should therefore strike before it was too late. Lichnowsky was in no doubt about Moltke's detrimental effect on Bethmann's thinking, telling the journalist Theodor Wolff in September 1915: 'Moltke had wanted the war, perhaps also Falkenhayn. Moltke had been of the opinion "better now than in two years' time", and had influenced Bethmann.'[14] Bethmann's secretary Kurt Riezler recorded the

[11] See Kronenbitter, '"Nur los lassen!"', p. 167.
[12] Berchtold Memoirs, 12 March 1914, quoted in Leslie, 'Antecedents of Austria-Hungary's War Aims', p. 321, note 51. Conrad's was not the only voice advocating war against Serbia, as Kronenbitter shows ('"Nur los lassen!"', pp. 167ff.).
[13] Geiss, *Julikrise*, vol. 1, doc. 6, pp. 60ff. Victor Naumann had travelled to Vienna on 26 June, after a conversation with Wilhelm von Stumm at the Auswärtiges Amt. After the assassination, Naumann spoke to several Austrian statesmen, and must have regarded his views as being in accordance with those of the Auswärtiges Amt. See Fischer, *Illusionen*, p. 686.
[14] Theodor Wolff, *Tagebücher 1914–1919*, ed. Bernd Sösemann, 2 vols., Boppard/Rhein 1984, 10 September 1915, p. 284. See also 16 March 1915, p. 181: 'L[ichnowsky] says that Moltke had been among those who were primarily in favour of the war.'

Chancellor's fear quite strikingly, especially as he (Riezler) was surprised at the apparent seriousness of the situation, of which Riezler, as an outsider to actual decision-making, had not been aware. On 7 July, he noted: 'One does not get the secret news if one does not belong properly to the "guild" – and everything that is highly political and in addition of a military nature is "top secret".' Bethmann was concerned about the news of Anglo-Russian naval negotiations and Russia's increasing military potential, so frequently pointed out by Moltke in the pre-war years. In Bethmann's words, 'the future belongs to Russia, which is growing and growing and is becoming an increasingly burdensome nightmare for us'.[15] This was a nightmare that Moltke and the Chancellor shared, and a view that was echoed in the Auswärtiges Amt. In February 1915, Stumm remembered his own fears of the future in the days of July 1914, telling Wolff: 'If the war had not come then, then we would have had to wage it in two years' time under worse conditions.'[16] In 1917, shortly after his dismissal, Bethmann Hollweg made explicit the significant influence that military concerns had had over his decisions in 1914, when he told Conrad Haussmann:

Yes, by God, in a way it was a preventive war. But if war was in any case hovering above us; if it would have come in two years' time, but even more dangerously and even more unavoidably, and if the military leaders declared that then it was still possible without being defeated, in two years' time no longer! Yes, the military![17]

Later in the crisis, Bethmann returned to the Russian threat, as Riezler recorded on 20 July: 'Again the topic is the entire situation. Russia's increasing demands and amazing potential. In a few years no longer possible to fend off, especially if current European constellation remains.'[18] In the light of these perceived future threats, it is important to note that the military decision-makers considered in July 1914 that the enemy armies were not yet ready. In their eyes, this might make Russia and France more inclined to seek a diplomatic solution to the crisis, as the military attaché of Württemberg, Graevenitz, reported from Berlin: 'The general unreadiness in Russia and the damage exposed in France [following the revelations of Senator Humbert] would contribute

---

[15] Riezler, *Tagebücher*, 7 July 1914, pp. 181ff. On the debate about the authenticity of Riezler's diary, see Bernd-Felix Schulte, *Die Verfälschung der Riezler Tagebücher: Ein Beitrag zur Wissenschaftsgeschichte der 50er und 60er Jahre*, Frankfurt/M. 1985, Fritz Fischer, *Juli 1914: Wir sind nicht hineingeschlittert. Das Staatsgeheimnis um die Riezler-Tagebücher*, Reinbek 1983.

[16] Wolff, *Tagebücher*, 17 February 1915, p. 167.

[17] Quoted in Fischer, *Illusionen*, p. 671. Haussmann was member of the Reichstag for the Progressive People's Party.   [18] Riezler, *Tagebücher*, 20 July 1914, p. 187.

towards making the Russians and the French more inclined towards solving the matter in a diplomatic way.'[19]

Moreover, Austria's planned secret ultimatum kept her neighbours in the dark. The surprise was intended to ensure that France and Russia in particular would not be able to co-ordinate their response and might thus be less willing to go to war. If, however, war resulted from the crisis, then this would provide a good opportunity for Germany to defeat her enemies while they were still thought to be weak. This view had almost become common currency. Thus Lerchenfeld informed Hertling on 3 August that 'Germany has to pass a difficult test. . . . It is a consolation that we would never have been able to avoid that test and that it is better that we fight now than in a few years' time, when our enemies would have completed their armaments.'[20] In the early days of July, however, these thoughts were still peripheral. First there was a need to establish whether Austria-Hungary was determined to push for action against Serbia. Nothing could come of the crisis without the ally's resolve.

Both Moltke and Waldersee were away from Berlin, and could not be consulted by the Kaiser after Szögyény's fateful audience on 5 July, during which Wilhelm II had assured the Austrian ambassador of Germany's total support for any action Vienna might take against Serbia.[21] On 4 July Waldersee had gone to Hanover, where his aunt was critically ill,[22] and Moltke was in Karlsbad. Wilhelm spoke to those key advisers that were available: characteristically he consulted his military advisers first, namely the generals Plessen, Lyncker and Falkenhayn, as well as Captain Zenker of the Navy.[23] Then he met with Bethmann

---

[19] Graevenitz, 26 July 1914. A copy of this letter can be found in BA-MA, w-10/50890. See also Lerchenfeld to Hertling, 28 July 1914: 'Here, as well as in Vienna, the military are of the opinion that the Russian army is not yet ready' (Deuerlein, *Briefwechsel*, doc. 108, p. 316). (See footnote 44 below for the revelations of Senator Humbert.)

[20] Lerchenfeld to Hertling, 3 August 1914, in Deuerlein, *Briefwechsel*, doc. 116, p. 326.

[21] On 5 July, the Austrian ambassador Szögyény had delivered an Austrian memorandum and letter from the Austrian Emperor to Wilhelm II, asking the German ally for support for any action that Austria might decide on to avenge the Serbian-led assassination at Sarajevo. It was on this occasion that the famous 'blank cheque' was presented to Austria in the shape of a pledge of unconditional support.

[22] See PA Bonn, R996, 'Mitteilungen des Generalstabes der Armee und des Admiralstabes der Marine über die militärische Leistungsfähigkeit anderer Staaten', Waldersee to the Secretary of State for Foreign Affairs, Zimmermann, 4 July 1914.

[23] See Geiss, *Julikrise*, vol. 1, p. 79; Klein, *Deutschland*, p. 220. Falkenhayn's evidence to the parliamentary inquiry in Hölzle, *Quellen*, doc. 131, pp. 308–309. Falkenhayn recalled that Plessen and Lyncker were also present at the meeting with the Kaiser, but mentioned no other participants. This meeting between the monarch and the three generals hardly amounts to the mythical 'Kronrat' (crown council) that reputedly took place that day. Rather, the Kaiser consulted military and civilian advisers separately. For an example of such a claim see Gerhard Hecker, *Walther*

Hollweg (who had briefly returned from Hohenfinow) and Zimmermann. The Kaiser informed them of Austria's intentions to act against Serbia in retaliation of the assassination and of the ally's request for German support. He asked the Minister of War if the army was ready, as Falkenhayn told the Parliamentary Commission after the war: 'Based on my convictions I briefly confirmed this was the case without any reservations, and only asked whether any preparations were to be made. H.M. declined this equally briefly and dismissed me.'[24]

Although Moltke was not present at any of these discussions, he was subsequently briefed in detail about them. Falkenhayn wrote to him at Karlsbad, informing him unofficially of his impression that Vienna might not be quite as resolved on war as the Kaiser had deduced from the memorandum and letter that Szögyény had presented:

The Chancellor . . . appears to have as little faith as I do that the Austrian Government is really in earnest, even though its language is undeniably more resolute than in the past. . . . Certainly in no circumstances will the coming weeks bring any decision. . . . Nonetheless, although I have not been authorized to do so, I consider it advisable to inform you of the gravity of the situation so that anything untoward – which could, after all, occur at any time – should not find you wholly unprepared.[25]

Falkenhayn was sceptical that war would really result from the current crisis,[26] and as long as the Kaiser shared this notion (on 6 July he told Tirpitz's deputy Capelle as well as General von Bertrab that he did not think war would occur),[27] the military's wishful thinking could not come to much. The military were unaware of Bethmann Hollweg's resolve and underestimated his determination to encourage the Austrian ally. That Falkenhayn, as well as the absent Moltke, did not yet consider war unavoidable is also clear from their exchange of letters between 8 and 18 July on the matter of further army increases.[28]

There was no need for immediate action, and therefore no need to

Rathenau und sein Verhältnis zum Militär, Boppard/Rhein 1983, p. 157, who refers to a 'Gesprächsrunde' on 5 July between Wilhelm II, Bethmann Hollweg, Zimmermann, Plessen, Lyncker and Falkenhayn.   [24] Hölzle, *Quellen*, pp. 308–309.   [25] Geiss, *Julikrise*, vol. 1, doc. 23a.

[26] See Afflerbach, *Falkenhayn*, p. 150; Alfred von Wegerer (ed.), *Der Ausbruch des Weltkrieges 1914*, 2 vols., Hamburg 1939, vol. 1, p. 132.

[27] Geiss, *Julikrise*, vol. 1, docs. 32a and 32b, p. 95. See also Hopman's letter to Tirpitz, in which he passed on information about this talk from Capelle. According to this document, the Kaiser claimed to have spoken about the current situation with the Chancellor, Chief of the General Staff, Minister of War and the deputy of the Chief of the Admiralty Staff on the previous day. Either Hopman was mistaken or the Kaiser must have spoken with Moltke on the telephone, for he was not in Berlin at this time. Hopman to Tirpitz, 6 July 1914, in Berghahn and Deist, 'Kaiserliche Marine', *MGM*, 1/1970, doc. 1, p. 45.

[28] See also Afflerbach, *Falkenhayn*, p. 151.

recall Moltke or cancel already-arranged holidays. Falkenhayn, like most military decision-makers, went on vacation as scheduled; he was absent from Berlin from 8 July onwards.[29] Wilhelm Groener, head of the General Staff's Railway Department, was in Bad Kissingen, and Oberst Walter Nicolai, head of Section IIIb, was in the Harz mountains, and only returned to Berlin on 25 July.[30] Tappen cancelled his planned holiday on the island of Langeoog, but only because his children fell ill, and he left Berlin on 15 or 16 July to spend a few days in Goslar before returning to Berlin on 23 July.[31] The responsible political leaders, Bethmann Hollweg and Jagow, were also absent from Berlin, giving the crisis – quite deliberately – a 'leaderless appearance'.[32]

Before leaving for his annual North Sea cruise on 6 July, the Kaiser instructed General Hermann von Bertrab, the most senior General Staff officer in Berlin during Moltke's and Waldersee's absence, to inform Moltke of the events at Potsdam. Bertrab wrote to Moltke about the Austrian memorandum and the Kaiser's decision to back Austria's demands and to support her, should Russia get involved in the conflict. His impression was that the Kaiser did not consider such a Russian involvement likely, and that he viewed the matter as a purely Balkan affair, at least for the moment. He informed Moltke that the Kaiser's departure for his cruise was to be seen in that light.[33] When Waldersee briefly returned to Berlin on 8 July, Bertrab advised him of his talk with the Kaiser and his letter to Moltke. Waldersee felt no need to take further action at that point, as he recalled after the war:

For my part, being the deputy of General von Moltke in all matters relating to war, there was nothing to be arranged as a result of the audience of General von Bertrab in Potsdam. The scheduled mobilization work had been completed on 31 March 1914. The army was ready, as always.[34]

The General Staff was ready; and as nothing could be done while events in Vienna were taking their course, the key decision-makers might as

---

[29] After the war, Theobald von Schäfer of the Reichsarchiv accused Bethmann of issuing the blank cheque 'without first asking the leading people in the army and navy whether they could wage a possible war with a prospect of success.' This is not a tenable charge, not only because it was the Kaiser, rather than Bethmann, who issued the 'cheque' (admittedly subsequently approved by Bethmann), but also because in the first place it was the constant insistence on German military superiority that led the civilian decision-makers to believe that Germany stood a real chance in a future war. Schäfer, *Generalstab und Admiralstab. Das Zusammenwirken von Heer und Flotte im Weltkrieg*, Berlin 1931, p. 10.   [30] Trumpener, 'War Premeditated?', p. 62.

[31] BA-MA, W-10/50661, Tappen, 'Kriegserinnerungen', p. 10.

[32] Geiss, *July 1914*, pp. 60/1.

[33] Geiss, *Julikrise*, vol. 1, doc. 33, pp. 97–98; Müller, *Diary*, p. 32.

[34] Geiss, *Julikrise*, vol. 1, doc. 32c, pp. 96–97.

well wait at their various holiday destinations, while their absence helped to create the impression of calm that both Berlin and Vienna wanted to convey to the outside world. The government in Berlin deliberately used the absence of the Kaiser, Moltke and Falkenhayn to pretend that Germany was just as surprised by Austria's ultimatum as the other European governments and had not known about its contents prior to it being delivered, as the Bavarian *chargé d'affaires* Schoen reported to Munich on 18 July.[35] During their absence, Moltke and Waldersee were being kept informed about the events in Vienna by the German military attaché Karl von Kageneck, and about general developments by the Auswärtiges Amt, with whom they were 'in constant touch'.[36] Tappen was also able to brief Moltke in person when he visited him in Karlsbad on 7 July.

From Kageneck Moltke learned of the decisions taken by the Austro-Hungarian ministerial council of 7 July. Kageneck had found out from an Austrian General Staff officer that an unacceptable ultimatum to Serbia was planned, and that it was considered probable that Russia would become actively involved in the ensuing conflict. His informant had declared 'with a triumphant smile: "This time war is certain."'[37] German decision-makers, military and political, were not convinced, however, that Austria would not back down at the last minute. Thus Hopman wrote to Tirpitz on 9 July: 'Personally I am of the opinion that the Austrians were never quite as fired up as H.M. has portrayed it, and that they have already lost steam and are still losing it.'[38] A similar concern existed within the Auswärtiges Amt, as Schoen reported to Hertling: 'Here [in Berlin] they are quite in favour of Austria using this favourable hour, even given the danger of further complications. Whether, however, they will ultimately show resolve in Vienna still seems doubtful to Herr von Jagow and Herr von Zimmermann.'[39]

[35] *Bayerische Dokumente zum Kriegsausbruch und zum Versailler Schuldspruch, herausgegeben im Auftrage des Bayerischen Landtages*, o.D. (1922), Schoen to Hertling, report no. 386, pp. 4ff. Schoen pointed out that not even Italy had been confided in.

[36] BA-MA, W-10/50661, Tappen, 'Kriegserinnerungen', p. 10.

[37] Geiss, *Julikrise*, vol. 1, doc. 44, p. 116. For this and other letters from and to Kageneck see now also Günther Kronenbitter, 'Die Macht der Illusionen. Julikrise und Kriegsausbruch 1914 aus der Sicht des deutschen Militärattachés in Wien', *MGM*, 57, 1998.

[38] Berghahn/Deist, 'Kaiserliche Marine', doc. 4, Hopman to Tirpitz, 9 July 1914.

[39] Deuerlein, *Briefwechsel*, Schoen to Hertling, 18 July 1914, doc. 104. See also Soden to Hertling, 9 July 1914, doc. 103: 'Zimmermann would consider the current point in time as very favourable for, as he put it, launching a "war of revenge" (*Rachezug*) against the southern neighbour, and he believes firmly that it would be possible to localize the war. But he doubts that they would decide on this in Vienna.'

On 13 July, Kageneck informed Moltke that, according to inside information from the Austrian War Ministry, Emperor Franz Joseph was still determined to send an unacceptable ultimatum to Belgrade, and that a ministerial council meeting the following day would decide the date for the delivery of such a note. 'That Russia, possibly also Romania, will interfere is considered 50 per cent likely by the military.'[40]

Kageneck also received specific questions from Waldersee. On 11 July, he requested information about Conrad's strategic intentions: 'Is the entire army to be mobilized? Is it planned to march into Galicia at the same time? Or are only a few corps, partially strengthened, to march into Serbia? Or is nothing decided yet?'[41] Waldersee requested this information soon, in order to advise Moltke accordingly. It is clearly not true to claim, as Turner does, that Waldersee 'did nothing at all' during the crucial days of July.[42] In his reply of 15 August Kageneck explained that he had been unable to consult Conrad, who was on holiday in Innichen in the Tyrol, but had spoken to his deputy, General von Höfer.[43] He was able to ascertain that Austria planned to mobilize against Serbia only (*Mobilmachung Balkan*), and not to deploy any troops in Galicia, not least to ensure that Russia would have no pretext for becoming involved. Höfer was concerned, however, about the length of Austrian mobilization time, and about the possibility that Serbia's forces would stay far in the South, in the area of Nis, so that an engagement of Serbian troops could be delayed for about three weeks after the outbreak of hostilities. Kageneck suspected that Russia would stay out of a conflict, especially following the revelations by the French senator Humbert about the poor state of French armaments.[44] He informed Moltke that the date for the

---

[40] Geiss, *Julikrise*, vol. 1, doc. 84, pp. 158–159.

[41] Waldersee to Kageneck, in Kronenbitter, 'Die Macht der Illusionen', p. 533.

[42] Turner, 'The Role of the General Staffs', p. 312.

[43] This was an unfortunate result of the plan to demonstrate outward calm by sending key men on holiday. Key decision-makers, such as Conrad and Moltke, could not co-ordinate or confirm their strategies, and military discussions had to be conducted by less senior figures. See Kageneck to Waldersee in Geiss, *Julikrise*, vol. 1, p. 179, also in BA-MA, w-10/50891.

[44] On 13 July 1914, the French Senator Charles Humbert, in a speech to the Senate, had publicly revealed serious shortcomings within the French army, e.g. that France's field artillery was inferior to Germany's, that there was a shortage of officers, that fortification artillery was out of date, that France did not have the necessary means to cross the Moselle or Rhine, and that the fortifications between Toul and Verdun had not been improved since 1875. In the light of these revelations, Moltke composed a secret memorandum on 31 July 1914. It summarized that France only had a limited amount of heavy artillery, and that this did not meet modern requirements in terms of effectiveness, range and mobility. Substantial changes to the current M81 model were, however, planned for the end of 1914. Ammunition supplies in France's eastern fortifications had been increased over the last two years, but there was only limited bomb-proof storage space. France did not yet have any new-style mortars (*Minenwerfer*), and would instead use out-of-date

delivery of the ultimatum was set for the 25th (it was later changed to the 23rd), and that Austria wanted to wait until the end of the harvest holidays before taking any action. Clearly, then, for the German military there was no need to feel pressured by time. Moltke commented in the margin of Kageneck's report: 'If the *démarche* is not presented until 25 July a lot of water will flow down the Danube before it comes to anything further.'[45] Kageneck expressed concern that Serbia might back down once 'Mobilization Balkans' was under way: 'What then? Should this great attempt again come to nothing? Berchtold fears such a turn of events. In my opinion it should then be up to the military leaders to ensure that there can be no turning back.'[46] Waldersee received Kageneck's reply on 17 July. He immediately advised Moltke of its contents 'in the most careful manner', and passed on the information in a private letter to Jagow.[47] He informed the State Secretary that Austria intended initially to deploy six army corps against Serbia and none against Galicia, but that Austria would turn away from Serbia and towards Russia ('the main opponent') if the latter became involved in the conflict. Waldersee warned, however, that the Austrian military measures might be slow, for a partial mobilization was never without shortcomings; the change from the Serbian to the Russian front would take time, and no one yet knew where (i.e. how far to the South) the Serbs would face the Austrian army. However, he assured Jagow that there was no need for action from Germany's military authorities, adding: 'General Moltke plans to return to Berlin on the 25th of this month. I remain here [in Ivenak] ready to pounce; we in the General Staff are ready, in the meantime there is nothing for us to arrange.'[48] At this point in the crisis, Waldersee was not convinced that 'the current crisis would lead to actions of a greater sort', as he put it in a letter to Kageneck.[49] A few days later, with the day of the ultimatum almost reached, Moltke wrote to his wife: 'I am sorry not to be able to stay here another week,

ones (*glatte Mörser*) with out-of-date ammunition: BA-MA, PH3/629, pp. 12–13. This knowledge made the current crisis appear even more of a golden opportunity for Germany. On Humbert's revelations, see also Gerd Krumeich, *Armaments and Politics in France on the Eve of the First World War. The Introduction of the Three-Year Conscription 1913–1914*, London 1984, p. 214; John Keiger, *France and the Origins of the First World War*, London 1983, p. 149.

45 Quoted in Theobald von Schäfer, 'Generaloberst von Moltke in den Tagen vor der Mobilmachung und seine Einwirkung auf Österreich-Ungarn', *Die Kriegsschuldfrage. Berliner Monatshefte für Internationale Aufklärung*, August 1926, p. 515.

46 Geiss, *Julikrise*, vol. 1, doc. 102, p. 179.

47 Waldersee to Kageneck, in Kronenbitter, 'Die Macht der Illusionen', p. 534.

48 Geiss, *Julikrise*, vol. 1, doc. 124, pp. 198–199.

49 Waldersee to Kageneck, in Kronenbitter, 'Die Macht der Illusionen', p. 534.

but I have to return to Berlin. Tomorrow, the 23rd, is the critical day! I am eager to find out what will happen.'[50] Only a day earlier, Lyncker had telegraphed Moltke, warning that a war might result from the increasing Anglo-German tensions.[51] It was time to return to the centre of German decision-making.

As part of his attempt to play down the involvement of the military in the events of the July Crisis, Waldersee informed the Parliamentary Committee in 1919: 'I only returned to Berlin once the greatest political tension arose, on the 23rd of July.' It would be more accurate to say that he returned when he knew to *expect* the greatest political tension, namely on the 23rd, the day the ultimatum to Serbia was finally delivered. The military were informed about the date for the delivery of the ultimatum, as well as its unacceptable character, and Waldersee timed his return to coincide with it.[52] Waldersee was, however, lying in 1919 about the period of time he supposedly spent away from Berlin. While he went to Hanover on 4 July, he did not stay for his aunt's funeral, and was in fact not absent from the centre of decision-making for as long as he later suggested. In September 1914, he wrote:

I could not attend the funeral because I was recalled due to the political tension. After that, after discussion with Jagow and Zimmermann, I went to Ivennack [sic] for a bit in order to avoid attention, from where I was recalled three times, however; the last was on the 23rd.[53]

The key military decision-makers all returned to Berlin within hours of one another. Tappen was back in Berlin on 23 July. Falkenhayn returned from the island of Juist on 24 July, and was back at work at the War Ministry the next day.[54] Moltke's return was also timed to coincide with the expected rising of tension following the Austrian ultimatum to Serbia. He arrived back in Berlin on the evening of the 25th, and met

---

[50] Cited in Grone, 'Zum Kriegsausbruch 1914', p. 8. This letter is not included in the edited *Erinnerungen.*   [51] Cited in Stevenson, *Armaments*, p. 376.

[52] See Geiss, *Julikrise*, vol. 1, p. 96, note 3, who points out that no one other than the authorities in Berlin and Vienna knew about the soon-to-be delivered ultimatum and that 'the most severe political tensions' could not yet have occurred.

[53] BA-MA, w-10/51032, Waldersee's secret memorandum, September 1914, 'Meine Erlebnisse zu Beginn des Krieges 1914', p. 9. See also Klein, *Deutschland*, p. 222, who cites post-war letters from Waldersee to Jagow, in which Waldersee wrote that he returned repeatedly from Ivenak (in nearby Mecklenburg) to Berlin or had his adjutant visit him. As Klein points out, this is important evidence to suggest that military preparations were taken in Berlin following the meetings of 5/6 July. Trumpener maintains that Waldersee left Berlin on 8 July and did not return until the 23rd, and is unconvinced by Klein's allegations or the evidence he cites. Trumpener, 'War Premeditated?', p. 63. However, Waldersee's memorandum, as well as the letter Klein cites, prove without doubt that Waldersee did indeed return from the Mecklenburg countryside.

[54] Afflerbach, *Falkenhayn*, p. 153.

Waldersee the next morning for a discussion of the situation, later meeting Jagow in the Auswärtiges Amt.[55] Eliza von Moltke recalled that, upon his return to Berlin, her husband was 'overworked day and night, [and] very dissatisfied with the diplomatic preparations'.[56] Only now did the Entente states realize the gravity of the situation; 'the softly-softly approach' had worked in preventing Russia and France from initiating any military measures before the ultimatum was delivered.[57]

It was also on the 26th that Moltke passed on to the Auswärtiges Amt his draft for a notification to Belgium, which would be used by the diplomats, with only minor alterations, to initiate the violation of Belgian neutrality. It requested that the Belgian government allow German troops to march through Belgium because 'reliable news' suggested that France would march against Germany in this way. Brussels was given 24 hours to reply. Moltke also threatened, as he had done in November 1913, that the consequences for Belgium would be grave if her troops joined Germany's enemies. The timing of the drafting of the memorandum is important in evaluating Germany's decision for war, as Geiss points out:

> The note . . . clearly demonstrates that the German government reckoned so seriously with the eventuality of a war against Russia and France from 26 July at the latest that it began to adapt to that possibility – not, however, by trying with positive measures to prevent such a war from breaking out, but by considering how best to begin the war against France, for example by means of completely invented allegations of an apparent French threat to Belgian neutrality.[58]

On 26 July, Moltke also spoke with the Chancellor, who had spent most of July away from Berlin in his country estate at Hohenfinow.[59] Bethmann, too, had secretly travelled to Berlin on several occasions

---

[55] NL Moltke, N78/34, 'Dommes' Stellungnahme für Friedensverhandlungen, February 1919'. Geiss gives the date for Moltke's return as the 25th (Geiss, *Julikrise*, vol. 2, pp. 11–12), as does Wegerer (*Ausbruch*, vol. 1, p. 355). Ritter mistakenly claims that Moltke returned on 26 July (*Staatskunst*, vol. 2, p. 312) – this was in fact the day that he returned to the General Staff to direct future proceedings – and even that he was away until the 27th (ibid., p. 282). Similarly, Fischer falsely claims that Moltke, like Waldersee, only returned to Berlin on 26 July (*Illusionen*, p. 702). Turner also gives a wrong (later) date, and attaches significance to this alleged late return by claiming that Moltke arrived in Berlin after Austria's partial mobilisation ('The Role of the General Staffs', p. 312).

[56] Eliza von Moltke, Memorandum, 1 February 1915, quoted in Grone, 'Zum Kriegsausbruch 1914', p. 8.   [57] Stevenson, *Armaments*, pp. 337–338.

[58] Geiss, *Julikrise*, vol. 2, p. 12. The text can be found in *DD*, No. 376. See also Frank Wende, *Die belgische Frage in der deutschen Politik des Ersten Weltkrieges*, Hamburg 1969, pp. 17–18. Moltke also wrote a note to the Dutch government assuring them that Germany would respect Dutch neutrality: BA-MA, W-10/51063, Moltke to Freytag-Loringhoven, 26 July 1915.

[59] See Geiss, *Julikrise*, vol. 2, p. 12, note 3; Schäfer, 'Generaloberst von Moltke in den Tagen der Mobilmachung', p. 516; Wegerer, *Ausbruch*, vol. 1, p. 355.

during the crisis. In the tense days before and after the ultimatum was delivered, he spent most of his time on the telephone, as Riezler noted: 'Apparently preparations for all eventualities, discussions with the military leaders about which nothing is said.'[60] Bethmann and Riezler returned to Berlin on Saturday, 25 July.[61]

On 27 July, the Kaiser returned earlier than scheduled from his North Sea and Baltic cruise and was met at Wildpark station by the Chancellor, Moltke and Hugo von Pohl, the Chief of the Admiralty Staff.[62] Having read the Serbian reply to the ultimatum the Kaiser reacted as the decision-makers in Berlin had feared: he once again counselled peace. Count Dohna, who had accompanied the Kaiser on his cruise, recalled the scene of the arrival at the station: 'At Wildpark station there were H.M. the Kaiserin, Beethmann [sic] and many other important people. It was a moment during which peace seemed once again in the offing; the war-party seemed disappointed.'[63] Wilhelm invited his closest advisers, the Chancellor, Jagow, Moltke, Pohl and the Cabinet Chiefs, to the Neues Palais for a meeting. Falkenhayn was not present at the discussions, and only received information about them 'on the quiet'.[64] Although Falkenhayn was under the impression that the decision 'to fight the matter through to the end, whatever the cost' had been reached, when he approached the Chancellor the next day to demand the return of all troops back to their garrisons, Bethmann refused. Wenninger recorded on 29 July that Falkenhayn needed to point out that France had recalled her troops, and that he (Falkenhayn) had only managed to convince Bethmann with difficulty that Germany needed to do the same. He would not, however, allow recalling all officers on holiday leave, or soldiers away on harvest leave.[65] The Chancellor's problem was the Kaiser, whose mood, upon reading Serbia's conciliatory answer to Austria's ultimatum, had changed completely. He decided that all reason for war had been removed.[66] This was a reaction that the Auswärtiges Amt and the

[60] Riezler, *Tagebücher*, 25 July 1914, pp. 190–191.   [61] Ibid., 27 July 1914, p. 191.

[62] Müller, *Diary*, p. 35.

[63] Alfred Graf von Dohna, 'Der Feldzug in Ostpreußen 1914', 24 April 1920, in BA-MA, w-10/51032, pp. 136–137.

[64] Falkenhayn diary, 27 July 1914, in BA-MA, w-10/50635. Falkenhayn's diary was copied by Generalmajor von Tieschowitz for the Reichsarchiv in 1927; the original is lost. The copies were among the material returned from Moscow, and they are an invaluable source for the decision-making process during the July Crisis. See also Afflerbach, *Falkenhayn*, pp. 148ff.

[65] Geiss, *Julikrise*, vol. 2, doc. 704. Similarly, Leuckart wrote on 29 July about his briefing at the Ministry of War: 'It was added, as very secret, that the Minister of War had persuaded the Chancellor to agree to the recalling of the troops from the practice-grounds only with the greatest difficulty.' A copy of this letter can be found in BA-MA, w-10/50890.

[66] Geiss, *Julikrise* , vol. 2, doc. 575, Wilhelm II to Jagow, 28 July 1914.

military had anticipated and feared. The Bavarian General Krafft von Dellmensingen commented in his diary after his return from Berlin to Munich on 30 July on the 'unfortunately noticeably peaceful news. The Kaiser absolutely wants peace and the Kaiserin is working towards it with all her might. . . . He even wants to influence Austria and to stop her continuing further. That would be the gravest disaster! We would lose all credit as allies.'[67] The Kaiser no longer wanted Austria to provoke a conflict, and was even prepared to drop the ally to avoid it. Falkenhayn recorded coldly: 'I remind him that he is no longer in control of these matters.'[68] By delaying and altering the Kaiser's mediation proposal to Vienna (the idea of a 'Halt in Belgrade'), the Chancellor in the end ensured that the monarch was indeed no longer in a position to interfere.[69]

On 28 July, the day of Austria's declaration of war on Serbia, the Kaiser's mood had changed again: 'His Majesty . . . claims, as he says, that the ball that is rolling can no longer be stopped', Falkenhayn recorded. At this point, the Minister of War was already advocating the declaration of a state of 'imminent danger of war' ('drohende Kriegsgefahr'), but Bethmann favoured a delay of that measure, as it would make war unavoidable.[70] The Chancellor was intent on letting Germany's future opponents, and Russia in particular, put themselves in the wrong. It was paramount that Germany should 'appear to be the attacked', if public support were to be relied upon. Bethmann was also still motivated by the vain hope that Britain might stay out of a conflict if Germany appeared peaceable. He explained at the meeting with Falkenhayn, Moltke and Jagow that Germany had to await Russia's mobilization, 'because otherwise we will not have public opinion in our favour, either here or in England. The latter was desirable because in the Chancellor's opinion, England would not be able to side with Russia if

---

[67] BA-MA, w-10/50642, p. 2.

[68] BA-MA, w-10/50635, Falkenhayn diary, 28 July 1914.

[69] The substantial differences between the Kaiser's order and Bethmann's instruction to Vienna are analyzed by Geiss, *Julikrise*, vol. 2, pp. 164–165.

[70] The military leadership had three different stages of mobilizing measures at its disposal, 'Verstärkung, drohende Kriegsgefahr und Mobilmachung' (strengthening, imminent danger of war, mobilization). The first troop movements were expected within 36 hours of an initial declaration of the state of impending war. (See e.g. BA-MA, PH3/720, General von Below to Falkenhayn, 6 June 1914.) Bucholz distinguishes seven different stages of mobilization (*Moltke*, pp. 300–302). On 21 July 1914, the Ministry of War suggested speeding up the troop increases, as such a relatively long time span seemed potentially dangerous. Despite the date, however, this suggestion seems not to have been motivated by concern that a mobilization might be imminent, because a post-script to the document suggests that these matters should be discussed again at the end of August, with the aim of achieving a result by the winter of 1914/1915.

the latter unleashed a general war by attacking Austria . . .', Falkenhayn recorded in his diary.[71] The Minister of War, convinced of Britain's opportunism, did not share Bethmann's belief in the possibility of British neutrality. To Falkenhayn's surprise, Moltke also advocated a delay. It is much more difficult to explain why Moltke opposed this measure. Falkenhayn seems to have thought that Moltke still hoped for peace, for he noted:

I do, by the way, understand this decision; for anyone who still believes in the possibility of keeping the peace, or at least wishes for it, can, of course, not subscribe to the declaration of an imminent danger of war. Naturally, this decision leads to a military disadvantage for us, but if Moltke is willing to justify that then I cannot oppose it.[72]

It is doubtful, however, that Falkenhayn was right to suspect that Moltke wanted to preserve peace at that time. More likely, he agreed with Bethmann's view that they should wait as long as possible in order to let the Russians take the blame for being the first great power to declare a general mobilization. Moreover, he had received intelligence suggesting that Russia's mobilization preparations were not as extensive and systematic as he had previously been led to believe.[73] It is also possible that Falkenhayn painted a deliberately unfavourable picture of Moltke, for whom he had little respect. On the same day, other military observers had a very different impression of Moltke's resolve, and thought him far from peaceable. (Theirs were, however, second-hand opinions, and as such presumably less reliable than Falkenhayn's first-hand account.) Wenninger informed the Bavarian Minister of War, Kress von Kressenstein, that he was under the impression that there was a battle between the Ministry of War and the General Staff on the one hand, and the Chancellor and Auswärtiges Amt on the other. The Minister of War, with support from the Chief of Staff, was pushing for immediate military measures, in keeping with the current political tension. In fact, Wenninger observed that Moltke wanted to go even further:

he uses his whole influence towards ensuring that this unusually favourable military situation be used in order to strike; he points out that France was almost in a military quandary,[74] that Russia militarily felt anything but secure; in addi-

---

[71] BA-MA, w-10/50635, Falkenhayn diary, 29 July 1914, also Afflerbach, *Falkenhayn*, p. 157; Fischer, *Illusionen*, p. 711. On Britain's dithering during July 1914, see Ferguson, *Pity of War*, pp. 158ff.

[72] BA-MA, w-10/5063, Falkenhayn diary, 29 July 1914.

[73] See also Trumpener, 'War Premeditated?', p. 77; Geiss, *Julikrise*, vol. 2, p. 237.

[74] This view was clearly based on Humbert's revelations about the poor state of the French army. See note 44 above.

tion the favourable time of year, the harvest largely brought in, the annual training programme completed.[75]

General von Leuckart's impression of Moltke's resolve was strikingly similar:

There is no doubt that the Chief of the General Staff is for the war, while the Chancellor is holding back. Generaloberst v. Moltke is reported to have said that we would never again find a situation as favourable as now, when neither France nor Russia had completed the extension of their army organizations.[76]

On 28 July Moltke drafted a memorandum entitled 'Assessment of the Political Situation', which he gave to the Kaiser later that evening and sent to Bethmann the next day.[77] He argued that a Russian partial mobilization should be followed by a German general mobilization. In Albertini's words, the memorandum 'marks an invasion by the military authorities of the political field which lies outside their province', and indeed, Moltke felt entitled to comment on the political situation, as the title of the memorandum suggests.[78] He began to put pressure on the politicians, and attempted to influence foreign policy decisions by making them dependent on military necessities.

In his memorandum, Moltke outlined how a number of partial and general mobilizations would follow one another in a domino effect. Austria had so far only mobilized against Serbia, but when faced with Russian mobilization in the districts of Kiev, Odessa and Moscow, would have to mobilize her remaining forces against Russia. Once Austria mobilized her entire army, however, a clash between Austria and Russia would become unavoidable. This, in turn, would spell the *casus foederis* for Germany, who would have to mobilize herself, or break her alliance agreement and allow the ally to be destroyed by superior Russian forces. A German mobilization would lead to a general mobilization in Russia,

---

[75] BayHSTA-KA, MKr 1765, No. 2637, Wenninger to Kress, 29 July 1914, Report No. 1, 'Politische Lage und militärische Massnahmen', also in Geiss, *Julikrise*, vol. 2, doc. 704. The discrepancy between Wenninger's and Falkenhayn's accounts is also noted by the Reichsarchiv. Haeften concluded that Wenninger's view can only have been based on third-hand information, as he would not have had the opportunity for a discussion with Moltke (BA-MA, w-10/52106), 'Bericht über Besprechung mit Prof. Bernadotte Schmitt im Reichsarchiv', 31 July 1928.

[76] Geiss, *Julikrise*, vol. 2, doc. 705. Freiher von Varnbüler, the Württemberg ambassador, found out from the military attaché Graevenitz that there had been a pronounced difference between civilian and military decision-makers. While Bethmann still wanted to gain time, the Chief of Staff and Minister of War advocated immediate mobilization measures. Wegerer, *Ausbruch*, vol. 2, p. 112.

[77] 'Zur Beurteilung der politischen Lage'. See Schäfer, 'Generaloberst von Moltke', p. 516.

[78] Albertini, *Origins*, vol. 2, pp. 488–489; Geiss, *Julikrise*, vol. 2, pp. 235–236, doc. 659; Ritter, *Staatskunst*, vol. 2, p. 315.

who would secure French support by claiming that she was being attacked by Germany. Moltke urged that Germany begin her mobilization in the light of Russian and French mobilizing measures, saying that it was imperative to establish as soon as possible whether Russia and France were willing to go to war. His urgent pleas were motivated by his knowledge of the tight mobilization schedule for the German army. 'The longer our neighbours' preparations continue, the quicker they will be able to complete their mobilizations.' The result of such a head start was described in no uncertain terms by Moltke: 'the military situation is worsening for us day by day and may lead to fateful consequences for us if our likely opponents are allowed continue to prepare in peace and quiet.'[79]

Whereas the German politicians had previously not intended to mobilize in response to a Russian partial mobilization, Moltke's insistence led to a change of heart. In Geiss's words, Moltke's memorandum amounted to a serious intervention in the decision-making process, and he rightly concludes: 'on 29 July [Moltke] decisively contributed to bringing about this 'horrible war' [Moltke's term!] with his robust intervention in German politics'.[80] Yet the memorandum also highlights Moltke's ambiguous attitude to the coming war. He clearly felt the need to advocate military measures; he did not want Germany to back down, or to adopt a conciliatory policy. Moltke had no illusions about the result of these seemingly inevitable developments. Instead he anticipated the carnage of the coming war: 'the cultured states (*Kulturstaaten*) of Europe will begin to tear one another apart.'[81] Only a miracle, he wrote, could prevent war in the end, a war 'that would destroy the culture of almost the whole of Europe for decades to come'. Moltke was torn between feeling bellicose and apprehensive, and was perhaps more concerned about the nature of the impending tragedy than some of his military contemporaries. Certainly Falkenhayn did not have the same qualms. Callously, he declared on 4 August: 'Even if we perish over this, at least it will have been fun.'[82]

By 29 July Moltke was adamant that Germany needed to announce

---

[79] Ibid. Details of Russia's mobilization in Stephen J. Cimbala, 'Steering Through Rapids: Russian Mobilization and World War I', *The Journal of Slavic Military History*, 9, 2, 1996, pp. 376–398.

[80] Geiss, *Julikrise*, vol. 2, p. 236. See also Albertini, *Origins*, vol. 2, 489–490; Ritter, *Staatskunst*, vol. 2, p. 315.   [81] Geiss, *Julikrise*, vol. 2, doc. 659.

[82] Quoted in Afflerbach, *Falkenhayn*, p. 147. See also Albertini, *Origins*, vol. 2, p. 490: 'Though resolved to go to the ally's help, he [Moltke] seems at the critical moment to have perceived the terribleness of the tragedy towards which events were moving and to have been somewhat more cautious than the War Minister Falkenhayn.'

general mobilization, although Russia had not yet declared hers and Russia and Austria were not yet engaged in hostilities; whereas only the previous day, he had made a German mobilization dependent on those points. He was concerned about the speed that was needed to implement the first part of the Schlieffen/Moltke plan: initial success in Belgium depended on a surprise attack and the successful *coup de main* on Liège, and the plan's overall success depended on the capture of Belgian railway lines and on slow Russian mobilization. Germany could not afford to wait until her enemies mobilized – military concerns were now beginning to dictate political measures.

It is impossible to say what exactly triggered this change of heart; the fact that Austria had declared war on Serbia may have been a decisive factor. Moltke had also learned that Russian partial mobilization was 'far advanced', suggesting that full mobilization would be quicker than had previously been thought. Even more worrying must have been the news from Belgium. The Belgians were withdrawing troop units from training grounds and were calling up reservists. Worse still, they were preparing for action in and around Liège. The garrison was confined to quarters, bridges were being prepared for demolition, and the forts around Liège were being supplied with ammunition.[83] This is exactly the kind of bad news that would have stirred Moltke into action. From a military point of view, Germany could now afford to wait no longer.

Yet, according to Falkenhayn's diary, Moltke's confidence was shaken, and he did not feel he could support a decision that would amount to war, now that the war that he had so often demanded was imminent. Behind closed doors he was urging caution, but publicly he did not voice his concerns. This would explain the discrepancy between first- and second-hand accounts of Moltke's determination. He had doubts about Germany's chances of victory, and he knew – better than Falkenhayn, who did not know about the narrow time-scale for the planned *coup de main* on Liège – that hostilities would have to follow almost immediately once the 'impending danger of war' had been declared. The planned *coup de main* was thus an extra burden of responsibility for Moltke; what had looked good as a plan on paper must have appeared as a frightening gamble once it threatened to become reality. Being responsible for the implementation of the plan must have led to Moltke's hesitation. Moreover, Ludendorff, the co-author of this risky plan, was no longer

---

[83] Trumpener, 'War Premeditated?', pp. 79–80; see also Geiss, *Julikrise*, vol. 2, pp. 335–336.

around to provide moral support or act as a fellow conspirator. Moltke explained to the Austrian liaison officer Hauptmann Fleischmann[84] on 30 July that, unlike a Russian partial mobilization, German mobilization could be no half-measure and would automatically mean war. Moltke pointed out that a Russian partial mobilization

gave no occasion for a similar measure on the part of Germany, since German mobilization would only follow upon the beginning of a state of war between the Monarchy [i.e. Austria] and Russia. In contrast to the already customary Russian mobilizations and demobilizations, a German mobilization would inevitably lead to war.[85]

There was only one reason why war would become unavoidable once German mobilization was declared: because German troops would have to march into Belgium and take Liège immediately. The Schlieffen/ Moltke Plan, once in action, would significantly constrain Germany's political options and did not allow for a last-minute change of heart. Of all the influential decision-makers in those crucial last days of the crisis, only Moltke really knew just how much each hour counted.[86]

At a meeting at the Reichskanzlerpalais on 29 July, Falkenhayn again pushed for a decisive German response to Russia's partial mobilization. 'Against quiet, *very* quiet resistance from Moltke', Bethmann opposed a German mobilization at this point, because his policy relied on Russia mobilizing first, so that she would appear to the German population as the guilty party.[87] Moltke had still not found the resolve to demand what he knew to be a military necessity. Bethmann continued to resist a dec-

---

[84] Fleischmann had arrived in Berlin on 30 July as part of an effort to co-ordinate military matters between the German and Austrian General Staffs. Upon his arrival, a direct telephone line between the two staffs was established (BA-MA, w-10/50890, Reichsarchiv questionnaire, 9 June 1928).

[85] Quoted in Albertini, *Origins*, vol. 2, p. 672. See also Afflerbach, *Falkenhayn*, p. 156. Moltke also urged Fleischmann that Austria should refrain from declaring war on Russia, 'to avoid producing any appearance of an aggressive move on our part in the eyes of Europe and because in the event of a Russian declaration of war, England would in no case co-operate within the framework of the Triple Entente', thus hinting at Bethmann's views regarding the possibility of British neutrality. Conrad felt somewhat belittled by this advice and replied indignantly: 'We will not declare war on Russia and will not start the war' (Geiss, *Julikrise*, vol. 2, doc. 869).

[86] This is particularly true regarding the events of 1 August, which will be examined in detail below. The secrecy around the *coup de main* was extended to exclude the military cabinet, with further negative consequences. Because the General Staff refused, for reasons of secrecy, to explain why they wanted particular generals deployed on the western front (namely officers who knew of the plan and were familiar with the terrain around Liège), the cabinet refused to comply, and sent e.g. Waldersee to the eastern front. See Eugen Fischer-Baling's account of a post-war conversation with Waldersee, in 'Verfl . . . Kabinettswirtschaft' [sic], *Vossische Zeitung*, 18 September 1932.

[87] BA-MA, w-10/50635, Falkenhayn diary, 29 July 1914; Afflerbach, *Falkenhayn*, p. 157. Emphasis in the original.

laration of mobilization on 30 July.[88] Falkenhayn and Tirpitz tried to change his mind, both at a meeting at the Prussian State Ministry and afterwards, when Moltke was also present.[89] That evening, Moltke finally abandoned his cautious approach, and Falkenhayn recorded in his diary:

Late in the evening an argument between him [the Chancellor] and Moltke over who would carry the responsibility for a possible war. . . . Moltke declares himself decidedly in favour of war *sans phrase*. His changes of mood are hardly explicable, or not at all.[90]

At this late point in the crisis, in 'a stunning shift' of attitude, Bethmann Hollweg finally tried to restrain Vienna, because Russia's partial mobilization spelt the end of any hopes of localizing the conflict.[91] However, his attempts were not only too late but also arguably not forceful enough, considering the pressure Germany had put on the ally in the previous weeks. What the military had feared all along had indeed occurred: once war threatened to become reality, the civilian decision-makers were starting to counsel peace. At the same time as Bethmann was urging Vienna to consider negotiation proposals, Moltke was secretly liaising with the Austrian General Staff behind the Chancellor's back, demanding immediate general mobilization from the ally, and famously leading Berchtold to ask Conrad: 'Who rules in Berlin – Moltke or Bethmann?'[92]

In the evening of 30 July Moltke, Bethmann and Falkenhayn finally agreed on a deadline, following 'endless negotiations'. Falkenhayn recorded cynically in his diary:

---

[88] See ibid, p. 158, where Falkenhayn quotes from the minutes of a meeting of the Staatsministerium on 30 July 1914.

[89] According to Wenninger's report of 30 July 1914, the Chancellor had asked Falkenhayn and Tirpitz to a meeting, but not Moltke, who was notified by Falkenhayn and later appeared uninvited (Schulte, 'Neue Dokumente zum Kriegsausbruch und Kriegsverlauf 1914', p. 139). It is unclear why Moltke was not invited, but a probable reason was that Bethmann was trying to break up the military 'lobby' and attempting to avoid having Falkenhayn and Moltke both present at the same time.

[90] BA-MA, W-10/50635, Falkenhayn diary, 30 July 1914; Afflerbach, *Falkenhayn*, pp. 158–159. Theobald von Schäfer's apologetic account of Moltke in these crucial days cites the Chief of Staff's initial reluctance to demand action as proof that he did not want war, and dismisses Wenninger's incriminating accounts as unreliable because he would not have had direct access to Moltke during those critical days: 'Wollte Generaloberst von Moltke den Präventivkrieg?', p. 552.

[91] Trachtenberg, 'The Coming of the First World War', p. 84. See note 39 above on Zimmermann's certainty that the war would be localized, a clear prerequisite for the policy of the Auswärtiges Amt during July 1914.

[92] See David Stevenson, *The First World War and International Politics*, Oxford 1988, p. 28; Herwig, *First World War*, p. 28; Conrad, *Dienstzeit*, vol. 4, p. 152.

The Chancellor and his people (Jagow – Zimmermann) apparently still hope for a miracle. . . . Moltke and I finally manage to assert that the decision over the declaration of 'imminent danger of war' must be made by tomorrow midday at the latest.[93]

By midday on 31 July, Germany was to declare the state of 'imminent danger of war', whether or not Russia had mobilized.[94] Although such a measure would remove the pretext that Germany was being attacked, the deployment plan allowed for no further delay.

Hans von Haeften, Moltke's personal adjutant in 1914, was called to Moltke shortly after midnight in the night of 30/31 July. Moltke instructed him to draft the Kaiser's soon-to-be-delivered declaration to the people, the army and the navy. Haeften, who had only just returned to Berlin, requested a briefing on the current situation and, in addition to being given a copy of Moltke's memorandum of 28 July, was told that reliable news had been received about Russia's general mobilization. In fact, no such news was received until the next day and Moltke could not be certain that it would arrive before Germany's self-imposed deadline of 12 noon on 31 July for her own mobilization. Moltke was clearly concerned about the time pressure that Germany was under, for he told Haeften:

However, if we mobilize it will mean war. If Germany still continues to hesitate to implement this measure, for example in order to gain extra time for negotiations, then if the negotiations fail – which is to be predicted – it will mean that Germany will enter the war under the worst conceivable circumstances. We would thus allow our opponents to carry the war into Germany. If we hesitate with mobilization, our situation will worsen day by day and may lead to the most fatal results for us if our opponents are allowed to continue to prepare themselves undisturbed.[95]

Haeften's impression was that Moltke was suffering serious psychological turmoil ('seelisch ganz ausserordentlich litt')[96] under the pressure of having to advocate German mobilization against Russia, because only he realized the gravity of the situation. He made his fears plain to Haeften: 'This war will turn into a world war in which England will also intervene. Few can have an idea of the extent, the duration and the end of this war. Nobody today can have a notion of how it will all end.'[97]

---

[93] BA-MA, w-10/50635, Falkenhayn diary, 30 July 1914.   [94] Geiss, *Julikrise*, vol. 2, doc. 801.

[95] BA-MA, N35/1, p. 26, 'Generaloberst v. Moltke in der Nacht vom 30. zum 31. Juli 1914', Aufzeichnung v. Haeften.

[96] BA-MA, w-10/50897, Haeften to Reichsarchiv, 30 January 1926.

[97] BA-MA, N35/1, Aufzeichnungen v. Haeften, p. 27.

Haeften, who did not realize the extra pressure of time that Liège posed, considered Moltke's attitude at the time 'too pessimistic'.

As the 12 o'clock deadline was approaching on 31 July, there was uncertainty over whether Russia had already declared mobilization, and while Moltke, Falkenhayn and the Kaiser waited for news, Moltke appeared to Falkenhayn 'unfortunately very nervous'. Just before the deadline, news was received confirming Russia's general mobilization. The Kaiser could no longer refuse the military's demand for a state of imminent mobilization to be declared. He signed the order for a German general mobilization at 5 p.m. on 1 August in the 'Sternensaal' of his Schloss in Berlin. The first day of mobilization was to be 2 August.[98] Admiral von Müller recorded in his diary: 'Brilliant mood. The government has succeeded very well in making us appear as the attacked.'[99]

Bethmann, who arrived later on the scene in the Sternensaal, was furious that the military had usurped the centre stage of decision-making, even interfering in such 'civilian' matters as drafting the Kaiser's declaration to the German people. Falkenhayn described the scene in his diary:

The order about the imminent danger of war is being signed as I stand there with it in my hand. Then Moltke reads out the draft, written by Major v. Haeften, of a declaration to the people, delivered in such a way, sometimes in a voice that was almost suffocated by tears but yet energetic at the same time, that it made a superb impression. . . . The declaration to the people is taken over by the Chancellor, who appeared in the meantime, and who expressed his displeasure in no uncertain terms because Moltke had infringed here upon his prerogative, which leads to a clash between the Chancellor and H.M.[100]

This was a moment of triumph for the military. It had been worth waiting for Russia to be the first great power to declare mobilization, as had been Bethmann's intention all along. The Chancellor's patience had helped to avoid the odium of Germany being the first major power to mobilize. This apparent moral victory was, however, later jeopardized by Germany's ultimatum to Russia and subsequent declaration of war – upon Moltke's insistence but against Falkenhayn's advice – on 1 August, six days before Austria declared war on Russia.[101] Germany's

[98] Geiss, *Julikrise*, vol. 2, doc. 999, Falkenhayn to Jagow, 1 August; doc. 1000, 'Besprechung bei Wilhelm II', 1 August; Afflerbach, *Falkenhayn*, pp. 159–160. The events of 1 August are examined in detail below, pp. 216ff.   [99] Quoted in Röhl, 'Admiral von Müller', p. 670.

[100] BA-MA, w-10/50635, Falkenhayn diary, 31 July 1914; Afflerbach, *Falkenhayn*, p. 161.

[101] Bethmann Hollweg was later accused of being responsible for this diplomatic mistake. In July 1917, he justified his action to Theodor Wolff and claimed that Moltke had demanded the declaration of war: Wolff, *Tagebücher*, 19 July 1917, No. 578, p. 521.

declaration of war on Russia and France was also a grave mistake, because it exonerated Italy and Rumania from their alliance obligations.

Moltke accepted and co-operated for a while with Bethmann Hollweg's desire to let the Russians put themselves in the wrong, by waiting for Russian mobilization to be declared. Yet he was torn between such political considerations and the need for speed, which was essential for Germany's war plan. Knowledge of the time pressure must have made it extremely frustrating for him to see time being 'wasted' in catering for such political considerations. However, with the *coup de main* on Liège still a closely guarded General Staff secret, Moltke could not explain why speed was so important. Certainly German mobilization became a matter of urgency once Austria had declared war on Serbia on 28 July, and this event led Moltke to join Falkenhayn in his vociferous demands for mobilization.

THE LAST DAYS OF THE CRISIS

Upon his return to Berlin, Moltke had found that the Kaiser had lost much of his earlier resolve, and was now trying to calm the Austrians. The Kaiser's courage had waned much earlier than that of Bethmann, who sabotaged the monarch's attempts at arranging a compromise solution, following Serbia's almost complete acceptance of Austria's ultimatum.[102] In the light of the newly established certainty that Russia would become involved on Serbia's side, and that Britain would not remain a neutral onlooker, Bethmann, too, began to urge restraint on Austria in the last days of July. Now the military came into their own, pushing for the war that they had wanted for so long.[103] Falkenhayn in particular stands out as a belligerent advocate of war. As his recent biographer, Holger Afflerbach, has shown, Falkenhayn had become increasingly exasperated with every opportunity for war that Germany had missed, and desired a war almost for its own sake. There were times during the last days of July 1914 when Falkenhayn pushed for war even more than the Chief of the General Staff.[104] Falkenhayn's diary shows that Moltke swayed and changed his attitude – inexplicably to Falkenhayn, who did not know about the *coup de main* on Liège.

Once it became clear that the assassination in Sarajevo could serve as

---

[102] See Geiss, *Julikrise*, vol. 2, p. 164 for the 'halt in Belgrade', and p. 199 above.

[103] See Afflerbach, *Falkenhayn*, p. 153.

[104] Ibid., pp. 152–155. Afflerbach confirms Albertini's view that Moltke was more cautious than Falkenhayn in these last crucial days of July 1914. See also Albertini, *Origins*, vol. 2, pp. 490–491.

the desired 'trigger', the military decision-makers, and with them Moltke, were determined to put into action what they had so far painstakingly planned on paper. This was finally a chance to prove themselves; this was to be no longer merely 'playing at soldiers', but the fulfilment and climax of years of work and training. The circumstances for a war at the end of July were considered favourable, as the military leaders assured their civilian colleagues. Lerchenfeld, for example, noted on 31 July: 'In military circles here they are feeling very confident. Months ago [!] the Chief of the General Staff, Herr von Moltke, had already expressed the opinion that the point in time was militarily as favourable as it would not be again in the foreseeable future.' According to Lerchenfeld, the Prussian General Staff 'looked forward to war against France with great confidence [and] reckoned that it would be able to defeat France in four weeks; no great spirit in the French army, few howitzers (*Steilfeuergeschütze*) and worse guns (*Gewehre*).'[105]

Wilhelm von Dommes also recalled his delight when war seemed to become a certainty. In 1919, he wrote:

I have to admit that I was pleased about the developments. I was in no uncertainty about the horrors of a great European war, or about the difficulties that the war would entail for us considering the great numerical superiority of our enemies. However, I was . . . convinced that the clash would unavoidably come, but that our military situation would worsen every year. I felt a certain hope that superior leadership and efficiency would secure victory for us.[106]

That Britain would not remain neutral was a mere hiccough for the General Staff. In a conversation with Freiherr von Eckardstein on 1 June 1914, Moltke had dismissed the attaché's pessimistic assessment of Germany's diplomatic situation and claimed: 'You are also mistaken regarding England; in any case, we can wait calmly to see what she will do in the event of war.'[107] The General Staff completely underestimated the damage that the British Expeditionary Force could do, in the same way as they underestimated all their other future opponents.[108] There

---

[105] Lerchenfeld to Hertling, 31 July 1914, in Deuerlein, *Briefwechsel*, doc. 113, p. 322; *Bayerische Dokumente*, Telegram 31 July 1914, No. 67, p. 172. Moltke gave several reasons why the German army was still superior to the Russian and French, such as the superiority of German artillery and of the German infantry gun, as well as the inadequate training of French soldiers due to the recent change from two- to three-year service.

[106] BA-MA, NL Moltke, N78/34, 'Stellungnahme Generalmajors von Dommes für Friedensverhandlungen', February 1919.   [107] Eckardstein, *Lebenserinnerungen*, vol. 3, p. 186.

[108] See e.g. Wenninger's diary entry of 31 July, when rumours of an ultimatum to France led to speculation in the Ministry of War as to whether this was necessary, since France seemed to be shying away from an armed conflict. Wenninger recorded: 'General von Wild says: "Well, we would like to have the brothers take part, too"' (Schulte, 'Neue Dokumente', p. 140).

was also little concern over the likely consequences a British involvement would have for Germany's alliance partners. A hostile Britain would most probably lead Italy to opt for neutrality, if not in due course to join the Alliance's enemies.[109] Rather than being concerned, there was a sense in which the military looked forward to facing the British, as Oberst von Klewitz recalled in 1925: 'Every one of us was dying not only to defeat the English, but also to take every last one prisoner. How often was there talk about this in peace-time.'[110] Unlike the Chancellor, Moltke was under no illusion regarding Britain's attitude in case of a violation of Belgian neutrality, and unlike the Wilhelmstrasse, the General Staff was not concerned to keep Britain neutral.[111] Moltke did not regard Britain's decision to become involved as a reason to back down, to avoid the escalation from localized to European and ultimately world war. In 1908 or 1909, Moltke had told a surprised Bülow that he would rather see England as an open enemy than an unfavourable onlooker.[112] His only concession was his concern to keep the British out of the Netherlands. As he recalled in 1915: 'Because we spared Holland it became impossible for England to violate the neutrality of that country herself. After all, she had declared war on the basis of being protector of the small neutrals.'[113]

Moltke's reaction to the outbreak of war was two-fold. He was convinced of its inevitability, and was far from advocating peace. Once Moltke was certain that war would come, he was determined to see it through, and within the General Staff there was confidence that the German army was well prepared. The mobilization that went 'like clock-work', and the performance of the German troops in the first weeks of the war, seemed to confirm the military's pride in their achievements. However, Moltke was painfully aware that the war that was about

---

[109] See also Ludwig Beck, 'West- oder Ostoffensive 1914?' in idem, *Studien*, ed. Hans Speidel, Stuttgart 1955, p. 150.

[110] BA-MA, w-10/50897, Klewitz to Haeften, 16 January 1925, p. 125.

[111] Jagow suggested a curious plan to threaten Britain with a German occupation of Holland if Britain were to intervene in the war, a suggestion that was rejected by Admiral von Capelle. Berghahn and Deist, 'Kaiserliche Marine', docs. 10–11; Berghahn, *Approach*, p. 211.

[112] BA-MA, NL Tirpitz, N253/173, Bülow to Tirpitz, 11 June 1922. In this letter, Bülow condemned Bethmann for believing that British neutrality was a realistic option in 1914: 'The unfortunate Beth-mann (*der Beth- und Unglücksmann*) was caught up in the delusion that the English would be moved and embrace us again, if only we did not "provoke" them.' The underestimation of the British opponent continued right into the war. On 30 August, e.g., the Bavarian Crown Prince Rupprecht noted in his diary: '[Falkenhayn] said that 5000 English [troops] had landed in our rear at Ostend. That is fine by us. We'll get them!': Crown Prince Rupprecht of Bavaria, *Mein Kriegstagebuch*, vol. 1, p. 72, also in BA-MA, w-10/50659, p. 86.

[113] BA-MA, w-10/51063, Moltke to Freytag-Loringhoven, 26 July 1915.

to begin would be worse than anyone could imagine, and he was concerned about its consequences. Despite his bellicose words, he was not totally confident of German victory.[114] He desired it desperately, but he was not certain of it. Yet the image that he and his fellow officers gave to the outside was that of certainty of victory. Thus Lerchenfeld could report on 3 August: 'It seems to be settled that everyone will be going against us, but I share the confidence (*Zuversicht*) of the military that we will succeed.'[115]

Moltke was, however, already sowing some doubts as to the length of the expected war. Thus, he told Lerchenfeld on 5 August that 'England's joining with our opponents had no doubt worsened our situation, because it might become difficult to ensure supplies for the civilian population should the war last longer. This point was of some concern to him.'[116] Others, too, had a notion that the hope of a short war – lasting a matter of weeks – was perhaps wishful thinking. Bethmann Hollweg expressed concern about feeding the population in time of war: 'The future war, with its use of million-strong armies, will not be over as quickly as the war of 1870.'[117] Recently, Stig Förster has advanced the argument that, contrary to widely held beliefs, not everyone before the First World War was convinced that the fighting would be over by Christmas: in fact, the 'short war' doctrine failed to convince some military experts. The evidence he has gathered to support this thesis certainly suggests that the illusion of a short war was not wholeheartedly shared by everyone. Förster demonstrates that there was much more a desperate hope, rather than a belief, in a short war, because a long war between industrialized nations was inconceivable. Moltke was among those who expressed serious doubts whether the coming war would be as short as was widely anticipated.[118] As with his doubts about Germany's ultimate chances of victory, however, he did not make his fears about the prospects of a long-drawn-out war of attrition widely known, and failed to instigate any precautionary measures.[119] Optimistically, Lerchenfeld could report on 2 August: 'One can say

---

[114] Hermann v. Santen, officer in the General Staff's railway department, remembered the declaration that Moltke made in the morning of 31 July, when his impression was that Moltke 'was completely aware of the difficult, perhaps for him too difficult, task that fate had confronted him with'. Santen, 'Erinnerungen', vol. 10, p. 373.

[115] Lerchenfeld to Hertling, 3 August 1914, in Deuerlein, *Briefwechsel*, doc. 116, p. 325.

[116] Lerchenfeld to Hertling, 5 August 1914, in ibid., doc. 119, p. 330.

[117] Lerchenfeld to Hertling, 4 June 1914, in ibid., doc. 97, p. 296.

[118] Förster, 'Metakritik eines Mythos'. Holger Herwig also emphasises this point in his recent monograph *The First World War*, pp. 36, 49.

[119] See Ludwig Beck, 'Besass Deutschland 1914 einen Kriegsplan?' in idem, *Studien*, p. 98.

today that Germany and Austria will be opposed by the whole world in the impending war. Nonetheless, the mood in the military circle here is one of complete confidence.'[120]

While Moltke felt he could confide his doubts in his personal adjutant Haeften in the night of 30/31 July, when addressing a meeting of General Staff officers the next morning he made a confident impression. Hermann von Santen, an officer in the General Staff's Railway Department, recalled Moltke's declaration to his officers on the eve of war:

> The words that he directed toward us were sober and simple: the Reich probably stood facing the greatest war that world history had ever seen. We were entering a war on two fronts, for, even though the same news of mobilization measures as had been received from Russia had not yet been received from France, there could be no doubt regarding France's ultimate position.[121] Then Moltke declared in a loud voice: 'Gentlemen! I trust the army! I know that its soul is healthy. And now, gentlemen, go to your posts and do your duty, as His Majesty and your country expect from you.' . . . We parted under the impression that the man who had just spoken to us was fully aware of the difficult task . . . that fate had confronted him with.[122]

Whatever doubts Moltke may have harboured, outwardly the Chief of the General Staff maintained convincingly that Germany would be victorious in the coming war, as Kurt Riezler recalled on 25 May 1915: 'After all, Bethmann can blame the coming of the war on the problematic situation that he took over and on the answer that Moltke gave him at the beginning of July [!]. He did say yes! we would succeed.'[123] Together with the claim that this was a 'justified' war, a war that had been forced on Germany by envious and dangerous neighbours, these views helped to create the popular enthusiasm for war that carried away so many Germans in the first days and weeks of fighting.[124] Moltke's guilt lies as

---

[120] Lerchenfeld to Hertling, 2 August 1914, in Deuerlein, *Briefwechsel*, doc. 115, p. 324.

[121] Even when France's attitude seemed to offer a glimpse of hope for neutrality, Moltke did not consider a change of strategy that might turn the expected two-front war into one against Russia only. See below, pp. 216ff.   [122] Santen, 'Erinnerungen', vol. 10, p. 373.

[123] Riezler, *Tagebücher*, p. 275.

[124] Recent research into the so-called *Augusterlebnis* has revealed that the enthusiasm with which German people greeted the war in 1914 was less uniform than has often been assumed. Apprehension was just as prevalent as fervour, and any analysis of the phenomenon must consider differences of social and regional background and political persuasion, as recent local studies show. See e.g. Benjamin Ziemann, *Front und Heimat. Ländliche Kriegserfahrungen im südlichen Bayern*, Essen 1997, pp. 39ff.; Christian Geinitz, *Kriegsfurcht und Kampfbereitschaft. Das Augusterlebnis in Freiburg. Eine Studie zum Kriegsbeginn 1914*, Essen 1998; M. Stöcker, *'Augusterlebnis 1914' in Darmstadt. Legende und Wirklichkeit*, Darmstadt 1994; Roger Chickering, *Imperial Germany and the Great War, 1914–1918*, Cambridge 1998, pp. 13ff. Nonetheless, the German government did on

much in disguising his own doubts about Germany's ultimate chances at victory as in constantly advocating a war. Thus, German political decision-makers never felt the need to re-think or adapt their foreign policy, which they might have done if they had realized that such doubts existed in the highest military circles. Instead, they completely overestimated Germany's military strength. Wilhelm von Stumm expressed this overconfidence, as well as his complete ignorance of Germany's strategic plan, during the July Crisis, when he declared: 'I will force the Russians on to their knees in three days.'[125] Kurt Riezler, too, recalled that the military's optimism had influenced political decisions, when he tried to justify Germany policy of 1914 almost two years after the July Crisis in a conversation with Theodor Wolff:

R[iezler] thinks that some things appear differently today – back then we could not have known with certainty that Russia and England would strike. What is more, the General Staff had declared that the war against France would take 40 days. All that has to be taken into account.[126]

In February 1915, Stumm felt he had to defend his role in July 1914, claiming that 'nobody could have foreseen that militarily everything would not work out as we had believed'.[127] Rather, the Auswärtiges Amt had operated with a presumed certainty of military superiority. Zimmermann had even told Hoyos on 3 July that thanks to the large increases of the army bill of 1913, Germany's army was strong enough to fight the war without Austrian help, if the latter found herself tied up against Serbia and unable to deploy significant numbers of troops to the eastern front. 'That did not matter', Zimmermann confidently asserted, 'because Germany was strong enough to conduct the war on both fronts alone.'[128]

It was not only German decision-makers who based their policy-making on an allegedly strong, if not invincible army. The Austrian ally, too, was motivated in its decisions by a belief in German military strength. After the war, Count Hoyos recalled:

Nobody today can imagine just how much the belief in the German power, in the invincibility of the German army, determined out thinking and how certain

---

the whole manage to convince its people that Germany was acting defensively: an important prerequisite for achieving popular support for the war, and for the *Burgfriede* (truce) with the Social Democrats.   [125] Wolff, *Tagebücher*, 11 May 1916, p. 379.
[126] Ibid., 24 May 1916, p. 384.   [127] Ibid., 17 February 1915, p. 167.
[128] Quoted in Fritz Fellner, 'Die Mission Hoyos' in Wilhelm Alf (ed.), *Deutschlands Sonderung von Europa 1862–1945*, Frankfurt/M. 1984, p. 312. Conrad laughed at Hoyos when the latter told him this story, and told him that 'Zimmermann did not know what he was saying.'

we all were that Germany ~~would easily win the war against France~~ [*crossed out in the original*] would provide us with the greatest guarantee of our safety should a European war result from our action against Serbia.[129]

On the other hand, the Austrian ally's military measures were a source of anxiety for Moltke. On 15 July 1914, Kageneck's report from Vienna about the likely Austrian mobilization procedure was disheartening. 'However, it will all go slowly with the usual [Austrian] humdrum routine. . . .'[130] During the last week of July, further concerns were expressed about the expected length of time needed for Austrian mobilization. Forecast at between 12 and 16 days, it spelt a substantial delay before Austrian troops could actually engage their opponents and therefore threatened to delay German mobilization, too. Leuckart reported to the Saxon Minister of War on 29 July:

> On the Great General Staff they are of the opinion that the Austrian army will not be operational before 12 August. Rumour has it that the Austrian mobilization has been hindered by difficulties and that we might therefore also have to postpone our mobilization if possible, should mobilization become necessary.[131]

It must have seemed to Moltke that, when every hour counted for Germany, Austria was wasting precious time. Yet he did not get in contact with Conrad at any time in July. Their last meeting had occurred on 12 May in Karlsbad, and following the assassination they only exchanged thoughts once, on 30 July. On the previous day, Conrad's adjutant Hauptmann Fleischmann von Theissruck, had arrived in Berlin, and Hauptmann Hasse was in turn sent to Vienna.[132]

Matters were made worse when Moltke discovered on 30 July that Conrad intended to remain on the defensive in Galicia, while concentrating on an offensive against Serbia. Conrad had always regarded Serbia as the main enemy. The fact that Moltke and Conrad had not been completely honest with each other in their negotiations now began to take its toll. Each expected the alliance partner to bail him out in the theatre of war that they both considered less important, despite its obviously superior strength: Russia.

Moltke received this news at the same time as reports were arriving about Russian moves towards a general mobilization, and, in Gerhard Ritter's words, felt 'almost dizzy' in the light of his knowledge of the

---

[129] Quoted ibid., p. 313.   [130] PA Bonn, R8627, Kageneck to Waldersee, 15 July 1914.

[131] A copy of Leuckart's letter of 29 July can be found in BA-MA, W-10/50890.

[132] Fleischmann and Moltke met for the first time on 30 July. Schäfer, 'Generaloberst von Moltke in den Tagen vor der Mobilmachung', p. 522.

requirements of the German deployment plan. If Austrian troops did not engage Russian troops in Galicia, the careful time-tabling of German deployment in the West before turning against Russia would crumble.[133] As late as the afternoon of 31 July, Conrad intended to make the punishment of Serbia a priority, and Moltke tried frantically to achieve a change of heart in Austria. The Kaiser became involved, too, and in a telegram to Franz Joseph urged Austria not to get 'distracted' by Serbia, whose role in the forthcoming war he considered to be of minor importance:

In this difficult struggle it is of the utmost importance that Austria deploy her main troops against Russia and does not split them up by a simultaneous offensive against Serbia. This is all the more important because a large part of my army will be tied up by France. Serbia's role in this gigantic fight, in which we enter shoulder to shoulder, is completely peripheral and only requires the most basic defensive measures.[134]

Considering that Austria's intention at the beginning of the July Crisis had actually been to retaliate against Serbia, and that she still hoped that by some miracle Russia would, at the last minute, decide to stay out of the conflict, this was a lot to ask. The one-sided nature of Germany's military planning began to impose restrictions not just on Germany's options, but also on Austria's. In fact, it made a localized conflict impossible.

In those crucial final days of peace, the worries about Austria weighed heavily on Moltke, who was beginning to feel the strain of responsibility for the war that was about to begin. The lack of trust in the pre-war years was now taking its toll, and when war broke out, the secrecy in the relationship between the German and Austrian General Staffs had grave consequences. No concrete information had been exchanged, even as late as 1 August, when Kageneck wrote to Waldersee: 'It is high time that the two general staffs consulted with absolute frankness about mobilization, jump-off time, areas of assembly, and precise troop strength.'[135] Everyone in the two General Staffs had been relying on the belief that the two chiefs of staff had worked out these most intimate agreements between themselves. The crucially important question of a united supreme command between Germany and Austria had never even been

---

[133] Ritter, *Staatskunst*, vol. 2, pp. 324–325.
[134] *DD*, vol. 3, doc. 503, Wilhelm II to Franz Joseph, 31 July 1914.
[135] Quoted in Gordon Craig, 'The World War I Alliance of the Central Powers in Retrospect: The Military Cohesion of the Alliance', *Journal of Modern History*, September 1965, p. 338. See also Beck, 'Besass Deutschland 1914 einen Kriegsplan?', pp. 100ff.

raised before 1914. Gordon Craig sums up how the German General Staff embarked on the war, 'with only the most rudimentary knowledge of the strength, organization, command structure, national composition, and tactical forms of the Austro-Hungarian army'.[136] The lack of understanding was such that there was even surprise in Germany when it was 'discovered' that not all soldiers in the Austro-Hungarian army spoke German. Despite Moltke's desire to lead an 'alliance war', ignorance of Austro-Hungarian military affairs was a striking shortcoming in German military planning.

THE EVENTS OF I AUGUST 1914

In the last days of the crisis, military concerns began to supersede any political attempts at alleviating the situation. Military requirements made it impossible for the politicians to react to Russia's assurances that her mobilization did not have to result in war, and that Russian troops would not begin hostilities while Austria and Serbia were still negotiating. Nor could they support Britain's suggestion that Austria should make a negotiation proposal that Russia could not refuse. Britain even suggested that in such a scenario she would not support Russia, if a conflict proved unavoidable despite a genuine Austrian negotiation attempt. The restrictions of the Schlieffen/Moltke Plan meant that Germany could no longer accept such offers.[137] However, on 1 August a last-minute proposal was received that seemed to suggest the possibility of British neutrality. It was an opportunity the Kaiser and Chancellor felt they could not ignore. For Moltke, the events of 1 August spelt the first in a long chain of disasters that would lead to his downfall.

In the afternoon of 1 August, Russia had not replied to Germany's ultimatum, but Moltke and Falkenhayn insisted that German mobilization had to begin. Moltke's frustration at the delay this posed became particularly apparent. With reliable news from Russia still not forthcoming, Tirpitz suggested delaying action in the West, but Moltke 'urged we should proceed immediately'. Although the imminent arrival of an important telegram from Lichnowsky, Germany's ambassador to London, had been announced, Moltke did not even want to await it. Tirpitz expressed the opinion 'that an hour more or less did not matter

---

[136] Craig, 'World War I Alliance', pp. 338ff. See also Dennis E. Showalter, *Tannenberg. Clash of Empires*, Hamden, Conn. 1991, p. 143, who likens the two allies to a married couple going on holiday with each assuming that the other one had turned off the stove.

[137] See also Ritter, *Staatskunst*, vol. 2, pp. 329ff.

9 The mobilization order of 1 August 1914, signed by the Kaiser and Chancellor Bethmann Hollweg

10 The Kaiser, with hand-written declaration 'Ich kenne keine Parteien mehr, kenne nur noch Deutsche' ('I no longer know any parties, I know only Germans'); postcard from the beginning of the war

to our intended action. H.M. agreed with me, despite Moltke's protest.'[138] Of all the men present at the Schloss, only Moltke knew how much each hour counted.

At 5 p.m. on 1 August, the Kaiser signed the mobilization order in the presence of the Chancellor, Moltke, Falkenhayn, Tirpitz, Lyncker and Plessen.[139] Moltke had already left the Schloss when Lichnowsky's fateful telegram arrived that threatened to overthrow all the careful military arrangements for the initial days of the war. The ambassador reported that Grey had informed him not only that England would remain neutral, but also that she would guarantee French neutrality in a forthcoming war, if Germany refrained from hostilities against France.[140] In Lyncker's words, the news impacted 'like a bomb':

Immediately the opinion was prevalent that this request could under no account be turned down, even if the offer was only a bluff, which was after all possible. For firstly this might be the opportunity perhaps to have to face only 1 rather than 3 opponents, that is Russia, against whom war has already been declared today; and secondly the Kaiser must grasp the hand that is offered and may not repulse it for reasons of loyalty to the [German] people and the public.[141]

To the civilian decision-makers, the British offer seemed to present a real opportunity for avoiding the dreaded two-front war. The Kaiser and Bethmann Hollweg were concerned to preserve British neutrality. In fact, a détente with Britain had been the basic premise of Bethmann's policy all along, and when, for a short while, this seemed possible, the Kaiser insisted on a change of deployment. Instead of heading West, he wanted 'his' troops to go East.

Moltke was immediately recalled to the Schloss, where he found the Kaiser and Bethmann 'joyfully excited' over the news from Lichnowsky. 'There was a happy mood. Now we only had to conduct the war against Russia. The Kaiser said to me: "So we simply deploy the whole army in the East!"' Moltke replied that this was impossible. Lyncker recorded: 'There was general astonishment when Moltke declared that the deployment in the West could no longer be stopped and that war would have

---

[138] Tirpitz, quoted in Geiss, *Julikrise*, vol. 2, doc.1000e.

[139] Ibid., doc. 1000, Falkenhayn diary, 1 August 1914; Wegerer, *Ausbruch*, vol. 2, p. 187. See also Lerchenfeld to Hertling, 1 August 1914, in Deuerlein, *Briefwechsel*, doc. 114, p. 323.

[140] Geiss, *Julikrise*, vol. 2, doc. 983.

[141] Lyncker's diary, ibid., doc. 1000b. There are several testimonies to the events in the Kaiser's Schloss that day, collected in ibid., docs. 1000 a–e; see also Wegerer, *Ausbruch*, vol. 2, pp. 188ff. Haeften's accounts are particularly important: see BA-MA, N35/1, as well as his article in *Deutsche Allgemeine Zeitung*, 11 October 1921. For an analysis of these events, see also Albertini, *Origins*, vol. 3, pp. 172ff.; Trachtenberg, 'The Coming of the First World War', pp. 58ff.

to be forced on to France despite everything.' Admiral von Müller, who was also present at the meeting, recorded similarly:

The Kaiser says: 'Of course we must go along with this and therefore stop the deployment in the West for the time being.' General v. Moltke: 'We cannot do that; if that were to happen, we would disrupt the whole army and would give up any chance of success. Besides, our patrols have already entered Luxembourg and the Division from Trier is to follow immediately.'[142]

Could it be that at the last minute, the war that already seemed unavoidable would be averted? To the shocked Moltke, the Kaiser's interference demonstrated that the monarch still wanted to preserve peace. Outraged, he complained: 'The final straw would be if Russia now also fell away.'[143] He declared that he could not accept any responsibility for the war if the Kaiser's order to stop the Sixteenth Division from leaving Trier for Luxembourg were followed. Bethmann's response was that for his part he would not accept responsibility if the British offer were declined.[144] Falkenhayn, who had been called to the scene, was no less belligerent than Moltke, but he calmed the frantic Chief of Staff. Moltke was later to complain bitterly to Haeften that the Minister of War, 'instead of supporting him against the nonsensical plans of the Kaiser, had remained silent'.[145] Falkenhayn apparently did not believe that Lichnowsky's telegram would alter anything in the events that had been initiated with the signing of the mobilization order at 5 p.m. The outcome proved him right.

It was during these tense hours on 1 August that Moltke 'lost his nerve', as commentators put it, because he had no alternative to the deployment of troops in the West, and to the surprise attack on Liège before war was even declared. Railway time-tables and mobilization plans had been worked out meticulously by the General Staff. What had taken months to perfect could not simply be changed at the last minute, Moltke explained to the Kaiser: 'If His Majesty insisted on leading the entire army to the East then he would not have an army that was ready to strike but a messy heap of disorderly, armed men without supplies.'[146] Already in 1911 he had warned the Chancellor that there would come a point when military considerations would assume primacy over political concerns:

---

[142] Müller, *Diary*, pp. 38ff.; also in Geiss, *Julikrise*, vol. 2, doc. 1000d.

[143] Müller, *Diary*, p. 39; Geiss, *Julikrise*, vol. 2, doc. 1000d. Thomas Meyer, one of Moltke's apologists, credits the Chief of Staff with rather a lot of foresight when he claims that he had immediately recognized that the news had to be fake. In fact, Meyer tries to blame Britain for the outbreak of war: *Moltke*, vol. 1, pp. 16–17.   [144] Müller, *Diary*, p. 39.

[145] BA-MA, N35/1, Haeften, 'Meine Erlebnisse aus den Mobilmachungstagen 1914', p. 35.

[146] Moltke, *Erinnerungen*, p. 20; also in Geiss, *Julikrise* vol. 2, doc. 1000c.

The preparations for deployment and operations require long and careful work, they cannot be changed from one day to the next, and our political leadership will also have to bear them in mind. Even the precise point in time when politics are to be continued by force of arms can be of decisive importance for the outcome.[147]

Three years later he had not changed his opinion: he still maintained that a last-minute alteration was impossible. After all, on what basis would such a change be made? On a vague promise from Britain that might be revoked at any moment? And could France be trusted not to come to her ally's help once German troops were engaged in the East? German strategy could not be based on such an assurance, as Moltke had already outlined in a memorandum of January 1913:

I would consider it to be extraordinarily dangerous if we decided to do without the only chance that a speedy war against France would give us, based only on vague assurances from England. We would burden ourselves with the difficulty of a frontal attack on the French eastern front and have no guarantee that England would not intervene at a given moment anyway.[148]

In this memorandum, Moltke had speculated on the possibility of British neutrality – the very scenario that he was faced with on 1 August 1914. He had posed the question whether the march through Belgium should be abandoned if Britain guaranteed her neutrality, and had been quite adamant that this would not be possible:

It would be very dangerous, because it is quite uncertain whether England would keep her promise; at the same time we would abandon our only chance of the quick and resounding success we need so badly. To renounce the march through Belgium would only be possible if England went along with us. But that is out of the question, because England considers Germany stronger than France, is afraid of German hegemony and wants to preserve the balance in Europe.[149]

In August 1914, Moltke re-emphasized this point. Respecting Belgium's neutrality was too high a price to pay, even for British neutrality, he declared.[150] His refusal to comply with the Kaiser's order on 1 August

---

[147] Moltke to Bethmann, 2 December 1911, quoted in BA-MA, w-10/50279, also in w-10/50276: 'Die Militärpolitische Lage Deutschlands', pp. 57–58. For details of the memorandum and letter, see above, Chapter 3, p. 132.

[148] BA-MA, w-10/50276: 'Die Militärpolitische Lage Deutschlands', pp. 66–67. This important document of January 1913 probably did not survive the Second World War. It is also referred to by Gerhard Ritter, who saw it in 1943 and presumed that it was intended for the Chief of the Military Cabinet. The original document was entitled 'Germany's conduct in a Triple Alliance war' ('Verhalten Deutschlands in einem Dreibundkrieg'). Ritter's notes can now be supplemented with the Reichsarchiv study cited here (Ritter, *Schlieffen Plan*, pp. 68–69, note 50).

[149] Cited in ibid.

[150] Lerchenfeld to Hertling, 4 August 1914, in Geiss, *Julikrise*, vol. 2, doc. 1148.

led to the monarch snapping: 'Your uncle would have given me a different answer', and 'it must be possible, if I order it'. The 'Supreme War-Lord' prominently displayed his lack of military expertise and understanding in this situation.[151] He brushed Moltke's objections aside and told his *Flügeladjutant* Oberst von Mutius to stop the advance of the Sixteenth Division. Although Moltke tried to explain the strategic importance of the Luxembourg railways, which the Sixteenth Division was to occupy on the first day of mobilization, he was simply told that he would have to use different railway tracks instead.[152] Eventually, Moltke was able to achieve a compromise: deployment was allowed to continue as planned, but had to stop just before the border. Depending on the nature of French assurances, an orderly move to the East could then be undertaken, rather than halting the deployment immediately and creating chaos. As long as France's position was unclear, Moltke insisted that Germany would have to deploy the main part of her armies in the West. 'Only after a clarification of France's position, and after securing guarantees for her neutrality, would the transport of the German army to the East be possible.'[153] However, Moltke could not change the Kaiser's mind, or alter the fact that the march into Luxembourg and Belgium was to be postponed.[154]

That evening, when Moltke returned to the General Staff building from the Schloss, he was distraught, as Dommes recalled:

I found Gen. v. Moltke in a state of greatest excitement. His Majesty's order to stop the 16th Division (which was to occupy Luxembourg on the 1st day of mobilization) had affected him greatly. He was dark red in the face. It appeared as if he might suffer a stroke at any moment. Frau von Moltke also feared this; in her opinion he had already suffered a light stroke.[155]

In February 1915, Eliza von Moltke recalled her impression of the effect of these events on her husband. 'I saw immediately that something terrible had happened here. He was purple in the face, his pulse hardly countable. I had a desperate man in front of me.'[156]

To Moltke, the Kaiser's interference was disastrous, although perhaps not altogether unexpected. The Kaiser had always been a risk factor in

[151] See Ritter, *Staatskunst*, vol. 2, p. 336.
[152] Moltke, *Erinnerungen*, pp. 20–21; also in Geiss, *Julikrise*, vol. 2, doc. 1000c; Wegerer, *Ausbruch*, vol. 2, p. 190.
[153] Haeften, quoted in *Kreuz-Zeitung*, 10 October 1921, BA-MA, NL Tappen, N56/2.
[154] Wegerer, *Ausbruch*, vol. 2, p. 189.
[155] BA-MA, W-10/51061, Dommes to Reichsarchiv, 14 January 1926. Eliza von Moltke told Haeften the same thing: Haeften, 'Meine Erlebnisse aus den Mobilmachungstagen 1914', BA-MA, N35/1, p. 35.   [156] Quoted in Grone, 'Zum Kriegsausbruch 1914', p. 8.

military planning; his interferences, though less frequent by the time Moltke was Chief of the General Staff, were still unpredictable and potentially dangerous. Moltke had always been aware that, just as the Kaiser had been prone to interfere in army manoeuvres, he was likely to get involved in 'the real thing'. In September 1901, during army manoeuvres, Moltke had sent the following account to his wife:

As I see from the paper, the Kaiser has interrupted the big manoeuvres for a day because of the rain. A layman can hardly understand what this means for the leadership of the manoeuvres. All dispositions will be messed up . . . everything will be topsy-turvy, and all those difficulties aside, the impression in the army will be that soldiers cannot cope with rain when it matters. – Just imagine the results if such forceful intervention were to be made during the real thing.[157]

On 1 August 1914, Moltke's worst fears were confirmed, and even a layman can imagine his horror as he was faced with the Kaiser ordering a German deployment in the East rather than the West. As 'Supreme War-Lord', the Kaiser could insist on orders being carried out as he saw fit, regardless of the fact that he was ill-equipped to make such important decisions – and in this situation he did just that. Moltke complained bitterly to Haeften on 1 August: 'I want to wage a war against the French and the Russians, but not against such a Kaiser.'[158] He feared that the monarch would not even have signed the mobilization order if Lichnowsky's telegram had arrived half an hour earlier.[159] It is worth speculating that war could perhaps still have been averted in that case, because the time for finding a diplomatic solution to the crisis had not yet passed.

Later that night, Moltke and Dommes returned to the Schloss to try to effect a change of mind in the Kaiser. During their absence, he had received bad news from London. A second telegram from London spelt out the unacceptable conditions according to which Britain was willing to negotiate her neutrality: Belgium was to be spared, and those troops earmarked for the war against France were not to be used against Russia. Moltke was finally given the go-ahead for the occupation of Luxembourg.[160] The Kaiser, already in bed, told Moltke: "'As has now

[157] Moltke, *Erinnerungen*, pp. 245–246, 19 September 1901.
[158] BA-MA, N35/1, Haeften, 'Meine Erlebnisse aus den Mobilmachungstagen 1914', p. 34.
[159] See Heisterkamp, 'Lebensskizze', in Meyer, *Moltke*, vol. 1, p. 35.
[160] Lichnowsky's telegram has usually been regarded as based on a misunderstanding (See e.g. Geiss, *Julikrise*, vol. 2, p. 530; Bethmann Hollweg, *Betrachtungen zum Weltkrieg*, 2 vols., Berlin 1919/1921, vol. 1, p. 183), but Afflerbach, *Falkenhayn*, p. 166, note 82, argues it was in fact motivated by Grey's difficulty in getting approval from the Cabinet for intervention on the continent. On Britain's decision-making during the July Crisis see Zara Steiner, *Britain and the Origins of the First World War*, London 1977.

transpired, Lichnowsky's telegram was based on a misunderstanding."
Turning over in the bed, he continued: "Now do as you please; I don't
care either way.""[161]

Moltke's younger son Adam, in a post-war attempt to justify his
father's actions and to defend him from his numerous critics, described
the impact of the events of 1 August on his father quite dramatically:

He had to witness how the Kaiser and the Chancellor, in their blind belief in
England, fell for this 'misunderstanding' [i.e. the telegram from Lichnowsky] –
and 'misunderstanding' is putting it diplomatically. He had to witness how the
Kaiser laid bare the borders of the country whose protection, in view of the situation, had already been entrusted to the soldiers, and how he laid them open
for a hostile, mobilizing France to pounce. He had to witness how the Supreme
War-Lord, in a quite unbelievably dilettante way, demanded an immediate
change of direction of all the armed forces towards the East. . . . Eight years of
difficult and well-thought-out work were to be eradicated through the
monarch's capricious demand for power. What the outcome of this would be
was a clear vision for the Chief of the General Staff: the downfall of
Germany.[162]

Moltke was adamant on 1 August that the German army could not be
directed eastwards. After the war, some commentators, such as Groener
and Kuhl, felt that a deployment in the East 'to a certain degree' would
actually have been feasible.[163] It has been suggested not only that such a
change was indeed a possibility, but also, crucially, that it could have had
a positive effect on the outcome of the war. Both Ludwig Beck and
Gerhard Ritter have argued that the elder Moltke's strategy offered
more hope of military success than the Schlieffen Plan. Gordon Craig
rightly points out that, decades after the event, it is impossible to maintain this with any certainty, but he is also correct in suggesting that the
fraught relationship between the German and Austrian allies might have
been ameliorated by a joint success on the eastern front against a
common enemy.[164] Without any up-to-date deployment plans, however,
Moltke was right in thinking that the physical reality of moving the

---

[161] BA-MA, N35/1, Haeften, 'Meine Erlebnisse aus den Mobilmachungstagen 1914', pp. 35–36.

[162] Adam von Moltke's reply to Walter Görlitz, 'Eine Antwort an Herrn Walter Görlitz, das Kapitel
"Der Krieg ohne Feldherr" in seinem Buch "Der Deutsche Generalstab" betreffend', NL
Moltke, N78/37, pp. 18–19. Given the gravity of the situation, capricious (*launisch*) seems an
understatement for the Kaiser's last-minute efforts to try to limit the war and prevent a
European-wide escalation.

[163] Kuhl, *Der Weltkrieg 1914–1918*, vol. 1, pp. 15–16; Groener, *Lebenserinnerungen*, p. 145; Herzfeld, *Der
erste Weltkrieg*, pp. 50–51. Yet one wonders what Kuhl meant by a change of plan 'to a certain
degree', and whether these voices were not wise after the event. See also Beck, 'West oder
Ostoffensive?'   [164] Craig, 'World War I Alliance', p. 344.

German army to the East was an impossibility. The chaos that would have ensued would hardly have helped Germany against her numerically superior enemies. Perhaps, however, a different counter-factual speculation could be considered. It would seem that the reasoning behind the scrapping of the eastern deployment plan was that, strategically, it did not offer a realistic chance of winning in 1913.[165] However, if Moltke had spent effort on developing an alternative plan, rather than deciding to scrap it in 1913, the option to deploy troops in the East would have existed in 1914. If France and Britain had decided not to support Russia, then a deployment to the eastern front and a defensive stance could have prevented an escalation of the Austro-Serbian conflict. Moreover, such a plan would have allowed for more honesty with the Austrian ally, for Russia was the only major enemy they shared. Moltke's defenders have perhaps been too keen to blame the Kaiser for the disastrous events of 1 August 1914. He was no military expert, and as such unaware of the implications of his order; but his layman's instinct rightly suggested to him that there *should* have been an alternative to the almost suicidal mobilization plan in the West. It was up to the military experts to find such an alternative plan, rather than stake Germany's fate on the one card that they hoped would provide them with a chance of victory. Moltke's narrow war plan significantly restricted any options for peace in 1914; considering his frequently expressed desire for war 'the sooner the better', it is worth speculating whether the existing war plan did not even deliberately impose such restrictions.

On 1 August, Moltke's trust in his Kaiser was severely shaken, and he was never to recover from the shock of this potentially disastrous interference. According to his son, Moltke now had to expect at all times that there might be interference with in his strategic leadership.[166] He would most certainly have endorsed Varnbüler's view that 'indeed, our diplomacy cannot pride itself in having smoothed the German army's path or eased its gigantic task by even one enemy army corps'.[167] On 6 August, he had a further confrontation with the monarch, when he had the duty of reporting the initial failure to take Liège. The Kaiser

---

[165] See Chapter 2, pp. 100ff.

[166] BA-MA, NL Moltke, N78/37, Adam von Moltke, pp. 18–19; Eliza von Moltke: 'I saw immediately that something had happened here that could not be rectified, because his soul was too deeply wounded and shaken . . . That dreadful evening . . . he and I knew that there would be tragedy, and that feeling never left us after that moment.' Quoted in Grone, 'Zum Kriegsausbruch 1914', p. 8.

[167] A copy of the report by Varnbüler (Württemberg's ambassador) dated 2 August 1914 can be found in BA-MA, W-10/50890.

reproached him, and pointed out how he had always said the plan was nonsense and unworkable – whereas in fact the details had not been known to him. Later that day, when Moltke brought better news about Liège, the Kaiser hugged him and, according to Haeften, could not find enough words of praise for this success.[168] Müller recorded in his diary: 'Liège taken. Kaiser overjoyed'.[169]

The events of 1 and 6 August left Moltke feeling deeply disillusioned with his monarch and 'Supreme War-Lord'. Between 1 August and the Battle of the Marne, Moltke's health was impaired (he had already been to Karlsbad twice that year), and his confidence was badly shaken. It is not entirely surprising that the first major set-back, the battle of the Marne, would lead to his collapse and ultimate downfall. His final weeks in office, his replacement as Chief of the General Staff, and the months following his dismissal are the subject of the following chapter.

[168] BA-MA, N35/1, Haeften, 'Meine Erlebnisse aus den Mobilmachungstagen 1914', p. 36.
[169] Müller, *Diary*, p. 45.

CHAPTER FIVE

The General Staff at war

ATTACK IS THE BEST FORM OF DEFENCE: GERMAN
DEPLOYMENT AND THE FIRST WEEKS OF WAR

One cannot go to war with dreamers!

Generaloberst von Beseler, 15 September 1914[1]

When mobilization was finally declared and war had become a reality, the mood among the General Staff and the Ministry of War was one of elation. Wenninger recorded beaming faces everywhere in the Ministry when he went there following the declaration of war, and 'shaking of hands in the corridors, they congratulate each other on having jumped the ditch'.[2] The anxious period of waiting was over, as Major von Nida, who had been one of those troops immediately bound for Liège, recalled almost nostalgically in 1920:

On Saturday afternoon on 1 August I had returned home late, after we had waited for hours in vain at the General Staff for the Mob[ilization] Order. At 6 o'clock in the evening I sent my batman once again into Berlin, who suddenly appeared in front of me out of breath: Mobilization!! At last! At last! Went immediately to fetch the familiar secret maps for the attack from the General Staff, a brief instruction, a quick handshake, the last preparations in haste, a grave good-bye at home – and off we were carried by the train, away from tumultuous Berlin to the West, the starting point of our activities.[3]

When mobilization was declared, the details of the carefully guarded mobilization plan required only distribution. After the war, Tappen recalled this momentous occasion following years of preparation and anticipation as 'a strange feeling, when the big iron cupboards that contained the carefully guarded deployment material, to which our daily

---

[1] BA-MA, w-10/50631, Generaloberst von Beseler, diary entry, 15 September 1914, p. 12.
[2] Wenninger's report, 31 July 1914, in Schulte, 'Neue Dokumente', p. 140.
[3] BA-MA, w-10/50951, Major von Nida, 'Der Sturm auf Lüttich nach eigenen Erlebnissen'.

and often nightly thinking, worrying and working during countless hours had been dedicated, quickly began to empty'.[4]

According to contemporary commentators, the mobilization measures were carried out without a hitch, and 'the whole apparatus functioned like a well-oiled machine'.[5] Lerchenfeld was full of praise for the mobilization, which was being conducted 'exceptionally well'. 'The General Staff and the Ministry of War have not yet received a single enquiry from anywhere. Everybody knows what he has to do', he wrote on 4 August.[6] The success of the mobilization entirely justified the confidence of Moltke and his General Staff colleagues, who had felt they could afford to be absent from Berlin during the first weeks of the July Crisis because the mobilization plans were all finalized. It also did much to confirm the post-war belief in the apparent excellence of the German army and its General Staff. According to the Reichsarchiv, the mobilization in the West, which was completed within the space of 12 days, was 'an extraordinarily remarkable achievement. . . . The first great test of the reliability and thoroughness of the peacetime work of the German army could be considered to have been passed.'[7] Considering that a whole 'mobilization machine' was set in motion, in which approximately six per cent of the population had to be transported, equipped and kept supplied, the fact that this was achieved without any major hitches was indeed an impressive achievement.[8]

The German deployment plan of 1914 envisaged the following initial troop movements: nine divisions of the army were to remain in the East, 70 divisions to march immediately to the West. This left the German army with a reserve of eight and one third divisions, six and one third of which were 'Ersatz' divisions in the process of being formed. Moltke wanted to use five of these divisions in the East, raising the total there to 14. The remaining three and one third were to guard the German coast against possible landing attempts. The total number of divisions in the West was to be $73^{1}/_{3}$, to face a numerically superior alliance of French,

[4] BA-MA, w-10/50661, Tappen, 'Kriegserinnerungen', p. 13.

[5] BA-MA, w-10/50636, 'Erinnerungen des General der Infantrie a.D. Franke an seine Dienstzeit', o.D., pp. 7–8.

[6] Lerchenfeld to Hertling, 4 August 1914, in Geiss, *Julikrise*, vol. 2, doc. 1148. See e.g. also BA-MA, w-10/50661, Tappen, 'Kriegserinnerungen', p. 12. The competition between the Bavarian and Prussian General Staffs in boasting of how well their deployments were conducted is evidenced in Wenninger's reports to the Bavarian Minister of War, BayHSTA-KA, MKr 1765, 'Berichte des K.B. Militärbevollmächtigten, Mobilmachung 1914', No. 2779, 7 August 1914.

[7] *Der Weltkrieg*, vol. 1, p. 137.

[8] Figures from Stefan Kaufmann, *Kommunikationstechnik und Kriegsführung 1815–1945. Stufen telemedialer Rüstung*, Munich 1996, p. 145.

Belgian and British troops. The troops in the West were divided into seven armies: First Army (six corps) under the command of Generaloberst von Kluck; Second (six corps) under Generaloberst von Bülow; Third (four corps) under Generaloberst von Hausen; Fourth (five corps) under Duke Albrecht von Württemberg; Fifth (five corps) under the German Crown Prince; Sixth (five corps) under Crown Prince Rupprecht of Bavaria; Seventh (three corps) under Generaloberst von Heeringen. In the East, the Eighth Army (four corps) was under the command of Generaloberst von Prittwitz.[9]

In Moltke's opinion, inferiority in numbers did not need to affect German war planning. He relied, as he put it in a memorandum of November 1911, on the fact that 'the German people would take up arms unitedly and enthusiastically in a war that was forced upon them'. 'Mere numbers' were not as all-important as leadership skills, bravery, discipline – all attributes that Moltke associated with the German people and the German army, which, he believed, would display a unity of will unmatched by its opponents:

> Of course the number of military units (*Streitmittel*) is not by itself decisive in a war. Forces come to play that we cannot gauge in peacetime, and which lie in the realm not of mathematics but of morale. A whole nation's ability to fight (*Wehrhaftigkeit*), its readiness for war (*Kriegstüchtigkeit*), bravery, the will to make sacrifices, discipline, talent of its leadership, are to be valued more highly than mere numbers (*die tote Zahl*).[10]

Far from facing the implications of the expected *Volkskrieg* for Germany, Moltke was clearly not worried about the likely resistance by French and Belgian soldiers and civilians. Qualities assumed to be intrinsically German, such as bravery and discipline, were thought to make up for any numerical inferiority. Mobilization in 1914 meant that Germany's 'superior' character would finally be put to the test.

As part of the German war-plan, which relied on speed and surprise in advancing quickly towards Belgium,[11] neutral Luxembourg, whose

---

[9] Figures from Schäfer manuscript, BA-MA, w-10/50223, pp. 31–32; BA-MA, w-10/50661, Tappen, 'Kriegserinnerungen', p. 6; Kielmansegg, *Deutschland und der Erste Weltkrieg*, 1980, p. 33.

[10] Moltke's memoranda quoted by Schäfer, BA-MA, w-10/50223, pp. 31–32 and in w-10/50279, pp. 22–23.

[11] The surprise element was somewhat illusory, however, because a German attack on Belgium was widely expected. The French military attaché in Berlin, Serret, for example, expected Germany to attack France as soon as war broke out, and knew that Jagow had advised the German ambassador Cambon in late July 1914: 'Germany would . . . begin the fight with a *coup d'éclat* which would astonish the world.' Serret warned Paris to expect a well-prepared German attack on Belgium. See BA-MA, w-10/50349, 'Vorarbeit zum Weltkriegswerk 1914/18 über die Krise im Juli 1914' (1937), p. 20.

railway lines were essential for German strategy, was invaded on 2 August.[12] Luxembourg protested against this violation of her sovereignty, but offered no resistance.[13] The *coup de main* on Liège was the first major objective of the war. The ultimate success of Germany's strategic plan depended on a positive outcome to this first part of the offensive. The German advance into Belgium began on 4 August, and was already under way when Bethmann made his notorious Reichstag speech, in which he admitted that Germany's invasion of Luxembourg and Belgium was contrary to international law. Bethmann explained that Germany, unlike France, could not delay an invasion of Belgium for strategic reasons (i.e. the threat of a French attack on the south), and that Germany therefore had to ignore 'the justified protests of the governments of Luxembourg and Belgium'. He announced: 'We will try to make good the wrong – I speak openly – the wrong, that we have inflicted with this measure, as soon as our military goal has been achieved.'[14] Clearly, the military necessity of acting contrary to international agreements sat more uncomfortably with the Chancellor than it did with the military decision-makers, and he felt the need to adopt an apologetic tone – much to the disgust of some military commentators. Tappen, for example, remarked later that Bethmann's speech, and Germany's hasty declaration of war on Russia, had been grave and avoidable mistakes. 'They did us unending damage. Both were unnecessary.'[15]

On 5 August, Moltke responded to Bethmann's speech with a statement about Germany's initial strategy, outlining why it was impossible to spare Belgium, even if that might mean keeping Britain out of the war:

An attack [on France] from Reich territory would have cost the German army three months and would have assured Russia such a head start that it would then no longer have been possible to count on success on both fronts. We must attack France with all our might immediately via Belgium, in order to achieve a quick reckoning with France. This [is] the only way to victory.[16]

Moltke announced that Liège would be occupied the next day. In the event, the storming of one of the strongest fortresses in Europe proved

---

[12] Moltke drafted a note to Luxembourg, similar to the one to Belgium, thus clearly encroaching on the civilians' terrain. The Auswärtiges Amt did not use this memorandum, however. Cf. *DD*, vol. 3, doc. 639; also Ritter, *Staatskunst*, vol. 2, p. 386, note 21.

[13] *Der Weltkrieg*, vol. 1, pp. 105ff.; Stürgkh, *Hauptquartier*, p. 37.

[14] Bethmann Hollweg's address to the Reichstag quoted in Geiss, *Julikrise*, vol. 2, doc. 1146.

[15] BA-MA, w-10/50661, Tappen, 'Kriegserinnerungen', p. 14.

[16] Lerchenfeld to Hertling, 5 August 1914, in Deuerlein, *Briefwechsel*, doc. 119, p. 330.

more difficult than anticipated. The General Staff had only expected about 6000 garrison troops and about 3000 militia (*Bürgerwacht*): a serious, if characteristic, underestimate.[17] Manned with about 35,000 garrison troops, Liège put up strong resistance. The early mobilization of the Belgian army further impeded German hopes of a quick capture of the fortress town. As a result, it appeared initially as if the important *coup de main* was failing. Ludendorff, who as former head of the Second Department knew the details of the plan, was called upon to intervene, and under his leadership General von Emmich's troops entered the city and captured the central citadel on 7 August, although not without suffering heavy losses, particularly among officers.[18] However, all of the city's 12 concrete and iron forts still had to be overcome one by one. German troops were still fighting in Liège when the first British troops landed on the continent on 12 August. The last of Liège's forts was finally taken on 16 August, and only on the 17th, two days later than planned, was the right wing of the German army able to proceed with its enveloping move through Belgium.[19] Generalleutnant Max Hoffmann recorded in his diary at the time that taking Liège

was especially important. It had been long prepared for and the place had been thoroughly reconnoitred, so that it was depressing to learn that the first attack had failed. We were weeks behind in the entire campaign, and as everything depended on a speedy victory in the West, our joy over the success was doubly great.[20]

Liège had required 'an expenditure of men and munitions beyond all expectations'. Despite the meticulous planning, the operation was characterized by a lack of co-ordination and liaison between the troops and their leaders.[21] Great relief was felt in Berlin when the initial rumours of

---

[17] *Der Weltkrieg*, vol. 1, p. 108.

[18] Kielmansegg, *Deutschland*, p. 35. Wenninger's report of 9 August 1914 attaches great importance to the bombing activities of the Zeppelins in the success against Liège. He estimated German losses at that time as between 1000 and 3000: BayHSTA-KA, MKr 1765, No. 2820. According to Karl von Einem, the Fifty-Third Infantry Regiment had still not recovered from the loss of 'almost all its company commanders'. Cited in Kramer, 'Greueltaten', p. 89.

[19] Martin Gilbert, *The First World War*, London, paperback edn 1995, pp. 36–37, 43; Herzfeld, *Der Erste Weltkrieg*, p. 55; Herwig, *The First World War*, p. 96. Schlieffen had preferred to avoid Liège in his planning by marching through Holland, because he had anticipated that the fortress town would be difficult to take (Ritter, *Staatskunst*, vol. 2, p. 332). Waldersee maintained after the war that the Military Cabinet's decision not to deploy generals with knowledge of the area for the *coup de main* was to blame for the initial failure to capture Liège: *Vossische Zeitung*, 18 and 25 September 1932.

[20] Max Hoffmann, *War Diaries and Other Papers*, 2 vols., Engl. translation London 1929 (original *Aufzeichnungen des Generalmajors Max Hoffmann*, Berlin 1928), vol. 1, p. 38.

[21] Sewell Tyng, *The Campaign of the Marne 1914*, Oxford 1935, p. 58.

a German defeat at Liège were refuted, and the Kaiser was overjoyed. Emmich and Ludendorff were to receive the first *Pour le Mérite* of the war in appreciation of their important achievement, which Ludendorff considered his own personal triumph: 'I am justifiably proud of this honour because I have to say that the *coup de main* would not have succeeded without my own personal bravery outside Liège', he announced with characteristic lack of modesty.[22]

Liège's capture had cleared the way for the right wing of the German army to advance to meet their French and British opponents. Moltke now considered it time to move the key military decision-makers, who had remained in Berlin during these first weeks of August, closer to the main theatre of war, the western front. Moving the Military Headquarters (*Großes Hauptquartier*) to the front had, just like the initial troop deployments, been worked out meticulously.[23] According to Oberstleutnant von Natzmer of the Railway Department it had for years been that department's job to prepare annually the plans for transporting the headquarters to the front. The plan had been to set up the headquarters in Mainz. In the event, last-minute changes were made and the final destination was changed to Koblenz. Natzmer never found out what had prompted the change of plan, or whether it was indeed a last-minute alteration and not a planned measure to keep the real destination secret even from the Railway Department.[24]

Not everyone agreed with Moltke's decision to move the headquarters this early. Admiral von Müller, for example, asked Bethmann to postpone the Kaiser's trip to the front, only to learn that the Chancellor also opposed this move, but that the Chief of Staff's decision could not be overruled.[25] Others were, however, elated. Wenninger recorded his

---

[22] BHSTA-KA, HS 2665, 'Aufzeichnung Ludendorff', copy in NL Wenninger. Ludendorff's biographer Franz Uhle-Wettler agrees with his self-congratulatory assessment (*Ludendorff*, p. 110). On Ludendorff's role see also John Keegan, *The First World War*, London 1998, pp. 95ff. For details of the Kaiser's reaction to the good news see Chapter 4 above, pp. 225–226.

[23] The *Großes Hauptquartier* was a huge body, a blend of military headquarters and royal court. Apart from the Kaiser, Moltke and his deputy, Stein, it included Admiral von Pohl, Falkenhayn, Tirpitz, Bethmann Hollweg, Zimmermann and the Cabinet Chiefs Valentini, Lyncker and Müller, as well as Plessen as commander at Headquarters. In addition to this, there was the Kaiser's personal entourage, the staffs of the *Oberste Heeresleitung* (Supreme Army Command – OHL) and the military plenipotentiaries of the various German states and the alliance partners. Kielmansegg, *Deutschland*, p. 34.

[24] BA-MA, W-10/51063, 'Aufzeichnungen Oberstleutnant v. Natzmer', November 1920. Natzmer was First Staff Officer to Groener and acted as mediator (*Verbindungsoffizier*) between the Railway Department and the Operations Department. See Groener, *Lebenserinnerungen*, p. 189.

[25] Müller, *Diary*, pp. 46–48. Tirpitz and Valentini also opposed such an early move. According to Wenninger, there had been rumours of an even earlier move on 9 August (BayHSTA-KA, MKr 1765, No. 2779).

relief that they were finally moving to the front, and that the embarrassment of not yet being there was over at last.[26] He only wished the style
of the travel arrangements and the military headquarters themselves
had been less comfortable, more in keeping with being a 'warrior':
'Wonderful railway carriages, one compartment for every two gentlemen. . . . No sooner had we set off than a General Staff Major walked
along the corridors and allocated the seats for the dining-car!! Breakfast
at 12 o'clock, dinner at 7. . . . Are we indeed real warriors, or Sybarites?'
Krafft von Dellmensingen, Chief of Staff of the Sixth Army, had commented on the difficulty of communicating with Headquarters in far-
away Berlin. Written communications took two days to get there, and he
therefore considered it 'absolutely imperative' that it be moved closer.[27]
From a military point of view, Moltke could not have delayed the decision any longer.

At 8 a.m. on Sunday 16 August, 11 trains left Potsdam station for
Koblenz. This was the transport of the Supreme Headquarters to the
front. In the last two trains travelled the Kaiser, the Operations
Department, the Railway Department and the Chancellor, as well as the
Minister of War and the Admiralty Staff.[28] The three cabinet chiefs were
also present, as were the Austrian military attaché, Bienerth, and Josef
von Stürgkh, Austria's military plenipotentiary in the German headquarters. The mood of the departing officers was hopeful. Müller
recorded: 'Superbly optimistic mood of the Chief of the General Staff,
General v. Moltke, and the Austrian General Count Stürck [sic]. Moltke
says: "Today the last forts of Liège will be shot to pieces."'[29] Moltke even
expressed confidence in the abilities of the Austrian army, telling
Stürgkh: 'You have a good army. You will defeat the Russians.' Stürgkh,
quite rightly, considered this wishful thinking.[30] Moltke's parting words
to Generaloberst von Kessel demonstrated to what extent he also
seemed to be relying on fate, for he exclaimed: 'if there is any justice left
in this world, then <u>we</u> must win this war'.[31]

There was a slight hiccough before the trains could finally depart – a
last-minute, unscheduled, 'unpleasant' alteration, in Natzmer's words:
'On the order of His Majesty seats were to be "cleared" for Frau v.
Moltke and her maid. Eventually this was achieved, accompanied by the

---

[26] Wenninger, diary, 16 August 1914, in Schulte, 'Neue Dokumente', p. 146.
[27] BayHSTA-KA, NL Krafft von Dellmensingen, 'Kriegstagebücher 1914', 12 August 1914.
[28] BA-MA, W-10/51063, 'Aufzeichnungen Oberstleutnant v. Natzmer', November 1920. Natzmer
mistakenly gives the 14th as the departure date.   [29] Müller, *Diary*, p. 48.
[30] Stürgkh, *Hauptquartier*, p. 23.   [31] Ibid.

complaints of those concerned in train 8b.' The wife of the Chief of the General Staff accompanied the headquarters to Koblenz and later also to Luxembourg, where she even ate with the officers as the only woman present. As Natzmer recalled, 'the whole matter was regarded by most of the gentlemen as unspeakably embarrassing and disruptive, and her departure from Luxembourg, shortly before the move of the Supreme Headquarters to Mézières, was greeted with satisfaction.'[32]

According to Haeften's recollections, Eliza von Moltke had requested permission to accompany her husband to the front as early as 9 August, in the light of Moltke's frail state of health following the confrontations with the Kaiser on 1 and 6 August. The Kaiser had initially refused such a request as 'completely impossible . . . The Generaloberst is not that ailing, surely.' Only when the Kaiserin suggested that Eliza von Moltke could perhaps make herself useful in a Red Cross hospital in Koblenz was she allowed to board the Royal train.[33] Wenninger remarked sarcastically: 'On one compartment was written "Her Excellency v. M[oltke] with maid". So we are even being mothered!'[34]

In the morning of 17 August, the Supreme Headquarters arrived at Koblenz, where they set up office in a school building.[35] The next day was to mark the beginning of the right wing's offensive through Belgium. Finally installed at the front, the General Staff had to get down to work. While the first mobilization days had been planned meticulously long before war had been declared, the reality of warfare now had to be confronted. Peace-time generals finally had to live up to war-time demands. Immediately, organizational faults emerged within the General Staff that had escaped detection in peace-time. Only the experience of 'the real thing' was to show up such problems.[36] In Natzmer's view, these organiza-

---

[32] BA-MA, w-10/51063, 'Aufzeichnungen Oberstleutnant v. Natzmer', November 1920.

[33] Haeften had been informed about these events by Dommes, who had passed on Eliza von Moltke's request to the Kaiser: 'Meine Erlebnisse aus den Mobilmachungstagen 1914', BA-MA, N35/1, p. 37. According to Haeften, as a result of Eliza von Moltke's request Lyncker approached Falkenhayn that day to enquire whether he would be willing to take over Moltke's duties if the Chief of Staff proved unable to stand the strain.

[34] Schulte, 'Neue Dokumente', p. 146. Major Mewes recalled: 'Already in Koblenz [Moltke's] wife had arrived to care for him; during meals she sat at the table of the Chief of the General Staff, which caused much upset among the officers of the headquarters:' BA-MA, w-10/51063, 'Charakteristik der massgebenden Persönlichkeiten, ihr Anteil an den Ereignissen', p. 1.

[35] The OHL was billeted at the Hotel Union. Due to the large numbers, the headquarters were divided into two. The less important people were billeted in Bad Ems. On 30 August, Headquarters moved to Luxembourg, where they stayed in the Hôtel de Cologne and again had their offices in a school: Stürgkh, *Hauptquartier*, p. 22.

[36] BA-MA, w-10/51063, 'Aufzeichnungen Oberstleutnant v. Natzmer', November 1920: 'Organisation und Zusammenwirken bei der O.H.L. bezw. beim Gen[eral]stab des Feldheeres'.

tional shortcomings prevented proper co-operation among the various departments for the first two years of war, until Falkenhayn's replacement in 1916. The problem was one of subordination of the various departments. While the Operations Department and the Railway Department liaised directly with the Chief of the General Staff, all other departments were subordinated to the *Generalquartiermeister*, who was, however, at the same time in charge of the Railway Department as far as supplies were concerned. The chief of the Railway Department was thus answerable to two 'bosses'; luckily, as Natzmer explained, this had hardly any negative consequences, as the *Generalquartiermeister* rarely got involved, owing to the close working relationship that was established between the Railway Department and the Operations Department. Groener as head of the Railway Department became one of the best-informed generals, and the members of his department were, as a result, as well informed about events as the members of the Operations Department. Other departments were not so privileged, and due to this lack of co-operation the various OHL Departments frequently received news of the day's events after a long delay and were too inadequately informed for effective planning.[37]

Tappen was primarily blamed for this breakdown in communication. According to Natzmer, he had an exaggerated desire for secrecy regarding everything that happened in the Operations Department. Because the other departments realized that the Railway Department had all the information that the Operations Department was unwilling to part with, it was often approached for information about impending operations, troop movements and supply problems. This in turn created a problem for members of the Railway Department, who were torn between their duty to observe secrecy and the obvious need to inform the other departments about events that they needed to know about in order to perform their work properly. Natzmer remembered members of other departments approaching him 'in despair', trying to find out whether a particular corps or division was to be transported to another theatre of war, and he could only answer: 'My God, they already left yesterday!'[38] Krafft complained about the 'complete failure of the Operations Department', which did not pass on information even within the OHL.[39]

---

[37] Natzmer lists for example the '*Feldsanit.Chef, Feldmunitionschef, Generalintendant etc.*'. Ibid.

[38] Ibid. Groener refers to Tappen's secretiveness (*Geheimniskrämerei*) in his memoirs: *Lebenserinnerungen*, p. 189.

[39] BayHSTA-KA, NL Krafft von Dellmensingen, Kriegstagebücher 1914, 16 September 1914. Krafft blamed this secrecy for the failure of the attack on Troyou, because it had not been known that the Austrian 30.5 cm howitzer would be used there, and the appropriate ammunition was sent to Brussels instead.

The kind of *Ressortpartikularismus* (lack of co-operation between different decision-making bodies) that we have already examined for the pre-war years was so ingrained that it easily survived into the war, and Ministry of War and General Staff continued their policy of non-co-operation. On 16 August, for example, Wenninger reported on the War Ministry's plans to compose several new army corps by 10 October, thus increasing the entire army's strength to $50\frac{1}{2}$ corps, excluding the *Landsturm*. Incredibly, this plan was developed without consultation with the General Staff, who were not even told of it. 'The Prussian Minister of War wants to surprise the Great General Staff with this organization, therefore secrecy is demanded even vis-à-vis the [Bavarian] General Staff', Wenninger wrote.[40]

Between military and civilian decision-makers the pre-war lack of co-operation also continued once war had broken out. An apparent indiscretion of the Auswärtiges Amt in the early days of August even led to a worsening of this state of affairs. Wenninger reported that he had been informed by the Bavarian ambassador on 3 August that an invasion of Belgium was planned for the next day. Wenninger was shocked because the Auswärtiges Amt, which had given the ambassador this news, knew about this secret plan, and particularly because this information was revealed to civilians *before* the operation began:

I enquired immediately: 'Where does the Foreign Office get this from?' 'The General Staff, which asked the Foreign Office to ask Belgium how she would react if we were to march through while assuring her of full integrity.' My opinion was that this demand was understandable, but that I could not understand that the General Staff would announce such an important intended operation to a dozen civilians twenty-four hours in advance.

Wenninger clearly did not consider any diplomatic preparation of an operation of such magnitude to be essential. He asked the ambassador not to reveal this information to anyone, and informed Tappen about this 'dangerous circumstance'. Stumm, the person at the Auswärtiges Amt responsible for the indiscretion, was subsequently reprimanded by Moltke. The result of this event was a further worsening of the exchange of information between military and political bodies. As Wenninger recorded: 'Now everything is again going its regular course, except that the General Staff will be more careful about announcing military operations to the Auswärtiges Amt before they become historical fact.' In

---

[40] Schulte, 'Neue Dokumente', pp. 146–147. Wenninger also noted in his diary that the antagonisms that existed between the various decision-makers were to an extent resolved at a 'Bierabend' during the OHL's train journey to the *Großes Hauptquartier*.

other words, the lesson learned was that civilians could not be trusted with strategic information.[41] Not surprisingly, then, this lack of co-operation continued and worsened. In Müller's words of 13 September 1914, 'the Chancellor and the State Secretary for Foreign Affairs v. Jagow make up a sad picture of indecision and pessimism. They are very badly informed about the general military situation. . . . All co-operation is lacking. The Kaiser fails completely in this respect.'[42]

Kurt Riezler, who accompanied Bethmann to the military headquarters, similarly testified that civilians were kept uninformed, writing on 21 August that 'we learn little about the progress of operations. Only very generally that things are going well. The military are being terribly secretive. . . . The Chancellor has no talent for dealing with the military, impressing them, finding anything out from them.'[43] Even the Kaiser was kept uninformed. On 6 November, Müller overheard him saying: 'The General Staff tells me nothing and doesn't ask me anything, either. If they are under the impression in Germany that I am leading the army, then they are very much mistaken.'[44] Indeed, the Kaiser was *Oberster Kriegsherr* (Supreme War-Lord) only in theory. The person really in charge of military operations was the Chief of the General Staff, as Falkenhayn remembered after the war: 'The Kaiser had . . . granted the Chief of the General Staff the right to give operational orders in his name. Therefore . . . he had become the man actually in charge of the supreme army command and in any case the only one responsible for its actions and omissions.'[45]

MOLTKE'S WAR-TIME DECISION-MAKING

One of the problems that Moltke faced in war-time decision-making was to anticipate and respond to enemy action. Following the *coup de main* on Liège, it was difficult to predict where the French would concentrate their troops. Would they send considerable numbers north to counter the German advance, or would they concentrate their forces in Lorraine to attempt an offensive in the South? From the middle of August onwards,

---

[41] A copy of Wenninger's letter to the Minister of War, dated 6 August 1914, can be found in BA-MA, W-10/50890. See also his report of 6 August in Schulte, 'Neue Dokumente', pp. 143–144.

[42] Müller, *Diary*, p. 57. He added after the war: 'A very harsh judgement, but one that resulted from the situation at the time. The Kaiser still lived completely in his pre-war prejudices about the "stupid civilians"; he would not see that this war was to the highest degree a political one.'

[43] Riezler, *Tagebücher*, 21 August 1914, pp. 199–200.   [44] Müller, *Diary*, p. 68.

[45] Erich von Falkenhayn, *Die Oberste Heeresleitung 1914–1916 in ihren wichtigsten Entschließungen*, Berlin 1920, p. 3.

Moltke expected a French offensive between Metz and the Vosges. Moltke's pre-war planning had always anticipated such a move and he was prepared to engage the French in the South, rather than concentrating solely on the right wing, as the original Schlieffen Plan had demanded.

It was assumed that the French had amassed about one fifth of their entire army between Metz and the Vosges.[46] The plan was to lure the French beyond the River Saar and then launch a counterattack. In three days of fighting, the German *Südflügel* (southern wing), consisting of the Sixth and Seventh Armies, managed to achieve a victory in the Battle of Lorraine (20–23 August). Although they had not managed to envelop and destroy their opponents, the hasty retreat of the French was considered a victory and reported as such to the OHL.[47] When the news of the victory arrived at the headquarters on 22 August, the Kaiser's previously depressed mood lifted and the OHL was immediately led into exaggerated expectations. 'The strategic hopes are very wide-ranging', Müller recorded.[48] Plessen remembered after the war: 'On 24 or 25 of August Tappen literally said to me: "The whole thing will be over and done with in six weeks."'[49]

At the same time, the armies of Germany's right wing had begun their advance in accordance with the overall strategy of the Schlieffen/Moltke Plan on 18 August. Following the successful *coup de main*, German troops were progressing rapidly into Belgium and France through the narrow corridor at Liège. They were heading for Paris, reaching Brussels on 20 August, and engaging the French and British forces in the so-called 'Battles of the Frontiers' between 14 and 25 August.[50] Tappen recalled that the movement of the armies that had begun on 18 August had been progressing unstoppably. The ability of the armies to march and advance, particularly in the 'enveloping right army wing', was 'of a kind that we had never considered possible in peace-time.'[51] For the French, the Battles of the Frontiers spelt the end of their own deployment plan, Plan xvii; for the Germans, the Schlieffen Plan seemed to be delivering its promise of speedy and decisive victory.

---

[46] *Der Weltkrieg*, vol. 1, p. 184.
[47] BA-MA, n56/5, Tappen, 'Vor zwanzig Jahren. Generaloberst v. Moltke', pp. 262ff.; *Der Weltkrieg*, vol. 1, pp. 263ff.; p. 302.   [48] Müller, *Diary*, p. 50.
[49] BA-MA, w-10/50897, 'Mündliche Mitteilungen des Generalobersten von Plessen', 10 April 1923, p. 148.   [50] Herwig, *First World War*, p. 97.
[51] BA-MA, w-10/50661, Tappen, p. 27, 'Kriegserinnerungen'. The speed of advance of Kluck's army has become almost legendary. According to John Keegan, it was the very best that could be achieved by soldiers on foot (*A History of Warfare*, paperback edn, London 1993, p. 302). Ultimately, however, the speed and the need to go on marching due to the destruction of the railroads led to exhaustion, particularly among the inexperienced reservists.

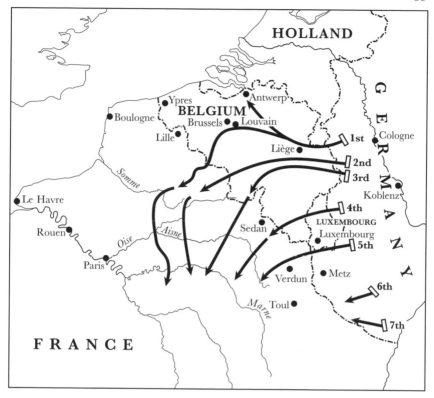

Map 3 The German advance of 1914

In the South, the Sixth and Seventh Armies managed to hold out against, and finally push back, a strong French offensive. Moltke faced the dilemma of deciding what to do, once victory had been achieved in Lorraine. Should troops from the South join the right wing to strengthen it for the intended enveloping move? Or should they press forward in Lorraine, in order to stop the French from bringing in reinforcements? Because Moltke expected a military decision on the right wing soon, he decided to engage the French further in Lorraine, in an attempt to drive the French armies apart and annihilate them. The right wing could then use its superiority to achieve an overall victory. After the war, Rupprecht and Krafft stressed their own surprise when they received the order to engage the French further. While Krafft's post-war notes were perhaps marred by his intention to justify his own actions, Rupprecht's diary confirms that they did not seek to continue the pursuit of the French at

11 Wilhelm Groener during the First World War

12 Alexander von Kluck, commander of the First Army, postcard *c.* 1914

v. BÜLOW

20
ROTOPHOT BERLIN

13 Karl von Bülow, commander of the Second Army, postcard *c.* 1914

that time.[52] Tappen argued after the war, when Moltke's choice was condemned by his critics, that transport problems were the main reason for the decision not to move troops north to strengthen the right wing. With the Belgian railways largely destroyed, troops from the South would have taken so long to get there that they would have been unable to make much of an impact on the fighting.[53]

Moltke had outlined how he meant to implement Germany's strategic plan in a manoeuvre critique of the pre-war years. His views on the future strategy were in fact more flexible than Schlieffen's had been:

> If the French come out of their fortress they come out into the open field. There is no sense in continuing the march in strength through Belgium, if the main French army is advancing in Lorraine. There can be only one thought: to attack the French army with all available forces and beat it wherever it may be. The march through Belgium is not an end in itself, but only a means to an end.[54]

Moltke's decision to pursue the enemy with the armies of the *Südflügel* amounted in effect to a strategy of 'double envelopment'. This has been interpreted, by both contemporary critics and some historians, as an adulteration of the Schlieffen Plan and as a serious misjudgement. Holger Herwig is a recent critic: 'Moltke's spur-of-the-moment decision to send the 16 divisions of the German sixth and seventh armies not north via Metz to join Bülow and Kluck but east towards Épinal, constituted one of his gravest errors during the Marne campaign.'[55] Tappen, however, in trying to counter allegations that Schlieffen, in the same situation, would have handled things not only differently from but also better than Moltke, argues that it was the Chief of Staff's right and duty to change the plan that he had taken over from Schlieffen, if he was convinced that such a change might lead to victory. Moreover, he claims that it was much harder to change the measures that had been prepared in peace-time, if and when that proved necessary, than to stick to them rigidly.[56] It could indeed be argued that Moltke could not have been expected to adhere to a plan that was developed years before the outbreak of war, rather than adapting it to changing circumstances.

The eastern front posed a further problem for Moltke in those critical

---

[52] Crown Prince Rupprecht of Bavaria, *Mein Kriegstagebuch*, vol. 1, p. 38.

[53] BA-MA, w-10/50661, Tappen, 'Kriegserinnerungen', p. 27; Tappen, *Bis zur Marne*, Oldenburg 1920, p. 14. But cf. Wilhelm Müller-Loebnitz, *Die Führung im Marne-Feldzug*, Berlin 1939, p. 24: this anti-Moltke publication claims that Groener had not even been asked about the possibility of transport, and that he thought it would have been possible.

[54] Quoted in Ritter, *Schlieffen Plan*, p. 55.   [55] Herwig, *First World War*, p. 99.

[56] BA-MA, w-10/50661, Tappen, 'Kriegserinnerungen', p. 27.

early weeks of the war, demanding his attention at that crucial point in time. It was against the enemy in the East that the anticipated 'racial struggle' would have to be waged – initially, of course, with insufficient numbers. Before the onset of fighting in the East, Moltke instructed General von Prittwitz, the commander of the Eighth Army, to rally his troops against the numerically superior enemy. He was to convey to them

that the eastern army was entrusted with the protection of German soil; that the task is to defeat an enemy to whom nothing is holy and who would save neither the lives nor the possessions of the peaceful inhabitants – that this meant a war of Asian barbarity against German civilization (*Gesittung*) – and that the eyes of the entire Fatherland were directed towards the soldiers of the eastern army in the unshakeable trust that all would do their duty.[57]

No doubt, these words of encouragement were also intended to make the eastern theatre of war appear more important and attractive. They were probably also intended for his peace-time deputy Waldersee, who had been disappointed at having been deployed to such a 'secondary' role in the war as Chief of Staff of the Eighth Army. Having been pre-occupied with developing the deployment plan for the West, he saw the eastern front as of minor significance. In September 1914, Waldersee recorded:

I can also not deny that I found it hard to leave behind all those matters of grand direction of war (*grosse Kriegführung*), all preparations against France and Belgium, those matters to which I had dedicated all my strength and interest over the two previous years.[58]

The eastern front was considered only 'second best', and Waldersee's disappointment at having been relegated to this lesser theatre of war is evident. General von Stein was disdainful, displaying 'a certain snobbery (*Süffisanz*) about my task', as Waldersee recalled. The western front had been and still was the real concern of the military planners, and even during mobilization, troops to be sent east were not regarded as particularly important. The Eighth Army's staff was, in Waldersee's words, 'of course completely jumbled together'.[59]

[57] BA-MA, w-10/51032, Dommes to Waldersee, 14 August 1914.
[58] BA-MA, w-10/51032, Waldersee, 'Meine Erlebnisse', p. 8. After the war, Waldersee even claimed that the delay in the capture of Liège in the early days of August had been because those General Staff officers who had been involved in working out the details of the plan had been sent to join the troops in the East. See Eugen Fischer-Baling, 'Verfl . . . Kabinettswirtschaft' [sic], *Vossische Zeitung*, 18 September 1932, and F. W. von Oertzen, 'Die Einnahme von Lüttich', *Vossische Zeitung*, 25 September 1932.
[59] BA-MA, w-10/51032, Waldersee, 'Meine Erlebnisse' p. 10.

However, Moltke attached more importance to the eastern front than Schlieffen had done, and he was not prepared to allow the Russians to enter into East Prussia. When war was about to begin, he was in fact so confident that a Russian invasion of Germany's eastern territories could be avoided that he told his nephew and niece, living on the Moltke family estate at Kreisau in Silesia, that they could stay there without anxiety.[60]

According to the orders given to the Eighth Army, it was to try to divert Russian forces away from the Austrian armies to make their initial engagement easier. This would easily be achieved if the Russian armies operated offensively against East Prussia. If they decided to remain in waiting or on the defensive, then a German offensive would have to ensure that Russian troops would be engaged away from the Austrians.[61] Moltke's order to Waldersee specified: 'When the Russians are coming, no defence under any account, but offensive, offensive, offensive.'[62] According to Dennis Showalter, Moltke was 'thinking in tactical and operational, rather than strategic terms'.[63] He considered it essential that within the overall strategy, and given Russia's numerical superiority, Germany should not be forced completely on to the defensive.[64] Despite the small number of troops deployed in the East, they were supposed to attempt limited offensives with the Austro-Hungarian army in the South.[65] While Schlieffen was even prepared to allow the Russians to occupy East Prussian territory while victory in the West was being sought, Moltke did not want to take the risk of surrendering territory. Waldersee had already hinted at this unwillingness to let the Russians seize the initiative in his memorandum of May 1914, when he wrote: 'We would relinquish any chance of victory from the start if we were to make do with an offensive to one side only [i.e. either France or Russia alone]. Though politicians may allow themselves to be forced on to the defensive, the German army may never do so.'[66]

The campaign on the eastern front would always be difficult, owing to Germany's numerical inferiority. Generalleutnant Max Hoffmann, First General Staff officer of the Eighth Army, recorded in his diary on 7 August: 'We have a hard task before us, harder, almost, than any in history.'[67] After initial favourable news from East Prussia on 20

---

[60] Dorothy von Moltke, *Ein Leben in Deutschland*, letter dated 31 July 1914, p. 42.
[61] *Der Weltkrieg*, vol. 2, p. 43. [62] BA-MA, w-10/51032, Dommes to Waldersee, 14 August 1914.
[63] Showalter, *Tannenberg*, p. 143. [64] *Der Weltkrieg*, vol. 2, p. 45.
[65] See BA-MA, w-10/50661, Tappen, 'Kriegserinnerungen', p. 5.
[66] Waldersee's memorandum of 18 May 1914, BA-MA, w-10/50279, doc. 94 (see also above, pp. 177–178.) [67] Hoffmann, *War Diaries*, vol. 1, p. 38.

August, the OHL learned a day later that Generaloberst von Prittwitz had discontinued the battle at Gumbinnen, which had already seemed almost won, and was contemplating a retreat, perhaps even beyond the Vistula. In three separate battles the Eighth Army had achieved only incomplete victories on the flanks and had been defeated in the centre. The Russians were threatening to cross the border into East Prussia.[68] In a telephone call the Eighth Army demanded urgent reinforcements if Prittwitz were to be able to defend the Vistula. Moltke ordered that a retreat beyond the river had to be avoided at all cost, and had an angry exchange with Prittwitz, who claimed that it would be impossible to defend the position with his 'handful of men'. Moltke snapped that this was Prittwitz's problem, and that he could hardly expect Moltke to be able to solve it for him from Koblenz.[69]

By 21 August it was beginning to look as if the only way to avoid a retreat and stop Prittwitz from dividing his forces was to replace him as supreme commander of the Eighth Army. Wenninger reported from the OHL to Munich: 'I may add <u>extremely confidentially</u> to the official reports: the unhappy combination (Prittwitz–Waldersee) is causing great concern here. . . . We hear of the "worry of being cut off", of a "hurried retreat behind the Vistula", which means giving up East Prussia.'[70] Similarly, Müller learnt from Plessen that the situation in the East was a cause for concern, recording in his diary: 'In Moltke's eyes Prittwitz had operated in a completely wrong way. The General Staff is said to be angry with him.'[71] On this important occasion, Moltke intervened forcefully, as even Groener had to admit after the war: 'The only time that I have seen him in determined yet tearful excitement was at the moment when he found out that the Oberkommando VIII [i.e. the Eighth Army] had broken off the battle at Gumbinnen and wanted to retreat behind

---

[68] This was the impression in the miltiary headquarters in Koblenz, following a telephone conversation with either Waldersee or Prittwitz. See Count von Dohna to Waldersee, 28 August 1914, BA-MA, w-10/51032; *Der Weltkrieg*, vol. 1, p. 431; Robert B. Asprey, *The German High Command at War. Hindenburg and Ludendorff and the First World War*, paperback edn, London 1994 (first edn 1991); Martin Kitchen, *The Silent Dictatorship. The Politics of the German High Command under Hindenburg and Ludendorff, 1916–1918*, London 1976; Showalter, *Tannenberg*, pp. 190ff.   [69] Ibid., p. 194.

[70] Schulte, 'Neue Dokumente', 21 August 1914, pp. 154–155.

[71] Müller, *Diary*, p. 50. It is possible that Moltke's reaction to Prittwitz's failure was particularly strong because Prittwitz had been not his choice, but the Military Cabinet's. After the war, Waldersee maintained that Moltke had objected to the intended appointment of Prittwitz as leader of the German forces in the East in the spring of 1914, but had not been able to change the Military Cabinet's mind. Waldersee felt that Moltke should have put his job on the line over this issue at the time (BA-MA, w-10/51032). On Moltke's anger at Prittwitz see also Showalter, *Tannenberg*, pp. 195ff.

the Vistula.'[72] Moltke had only authorized such a retreat in an extreme emergency, because its implications were that Russia would be free to turn on Posnan or Silesia, or even towards the Austrians. Such a potentially disastrous retreat had to be avoided at all costs: it was imperative that the Eighth Army stay east of the Vistula.

Against this background, Moltke had to decide whether more troops should be sent to the East straight away, as the Eighth Army so urgently requested, or whether they should be kept to strengthen the right wing for the decisive battle in the West. The mood in the OHL, judging by contemporary accounts, was desperate, as Plessen's diary confirms: 'But East Prussia! Gumbinnen and Allenstein occupied by the enemy! The Russians are burning and pillaging everything! – We must make haste to finish in the West as quickly as possible in order to come to the rescue of the East.'[73] News from the First and Second Armies gave the OHL the impression that victory in the West was almost achieved, and faced with the imminent threat of a Russian invasion of East Prussia, Moltke decided to move six corps from the western to the eastern front. In the event, this number was reduced to only two (the Guard Reserve Corps and the Eleventh Army Corps). The troops were moved east, although Ludendorff, who together with Paul von Hindenburg had replaced Waldersee and Prittwitz, had informed the OHL prior to the dispatch of the two corps that they would arrive too late to make any difference. Perhaps the OHL simply did not believe that Ludendorff would be able to turn around the situation which to them had seemed so desperate. Before the reinforcements arrived, Hindenburg and Ludendorff had managed to avert the threatening German defeat, eventually turning it into a victory at the Battle of Tannenberg (27–30 August). The two corps were, however, sorely missed in the decisive battle in the West. Not surprisingly, Moltke's critics have found in his decision to send troops East, rather than keeping them on the right wing in the West, further reason

---

[72] Groener to Oberstleutnant von Strube, 7 January 1931, BA-MA, NL Groener, N46/39, pp. 180–181. Moltke had demanded the removal (*Enthebung*) of Prittwitz and Waldersee, but the Military Cabinet interfered and instead issued a dismissal (*Verabschiedung*), which precluded any reinstatement at a later date. See Eugen Fischer-Baling, 'Fiel Lüttich rechtzeitig?', *Vossische Zeitung*, 9 October 1932. Oberst Max Hoffmann recalled later: 'The manner of the dismissal was unusually rough' (*Der Krieg der versäumten Gelegenheiten*, Leipzig 1929, p. 26). The official German history of the war maintains that Moltke dithered over the decision to replace Prittwitz and Waldersee, an allegation which is not confirmed by the available evidence: *Der Weltkrieg*, vol. 2, pp. 96ff.

[73] BA-MA, W-10/50676, Plessen diary, 24 August 1914. Plessen's diary of these crucial first weeks of the war had been presumed lost until copies were discovered among the archival material returned to Germany. See also Introduction, pp. 6ff.

for doubting his strategic competence. Again, however, this criticism benefits from hindsight, because Moltke could not have predicted that the dire state of the Eighth Army would so quickly be reversed and a major defeat avoided.[74] Moreover, as Dennis Showalter points out in Moltke's defence, German military doctrine had emphasized for the previous twenty years that troops needed to be sent East following initial, decisive victories in the West.[75] On August 25 and 26, this point in time seemed to have been reached.

Contemporary accounts were more positive in judging Moltke's decision. Plessen recorded in his diary:

Two further army corps will be sent east where a battle is taking place just now, a battle about whose outcome we are all very concerned because of the superior strength of the Russians. But I would attack, too! Nonetheless the quality of our troops and the capability and spirit of our officers justify the expectation of victory.[76]

Tappen explains how Moltke's decision was motivated by the 'exceedingly favourable news' which arrived from the right wing, together with the victory of the Sixth and Seventh Armies in Lorraine on 20–23 August. From the information he received, Moltke was under the impression that the French were virtually defeated.[77] Now, Moltke judged, the time had come to assist the troops on the eastern front, who were hard pressed by an overpowering Russian opponent. As Tappen summed up after the event:

It is an act of tragic fate that Generaloberst v. Moltke of all people, [a man] who considered every measure particularly seriously and gravely and who in any case did not tend towards optimism, should judge the situation on the western theatre of war too favourably on account of the messages received.[78]

Tappen failed to mention that he, too, had been inclined towards unwarranted optimism, at least according to Plessen's memories after the war.

---

[74] See *Der Weltkrieg*, vol. 1, pp. 604ff., vol. 2, pp. 206ff.; Showalter, *Tannenberg*, pp. 293ff.

[75] Ibid. p. 294.   [76] BA-MA, w-10/50676, Plessen diary, 26 August 1914.

[77] The diary of Crown Prince Rupprecht (Sixth Army) testifies to the delight with which the news of his victory was received by Moltke and Falkenhayn, who were 'moved to tears', and by the Kaiser, who was 'nearly ecstatic': BA-MA, w-10/50659, p. 19, 23 August 1914. Cf. Rupprecht, *Kriegstagebuch*, p. 41.

[78] BA-MA, N56/5, Tappen, 'Vor zwanzig Jahren. Generaloberst v. Moltke', pp. 267–268. Wenninger recorded in his diary for 22 August: 'Despite that great delight over the Sixth and Seventh Armies a day of crisis due to the miserable leadership in the East!' According to Wenninger, Moltke was particularly upset with their performance because he had suggested Prittwitz and Waldersee in the first place (Wenninger referred to them as 'Hungerwurm' and 'der Mann mit dem schönen Namen', the man with the pretty name). Schulte, 'Neue Dokumente', p. 156.

In Plessen's opinion, both Moltke and Tappen were of the impression that a decision in Germany's favour had already been reached in the West. It is this optimistic interpretation, based on the available information, that explains their decision to transport the two army corps to the eastern front.[79]

News of successes were almost always exaggerated, particularly by the Kaiser, whereas Moltke at least learnt from this mistake and in future displayed much more caution. For example, on 30 August Müller recorded the Kaiser's typical ranting, as well as Moltke's squirming reaction to it: 'The Kaiser was practically wading in blood – as so often recently – during the train journey [from Koblenz to Luxembourg]. Moltke, who sat beside him, was suffering torture.' Later Moltke spoke with Müller: 'Contrary to the Kaiser's fantasies he said very modestly: "We have pushed the French back, but they are not yet beaten. That has still to happen."'[80] Karl Helfferich also experienced how the Chief of Staff warned against over-optimism. In a conversation on 4 September, Moltke confirmed that German troops were within fifty kilometres of Paris, but that they were at the point of exhaustion:

We don't want to delude ourselves. We have had successes, but we have not yet won. Victory means the destruction of the opponent's strength to resist. Where million-strong armies confront each other, the victor has prisoners. Where are our prisoners? . . . Also the relatively low number of captured guns demonstrates to me that the French are conducting a planned and orderly retreat. The hardest task is still ahead of us![81]

If Moltke was over-optimistic on 23 August, he had clearly learnt the lesson since, and no longer considered a victory in the West to be imminent.

Contemporary accounts attest to the anxiety that was widely felt among military men about the precarious situation in the East, and only with hindsight can Moltke's decision to move troops from the western front can be condemned as a mistake. Critics have maintained that the two army corps that were sent to help the Eighth Army would have made a decisive difference to the fate of the German armies in the Battle of the Marne. However, a variety of reasons led to the defeat on the

---

[79] BA-MA, w-10/50897, 'Mündliche Mitteilungen des Generaloberst v. Plessen, die Se. Exzellenz bei einer mündlichen Besprechung mit dem Direktor v. Haeften am 10.4.1923 gemacht hat', p. 148.

[80] Müller, *Diary*, p. 53. The OHL was moved to Luxembourg closer to the front, on 30 August 1914.

[81] Karl Helfferich, *Der Weltkrieg*, 2 vols., Berlin 1919, vol. 2: *Vom Kriegsausbruch bis zum uneingeschränkten U-Bootkrieg*, p. 18.

Marne, and it can be argued that two additional army corps would not have made a decisive difference to the tragic events of September 1914.[82]

> I can hardly say with what nameless weight the burden of responsibility has rested on me over the last days and is still resting on me.
>
> Helmuth von Moltke, 8 September 1914[83]

> [Moltke] did not find salvation in giving orders – to use Goethe's words – but believed that the army commanders understood better than he did. He put up an inner resistance to any activity as supreme leader of the army.
>
> Wilhelm Groener, 7 January 1931[84]

The Battle of the Marne in September 1914 is generally seen as the beginning of the end for Germany's chances of victory in the First World War. With hindsight it has often been argued that the war was lost when the battle of the Marne was lost. Oberstleutnant von Egan-Krieger put this notion rather bluntly:

> If the pessimistic Oberstleutnant Hentsch had crashed into a tree somewhere on his journey on 8 [and 9] September, or if he had been shot by a French straggler, then we would have had a cease-fire two weeks later and afterwards would have received a peace in which we could have demanded everything.[85]

While regarding the battle as a grave set-back, contemporary commentators did not yet think that overall victory had become an impossibility.

---

[82] For a more favourable assessment of Moltke's impact on the events on the Marne, see Sebastian Haffner and Wolfgang Venohr, *Das Wunder an der Marne. Rekonstruktion der Entscheidungsschlacht des Ersten Weltkrieges*, Bergisch Gladbach 1982, pp. 13ff.

[83] Moltke to his wife, 8 September 1914, *Erinnerungen*, p. 384. Moltke was not the only one who found the carnage of war difficult to deal with. On 20 August, the Kaiser's *Oberstallmeister* Walter Frhr. von Esebeck committed suicide 'in an attack of nervous collapse', as Müller recorded in his diary. 'As Lyncker tells me, this was only one of many nervous breakdowns among officers, an occurrence that had also been observed in 1870 shortly after the outbreak of the war' (Müller, *Diary*, p. 50). For Esebeck's death, see also Stürgkh, *Hauptquartier*, p. 36. Not surprisingly, the cause of death was kept a secret at headquarters. Another high-ranking officer to be replaced was Generaloberst von Hausen, leader of the Third Army, due to 'nervousness'. Karl von Einem took over his duties following the Battle of the Marne: BayHSTA-KA, NL Krafft, 'Kriegstagebücher', vol. 48, 19 September 1914.

[84] BA-MA, NL Groener, N46/39, Groener to Oberstleutnant von Strube, 7 January 1931, pp. 180–181.

[85] Karl Lange, *Marneschlacht und deutsche Öffentlichkeit 1914–1939. Eine verdrängte Niederlage und ihre Folgen*, Düsseldorf 1974, p. 19.

Only as part of the post-war Schlieffen myth did the defeat on the Marne acquire such exaggerated importance. Oberst Nicolai explained to the Reichsarchiv in 1925 that it would be wrong to state that the OHL had believed 'that the result of the Battle of the Marne amounted to a decisive turning-point in the war or even the end of any hope of victory. In my opinion, this point of view is only the result of later developments.'[86] The events of September 1914, the first major German defeat, certainly destroyed all hopes of the Schlieffen/Moltke Plan fulfilling its promise of swift victory in the West.[87] Tirpitz commented after the war: 'Until that point the army had been imbued with one single thought: Cannae. . . . After the battle of the Marne the army had to re-think.'[88] The military's worst nightmare, a long-drawn-out war of attrition, a stalemate of trench warfare in which opponents of similar strength faced each other indefinitely, had become reality. The German war planners had no answers to the new problems that they were facing, no contingency plans or alternatives to the Schlieffen Plan. Germany was unprepared for a long war, both militarily and economically. Not surprisingly, the defeat was a closely guarded secret; even Conrad was not informed about it until late October 1914.[89] Throughout the war, the German public was ill-informed about the actual situation on the battlefields, leading to illusions about the country's chances of victory which continued right until the end.[90]

That the Battle of the Marne was lost was largely blamed on Moltke. Critics pointed to the changes that he had made to Schlieffen's strategic plans, and to the fact that his nerve had failed him once war had broken out. He was held responsible for ordering the retreat on the Marne. He had adulterated the certain recipe for victory and had never wholeheartedly endorsed Schlieffen's tactics. He had aimed for flexibility over where to meet and engage the French army, regardless of whether such a victory would be achieved on the right wing, in the middle or on the left wing. Unlike Schlieffen, who had wanted to force the French into battle where it suited him, Moltke was willing to alter his deployment in accordance with that of the French. If they were on the offensive in the

---

[86] BA-MA, w-10/51063, Nicolai's letter of 18 December 1925, p. 83. On the impact of the defeat (and the fact that this was initially kept secret and later denied), see Lange, *Marneschlacht*, passim.

[87] Although arguably a short war had already become unlikely given other diplomatic and military events, such as the Pact of London of 5 September, by which Britain, France and Russia had agreed not to conclude a separate peace with the Central Powers. See L. L. Farrarr, Jr., 'The Strategy of the Central Powers', in Hew Strachan (ed.), *The Oxford Illustrated History of the First World War*, Oxford 1999, p. 29.   [88] Tirpitz, *Erinnerungen*, p. 252.

[89] Asprey, *The German High Command*, p. 109.   [90] See also Ullrich, *Die nervöse Großmacht*, p. 410.

South, he wanted to be able to strike there, too. Because the German army did not have infinite manpower and resources available, however, such increased flexibility meant a potential weakening of the all-important right wing. Schlieffen's dying words had allegedly been: 'Be sure to strengthen the right wing!' That his hapless successor did not adhere to this was an unforgivable mistake in the eyes of Schlieffen's supporters.[91] From the point of view of the 'Schlieffen school', the matter was straight-forward enough: without Moltke, Germany would have been victorious on the Marne, and by implication would have won the war.

The exact events that led to the 'drama of the Marne' remain unclear. By 22 August, the invasion of Belgium was nearly completed. The First Army was approaching Mons, the Second had taken Namur and had reached the Sambre, and the Third Army was heading west towards the Meuse.[92] The fighting of 20–23 August had decided the Battles of the Frontiers in Germany's favour, and had led to the breakdown of the French Plan XVII. The armies of the Entente were retreating. However, the French were not beaten, and they were strengthening their left wing, whereas Germany's right wing was becoming significantly weakened, partly by the loss of two corps removed and sent east, as well as by the forces needed outside Antwerp and Maubeuge, and by the losses incurred in the battles so far. The leadership of the right-wing armies was impeded by differences of opinion between Kluck and Bülow. Their disagreements were temporarily overcome by Moltke's decision to subordinate the First Army to Bülow's leadership in order to achieve unity of command, but Bülow and Kluck continued to differ in their views on operations.

By the beginning of September, the German right wing had almost reached Paris. The Schlieffen Plan seemed to be delivering its promise, and expectations for an early victory were high. On 7 September, Moltke expressed his desire for a peace 'which could not be disturbed by any enemy for the foreseeable future'. Two days later, in the so-called 'September Programme', Bethmann Hollweg formulated his vision of Europe following a German victory, which he must have thought to be imminent.[93] However, that victory could not be achieved.

Following the rapid advance, Kluck thought that his army did not

[91] See BA-MA, NL Hahnke, N36/10, Hahnke to Freytag-Loringhoven, 5 March 1924.
[92] For the following, see Tyng, *Marne*, pp. 100ff., Erdmann, *Der Erste Weltkrieg*, pp. 113–114.
[93] Details on the 'September Programme', and Moltke's citation in Fischer, *Griff*, p. 90. But cf. Wayne C. Thompson, 'The September Program: Reflections on the Evidence', *Central European History*, 11, 4, 1978, p. 342, who claims that Riezler and Bethmann did not expect a victory to be imminent.

have the necessary strength to attempt to envelop the French capital. The enormous marching distances (the First Army had marched 500 kilometres in 30 days) had led to a serious reduction of the army's fighting power.[94] Moltke ordered a rapid advance to stop the French from reorganizing. When the German armies crossed the Marne to move towards Paris, on the extreme right wing, the balance of power had shifted to Germany's disadvantage, with 20 German divisions facing 30 French and British ones. The French had an advantage becauses the railways that they were able to use allowed them a more rapid deployment of troops and, crucially, of supplies to the front, while the Germans faced severe transport problems.[95] On 4 September, Joffre ordered a counter-attack against the flank of the First Army. Although Kluck's army defended itself successfully against this onslaught, a gap of almost 40 kilometres developed as a result between the First and Second Armies, into which the enemy was able to advance. Bülow and Kluck lost touch, partly due to a lack of adequate communications. With the First Army in danger of being outflanked by the enemy, the gap between the First and Second Armies had to be closed by way of a retreat. Consequently, the First and Second German armies withdrew on 9 September, although they had apparently so far been victorious in their campaigns.[96] In his diary entry for 10 September, Wenninger recorded the depressed mood in the headquarters following the retreat: 'It is as quiet as a mortuary in the school building in Luxembourg – we tip-toe around, the General Staff officers rush past me with their eyes downcast – best not to address them, not to ask.'[97] There could be no starker contrast to the optimism and the 'beaming faces' of the first days of war.

Essentially, the retreat behind the Marne was the result of misunderstandings, and of communications so bad that they were at times non-existent. On 9 September, which in Lyncker's words was 'the most critical day of the war so far', Moltke suggested a retreat, while Stein and Plessen opposed such a measure. Resignedly, Lyncker concluded: 'All of this is meaningless however, because there is no communication with the First and Second Armies at the present time.'[98] The military headquarters

[94] Kaufmann, *Kommunikationstechnik*, p. 148.   [95] Ibid., p. 149.

[96] See 'Bericht der OHL zum Ende der Marne-Schlacht', 10 September 1914, in Wolfdieter Bihl (ed.), *Deutsche Quellen zur Geschichte des Ersten Weltkrieges*, Darmstadt 1991, p. 63.

[97] Schulte, 'Dokumente', p. 172. Similarly Hermann von Santen recorded: 'Everyone is aware of the seriousness of the moment, although no-one can yet understand the final outcome of the changed situation. Without a word each of us stares at the next person, or preferably past him. There is a feeling of embarrassment' ('Erinnerungen', vol. 11, p. 77).

[98] BA-MA, w-10/50676, Lyncker diary, 9 September 1914, p. 27.

in Luxembourg were in touch with the *Oberkommandos* of the Fourth, Fifth, Sixth, and Seventh Armies by telephone, but with the crucial 'right wing' armies, the First, Second and Third, they had only radio contact which was becoming increasingly unreliable. With the First Army communication was often only possible via the Second. Unfortunately, no attempts were made to improve communications by mending already existing wires.[99] Even on the left wing, where telephone connections did exist, communication was not straightforward. No separate communication system for the army had been established, and civilian lines (including civilian operators) had to be used. No direct lines existed to the military headquarters, exposing any telephone conversations to the risk of espionage. All conversations had to be conducted in code, which did not ease the communication difficulties. It took a long time for connections to be established, and the coded messages were difficult to hear and always conducted under time pressure, leading to mistakes.[100] Nor were the headquarters moved closer to the front, another measure which would have aided communication. According to Tappen, Moltke had wanted to move the headquarters, but 'technical difficulties', as well as a reluctance to separate a small *Operationsstaffel* from the headquarters as a way of leaving the Kaiser behind in safety, prevented this. Moltke had considered moving the headquarters to Namur, but had to change his mind due to considerations of the Kaiser's safety.[101] Although the Kaiser, too, demanded that the headquarters be moved, his wish was refused on the pretext of 'technical grounds'.[102] Moltke later defended himself against criticism from the former Minister of War, Karl von Einem: 'But my dear Einem, I couldn't have travelled through half of France with the Kaiser during the advance.'[103]

Moltke had given the individual army leaders the freedom to make

[99] Reichsarchiv, *Der Weltkrieg*, vol. 4, p. 139. Erich Ludendorff also commented on the lack of communication between the supreme commanders of the First and Second Armies, and in particular on the fact that the Second Army did not learn of the intention of the First to attack: *Das Marne-Drama. Der Fall Moltke–Hentsch*, Munich 1934, p. 13. See also Müller-Loebnitz, *Die Führung*, p. 41.

[100] BA-MA, w-10/50076, Krafft von Dellmensingen, 'Kommentar zum Weltkriegswerk', p. 95, also in BayHSTA-KA, NL Krafft, vol. 186, p. 9. On the lack of adequate communication, see also Dieter Storz, *Kriegsbild und Rüstung vor 1914. Europäische Landstreitkräfte vor dem Ersten Weltkrieg*, Herford, Berlin, Bonn 1992, p. 321.

[101] BA-MA, w-10/50897, 'Mündliche Mitteilungen des Generalobersten von Plessen', p. 147. Dommes recalled in March 1921 that Moltke apparently wanted to move the HQ to Rethel, but changed his mind because he did not want to separate the General Staff from the Kaiser. See Jürgen von Grone, *Wie es zur Marneschlacht 1914 kam*, Selbstverlag des Autors, Stuttgart 1971, p. 16.

[102] Reichsarchiv, *Weltkrieg*, vol. 4, p. 129; also pp. 138–139.

[103] Einem, *Erinnerungen*, p. 177.

their own decisions within the confines of the overall strategy. Although critics have since condemned this as another of his mistakes, it was in fact a long tradition in the German army, going back to the elder Moltke's practice.[104] Practical reasons were also to blame. Apart from the extensive communication difficulties, Moltke was simply too far away from the front to be able to intervene, and he lost control over his leading generals very quickly. Not surprisingly, Moltke's critics also focused their strictures on the way in which Moltke had led the troops. Again, critics like Groener alleged that Schlieffen would have done a better job:

Whoever witnessed in 1914 how the armies rushed forward without any regard for the whole, how each wanted to achieve its own goal, and in so doing always pushed left instead of extending to the right, will agree with Count Schlieffen in his view that the great envelopment by the army must be governed by strict orders.[105]

Some post-war critics were quick to put all the blame on Moltke's lack of assertiveness, rather than any circumstances that might have hindered his involvement. Thus Krafft von Dellmensingen, who in 1914 had been Chief of Staff under Crown Prince Rupprecht, criticized: 'Moltke practised an exaggerated restraint, because he . . . lacked all self-assurance and thus all self-confidence. He was afraid to lead by himself.'[106] It is certainly true that he put a lot of trust in the army leaders, especially considering that many of them had not been chosen for any merit or skill, but rather on grounds of seniority. Allowing for the fact than many of the army commanders were ambitious senior generals who resented being told what to do, we must ask how great Moltke's opportunity to lead and rule them actually was. Some of the leading general were unwilling to accept Moltke's authority. Contemporaries also commented on the detrimental role of Moltke's most intimate advisers in the OHL. Krafft's diary of September 1914 detailed the importance of Tappen, Hentsch, Fabeck and Dommes, who formed a kind of 'war council and pulled Moltke to and fro. All unity of command went out of the window that way.'[107]

---

[104] On directive command in the German army, see Martin Samuels, *Command or Control*, pp. 15ff.

[105] Groener, 'Über den Schlieffenplan', in BA-MA, NL Hahnke, N36/11. See also Leppa, *Moltke und Conrad*, pp. 20–21.

[106] BA-MA, W-10/50076, Krafft von Dellmensingen, 'Kommentar zum Weltkriegswerk', p. 94.

[107] BayHSTA-KA, NL Krafft, 'Kriegstagebücher', 16 September 1914. Tappen was head of the Operations Department; Hentsch led the Information Department (*Nachrichtenabteilung*); Dommes was chief of the Political Department (which, according to Groener consisted almost solely of him and had been created to enable Dommes to be in close contact with Moltke and the Kaiser); and Fabeck was head of the Central Department. For the role of the 'camarilla' under Moltke, see also Schulte, 'Neue Dokumente', p. 174; Groener, *Lebenserinnerungen*, p. 188.

Too much leeway, inadequate communications, and the ambitions of military leaders who wanted a glorious campaign victory associated with their name meant that the OHL in Luxembourg lost touch. The German method of command allocated a predominant role to the individual army chiefs of staff, who exercised authority far in excess of those in the French and British armies and were able to make important decisions with strategic consequences independently from their superiors.[108] The determination of individuals to portray themselves in as good a light as possible was one of the most important factors in this 'drama', in which the main actors regarded the retreat of 'their' army, or any lost battle, as a personal loss; similarly, victories were seen as personal victories, and they were keen to appear as successful commanders.[109] Retreat, however strategically necessary, did not fit into this scheme, and news, when it was received from the front, was often either euphemistic or too pessimistic, rarely reflecting the actual situation.

Some army leaders simply did not agree with the overall strategy, and therefore ended up not complying with it. General von Bülow, though one of Schlieffen's pupils, was no believer in envelopment. In 1905, this had been one of the reasons why he was not promoted instead of Moltke.[110] After the war Krafft commented that Moltke should 'never have attempted a Schlieffen operation with Bülow'.[111] The differences between Bülow's and Kluck's views on strategy became increasingly pronounced during the Marne campaign.[112] Moltke also asserted after his dismissal that in the years prior to the outbreak of war he had warned Kluck repeatedly in war games that he was advancing too quickly on the right wing, telling him: 'If you do this during the real thing, we will lose the war.'[113] It would seem as if individual decisions and mistakes were as much to blame for the failure of Germany's strategic plan as Moltke's lack of assertiveness.

Another alleged mistake of Moltke's was that he did not travel to the front himself in order to establish the seriousness of the situation. On 8 September, Moltke wrote to his wife: 'The terrible tension of these days, the lack of news from far-away armies, the knowledge of what is at risk here, almost exceeds human strength.'[114] Moltke feared that the enemy

---

[108] Tyng, *Marne*, p. 37.
[109] Wallach suspects that Hermann von Kuhl, Chief of Staff of von Kluck's First Army, was motivated by personal ambitions (*Dogma*, p. 169), while Wenninger's report of 10 September 1914 commented on Kluck's 'egotistical manoeuvres' (Schulte, 'Dokumente', p. 171). See also Wolfgang Lautemann, *Studien zu Marnefeldzug und Marneschlacht 1914*, Berlin 1933, p. 48.
[110] See also Chapter 2, p. 68.   [111] BayHSTA-KA, NL Krafft, vol. 186, p. 9.
[112] Kluck, *Wanderjahre*, p. 179.   [113] Quoted in Grone, *Marneschlacht*, p. 7.
[114] Moltke, *Erinnerungen*, p. 384.

might advance into the gap that had developed between the First and Second Armies. Rather than go to the army headquarters himself, he chose Oberstleutnant Richard Hentsch[115] as his envoy to report back on the situation at the front, as no news had been received. When Hentsch reached the Second Army at 7 p.m., Bülow was optimistic and there was no thought of a retreat, although there was concern over the gap that had developed between the two armies of the right wing. Hentsch advised him that because of the seriousness of the situation of the First Army, both armies would have to retreat behind the Marne. What is perhaps most puzzling about this much-debated order is the fact that Hentsch had not even been to the First Army yet. He only went there the next morning.[116] If this was indeed the order that he gave, then it was based on nothing but speculation. It has never been firmly established whether Hentsch had been authorized by Moltke to order the retreat, or whether it was his decision, based on his own assessment of the situation. Claims have even been made that Hentsch acted in defiance of clear instructions to avoid a retreat at all cost. Moltke finally travelled to the army head-quarters of the right wing on 11 September, together with Tappen and Dommes, when it appeared as if the enemy would break through between the Second and Third Armies. Confronted with the situation as it presented itself, Moltke had to give the order to withdraw the Third, Fourth, and Fifth Armies so as to re-establish a united front. He wrote after the event: 'It was a difficult decision that I had to take without being able to get His Majesty's approval first. It was the hardest decision of my life, one that made my heart bleed.'[117] That night, he returned to head-quarters a broken man. Lyncker recorded in his diary on 12 September: 'Moltke returned, very depressed, came back with bad impressions. Should he fade away (*ausspannen*), Falkenhayn will have to take over.' The next day, his verdict was even more damning: 'Moltke is completely crushed by the events, his nerves are not up to this situation.'[118]

Because of the immense importance that has been attached to the loss of this particular campaign, much effort has gone into discovering how and why such a 'drama' could develop, and much care was taken by the

---

[115] Hentsch was Head of the *Nachrichtenabteilung* from 2 August 1914 until 28 May 1915. Oberst von Dommes had also volunteered himself for the trip, but Moltke chose Hentsch because the latter had already recently visited the First and Second Armies. Reichsarchiv, *Weltkrieg*, vol. 4, p. 223.

[116] See Müller-Loebnitz, *Die Führung*, pp. 89ff.   [117] Moltke, *Erinnerungen*, p. 24.

[118] BA-MA, w-10/50676, Lyncker diary, pp. 29ff. See also Crown Prince Rupprecht's account of 8 September: 'Gen.v. Moltke appeared to me like a sick, broken man. His tall figure was hunched, he looked incredibly worn out' (BA-MA, w-10/50659, p. 207); Rupprecht, *Kriegstagebuch*, vol. 1, p. 103.

men involved in the decision-making to disclaim their own responsibility for ordering the 'fateful' retreat. The files of the Reichsarchiv contain
numerous documents and studies relating to the Battle of the Marne and
the so-called 'Hentsch Mission' that preceded the German retreat.[119]
The Archive was keen to establish the exact events of those crucial days.
Had Moltke, ever pessimistic, ordered the retreat because he had 'lost
his nerve'? Or did his nerves 'crumble' as a result of the unsuccessful
battle? Had Hentsch, without explicit instructions to do so, ordered the
retreat because he judged the situation to be precarious and insoluble?
Or was the situation out of hand when he arrived at the front, with
retreat already ordered by the commanders of the armies concerned?

According to an enquiry conducted in April 1917, Hentsch's orders
were to direct and co-ordinate a retreat if one had already been started
by the First Army, in order to close the gap that had developed between
the two armies. However, Hentsch ordered a full retreat for both armies,
claiming that he had been authorized to do so by Moltke – an allegation
that was denied by Moltke as well as other commentators. According to
Hentsch, the mood at headquarters had been very despondent before he
left for the front (a point which is frequently emphasized because of both
Moltke's and Hentsch's alleged tendencies towards pessimism). In the
margin of the war diary of the First Army, Moltke commented after the
fateful mission (probably in February 1915):

Oberstleutnant Hentsch only had the order to tell the First Army that – if its
retreat became necessary – it should go back to the Soissons–Fismes line, in
order to reconnect with the Second Army. He did not have the order to say that
the retreat was <u>unavoidable</u>. . . . I did not give <u>an order</u> for the retreat of the
First Army. Nor was an order given for the retreat of the Second Army.[120]

This is confirmed by Tappen, who recalled in 1925: 'During the discussion it was again and again pointed out that the armies absolutely must
hold their positions.'[121] Dommes even informed the Reichsarchiv that
Moltke's order to Hentsch had demanded that he go and *prevent* a retreat
of the armies, unless he arrived too late, in which case he should direct
them to Fismes.

The Reichsarchiv also tried to establish whether Hentsch had

[119] See also Reichsarchiv, *Weltkrieg*, vol. 4, p. 545, Anlage 1: 'Quellenkritische Bewertung des zur
Darstellung der "Sendung Hentsch" benutzten Materials'. On the Battle of the Marne, see also
Reichsarchiv (ed.), *Schlachten des Weltkrieges*, vols. 22–23, *Das Marnedrama 1914*, Berlin 1928.

[120] Reichsarchiv, *Weltkrieg*, vol. 4, p. 223. Also in BA-MA, N56/2, NL Tappen, Reichsarchiv (v.
Haeften) to Tappen, 29 February 1920.

[121] Dommes to the Reichsarchiv, quoted in BA-MA, N56/2, NL Tappen, Haeften to Tappen, 29
February 1920. Tappen's letter of 1925 quoted in Reichsarchiv, *Weltkrieg*, vol. 4, p. 224.

received secret instructions from Moltke in a separate meeting. While the Reichsarchiv suspected this might have been the case, based on some involved detective work in the early years after the war,[122] Tappen ruled out the possibility of such a second secret meeting.[123] Ludendorff was also sceptical. Had such a meeting taken place, would it not have been referred to by either Hentsch or Moltke, and moreover, would not Moltke, due to his upright character ('vornehmen Charakter') have cleared Hentsch, if such a meeting and subsequent authorization had indeed occurred?[124] Ultimately, the Reichsarchiv found it impossible to solve the riddle of who gave which order to whom. The evidence that the Archive amassed was often contradictory and marred by apologetic or justificatory accounts and accusations. The order to Hentsch was never recorded in writing, and the two main protagonists, Moltke and Hentsch, were both dead by the time the Archive made its investigations.[125] Hentsch died in Bucharest on 13 February 1918 after a gall-bladder operation (but he had been able to assist in the investigation of April 1917). Moltke had compiled a report about the retreat at the Marne in July 1915, but it was, of course, no longer possible to question him by the time serious investigation into the events began. After the death of Hentsch, only Dommes and Tappen remained as eye-witnesses to the events, and the Reichsarchiv made extensive use of their testimonies. They both agreed that Hentsch had not been authorized to order a retreat. As Dommes points out, the fact that no order was recorded in writing further underlines this point of view, for they would have wanted to record such an important and unusual order.[126]

In conclusion, it is unlikely that Moltke authorized Hentsch to order a retreat, particularly considering the fact that the Kaiser had given strict orders against it. When he returned from a trip to the front on 7 September, he demanded: 'Attack, as long as it is possible – not a step back under any circumstances.'[127] Wilhelm II may have been 'Supreme War-Lord' in principle; in practice, his orders could not always be adhered to. Nonetheless, it is unlikely that Moltke would have authorized

---

[122] For the results of their detailed investigation, see ibid., p. 222.

[123] BA-MA, N56/2, NL Tappen, Haeften to Tappen, 29 February 1920.

[124] Ludendorff, *Marne-Drama*, pp. 15–16. Müller-Loebnitz agrees that there is no basis for such speculations (*Die Führung*, p. 89).

[125] The Reichsarchiv published its findings in *Weltkrieg*, vol. 4, pp. 220ff., where some of the available evidence is also reviewed. Müller-Loebnitz also concludes that Moltke's account of events is to be believed over Hentsch's *Die Führung*, p. 88.

[126] Reichsarchiv, *Weltkrieg*, vol. 4, p. 226.

[127] Ibid., p. 144. After the war, Plessen and Lyncker confirmed that the Kaiser had indeed given this order.

a subordinate to order a retreat that went completely counter to the monarch's wishes. Whatever order he gave, and whatever Hentsch's role in the events, the Chief of the General Staff would bear the blame for the lost Battle of the Marne. Of all the charges brought against him, this is the most serious, for the consequences of the defeat were grave.

THE CONSEQUENCES OF THE RETREAT BEHIND THE MARNE

The massive, historic battle on the Ourcq and the Marne was stopped! The German right army wing made a retreat out of a certain victory!

Reichsarchiv, *Der Weltkrieg 1914–1918*[128]

The army was not defeated on the Marne in 1914. It was the victor.

Erich Ludendorff, 1934[129]

The results of the German retreat were immediately noticeable. Moltke feared that 'the French elan, [now] on the point of fading, will flare up forcefully again',[130] and indeed, as the Reichsarchiv concluded, the retreat not only resulted in a revival of the will to fight in both the French and English armies, but particularly among the French people. Worse still, the German retreat from the Marne spelt the end for the Schlieffen Plan. It was now impossible to avoid fighting a long-drawn-out war on two fronts. Whether it meant that Germany's chances of winning the war had been gambled away, as has been maintained, is doubtful. A short war had already become unlikely following other dip-lomatic and military events, such as the agreement of the Entente powers not to conclude a separate peace (the Pact of London).[131] Perhaps the question should be posed differently: would Germany have won the war if she had won the Battle of the Marne? Naturally, believ-ers in the Schlieffen Plan would maintain that this would indeed have been the case. However, the lessons from the Franco-Prussian war tell a different story, and had already warned of the inherent dangers of *Volkskrieg*. French resistance would probably not have waned following a German victory on the Marne, and even if the German armies had reached Paris, the French could have continued fighting as they had in 1871. A complete annihilation of the enemy's army, as the Schlieffen

---

[128] Reichsarchiv, *Weltkrieg*, vol. 4, p. 270.
[129] Ludendorff, *Marne-Drama*, p. 1.
[130] Moltke to his wife, 9 September 1914, *Erinnerungen*, p. 385.
[131] Farrar, 'The Strategy' p. 29.

Plan envisaged, was not really feasible. What is more, would a victory against France really have spelt the end of the war? Britain had entered the war in order to maintain the status quo on the continent and would not have abandoned her French ally. Even if her army was still numerically weak at this point, her support would have bolstered French morale and, more importantly, kept her supply lines open. Moreover, the three Entente partners had agreed not to enter into separate peace agreements. In addition, Russia was a strong opponent in the East that still needed to be defeated. It had always been a fallacy to assume that the majority of German troops could be moved east in such a scenario. Ultimately, all of this is speculation and we do not know if the narrow Schlieffen Plan would ever have delivered its promise of victory against two opponents; but the available evidence suggests that the war would not have been 'over by Christmas', whatever the outcome of the Battle of the Marne. Victory on the Marne would not have altered the outcome of the war. If not on the Marne, then the plan's shortcomings would have revealed themselves elsewhere.

There can be no doubt, however, that on a personal level the results of the defeat on the Marne were grave for Moltke. It spelt the end of his military career. Contemporary observers have left numerous descriptions and accounts of Moltke's physical and mental state following these fateful events, and the overall impression was that the Chief of Staff collapsed as a result of his perceived failure as a military leader. Both friends and foes stressed that Moltke clearly suffered under the burden of coordinating and leading this massive army once the strategic 'blueprint' of the first weeks of fighting had expired.

Ludendorff's post-war publication *Das Marne-Drama – Der Fall Moltke–Hentsch* (The Drama of the Marne – the Moltke–Hentsch Case) is a good example of a typical anti-Moltke account, and as such deserves attention. During Moltke's lifetime, Ludendorff and Moltke had been on friendly terms, and had collaborated closely in the years following Ludendorff's appointment in 1908. They had also been fellow conspirators against Falkenhayn during the early months of the latter's tenure as Chief of Staff.[132] In his publication Ludendorff explained that his

---

[132] The correspondence of 1915 that survives in Moltke's papers (see also Zechlin, 'Ludendorff') testifies to the close relationship between the two generals. For Moltke the correspondence was of particular importance, being one of the few remaining links with military decision-makers and thus his only chance to keep himself informed about events on the fronts. Moltke even requested briefings about the current situation from Ludendorff, who was only too happy to oblige. See e.g. Ludendorff to Moltke, 27 January 1915, in Zechlin, 'Ludendorff', p. 328.

14 Ludendorff with Hindenburg during the First World War

change of attitude towards Moltke was due to 'my realization of the seriousness of the circumstances. . . . Not in order to devalue the army, but in honour of the old army and as a warning to coming generations, do I lay a finger on the wound that is Moltke.'[133]

While Ludendorff's portrayal of Moltke's character is interesting, he is not a reliable witness. His post-war writings are marred by his obsession with the 'secret forces of freemasonry' on which he ultimately blamed the loss of the war. Thus, in Ludendorff's opinion, Moltke was subjected to 'secret powers', and Hentsch was almost certainly a freemason – implicit proof, Ludendorff alleged, that Hentsch had deliberately overstepped his authority and ruined Germany's chances of victory. In the 1930s, such allegations were only too gladly taken up, when Jews and freemasons were blamed for stabbing the 'undefeated' German army in the back. Of all the interpretations of the Hentsch Mission, this is without doubt the furthest from the truth, and Ludendorff's allegations and conspiracy theories cannot be taken seriously. Ludendorff emphasized Moltke's connection with Rudolf Steiner, and particularly Eliza von Moltke's influence on her husband's Anthroposophical and 'occult' beliefs. He alleged that 'strangely enough, the importance of his wife . . . in this is underrated and never emphasized'.[134] Ludendorff's allegation that Eliza von Moltke had assured her husband, even before her arrival in Koblenz, that 'the whole operation of the German Army would end unhappily, according to Lisbeth Seidler [a spiritualist medium]', is important particularly in the context of Moltke's alleged pessimistic tendencies. Such warnings, if they were really given, might indeed have influenced his decision-making in the crucial days of September. Whether they actually occurred is impossible to affirm.[135] In terms of creating a particular post-war image of Moltke, however, the importance of Ludendorff's account cannot be rated too highly.

Whatever the truth behind Ludendorff's allegations, Eliza von Moltke's role and influence should certainly not be underestimated. Not only did she accompany her husband to the headquarters in Koblenz, but she also went along when the headquarters were moved to

---

[133] Ludendorff, *Marne-Drama*, p. 1.

[134] Ibid., p. 6. Ironically, the importance of Ludendorff's second wife Mathilde similarly deserves highlighting. Under her influence his writings became ludicrously dominated by conspiratory theories (Zechlin, 'Ludendorff', p. 319). Ludendorff divorced his first wife and married Mathilde in September 1926. Wolfgang Venohr describes them as having been in a 'dependent relationship' with each other. They jointly led a fanatical struggle against freemasons, Jews, Jesuits and the Vatican (*Ludendorff*, p. 17).

[135] According to Ludendorff, an aquaintance of his had been told this story by Eliza von Moltke herself: *Marne-Drama*, p. 6.

Luxembourg, apparently as a nurse, for whom Ludendorff claims Moltke had good use. The medium Lisbeth Seidler [the so-called 'Heeres-Sybille'] was allegedly also present as a nurse. Ludendorff maintains that Rudolf Steiner had also arrived in Koblenz, 'to increase the influencing of General v. Moltke'.[136] Steiner and Moltke did indeed meet in August 1914, when Steiner was staying in Niederlahnstein near Koblenz, and Moltke visited him there on 26 August.[137] However, Ludendorff's phrasing suggests more influence than Steiner actually had at the time, and his views have given credence to the widely held assumption that Moltke was in some way under Steiner's spell during those crucial first weeks of the war.

Ludendorff dates Moltke's 'loss of nerve' to even before the Battle of the Marne. During a brief stay in the General Headquarters on 22 August, he claims to have noticed that Moltke had 'completely lost his nerve.'[138] At that date Plessen, a more reliable witness, considered Moltke still to have been in control of events. Plessen detected a worsening of Moltke's condition only *after* the retreat on the Marne. Admiral von Müller, who was alert to mood swings, also did not record that Moltke was deteriorating as early as Ludendorff suggests. With hindsight at least, however, the image of Moltke that contemporaries remembered was that of a nervous man who was increasingly losing control, and such accounts are certainly true following the Battle of the Marne. Major Mewes recalled a striking image of the Chief of Staff:

The nervousness of the General was displayed outwardly, particularly in that he walked ceaselessly up and down the room and exhaled with a whistling sound through his teeth. Within the General Staff there was the general point of view that General von Moltke was unequal to his great task on account of his physical condition, and that he let the heads of departments do as they pleased.[139]

---

[136] Ibid., p. 4.

[137] Heisterkamp, 'Lebensskizze', in Meyer, *Helmuth von Moltke*, vol. 1, p. 39. The Reichsarchiv was particularly keen to establish the truth behind these events. See e.g. BA-MA, NL Tappen, N56/5, Foerster to Tappen, 8 March 1934. Tappen declared he had no knowledge of any meeting between Moltke and Steiner during the months of August/September 1914. We can be certain that such a meeting took place, because Steiner confirmed it after the war. It is untrue, however, that Steiner visited the military headquarters. Steiner was in Niederlahnstein by coincidence, and Moltke left the headquarters to visit him. Steiner asserted after the war that no military topics were discussed at the meeting.

[138] Ludendorff, *Marne-Drama*, p. 4. Groener's war-time diary seems to confirm that all was not well with Moltke, at least by 25 August. 'There is talk of Moltke's successor – Lauenstein or Knobelsdorf' (*Lebenserinnerungen*, p. 161).

[139] BA-MA, W-10/51063, 'Charakteristik der massgebenden Persönlichkeiten, ihr Anteil an den Ereignissen', by Major a.D. Dr. Mewes, p. 1.

Following the fateful events on the Marne, Moltke suffered something resembling a nervous breakdown. Contemporary accounts confirm this impression. During the fateful events, 'Moltke was reported to have been terribly agitated and had been quite harsh (*grob*) in his excitement. His wife! [sic] had continually remained in the room next door in order to be able to calm him.'[140] Hermann von Santen recorded the following image in his diary on 10 September, following a conversation that he witnessed between Moltke and another officer, in which Moltke outlined the need to withdraw troops even further. Santen's vivid description deserves to be quoted at length:

> The condition of the Chief of the German General Staff is disheartening (*niederschmetternd*): he is the image of a man whose nerves have completely crumbled. His excitement is such that he is unable to point on the map to the position that the army is now to hold. His trembling finger oscillates wildly on the map. Oberstleutnant Hasse has trouble understanding the new order for the army from the words which are uttered with such strong emotion. To [Moltke's] visible relief (*Beruhigung*) [Hasse] assures him repeatedly that he would deal with everything else through direct contact with the two neighbouring armies, and soon after the Chief of the German General Staff leaves us to continue on to the Fourth AOK. I am glad to know that there were only a few witnesses to this spectacle, which was far from uplifting. My Prussian pride has received another blow.[141]

At the end of August, Moltke had given Plessen the impression of a man in control of events, even a man who made decisions single-handedly. Thus the latter recorded on 29 August how he was being beseeched to ensure that the general headquarters was not moved to Luxembourg because of possible danger to the Kaiser. Plessen noted: 'It was not I who chose this place, but Moltke, who is doing everything himself – and a good thing, too, in war-time.'[142] As Plessen explained to Haeften after the war, the choice of military headquarters was always the Chief of Staff's domain. When a move to Luxembourg was suggested by Moltke, the Chancellor, the Foreign Secretary and the Chief of the Civil Cabinet expressed serious objections, because the population's attitude could not be gauged, and because His Majesty's safety might be endangered. They suggested Trier as a possible alternative.[143] Ultimately, however, it was Moltke's choice that was decisive.

---

[140] BayHSTA-KA, hs2642, diary of Crown Prince Rupprecht, 18 September 1914, p. 1.
[141] Santen, 'Erinnerungen', vol. II, p. 81.
[142] BA-MA, w-10/50676, Plessen diary, p. 57, also excerpts in w-10/51063, pp. 104ff.
[143] BA-MA, w-10/50897, 'Mündliche Mitteilungen des Generaloberst v. Plessen, die Se. Exzellenz bei einer mündlichen Besprechung mit dem Direktor v. Haeften am 10.4.1923 gemacht hat.',

On 12 September, the Kaiser feared that Moltke 'seemed somewhat nervous', an observation which Plessen could only endorse. The Kaiser wanted the Minister of War, Falkenhayn to assist Moltke, a change of personnel that Lyncker had been advocating strongly, but Plessen was worried that Falkenhayn was too much of a pessimist – 'impossible as a soldier, never mind a Chief of the General Staff'. When they met Moltke for his daily briefing, the first impression was not as bad as Plessen had feared. Moltke was 'indeed nervous', Plessen conceded, but not to the extent that one would have to think of an immediate replacement. Later that day, however, Moltke was to lose control completely. Plessen went to see him, urged by the Kaiser to check on his condition and to find out what Moltke thought of the recently received news that the First and Second Armies had again been attacked by the enemy. Plessen recorded:

[At] 10 p.m. I find him in his hotel, in the large dining room, which is completely filled with General Staff officers – at a small table with his wife (!!!) [sic], who unfortunately followed him here, too. . . . M[oltke] was very excited, nervous and very pessimistic, I stayed with him until 12 o'clock and tried to calm him . . .[144]

For Moltke, the Marne was more than the first set-back in the hitherto victorious German campaign – it was his personal defeat. Voices demanding his dismissal, which had made themselves heard in influential places even before this disaster, now found willing listeners, especially as it was easier to blame Moltke for the turn of events than address other possible shortcomings. Müller recorded on 14 September: 'Apparently the news has been received from the General Staff that things cannot go on with Moltke, while Moltke himself is of a different opinion. Lyncker should convince him.'[145] Lyncker had asked Falkenhayn as early as 10 August if he were willing to replace Moltke. It is a possibility that these intrigues were one of the reasons why Moltke did not leave the headquarters; knowing about them would certainly

---

footnote 143 (*cont.*)

　　p. 147. See also BA-MA, w-10/50676, Plessen diary, 28 August 1914. Following the defeat on the Marne, the OHL was moved to Mézières-Charleville, partly because the Luxembourg premises were too far away from the front and had always been considered cramped, and partly because they wanted the headquarters to be in French territory for reasons of prestige after the embarrassing defeat (Stürgkh, *Hauptquartier*, p. 52).

[144] BA-MA, w-10/51063, Plessen diary, August/September 1914, pp. 104ff. See Reichsarchiv, *Weltkrieg*, vol. 4, p. 482.

[145] Müller, *Diary*, p. 59. It is worth noting that Moltke clung to his position even when things were going so badly wrong. Görlitz comments that this is surprising, considering that he initially did not want the position (*Generalstab*, p. 229). Given his ambition, this is in fact hardly surprising, and ties in with his attempts to regain the post after his dismissal.

have added to his growing sense of insecurity.[146] When, in the aftermath of defeat, the Chief of the General Staff suffered a nervous breakdown, Lyncker's and Falkenhayn's time had come and they succeeded in convincing the Kaiser that Moltke should be replaced. Plessen recorded on 14 September:

Big crisis in the evening. The Chief of the Military Cabinet Lyncker and his head of dept. Marschall urged H.M. – without my knowledge – immediately before dinner, to dismiss Moltke and to entrust the Minister of War, Falkenhayn with the business of the Chief of the General Staff of the Field Army. H.M. agreed straight away.[147]

At the same time Moltke's deputy, Hermann von Stein, was demoted to commander of the Fourteenth Reserve Corps. Officially, Falkenhayn took over Stein's position, although in reality he replaced the Chief of the General Staff. Müller commented on 14 September that Stein's disappearance from the General Staff 'is being greeted with joy by many'.[148] Apparently, Moltke had already excluded the unpopular Stein from military decision-making. Stein took revenge on Moltke by travelling to the front without orders and arranging troop movements without authorization.[149] Personal animosities and the wish for revenge superseded the overall concern for the war effort in some quarters – an astonishing lack of professionalism in the acclaimed German leadership. As will be seen, the intrigues against Moltke's successor Falkenhayn display a similar preoccupation with personal advancement. Against the background of such personal concerns, 'ordinary soldiers' in their hundreds of thousands were being sent into battle.

The lost Battle of the Marne confirmed to critics their suspicion that Moltke had failed, that he had proved unable to stand up to the pressures that the war had placed on him. Wenninger judged harshly in his diary: 'Without doubt Falkenhayn has his own thoughts, whereas Moltke and his helpers were completely sterile. All they could do was turn the handle and roll Schlieffen's film, and they were clueless and beside themselves when the roll got stuck.'[150] Observers started to remember doubts

---

[146] Wallach, *Dogma*, p. 156.　　　[147] BA-MA, w-10/50676, diary entry, 14 September 1914.

[148] Müller, *Diary*, p. 59. Krafft considered Stein a 'weak personality and already mentally exhausted': BayHSTA-KA, NL Krafft, diary vol. 186, p. 29. See also Wenninger's account of these events, diary 14–15 September 1914, in Schulte, 'Dokumente', p. 174. The Kaiser was later to claim that the decision to replace Moltke had been entirely his. See a conversation between Conrad Haussmann and Walther Rathenau on 16 February 1915, Walter Rathenau, *Hauptwerke und Gespräche*, ed. Ernst Schulin, Munich 1977 (Walther Rathenau Gesamtausgabe, vol. 2).

[149] Wenninger report, 14 September 1914, Schulte, 'Dokumente', p. 175.

[150] BayHSTA-KA, HS2662, NL Wenninger, diary entry, 16 September 1914.

15 Erich von Falkenhayn, postcard *c.* 1915

they had had ever since Moltke had been appointed Chief of Staff. Moltke's breakdown – both mental and physical – following these events confirmed their worst expectations. Wenninger was a particularly harsh critic: 'Shame, but one should not try to force epigones to live up to the names of their fathers and uncles – Napoleon III, Siegfried Wagner, Moltke II.'[151]

Moltke was told by the Kaiser to report sick, on account of his 'fragile state'.[152] After some debate, during which Moltke vehemently refused the request, it was agreed that Moltke would stay at headquarters, but he was in effect replaced by Falkenhayn. The energetic Minister of War had secured the Kaiser's favour with his decisive anti-parliamentary stance during the Zabern Affair of 1913.[153] The Kaiser's choice of successor, a general who at 53 was younger than most other commanding generals in the German army and with little experience of General Staff work, was not widely popular, but, as in the case of Moltke's appointment eight years previously, the Kaiser's decision could not be overruled. Tirpitz, for example, commented in a letter of 15 September: 'I might be wrong, but I would not have chosen Falkenhayn, especially with such great authority.'[154] Tirpitz was alluding here to the fact that Falkenhayn would combine the office of Chief of the General Staff with that of Minister of War, which was indeed a powerful combination. From the viewpoint of the Chief of the Reich Navy Office, this was a dangerous amassing of authority; for military decision-making, it would actually have beneficial consequences, because the competition between these two bodies that had impeded peace-time military planning would be finally eradicated.

The replacement was initially secret, to avoid alerting the German public to the defeat or giving Germany's enemies an opportunity for triumph; it was only made public in November when Moltke actually left the headquarters. This led to some confusion, particularly on the part of the uninformed Austrian ally. Stürgkh recorded his bewilderment at the changes. Neither he nor Conrad had been told about

---

[151] Ibid., diary entry, 21 September 1914.

[152] BA-MA, w-10/50676, Plessen diary, 14 September 1914, p. 68.

[153] Stürgkh, *Hauptquartier*, p. 26. On Falkenhayn and the Zabern Affair, see Afflerbach, *Falkenhayn*, pp. 115ff. It was because of the Kaiser's favour that Falkenhayn managed to stay in office as Chief of Staff until 1916, against widespread opposition, from (among others) Hindenburg and Ludendorff, the Chancellor and, of course, Moltke himself.

[154] Tirpitz, *Erinnerungen*, p. 403. Wenninger, by contrast, had a very positive opinion of Falkenhayn: BayHSTA-KA, HS2662, NL Wenninger. On Falkenhayn's controversial appointment, see also Afflerbach, *Falkenhayn*, pp. 179ff.; Robert T. Foley, 'Attrition: Its Theory and Application in German Strategy, 1880–1916', Ph.D. Dissertation, King's College, University of London, 1999, p. 89.

Moltke's dismissal or the defeat on the Marne.[155] Falkenhayn maintained after the war that it had been his wish that the change be kept a
secret.[156] From 14 September onwards, Moltke's position had been
reduced to that of an onlooker who had to stand aside and let
Falkenhayn, promoted to *Generalquartiermeister*, do his work. Already on
15 September, it was Falkenhayn who gave the daily General Staff talk.
Plessen recorded: 'Moltke says almost nothing. Falkenhayn delivers the
talk very well.'[157] On one occasion, Moltke did speak up against
Falkenhayn, when he criticized his order to the Sixth Army 'to throw
troops, if need be, battalion by battalion, against the enemy', whom
Falkenhayn considered in the process of collapse. Moltke stressed on
this occasion that the main task was to get a decision on the right
wing.[158] A few days later, Moltke complained to the Kaiser in front of a
large group of officers: 'Your Majesty, nobody tells me anything any
more!', to which the Kaiser replied that he was in the same position.
Wenninger commented: 'A sad ending!'[159] Falkenhayn's lack of tact
made the situation all the more difficult to bear.[160] It is not difficult to
imagine the humiliation this meant for Moltke. In January 1915, Moltke
wrote to the Chancellor, describing the impact the replacement had had
on his role as decision-maker:

Since the moment when His Majesty told me via the Chief of the Military
Cabinet that I should report sick and go to Berlin, because the running of operations was to be given over to General v. Falkenhayn, I have had no influence
over the direction of the war. Because General v. Falkenhayn explained to me
at the same time that he could only accept the responsibility if I did not intervene in any way, I have restrained myself and have since neither been asked my
opinion nor been informed about intended measures by the army leadership.
Moreover, since I went to Homburg on 1 November at the Kaiser's wish and
received there after two days the order dismissing me from my previous position, I have been unable to inform myself about the situation by asking around
in the General Staff, because I have been completely eliminated.[161]

For the rest of his life, a bitter and resentful Moltke attempted to
justify his actions, and to refute his numerous critics. In a letter to Plessen
on 2 May 1915, he admitted having been nervous 'in the critical

[155] Stürgkh, *Hauptquartier*, p. 45; Herwig, *First World War*, p. 106.
[156] Falkenhayn, *Oberste Heeresleitung*, p. 1.
[157] BA-MA, w-10/50676, Plessen diary, 15 September 1914, p. 68. Cf. Lyncker's diary for the same
day: 'At today's report Falkenhayn alone spoke. Moltke just listened.'
[158] BayHSTA-KA, NL Krafft, diary, vol. 48, 18 September 1914.
[159] BayHSTA-KA, HS2662, NL Wenninger, diary entry, 21 September 1914.
[160] BayHSTA-KA, NL Krafft, diary, vol. 48, 18 September 1914.
[161] Moltke, *Erinnerungen*, pp. 396ff., 8 January 1915.

September days', blaming this on the events of the first days of mobilization (the scene in the Kaiser's Schloss on 1 August).[162] Moltke contended that future commentators would agree that his decision to withdraw troops on the Marne had been the right one: 'I look forward with a clear conscience to the judgement of military history on this episode.'[163] Similarly, he wrote in May 1915 that he had heard that the retreat on the Marne was being blamed on his nervousness, an allegation that he considered completely wrong. 'Given the situation, the retreat was a completely unavoidable necessity that I had to order after full consideration – though with a heavy heart – and I am certain that military history will one day prove me right.'[164]

Moltke was wrong, of course. After his death, and particularly after the war was lost, Moltke's critics became increasingly vociferous, often forgetting or glossing over their own mistakes in the process.[165] Moltke provided a convenient scapegoat, for they could argue that it was not German war planning, or the execution of that planning when war came, that had failed Germany, but rather the hapless successor who had followed the great military leader Schlieffen. Germany's infamous deployment plan had not been at fault, but rather Moltke had been wrong in his implementation of the allegedly brilliant strategy that he had inherited from his predecessor.

MOLTKE OUT OF OFFICE

> You know that I refused to report in sick and depart. You know that
> I said to you, 'My place is here, I stand and fall with this army.'
> Helmuth von Moltke, 3 October 1914[166]

Following his replacement, Moltke initially stayed at military headquarters, arguing that a public replacement would make apparent the scale of the disaster of the retreat on the Marne. However, he soon found the situation intolerable; being reduced to the position of an onlooker did nothing to improve his mental or physical health. Already on 21 September, Tirpitz had commented in a letter: 'Physically Moltke has collapsed.'[167] Moltke wrote to his wife from Mézières about his attempts

---

[162] See Chapter 4, pp. 216ff.
[163] BA-MA, NL Moltke, N78/6, p. 13.   [164] Moltke, *Erinnerungen*, 4 May 1915, p. 424.
[165] See e.g. Oberst von Mantey to Foerster, 30 June 1931: 'Kuhl [First Army] is complaining terribly about Moltke, but has himself made such severe mistakes that I would say he has spoilt many an idea for Moltke . . .'. BA-MA, RH61/v.68, pp. 56ff.
[166] Moltke to his wife, Mézières, 3 October 1914, Moltke, *Erinnerungen*, p. 387.
[167] Tirpitz, *Erinnerungen*, p. 405.

'to keep myself informed about everything that is being done and to keep up the relationship between Falkenhayn and myself, it is not easy but I am doing what I can. I believe that a more difficult test could hardly be imposed on a human being.'[168] Groener's recollection of Moltke at that time is uncharacteristically sympathetic – he considered the way he was treated 'humiliating'. Moltke no longer ate with the others, and Falkenhayn lacked the tact to ease the difficulty of the situation.[169]

Moltke found an immediate distraction when he joined Generaloberst von Beseler in Belgium. Beseler's Third Reserve Corps had the task of laying siege to the fortress town of Antwerp, into which the Belgian Army had retreated. Moltke pushed for a speedy capture of the town. In the afternoon of 24 September, Beseler and his staff had a conference, 'where I warned that Moltke was pushing terribly, and that I therefore approved of the utmost speeding up. Unfortunately ammunition is sorely lacking.'[170] The Kaiser was impatiently awaiting positive news, and Moltke probably felt that he could redeem himself with a success at Antwerp. He must still have remembered the monarch's delight following the capture of Liège. Moltke and Beseler met on several occasions over the next few days. On 4 October, Beseler's diary reads: 'Moltke visits me again; he is friendly and helpful and is helping me where he can. . . . Moltke promises ammunition and bridging trains (*Korpsbrückentrains*), both enormously important. He talks of the impatience of the Kaiser. . . .'[171] The next day, Krafft recorded in his diary:

General von Moltke is still sitting in Brussels. We still report to him pro forma. In reality, he is sadly excluded. It is a rather disgraceful end for the unfortunate man whose – apparently – gigantic shoulders had been burdened with a huge task against his will; I feel deeply sorry for him. – But the Fatherland now needs <u>men</u>![172]

The capture of Antwerp on 9 October was a much-needed military success and helped to improve the Kaiser's mood. For Moltke, it was also a welcome personal success. Müller recorded in his diary the Kaiser's toast on the capture of Antwerp 'to "the Generaloberst von Moltke, who thought up the plan, and to General von Beseler, who executed it" – a slight cover-up for the failure of Moltke as Chief of the General Staff.'[173] On 11 October, back at headquarters, Moltke informed his wife about

[168] Moltke, *Erinnerungen*, 11 October 1914, pp. 387–388.
[169] Groener, *Lebenserinnerungen*, p. 191.   [170] BA-MA, w-10/50631, Beseler diary, p. 15.
[171] Ibid., p. 18.
[172] BayHSTA-KA, NL Krafft, diary, vol. 48, 5 October 1914.
[173] Müller, *Diary*, p. 64. Tirpitz also commented how strange it appeared to him that Moltke was singled out for extra praise next to Beseler: Tirpitz, *Erinnerungen*, letter of 10 October, pp. 416–417.

Antwerp. 'At least I was able to be of some help there, whereas I am only a spectator here. – At least the fall of Antwerp was one success in a long time.'[174] As a result of the recent successes, the optimistic mood of the early days of the war had returned to the headquarters, as Wenninger noted: 'In the General Headquarters the bad mood had only lasted for a few days (from 10–15 Sept.). Now we have quite decisively regained the upper hand and have superiority in a decisive place.'[175]

It took Moltke and his wife some time to resign themselves to the fact that his dismissal was to be permanent, as they seem to have believed that he would be reinstated once his health had improved.[176] The official term 'leave of absence' ('Beurlaubung'), rather than 'dismissal', may have given Moltke a false impression. On 21 October, Moltke had a conversation with the Kaiser about his unhappy new position, as he told his wife: 'It was exactly as I had thought. The Kaiser was under the impression that I was actually directing things and that Falkenhayn was only a kind of deputy. I have now clarified the matter and I have told him that I am completely excluded.' Contrary to Moltke's impression, it is unlikely that the monarch ever considered the replacement to be only temporary. He simply did not have the heart to be frank with Moltke.

The following day, Moltke fell seriously ill, suffering from problems with his gall bladder and liver. 'Now I have collapsed after all, though my body has stood up so well until now.'[177] Moltke's various illnesses became a subject of much discussion after the war, and periods of illness well before the events on the Marne and their aftermath were frequently highlighted by post-war commentators. Moltke's son Adam von Moltke refuted most vehemently, as 'an outrageous lie', the allegation that the Chief of Staff had been seriously ill as early as 1911: 'It was just that the excitement brought about the events following the Battle of the Marne and the humiliating events following his exclusion from the military leadership brought on another gall-bladder infection.'[178] However, Adam

---

[174] Moltke, *Erinnerungen*, pp. 387–388. On Antwerp, see also Reichsarchiv (ed.), *Schlachten des Weltkrieges*, vol. 3, *Antwerpen 1914*, Berlin 1925.   [175] Schulte, 'Dokumente', p. 177.

[176] See Rathenau's diary entry, 2 November 1914. Frau von Moltke had asked him to visit her, and he went to see her in the General Staff building. According to Eliza von Moltke, the Kaiser had been under the impression that Moltke had only been replaced temporarily. Rathenau thought this was probably the Moltkes' mistake, as the Kaiser had been definite about replacing Moltke, but had probably felt too sorry for Moltke to say so outright. Walther Rathenau, *Tagebuch 1907–1922*, ed. Hartmut Pogge von Strandmann, Düsseldorf 1967, pp. 189–190. See also Wallach, *Dogma*, p. 191 on how Moltke continued to hope that the Kaiser would reappoint him.

[177] Moltke, *Erinnerungen*, Mézières, 22 October 1914, p. 388.

[178] See BA-MA, N78/37: Adam v. Moltke 'Eine Antwort an Herrn Walter Görlitz, das Kapitel "Der Krieg ohne Feldherr" in seinem Buch "Der Deutsche Generalstab" betreffend Gen. Oberst Helmuth von Moltke', 1958, pp. 10–11.

von Moltke offers no explanation of why his father had gone to Karlsbad twice in 1914, a fact that clearly attests to some health problems.

On 23 October, the Kaiser visited Moltke, who was still in Mézières.[179] On this occasion, he invited Moltke to go to his *Jagdschloss* at Bad Homburg to recover from his illness. Müller also visited him on 27 October. He recorded: 'I found a broken man, physically as well as spiritually.'[180] Moltke stayed in Mézières until his official dismissal from his duties as Chief of the General Staff on 1 November 1914. Only then did he accept the Kaiser's offer to retire to Bad Homburg. Major von Redern commented in his diary: 'This will be a relief both to him and to the headquarters.'[181] In Homburg, Moltke proceeded to write justificatory accounts of his actions, including in November 1914 the pamphlet 'Betrachtungen und Erinnerungen. Die "Schuld" am Kriege' (Thoughts and Memoirs. The War 'Guilt').[182] He also received a visit from Rudolf Steiner.[183]

On 30 December 1914, after convalescing at Bad Homburg, Moltke was made Chief of the Deputy General Staff of the Army (*Stellvertretender Generalstab der Armee*) which meant he would be based back in Berlin, in charge of supplies.[184] This was a position without any actual authority, and a real embarrassment for the former Chief of Staff.[185] Moltke can have been in no doubt that this was at best a consolation prize, and seems to have accepted it with the intention of trying to regain his old position as soon as possible. The Austrian military attaché Stürgkh was full of admiration and felt 'deeply moved' that Moltke did not find it beneath him to accept this inferior position. Not everyone would have been able to accept 'an office that, in comparison with his previous field of influence, can only be described as very modest and meaningless', he commented. Stürgkh visited Moltke in Berlin, where the topic of conversation was, among other things, the death of Conrad's son. Moltke felt very sorry for himself, telling Stürgkh that even the death of a son would have been preferable to the fate he had suffered:

---

[179] Moltke's letter to his wife, 24 October 1914, *Erinnerungen*, p. 388.   [180] Müller, *Diary*, p. 66.

[181] BA-MA, w-10/50676, excerpts from the diary of Major von Redern, 31 October 1914, p. 92.

[182] See Introduction, p. 8.

[183] Heisterkamp, 'Lebensskizze', p. 38. Steiner confirmed in a speech of May 1921 that he saw Moltke again occasionally from October 1914 onwards, after only having seen him once since the outbreak of war, on 26 August near the military headquarters at Koblenz (public speech, 25 May 1921, delivered in Stuttgart). My thanks to Konrad Donat for providing me with a summary of this unpublished speech. See also Walter Beck, *Rudolf Steiner. Sein Leben und Werk. Eine Biographie mit neuen Dokumenten*, Dornach 1997, p. 138.

[184] Kabinettsorder, 30 Dezember 1914, Moltke, *Erinnerungen*, p. 392.

[185] Wallach, *Dogma*, p. 174.

And yet I envy him [Conrad], when I compare myself to him. What is his loss compared to the blow that has struck me! Just consider from what position, from what field of influence a tragic fate has torn me; no one has ever experienced anything like it. Now I sit here in this position which I accepted because it is my belief that everyone has to serve the Fatherland at the present time, wherever he may be placed or be of use, but I will never get over it.[186]

After the initial hurt and disappointment following his dismissal, Moltke had not buried all hope of reclaiming his influential position. He tried to keep in touch with events at the front by corresponding with friends such as Ludendorff and Colmar von der Goltz.[187] His position in the Stellvertretender Generalstab did not make him privy to information from the OHL. Neither this institution nor the deputy Ministry of War had received any news from the OHL since its departure to the front, and had to glean information from newspapers.[188] In the intrigues surrounding his successor, which began with Falkenhayn's take-over in September 1914 and continued until his dismissal and fall from grace in 1916, Moltke played an important part.[189] First, he became involved in the debate over the fact that Falkenhayn now occupied both the positions of Prussian Minister of War and Chief of the General Staff. Moltke wrote to Bethmann Hollweg in January 1915 that he did not consider such a union of offices advantageous, a view that he thought was widely shared in the country, arguing that the Ministry and the General Staff should counterbalance each other. Presumably this was a euphemistic way of describing their state of rivalry in peace-time. Moreover, Moltke felt that the Minister of War should be in Berlin, not at the front.[190] He even speculated on the suitability of possible replacement candidates for the position of Chief of Staff. Ludendorff he considered 'probably too young', well suited as Chief of an operations department or *Oberquartiermeister*, but too stubborn to be able to work alongside Falkenhayn. 'He is very talented and ambitious, and has reason to be,

---

[186] Stürgkh, *Hauptquartier*, p. 89.
[187] BA-MA, NL Moltke, N78/40, letters from Goltz to Moltke, 1915.
[188] BayHSTA-KA, MKr1765, No. 2909, report of Bavarian deputy military plenipotentiary in Berlin, 21 August 1914.
[189] Criticisms of Falkenhayn were voiced almost as soon as he had taken over. Krafft accused Falkenhayn of 'dilettantism'. He also disliked Dommes and Tappen, whom he considered the most guilty in the failure of the OHL (BayHSTA-KA, NL Krafft, diary entries 23–24 September 1914, vol. 48). The intrigues against Falkenhayn are analysed in Afflerbach, *Falkenhayn*, pp. 218ff. See also Heinz Krafft, *Staatsräson und Kriegsführung im kaiserlichen Deutschland 1914–1916: Der Gegensatz zwischen dem Generalstabschef von Falkenhayn und dem Oberbefehlshaber Ost im Rahmen des Bündniskrieges der Mittelmächte*, Göttingen 1980.
[190] Moltke, *Erinnerungen*, p. 395.

but he would only submit to a personality he respected.' Moltke considered Generaloberst von Bülow the most suitable candidate. Although he must have hoped to be a possible candidate himself, Moltke did not put himself forward. Perhaps he expected that Bülow, to whom he referred Bethmann for 'a competent judgement', might in turn suggest him.[191]

In letters to both Bethmann and the Kaiser, Moltke also felt compelled to express his views regarding the current debate within the army on whether the main focus of operations should be the eastern or western front. Falkenhayn on the one hand, and the victors of Tannenberg, Hindenburg and Ludendorff on the other, could not agree on a strategy. Falkenhayn was an 'Ermattungsstratege', who hoped to exhaust the opponent with a war of attrition, whereas Hindenburg and Ludendorff wanted – and thought possible – a complete annihilation of the opponent, in this case Russia. They were 'Vernichtungsstrategen'.[192] Falkenhayn was determined to continue the campaigns in the West, while the Supreme Command in the East (Oberbefehlshaber Ost – OberOst) insisted on the East for further offensive action, arguing that the situation in the West had become a stalemate. Falkenhayn had decided as early as November 1914 that military victory over the Russians would be an impossibility – whereas OberOst insisted until February/March 1915 that such a victory was possible. Only then did Oberstleutnant Hoffmann of the Eighth Army staff write in his diary: 'The Russian army cannot be completely defeated.'[193]

Not surprisingly, Moltke joined the camp of Falkenhayn's opponents, and declared that the most important theatre of war was now in the East. When Bethmann asked his opinion on Falkenhayn's strategy, Moltke replied on 10 January 1915 that he considered Germany's main goal to be a decision against Russia, which would open up the opportunity for peace with her. 'If this were achieved', Moltke wrote, 'the war would in my opinion be as good as won.'[194] Similarly, he recommended to the Kaiser on the same day:

It is my innermost conviction that the decision of the war lies in the East. If we succeed, even now, in defeating the Russians in such a way that would make it possible to arrive at a peace with them, then France will give up her resistance very soon. Your Majesty would then have as good as won the war. As long as

---

[191] Moltke to Bethmann, 8 January 1915, ibid. It is possible that Ludendorff's post-war antipathy has its roots in the fact that Moltke did not recommend him as a Chief of Staff.

[192] Afflerbach, *Falkenhayn*, pp. 307–308.

[193] See ibid., p. 259 (here also Hoffmann's quote); Kitchen, *Silent Dictatorship*, p. 20.

[194] Moltke, *Erinnerungen*, p. 399. Bethmann had wanted some military opinions to substantiate his suspicions regarding Falkenhayn. See Afflerbach, *Falkenhayn*, p. 223.

Russia stands in the field, France will not agree a peace. . . . Therefore I consider it to be absolutely essential to deploy all available powers to defeat Russia, all the more so because it appears that Austria is steadily weakening militarily.[195]

Moltke was putting himself forward as the person who knew how to manoeuvre Germany out of the current stalemate, while outwardly protesting that he did want his old position back, as in a letter dated 12 January:

Your Excellency knows that I do not make this judgement [on Falkenhayn's leadership] in order to recommend myself by you by criticizing my successor. I have finished with my life and my work and would never be able to resume my old position.[196]

These protestations seem hardly convincing in the light of the available evidence. Moltke almost certainly hoped to regain his position, or at least to see one of his preferred candidates replace the despised Falkenhayn. At the very least, he hoped to be able to play a more active role as an army commander when his health was restored. He was to be very disappointed. In April 1915, he wrote to Plessen from Berlin:

When I arrived here I had the foolish hope that my position here would only be a temporary one and that I would be employed as an army commander when the opportunity arose. But nobody has asked for me. Am I really considered incapable of assuming a position in front of the enemy?

He probably hoped that Plessen, thanks to his closeness to the monarch, might be able to put a word in for him. He refuted allegations that his state of health precluded him from active service, arguing that he was as healthy as ever. His resentment at his current situation is evident. 'All of my comrades are standing in front of the enemy, only I am buried alive and excluded in a job that could equally be done by a higher civil servant.'[197]

Against his successor he found a powerful ally in Hindenburg, who suggested to the Kaiser in January that Moltke should replace Falkenhayn. Hindenburg intended Ludendorff to take over from him in due course, a plan of which Moltke was evidently not aware.[198] The Kaiser was not to be swayed, however, and Bethmann, too, objected to Moltke as a choice, arguing that Moltke was in his opinion 'a physically

[195] Moltke, *Erinnerungen*, letter to Wilhelm II, 10 January 1915, p. 406.

[196] Ibid., p. 409. The name of the recipient was omitted from the published version. It was probably Plessen.

[197] BA-MA, NL Moltke, N78/6, Moltke to Plessen, 21 April 1915, p. 7. In Groener's opinion, Moltke could have served the German people and army well as an army leader and had not deserved such treatment (*Lebenserinnerungen*, p. 191).

[198] See Zechlin, 'Ludendorff', p. 325.

and mentally broken man' and that he 'lacked on the entire western front that kind of trust which he absolutely needs.'[199] The Chancellor considered it necessary that a different person be chosen.

Hindenburg objected to Below and Knobelsdorff[200] as substitutes for Falkenhayn. Instead, if Moltke could not be agreed on, he considered Ludendorff, 'who is not much younger than Falkenhayn, to be absolutely the best'.[201] In answer to Bethmann's objections, he advised:

If the concerns about M[oltke] remain, then L[udendorff] is by far the best. If the latter is too young, then I myself would have to take the burden upon me, even if only very reluctantly, but only with L. as an aide. The place for the Minister of War would then have to be Berlin.[202]

Moltke attempted to seize the opportunity that presented itself when he was suddenly recommended in such high quarters as a replacement for Falkenhayn. On 17 January 1915, he wrote to the Kaiser that he had found out 'by chance' that Hindenburg had recommended his recall to his old position. Moltke's following protestations seem hardly credible: 'I beg of Your Majesty not to accept this under any circumstances. Not because of my health, which is completely restored, but because I am under the impression that Your Majesty no longer retains the old trust in me.'[203] With this letter Moltke clearly intended not only to alert the monarch to the fact that certain people still considered him suitable as Chief of Staff and that he had regained his health, but also to invite confirmation that the Kaiser still had faith in his abilities. At a time when it was common practice to offer a resignation that one did not necessarily want to be accepted, and to profess a lack of interest in positions that one really wanted, Moltke's protestations could hardly be taken at face value.

This was not the only occasion when Moltke emphasized that he had recovered his health completely. In a letter to Hindenburg on 23 January 1915 he wrote that the Kaiser had turned down Hindenburg's suggestion on the grounds that Moltke was too ill. He assured Hindenburg that he was well and 'completely restored'.[204] To

---

[199] Copies of telegrams between Bethmann and Hindenburg, January 1915, in BA-MA, w-10/50688. Bethmann to Hindenburg, 14 January 1915, p. 22.

[200] General Fritz von Below was Plessen's preferred candidate: BA-MA, w-10/50897, 'Mündliche Mitteilungen des Generalobersten von Plessen', p. 148. General Schmidt von Knobelsdorff was Chief of Staff of the Fifth Army under Crown Prince Wilhelm.

[201] BA-MA, w-10/50688, copies of telegrams between Bethmann and Hindenburg, January 1915, Reichskanzler to Hofrat Ostertag, relaying Hindenburg's telegram, received 14 January, p. 21.

[202] BA-MA, w-10/50688, Wahnschaffe to Reichskanzlei, 14 January 1914, p. 24.

[203] Moltke, *Erinnerungen*, pp. 413ff.   [204] Ibid., p. 418.

Ludendorff he complained a few days later of his isolation since the day of his dismissal: 'nobody, not the Kaiser or anyone else, has asked after me since then. The Kaiser has not even considered it worth the effort to enquire whether I was well or ill, whether I had the wish to return to my old position or not.'[205]

The intrigues surrounding Falkenhayn against the background of the developing trench warfare demonstrate that, instead of pursuing unity of command, the men in charge of military operations had time and energy for quarrels and in-fighting, displaying in times of crisis the same lack of co-operation that had been prevalent before the outbreak of war. Personal ambitions and animosities, but also differences in opinion over Germany's strategy and war aims, motivated and divided Germany's main military decision-makers. Thus Ludendorff wrote to Moltke on 2 January 1915: '[Your] Excellency knows my feelings, I can hate, and this man [Falkenhayn] I do hate.'[206] Hindenburg went as far as to threaten to resign because of plans to remove Ludendorff from his staff and away from the East. The Kaiser considered court-martialling the aged general for his tantrums ('Allüren eines Wallenstein').[207] Moltke was determined to convince the Kaiser that his choice for Moltke's successor had been wrong, and he even went as far as to suggest that Falkenhayn was dangerous for Germany. In his letter of 17 January 1915, he asserted that 'neither Falkenhayn's character nor his talent equip him to be Your Majesty's first adviser in military matters in these grave times. He is a serious danger for the Fatherland.'[208]

The Kaiser was outraged by Moltke's interference. Ritter claims that he even considered dismissing Moltke from his duties in Berlin, a fate that was only averted by Plessen's intervention.[209] Wilhelm II trusted Falkenhayn and kept him in office despite widespread criticism. Against the background of these intrigues, in which the Chancellor and even the Kaiserin got involved on the side of Falkenhayn's opponents, the unpopular general was promoted on 20 January to *General der Infanterie*. Ludendorff commented acidly: 'Herr v. F[alkenhayn] fell upstairs.'[210] The only concession that was made to Falkenhayn's many critics was the appointment of General Wild von Hohenborn, Falkenhayn's preferred candidate and a school-friend of the Kaiser, as Minister of War on 21 January 1915, ending Falkenhayn's dual role. Hindenburg wrote to

[205] Ibid., January 1915, pp. 420–421.   [206] Zechlin, 'Ludendorff', p. 325.
[207] Ibid., pp. 320, 327.
[208] Moltke, *Erinnerungen*, pp. 413ff.   [209] Ritter, *Staatskunst*, vol. 3, p. 70.
[210] Zechlin, 'Ludendorff', letter of 27 January 1915, p. 330.

Moltke three days later that some success had been achieved because Falkenhayn had been forced to give up one of his posts. He was happy that the attempt to get rid of Ludendorff had failed and content with the result the intrigues had achieved.[211]

Strategy was the main bone of contention between Falkenhayn and the duo Hindenburg and Ludendorff. On the eastern front, there was a lack of regard for the concerns and problems facing the German armies in the West. Even a year later, these differences had not been resolved, as Minister of War Wild von Hohenborn commented following a visit to OberOst in December 1915: 'There is no understanding among this staff of the West, of Belgium or Serbia; they want to bring their Russian battle to an end and hope that this will bring the war to an end.'[212]

Virtually everyone of importance was drawn into the quarrel: the Kaiser, the Chancellor, the Chief of the Military Cabinet, Tirpitz, Moltke, and, of course, Falkenhayn, Hindenburg and Ludendorff. As is well known, Hindenburg and Ludendorff eventually won, being placed in charge of military operations in August 1916. Falkenhayn did however, succeed in remaining in office for almost two years thanks to the Kaiser's trust in him. Eventually, Falkenhayn's fate was similar to Moltke's. Like Moltke, he had not been an unopposed candidate when the Kaiser decided to appoint him, and like Moltke, he was accused of not following the lead of the 'genius' Schlieffen.[213] The post-war writers of the Schlieffen school were hardly more charitable towards Falkenhayn than they were to Moltke. Their writings painted Falkenhayn as indecisive and self-doubting, and ultimately unsuited to high command.[214]

In addition to his self-pitying statements and accusations of his successor, Moltke was constantly warning about the worsening economic situation in the months following his replacement. The effects of the British naval blockade were becoming increasingly serious, and supplies within Germany were diminishing fast. An additional cause for concern was the bad harvest, which had been approximately 20–30 per cent below that of previous years.[215] The imports that could still be obtained via neutral countries were not enough.[216] However, Moltke's warnings did not increase his

---

[211] NL Hindenburg, N429/3, Hindenburg to Moltke, 24 January 1915.

[212] Wild von Hohenborn, diary, 16 December 1915. Quoted in Afflerbach, *Falkenhayn*, p. 309.

[213] See Afflerbach, *Falkenhayn*, p. 213.

[214] See e.g. Foley, 'Attrition: Its Theory and Application', p. 133; Afflerbach, *Falkenhayn*, p. 3.

[215] BA-MA, W-10/50374, 'Die Bedeutung der Kriegswirtschaft und Kriegsrüstung im Rahmen der Gesamtkriegsführung', p. 10.

[216] On the economic problems caused by the British blockade, see e.g. Ferguson, *Pity of War*, pp. 248ff.

popularity and he fully expected to be considered a 'trouble-maker'. In April 1915, he complained: 'But of what value is the voice of an outcast?'[217]

Indeed, it seems as if the recipients of such letters felt that Moltke was panicking unduly. Plessen advised Moltke that his warnings regarding the economic situation were regarded as further signs of his nervous disposition ('nervöser Reizbarkeit').[218] In his answer to Plessen, Moltke commented that this interpretation had been cause for some amusement on his part, and proceeded to explain how he came to be involved in the economic debate:

> When I arrived here [in Berlin], several gentlemen from the realms of industry, the economy, and agriculture visited me, all with the same request: Help us, our warning voice is not being heard. We are heading for a catastrophe, if there is no immediate intervention at the eleventh hour.[219]

Moltke felt indignant and misunderstood. As it looked increasingly likely that the war would drag on, he was indeed right to raise a warning finger about Germany's increasingly desperate economic situation. However, no one would listen to a man who was renowned for his pessimism. In any case, his sudden interest in economic matters came too late to be of any real value to the German army.

Much to his resentment, Moltke remained Chief of the Deputy General Staff. Frustrated, he complained to his friend Colmar von der Goltz: 'It is dreadful to be condemned to inactivity in this war which I prepared and initiated.'[220] In August 1915, Falkenhayn suggested that Moltke become the Governor General in newly conquered Russian Poland. Bethmann Hollweg objected, and Beseler was eventually appointed to that position.[221] In the same month, Moltke was awarded the Pour le Mérite, on the anniversary of the *coup de main* on Liège, in recognition of his efforts in preparing the army in peace-time and in the organization of mobilization and deployment.[222]

On 18 June 1916, immediately after giving a memorial speech for the recently deceased Colmar von der Goltz in the Reichstag, Moltke suffered a fatal stroke, never having regained his influential position or any other leading position within the army. In letters of support written to Moltke by old friends and colleagues when the news of his dismissal had become public in November of 1914, Generaladjutant von Plessen

---

[217] Moltke to Plessen, 29 January 1915, *Erinnerungen*, p. 421.
[218] BA-MA, NL Moltke N78/6, Plessen to Moltke, 30 April 1915, p. 10.
[219] Moltke to Plessen, 2 May 1915, ibid., p. 13.
[220] Moltke to Goltz, 14 June 1915, cited in Röhl, 'Germany', in Wilson (ed.), *Decisions for War*, p. 27.
[221] Afflerbach, *Falkenhayn*, p. 311.   [222] Zechlin, 'Ludendorff', p. 346.

had confidently forecast that 'the world will say that the war was bril-
liantly prepared by Moltke, and as along as he was involved, everything
went well.'[223] Plessen meant well, but he could not have been more
wrong. After Moltke's death, letters to his widow similarly underlined
that history would prove that Moltke had been a great military leader.
Instead, Moltke has always been portrayed as a bad substitute for more
famous Chiefs of Staff. Even in his obituary, comparisons were made
with his 'great' predecessors. The *Berliner Zeitung* reminded its readers of
Moltke's alleged reluctance to be a military leader:

When the trust of his King called him to be the successor of Schlieffen, of that
very unique *praeceptor exercitus*, he took on the position even though he told
himself that it would be inestimably difficult after Moltke and Schlieffen, two
princes in the realm of the art of war, to keep the army at the same height to
which those great men had led it.[224]

In a letter of condolence to Moltke's widow, Fritz Bronsart wrote from
Constantinople in July 1916:

I do not think that His Majesty had a more faithful and more honest man in his
entourage; and I can imagine how much this man of honour had to bear when
he had to accept a position that had so little resemblance to his past, motivated
by pure love for the Fatherland. Was his early death a salvation for him? But
what tragedy lies in the fact that he will not live to see the final victory, [a victory]
which we do not doubt will happen![225]

When Moltke died in 1916, he was a broken man. The war that he and
his colleagues had conjured up was supposed to lead to the triumph of
the stronger forces over the weaker, much in keeping with his own Social
Darwinist beliefs. It had found a victim in this military leader who was,
judging by overwhelming contemporary evidence, too weak for the task
he was given. Although he had been aware that the next war would
resemble nothing the world had ever seen, the full extent of the disaster
that resulted from his decision-making was worse than anything he could
possibly have imagined.

[223] BA-MA, NL Moltke, N78/6, Plessen correspondence, 13 November 1914.
[224] *Berliner Zeitung*, 19 June 1916.
[225] BA-MA, NL Moltke, N78/8, 'Privatkorrespondenz Eliza von Moltke mit verschiedenen
Persönlichkeiten', Fritz Bronsart to Eliza von Moltke, 15 July 1916.

Myths and realities: Helmuth von Moltke and the origins of the First World War

> The spiritual progress of mankind is only possible through Germany. This is why Germany will not lose this war; it is the only nation that can, at the present moment, take charge of leading mankind towards a higher destiny.
>
> Helmuth von Moltke, November 1914[1]

Helmuth von Moltke was one of Imperial Germany's leading military decision-makers. Far from being an ineffectual and reluctant military leader, justifiably marginalized by historians, through his constant advocacy of war 'the sooner the better' he did much to heighten the increasingly bellicose mood in Wilhelmine Germany, where war came to be regarded as inevitable. Moltke's fears for Germany's future, and his consequent desire for a preventive war, influenced other decision-makers in military as well as civilian quarters.

It can no longer be maintained that Moltke was the reluctant military leader that his post-war critics have claimed. This study confirms the view that Moltke benefitted from his close friendship with the Kaiser when acceding to the position of Chief of the General Staff, and demonstrates that there were positive, as well as negative, voices when his candidacy was first announced. The circumstances surrounding his appointment were therefore less clear-cut than has previously been suggested. Moltke was an ambitious careerist who, once in office, tried to cling to his influential position even after the Kaiser and his military entourage had lost faith in him. His inglorious dismissal did nothing to stop him from trying desperate measures in order to return to his old position.

Foremost among the myths, and most damaging to Moltke's reputation, has been the Schlieffen Plan and Moltke's alleged adulteration of it. The Schlieffen Plan, as well as its creator, have too readily been

---

[1] Helmuth von Moltke, 'Betrachtungen und Erinnerungen', November 1914, *Erinnerungen*, p. 14.

elevated to a mythical status by the historians of the Reichsarchiv and many subsequent commentators. A reassessment of Schlieffen and his strategic plan leads to a fairer appraisal of Moltke's abilities.

Politically, the Schlieffen/Moltke Plan proved disastrous, due to the violation of the neutrality of Luxembourg and Belgium.[2] The odium associated with the violation of her neighbours' neutrality, and of starting hostilities before war was officially declared, burdened Germany with guilt after 1918. And yet, contemporaries such as Groener had no problem in explaining away the plan's shortcomings. He regarded the violation of Belgian neutrality, for example, merely as 'politically uncomfortable'.[3] Groener was perhaps right when he stated with astonishing audacity that 'if the German army had been granted victory, then nobody would have wasted another word on the violation of Belgian neutrality, and the critics after the event would have been full of praise for the superb plan.'[4] While this may perhaps have been true of observers at home, internationally the violations of neutrality would in any case have created justified outrage. However, to Schlieffen such considerations had been of no concern. He had considered his duties to be purely military, and had conducted his planning in a vacuum that disregarded political considerations.[5] Moltke displayed a different attitude on strategic planning and tried, albeit with only limited success, to take non-military considerations into account whenever possible. While the 'Schlieffen school' would characterize this as a lack of courage or conviction, he was, in fact, more willing to make allowances for political and economic considerations. It needs to be stressed, however, that even under Moltke military priorities always took precedence over such 'secondary' concerns. This is exemplified by the violation of the neutrality of Holland and Belgium. While it was militarily possible to avoid a violation of Dutch neutrality if this brought political and economic advantages, the same could not be said of Belgium. The violation was determined by military reasoning. There simply seemed no alternative, if a swift victory in the West was to be sought.

The plan thus imposed a pattern of strategic thinking from which

---

[2] Even Wolfgang Förster, an ardent defender of Schlieffen, had to agree with Ritter on this point: 'Einige Bemerkungen zu Gerhard Ritters Buch "Der Schlieffenplan"', p. 43.

[3] Groener, *Testament*, p. 80: 'Nothing is . . . more unfair than to criticize Count Schlieffen because of the politically uncomfortable [!] march through Belgium.'

[4] Ibid., p. 81.

[5] See also Liddel Hart, Foreword to *Schlieffen Plan*, p. 5, who deplores Schlieffen's 'tendency to view strategic problems in a purely military way, disregarding political factors'. Also Ritter, *Schlieffen Plan*, p. 46; Wallach, *Kriegstheorien*, p. 95.

Moltke was unable to break free. It was based on the assumption that hostilities with France would precede a war with Russia and, consequently, in 1914, the military attempted to enforce this order of events. As a result, political considerations were subjugated to a tight formula, and strategy was not adapted to the actual political situation, but rather dictated it.[6] The serious consequences of this inflexibility during the July Crisis are obvious. Diplomatic solutions late in the crisis were rendered impossible by the deliberate narrowness of military planning.

Rather than accusing Moltke of changing the Schlieffen Plan, which was after all not only his right, but also his duty as Chief of the General Staff, Moltke can be blamed for not devising a suitable alternative, and for not admitting that in fact war was no longer a viable option for Germany's decision-makers in their quest for a position of hegemony in Europe. Moltke had doubts about this 'certain recipe for victory', and it appears as if he regarded the plan only as an initial step in a longer war. Unlike Schlieffen, who thought it possible that his strategy would deliver a quick victory, Moltke was not convinced that the war could be decided in the first few weeks of fighting.[7] However, despite this crucial realization, Moltke never undertook the necessary actions to address the problem.

Moltke's contribution to German decision-making was more wide-ranging, however, than simply the changes that he made to Germany's deployment plan. We have seen that he was more aware of the importance of the relationship between military and political decision-makers than many of his military contemporaries, and he was better placed than most of them to make his views heard in high places. This distinguished him clearly from his predecessor. He was also conscious of the importance of public opinion in supporting a decision to go to war, and he endorsed an active press policy to achieve this aim. On this crucial point Moltke and the Chancellor agreed. In fact, there were other similarities. Both believed in the inevitability of an armed conflict in the very near future, and both envisaged a racial struggle against the Slavs, emphasizing racial differences (*Rassengegensätze*) which they both considered unbridgeable. Both advocated army increases after 1911, although Bethmann's agenda was more extensive than Moltke's, for he wanted to curb the navy's influence at the same time. They shared a fear of Russia's increasing potential, and agreed in July 1914 that it was imperative that Russia and France should be made to appear the aggressors. Berchtold's

[6] Wallach, *Kriegstheorien*, p. 96.
[7] Stig Förster, 'Metakritik', p. 150; Müller, 'Anmerkungen', p. 434.

famous question 'Who governs in Berlin – Moltke or Bethmann?' is perhaps best answered in the light of these similarities, for, in the end, it was almost immaterial who was in charge. The two men at the summit of military and political decision-making in those crucial months essentially shared the same aims and were motivated by the same desires, not only in July 1914, but also in the months preceding and following the outbreak of war. Post-war attempts by the military leaders to blame civilians and vice versa have confused the issue by suggesting that differences of opinion existed where there was in fact a great resemblance. In the light of these similarities, some of the interpretations advanced regarding Bethmann Hollweg's role in the events leading to the outbreak of war should also be re-examined. To deny Bethmann the same 'aggressive self-confidence' as other German decision-makers, as, for example, Konrad Jarausch does, and to suggest that the Chancellor followed Germany's 'perilous course' only reluctantly and under pressure from the military leaders and the Kaiser, is to undervalue the strong convictions that Bethmann harboured and that mirrored so closely those of Moltke.[8] Only when it was certain that a localized war between Serbia and Austria-Hungary would escalate into a European war did Bethmann lose his courage – unlike the military, who were still as keen as ever for war to result from the current crisis.

In examining the military leaders in the July Crisis, this investigation has highlighted the role that the military decision-makers played in the crucial last days of peace. Although physically absent from Berlin for most of the crisis, they were thoroughly well informed about the events in Vienna and Berlin and were ready to become involved when the time was right. New evidence confirms that the military leaders considered the crisis a golden opportunity, and that their views were adopted by political decision-makers and significantly influenced them. The responsibility of the German military, and of Moltke in particular, for demanding war cannot be denied. Moltke has all too readily been dismissed as a pessimist. He certainly was prone to pessimistic tendencies; the realization of the narrow gamble that was Germany's strategic plan weighed heavily on his mind. However, this did not stop him from actively endorsing a bellicose policy.

Historians have perhaps too easily dismissed Moltke's importance due

---

[8] Konrad Jarausch, 'The Illusion of Limited War: Bethmann Hollweg's Calculated Risk, July 1914', *Central European History*, 2, 1969, p. 61; idem, *The Enigmatic Chancellor. Bethmann Hollweg and the Hubris of Imperial Germany*, New Haven and London 1973, p. 58. Alternative interpretations have been advanced by e.g. Fritz Fischer and Imanuel Geiss.

to his apparent interest in Spiritualism, his reputed 'softness', his alleged reluctance to accept the influential office that he occupied when war broke out. While there is some truth in all of these allegations, it should not detract from the fact that Moltke was also a hard-headed realist who had no qualms about pursuing and advocating war, whose decisions were based on his Social Darwinist beliefs, who advocated a racial struggle and who was willing to resort to ruthless intrigues to get rid of his successor Falkenhayn. It is true that he was shocked by the full extent of the disaster of the war for which he, quite rightly, felt responsible. However, he had steered Germany into this catastrophe while clearly realizing its potential dangers, or even in spite of this realization. Moltke was, of course, aware that his many critics did not rate his abilities highly. Moreover, his famous name put further pressure on him to live up to people's expectations. He may have been tempted to appear even more bellicose so as to prove his critics wrong.[9]

The evidence now available confirms without a doubt that Moltke and his colleagues wanted war and had sufficient influence over their political colleagues to achieve their aim. The frightening images of an uncertain future that the 'demigods' in the General Staff conjured up, and their frequent assurances that Germany was still superior to her enemies at present, equipped the civilian decision-makers with the necessary bravado to implement the aggressive foreign policy of the pre-war years and not to shy away from the ultimate manifestation of that policy: war. Partially, at least, the system which allowed military authority to overrule the responsible political decision-makers, rather than being under the control of the civilian leaders, is to blame for this development, and helped to bring about the war of 1914. Only the Kaiser was in a position to place demands on the military, but he was not well-informed or committed enough to put checks on them. After all, his own overestimation of everything military had helped to create this fateful system in the first place.

Moltke was in many ways no better and no worse than his military contemporaries. In fact, as we have seen, Falkenhayn was the more bellicose of the two, especially towards Britain. However, Moltke had doubts about the nature of the coming war, anticipating that it would be a long struggle, rather than the desired short war on which German planning was based. He *hoped* it would be short and manageable, just as

---

[9] Stig Förster also makes the point of the pressure ('Erwartungsdruck') resulting from the famous name ('Metakritik', p. 157). Dennis Showalter similarly refers to an 'overcompensation through posturing' (*Tannenberg*, p. 89).

he hoped that Germany's forces would win due to their superiority in morale and training. He was not certain of victory, but he believed that any delay in the 'big fight' would further decrease Germany's chances of victory. Soon, Germany would no longer be able to fight a successful war; war itself might become redundant. What would become of the 'warrior state' of Prussia-Germany in such a world? What would the prospects be for the military élite, the men whose job it was to prepare the future war? Would they not also become redundant, if war ceased to be an option for the continuation of policy with other means? From Moltke's point of view, the opportunity offered by the crisis of July 1914 really was a case of 'now or never'. One can only agree with Stig Förster's recent indictment of Moltke's decision for war in 1914 as representing 'almost criminal irresponsibility'.[10]

When evaluating Moltke's role in the events leading to the outbreak of war, his alleged inability has too long been an easy excuse. The evidence available today is incriminating and demonstrates that more was at work than simple incompetence. Moltke's main share of responsibility lies in encouraging, almost to the point of deception, an aggressive foreign policy although he was not certain that Germany's military potential could guarantee success in a coming conflict. Increasingly, the option for Germany under Moltke's leadership had become 'war now or never'. For the civilian leaders to decide that war was no longer an option – for them to opt for the 'never' – was something the military wanted to avoid at all costs. Perhaps one of the most important conclusions to be drawn from this investigation is that war was not inevitable and that it certainly was no accident. Until the very last moment, individual decision-makers could have stopped an escalation of the crisis.

Moltke himself, at least, was fully aware of this responsibility, and when it began to dawn on him that his planning had been too optimistic in anticipating a speedy victory, he confessed his feelings of guilt in a letter to his wife:

What rivers of blood have already flowed, what nameless sorrow has come over the countless innocents whose houses have been burnt and pillaged! I am often overcome by dread when I think of this and I feel I should take responsibility for this horror; and yet, I could not have acted otherwise than I did.[11]

---

[10] Förster, 'Metakritik', pp. 157–158. Förster argues that the General Staff could not possibly have concluded that war was no longer a feasible option, and that Moltke's decision for war was 'a kind of suicide for fear of death'.

[11] Moltke to his wife, 7 September 1914, *Erinnerungen*, p. 384.

He was right to feel responsible. He had repeatedly advocated war; he had pressurized the civilian decision-makers into pursuing an aggressive foreign policy (although arguably they had not needed much convincing). He had painted a picture that was at different times either so gloomy as to suggest that only a war now could save Germany from a fate that would inevitably lead to her defeat in the future, or so overconfident that it led the civilian statesmen to assume that they could undertake an aggressive foreign policy that was backed up by a seemingly invincible military force.

Little wonder, then, that Moltke felt responsible for the suffering the war had caused. His anthroposophical belief in karma would have made him anticipate an atonement for the wrongs he committed in his lifetime, which must have made the burden of responsibility even harder to bear. His death in 1916 spared him the realization of the full extent of the horrors of the war that he willed, let alone its poisonous legacy. He should certainly not be remembered as a reluctant military leader, but rather for his decisive role in the events that led to war in 1914. Once the horrors of war had become inescapable reality, at least Moltke himself did not deny that responsibility.

Bibliography

A. UNPUBLISHED PRIMARY SOURCES

POLITISCHES ARCHIV DES AUSWÄRTIGEN AMTES, BONN (PA-BONN)

Nachlässe

Gottlieb von Jagow
Heinrich von Tschirschky und Bogendorff
Karl von Eisendecher
Friedrich von Pourtalès

Akten des Auswärtigen Amtes

R776–789, R849ff., R794, R852/853, R901/902, R929, R995–998, R1358, R2408, R4463, R6916, R8627, R10434, R10450, R20171, R20282/3, R20551–20555, R22094, R22367–22372, R22388, R22369, R22373.

BUNDESARCHIV-MILITÄRARCHIV, FREIBURG (BA-MA)

Nachlässe

Max Hoffmann	N37
Gerhard Tappen	N56
Helmuth von Moltke	N78
Paul von Hindenburg	N429
Hans von Haeften	N35
Colmar von der Goltz	N737
Wilhelm von Hahnke	N36
Franz von Wandel	N564
Wilhelm Groener	N46
Alfred von Tirpitz	N253
Georg Alexander von Müller	N159
Hans von Seeckt	N247
Theobald von Schäfer	N501
Alfred von Schlieffen	N43
Adolf Wild von Hohenborn	N44
Hans von Beseler	N30

Wilhelm von Dommes   N512
August von Mackensen   N39
Karl von Einem   N324
Erich Ludendorff   N77
Albert Hopman   N326

Bestand Kriegsgeschichtliche Forschungsanstalt des Heeres

W-10/50001, 50005, 50017, 50021, 5006off., 50069, 50076ff., 50125, 50128, 50131, 50133, 50136, 50137, 50140, 50146, 50156–50157, 50168, 50172, 50195–50196, 50197ff., 50205, 50211, 50220–50223, 50226, 50276, 50279, 50281, 50284, 50285ff., 50293, 50300f., 50310, 50313, 50315, 50322–50323, 50337–50338, 50349–50350, 50355, 50374, 50378, 50415, 50417, 50419, 50593–50594, 50600, 50629, 50631, 50635–50636, 50641–50651, 50656, 50659, 50661–50662, 50676, 50687–50688, 50706, 50709, 50721, 50728–50732, 50738, 50743–50744, 50890–50891, 50894, 50897, 50910ff., 50943, 50951, 50962, 51032, 51048, 51053, 51060–51064, 52106.

KGFA des Heeres, new classmark: RH 61/v.16, v.61, v67f., v.71.
Bestand Kriegsministerium: PH2/363–368, 400–402, 413, 433–434, 549–470.
Bestand Generalstab: PH3/256, 443, 444, 445, 447, 508 – 510, 528–531, 608, 628, 629, 642, 653, 654, 656, 657, 720, 721.
Bestand Reichsmarineamt: RM2/60, 1555, 1615.
Miscellaneous: RH16/v.99, RH18/v.255, RH18/v.542, RH19/v.27, MSg2/3096.

BUNDESARCHIV, ABTEILUNG POTSDAM
Nachlässe

Otto Hammann   90 Ha 6
Herwarth von Bittenfeld   90 He 5
Ernst von Falkenhausen   90 Fa 1
Erich von Falkenhayn   90 Fa 2
Konstantin von Gebsattel   90 Ge 4
Gustav Frhr. von Senden-Bibran   90 Se2
Bogdan von Hutten-Czapski   90 Hu 2
Bestand Auswärtiges Amt, Politische Abteilung, 1869–1920: R901, 54499, 55352, 54498, 54499, 54893, 55352, 55353.
Bestand Reichskanzlei: R43, 11813, 11814, 12411, 12412, 12413, 12414, 12423, 12424, 12425, 12426, 12837.

BAYERISCHES HAUPTSTAATSARCHIV-KRIEGSARCHIV MUNICH (BAYHSTA-KA)
Nachlässe

Krafft von Dellmensingen
Karl Ritter von Wenninger

Nikolaus von Endres
Franz von Epp
Wolfram Ebner von Eschenbach
Eugen von Frauenholz
Kronprinz Rupprecht von Bayern
Rudolf Ritter von Xylander

Bestand Generalstab 146, 151, 161, 645, 647, 925, 1237
Bestand Militärbevollmächtigter Berlin MKr 41, 42, 43, 45, 983, 998, 1731, 1765,
    1829/1, 1830

SÄCHSISCHES HAUPTSTAATSARCHIV, DRESDEN

Sächsischer Militärbevollmächtigter in Berlin, 1426, 1427, 1430, 1433, 1434,
    4222.

OTHER UNPUBLISHED PRIMARY SOURCES

Public Record Office, Kew: wo106/6182, 6171
Hermann von Santen, 'Erinnerungen', unpublished diaries in family's
    possession, Wennigsen, Hanover (courtesy of Professor John C. G.
    Röhl)
NL Alfred von Waldersee, Geheimes (ehem. Zentrales) Staatsarchiv Merseburg
    (exerpts from the orginal diary courtesy of Professor John C. G. Röhl)

NEWSPAPERS

Berliner Zeitung
Berliner Tageblatt
Deutsche Allgemeine Zeitung
Frankfurter Allgemeine Zeitung
Frankfurter Rundschau
Rheinisch-Westfälische Zeitung
Spectator
Vossische Zeitung
Die Zeit

B. PUBLISHED PRIMARY SOURCES

Document Collections, Memoirs, Diaries and Contemporary Literature,
mostly published before 1939

Bauer, Max, *Der große Krieg in Feld und Heimat, Erinnerungen und Betrachtungen*,
    Tübingen 1921
*Bayerische Dokumente zum Kriegsausbruch und zum Versailler Schuldspruch, herausgegeben
    im Auftrage des Bayerischen Landtages*, Munich o.D. (1922)

Behnen, Michael (ed.), *Quellen zur deutschen Außenpolitik im Zeitalter des Imperialismus, 1890–1911*, Darmstadt 1977

Bergh, Max van den, *Das deutsche Heer vor dem Weltkriege*, Berlin 1934

Berghahn, Volker R. and Deist, Wilhelm (eds.), *Rüstung im Zeichen wilhelminischer Weltpolitik. Grundlegende Dokumente 1890–1914*, Düsseldorf 1988

'Kaiserliche Marine', *MGM*, 1/1970

Bernhardi, Friedrich von, *Deutschland und der nächste Krieg*, Stuttgart 1912

Bethmann Hollweg, Theobald von, *Betrachtungen zum Weltkrieg*, 2 vols, Berlin 1919/1921

Beyerhaus, Gisbert, *Einheitlicher Oberbefehl. Ein Problem des Weltkrieges*, Munich 1938

Bihl, Wolfdieter (ed.), *Deutsche Quellen zur Geschichte des Ersten Weltkrieges*, Darmstadt 1991

Boos, Roman (ed.), *Rudolf Steiner während des Weltkrieges. Beiträge Rudolf Steiners zur Bewältigung der Aufgaben, die durch den Krieg der Welt gestellt wurden*, Dornach 1933

Bülow, Bernhard Fürst von, *Denkwürdigkeiten*, 4 vols., Berlin 1930–1931.

Chernavin, Victor, 'What the Allies knew of the German Military Plan before the Outbreak of the Great War', *The Army Quarterly*, 29, January 1935

Claß, Heinrich, *Wider den Strom. Vom Werden und Wachsen der nationalen Opposition im alten Reich*, Leipzig 1932

Clausewitz, Carl von, *On War*, ed. Michael Howard and Peter Paret, Princeton 1984

Cochenhausen, Friedrich von (ed.), *Von Scharnhorst zu Schlieffen, 1806–1906: Hundert Jahre preußisch-deutscher Generalstab*, Berlin 1933

Conrad von Hötzendorf, Franz, *Aus meiner Dienstzeit 1906–1918*, 5 vols., Vienna, Leipzig, Munich 1921–1925

Private Aufzeichnungen. Erste Veröffentlichungen aus den Papieren des k.u.k. Generalstabschefs, ed. Kurt Peball, Vienna and Munich 1977

Cramon, August von, *Unser Österreichisch-Ungarischer Bundesgenosse im Weltkriege. Erinnerungen aus meiner vierjährigen Tätigkeit als bevollmächtigter deutscher General beim k.u.k. Armeeoberkommando*, Berlin 1920

Deimling, Berthold von, *Aus der alten in die neue Zeit*, Berlin 1930

Delbrück, Hans, *Geschichte der Kriegskunst im Rahmen der politischen Geschichte, 1. Teil: Das Altertum*, Berlin 3rd edn. 1920 (1st edn 1900)

'Die deutsche Kriegserklärung und der Einmarsch in Belgien', *Preußische Jahrbücher*, 175, January–March 1919

Deuerlein, Ernst (ed.), *Briefwechsel Hertling–Lerchenfeld 1912–1917. Dienstliche Privatkorrespondenz zwischen dem bayerischen Ministerpräsidenten Georg Graf von Hertling und dem bayerischen Gesandten in Berlin Hugo Graf von und zu Lerchenfeld*, 2 vols., Boppard/Rhein, 1973

Die Deutschen Dokumente zum Kriegsausbruch. Vollständige Sammlung der von Karl Kautsky zusammengetragenen amtlichen Aktenstücke mit einigen Ergänzungen. Im Auftrage des Auswärtigen Amtes nach gemeinsamer Durchsicht mit Karl Kautsky herausgegeben von Graf Max Montgelas und Walter Schücking, 5 vols., Berlin 1919

Eckardstein, Hermann Frhr. von, *Lebenserinnerungen und Politische Denkwürdigkeiten*, 3 vols., Leipzig 1921

Einem, Karl von, *Erinnerungen eines Soldaten 1853–1933*, 2nd edn Leipzig 1933

Elze, W., *Tannenberg. Das deutsche Heer von 1914, seine Grundzüge und deren Auswirkung im Sieg an der Ostfront. Im Einvernehmen mit dem Reichsarchiv*, Breslau 1928

Falkenhayn, Erich von, *Die Oberste Heeresleitung 1914–1916 in ihren wichtigsten Entschließungen*, Berlin 1920

Förster, Wolfgang, *Graf Schlieffen und der Weltkrieg*, Berlin 1925
    'Die deutsch-italienische Militärkonvention', *Berliner Monatshefte*, 5/1, 1927
    Aus der Gedankenwerkstatt des deutschen Generalstabes, Berlin 1931

Freytag-Loringhoven, Gustav Frhr. von, 'Generalfeldmarschall Graf von Schlieffen. Lebensgang und Lebenswerk', in Alfred von Schlieffen, *Gesammelte Schriften*, Berlin 1913, pp. VII–XLIII
    Menschen und Dinge, wie ich sie in meinem Leben sah, Berlin 1923

Gackenholz, H., *Entscheidung in Lothringen 1914. Der Operationsplan des jüngeren Moltke und seine Durchführung auf dem linken deutschen Heeresflügel*, Berlin 1933

Geiss, Imanuel (ed.), *Julikrise und Kriegsausbruch. Eine Dokumentensammlung*, 2 vols., Hanover 1963/1964
    Juli 1914. Die europäische Krise und der Ausbruch des Ersten Weltkrieges, 3rd ed. 1986 (^{1}1965) (English transl. *July 1914. The Outbreak of the First World War. Selected Documents*, New York 1967)

Generalstab des Heeres, Kriegswissenschaftliche Abteilung (ed.), *Dienstschriften des Chefs des Generalstabes der Armee Generalfeldmarschall Graf von Schlieffen*, vol. 1. *Die taktisch-strategischen Aufgaben aus den Jahren 1891–1905*, Berlin 1937

Goltz, Colmar Frhr. von der, *Denkwürdigkeiten*, ed. Friedrich Frhr. von der Goltz and Wolfgang Förster, Berlin 1929

Görlitz, Walter (ed.), *Regierte der Kaiser? Kriegstagebücher, Aufzeichnungen und Briefe des Chefs des Marinekabinetts Admiral Georg Alexander von Müller 1914–1918*, Göttingen, Berlin, Frankfurt, 2nd edn 1959

Görlitz, Walter (ed.), *Der Kaiser . . . Aufzeichnungen des Chefs des Marinekabinetts Admiral Georg Alexander von Müller über die Ära Wilhelms II*, Göttingen 1965

Granier, Hermann, 'Eine Denkschrift des Generals Edwin von Manteuffel über das Militär-Kabinett', *Forschungen zur Brandenburg-Preußischen Geschichte*, vol. 47, Berlin 1935

Groener, Wilhelm, *Das Testament des Grafen Schlieffen. Operative Studien über den Weltkrieg*, Berlin 1927
    Der Feldherr wider Willen. Operative Studien über den Weltkrieg, Berlin 1930
    Lebenserinnerungen. Jugend, Generalstab, Weltkrieg, Göttingen 1957

Haller, Johannes, *Aus dem Leben des Fürsten Philipp zu Eulenburg-Hertefeld*, Berlin and Leipzig 1926

Hammann, Otto, *Um den Kaiser. Erinnerungen aus den Jahren 1906–1909*, Berlin 1919

Helfferich, Karl, *Der Weltkrieg*, 2 vols., Berlin 1919

Hölzle, Erwin (ed.), *Quellen zur Entstehung des ersten Weltkrieges. Internationale Dokumente 1901–1914*, Darmstadt 1978

Hoffmann, Max, *War Diaries and Other Papers*, 2 vols., London 1929 (Engl. transl.

of *Die Aufzeichnungen des Generalmajors Max Hoffmann*, ed. Karl-Friedrich Nowak, Berlin 1928)

Hoffmann, Max, *Der Krieg der versäumten Gelegenheiten*, Leipzig 1929

House, Edward, *The Intimate Papers of Colonel House*, 2 vols., London 1926, vol. 1, *Behind the Political Curtain, 1912–1915*

Hutten-Czapski, Bogdan Graf von, *Sechzig Jahre Politik und Gesellschaft*, 2 vols., Berlin 1936

Jagow, Gottlieb von, *Ursachen und Ausbruch des Weltkrieges*, Berlin 1919

Justrow, Karl, *Feldherr und Kriegstechnik. Studien über den Operationsplan des Grafen Schlieffen und Lehren für unseren Wehraufbau und unsere Landesverteidigung*, Oldenburg 1933

Kanner, Heinrich, *Kaiserliche Katastrophenpolitik*, Vienna 1922

Keim, August, *Erlebtes und Erstrebtes. Lebenserinnerungen*, Hannover 1925

Kluck, Alexander von, *Wanderjahre–Kriege–Gestalten*, Berlin 1929

Kuhl, Hermann von, *Der Deutsche Generalstab in Vorbereitung und Durchführung des Weltkrieges*, Berlin 1920

Der Weltkrieg 1914–1918. Dem deutschen Volke dargestellt, 2 vols, Berlin 1929

Der Marnefeldzug 1914, Berlin 1921

Lautemann, Wolfgang, *Studien zu Marnefeldzug und Marneschlacht 1914*, Berlin 1933

Leppa, Konrad, *Moltke und Conrad. Die Heerführung des Generaloberst v. Moltke und des Generals der Infantrie Frhr. v. Conrad* [*sic*] *im Sommer 1914*, Stuttgart 1935

Lepsius, Johannes, Mendelsohn-Bertholdy, Albrecht and Thimme, Friedrich (eds.), *Die Große Politik der Europäischen Kabinette 1871–1914. Sammlung der Diplomatischen Akten des Auswärtigen Amtes*, 40 vols, Berlin 1922–1927

Lewinski, Hauptmann von and Brauchitsch, Leutnant von, *Geschichte des Grenadier-Regiments König Wilhelm I (2. Westpreußisches) Nr. 7*, 2 vols., Glogau 1897

Lichnowsky, Karl Max Fürst von, *Meine Londoner Mission 1912–1914*, Berlin 1919

Liddell Hart, B. H., *The Real War 1914–1918*, London 1930

Litzmann, Karl, *Lebenserinnerungen*, 2 vols., Berlin 1927/28

Loßberg, Fritz von, *Meine Tätigkeit im Weltkriege 1914–1918*, Berlin 1939

Ludendorff, Erich, *Meine Kriegserinnerungen 1914–1918*, Berlin 1919

Mein militärischer Werdegang. Blätter der Erinnerung an unser stolzes Heer, Munich 1933

Das Marne-Drama. Der Fall Moltke–Hentsch, Munich 1934

Manstein, E. von, *Aus einem Soldatenleben 1887–1939*, Bonn 1957

Mantey, Friedrich von, 'Graf Schlieffen und der jüngere Moltke', *Militär-Wochenblatt*, 10, 1935, pp. 395–398

Mantey, Friedrich von, 'Schlieffen-Plan von 1905, Moltke-Pläne von 1908 bis 1914 und Schlieffen-Plan 1912', *Militär-Wochenblatt*, No. 16, 1935, pp. 652ff.

Meisner, H. O. (ed), *Denkwürdigkeiten des Generalfeldmarschalls A. Grafen von Waldersee*, 3 vols., Stuttgart 1923–1925

'Militärkabinett, Kriegsminister und Reichkanzler zur Zeit Wilhelms I', *Forschungen zur Brandenburg-Preußischen Geschichte*, 50, 1938

Meyer, Thomas, *Helmuth von Moltke 1848–1916. Dokumente zu seinem Leben und Wirken*, 2 vols., Basel 1993

Moltke, Dorothy von, *Ein Leben in Deutschland. Briefe aus Kreisau und Berlin, 1907–1934*, ed. Beate Ruhn von Oppen, Munich 1999

Moltke, Helmuth von, *Erinnerungen, Briefe, Dokumente 1877–1916. Ein Bild vom Kriegsausbruch, erster Kriegsführung und Persönlichkeit des ersten militärischen Führer des Krieges*, ed. Eliza von Moltke, Stuttgart 1922

Mühlmann, C., 'Die Einstellung des deutschen Großen Generalstabs zum Balkan- und Orientproblem in der Vorkriegszeit', *Wissen und Wehr*, 1927

Müller-Loebnitz, Wilhelm, *Die Sendung des Oberstleutnant Hentsch am 8.-10. September 1914. Auf Grund von Kriegsakten und persönlichen Mitteilungen, bearbeitet*, Berlin 1922

Müller-Loebnitz, Wilhelm, *Die Führung im Marne-Feldzug 1914*, Berlin 1939

Nicolai, Walter, *Nachrichtendienst, Presse und Volksstimme im Weltkrieg*, Berlin 1920

Niemann, Alfred, *Kaiser und Heer: Das Wesen der Kommandogewalt und ihre Ausübung durch Kaiser Wilhelm II*, Berlin 1929

Oertzen, F. W. von, 'Die Einnahme von Lüttich', *Vossische Zeitung*, 25 September 1932

Pomerin, Reiner and Fröhlich, Michael (eds.), *Quellen zu den deutsch-britischen Beziehungen, 1815 – 1914*, Darmstadt 1997

Rathenau, Walter, *Hauptwerke und Gespräche*, ed. Ernst Schulin, Munich 1977 (Walther Rathenau Gesamtausgabe, vol. 2)

Rathenau, Walther, *Tagebuch 1907–1922*, ed. Hartmut Pogge von Strandmann, Düsseldorf 1967

Reichsarchiv (ed.), *Der Weltkrieg 1914–1918*, 14 vols, Berlin 1925ff., vol. 1: *Die Grenzschlachten im Westen*, Berlin 1925, vol. 2: *Die Befreiung Ostpreußens*, Berlin 1925

Schlachten und Gefechte des Krieges 1914–1918, Berlin 1920

Schlachten des Weltkrieges, 38 vols., Berlin 1922ff. Vols. 22–23, *Das Marnedrama 1914*, Berlin 1928; vol. 3, *Antwerpen 1914*, Berlin 1925

Reichsarchiv (Abteilung 3) (ed.), *Der Weltkrieg 1914–1918. Kriegsrüstung und Kriegswirtschaft*, 2 vols., vol. 1: *Die militärische, wirtschaftliche und finanzielle Rüstung Deutschlands von vor der Reichsgründung bis zum Ausbruch des Weltkrieges*; + *Anlagen*, Berlin 1930

Riezler, Kurt, *Tagebücher, Aufsätze, Dokumente*, ed. Karl Dietrich Erdmann, Göttingen 1972

Röhl, John C. G. (ed.), *Philipp Eulenburgs Politische Korrespondenz*, 3 vols., Boppard/Rhein 1976, 1979, 1983

Rüdt von Collenberg, Ludwig, *Die Deutsche Armee von 1871–1914*. Forschungen und Darstellungen aus dem Reichsarchiv, No. 4, Berlin 1922

'Die staatsrechtliche Stellung des preußischen Kriegsministers von 1867–1914', *Wissen und Wehr*, 5, 1927

'Die deutschen Heeresverstärkungen 1871–1914', *Berliner Monatshefte*, 11, 1930

Rupprecht of Bavaria, Crown Prince, *Mein Kriegstagebuch*, ed. Eugen von Frauenholz, 3 vols., Berlin 1929

Schäfer, Hugo, 'Die militärischen Abmachungen des Dreibundes vor dem Weltkriege, *Preußische Jahrbücher*, 188, 1922, pp. 203–214

Schäfer, Theobald von, *Generalstab und Admiralstab. Das Zusammenwirken von Heer und Flotte im Weltkrieg*, Berlin 1931

Ludendorff. *Der Feldherr der Deutschen im Weltkriege*, Berlin 1935

'Wollte Generaloberst von Moltke den Präventivkrieg?' *Berliner Monatshefte*, 5, 1, 1927

'Generaloberst von Moltke in den Tagen vor der Mobilmachung und seine Einwirkung auf Österreich-Ungarn', *Berliner Monatshefte*, August 1926

Schlieffen, Alfred von, 'Der Krieg der Gegenwart', *Gesammelte Schriften*, vol. 1, Berlin 1913

'Die Schlacht bei Cannae', *Gesammelte Schriften*, vol. 1, Berlin 1913

Briefe, ed. Eberhard Kessel, Göttingen 1958

Schlopp, Eugen von, *Geschichte des Königs-Grenadier-Regiments (2. Westpr.) Nr. 7*, Berlin 1877

Schmidt-Bückeburg, Rudolf, *Das Militärkabinett der preußischen Könige und deutschen Kaiser, Seine geschichtliche Entwicklung und staatsrechtliche Stellung 1787–1918*, Berlin 1933

Schneider, Paul, *Die Organisation des Heeres*, Berlin 1931

Schwinn, Erich, 'Die Arbeit des deutschen Wehrvereins und die Wehrvorlage Deutschlands vor dem Weltkrieg', Ph.D. Dissertation, Heidelberg 1938

Seyfert, Gerhard, 'Die militärischen Beziehungen und Vereinbarungen zwischen dem deutschen und dem österreichischen Generalstab vor und bei Beginn des Weltkrieges', Ph.D. Dissertation, Leipzig 1934

Sösemann, Bernd, *Theodor Wolff. Der Chronist. Krieg, Revolution und Frieden im Tagebuch 1914–1919*, Düsseldorf and Munich 1997

Staabs, Hermann von, *Aufmarsch nach zwei Fronten: Auf Grund der Operationspläne von 1871–1914*, Berlin 1925

Stein, Hermann von, *Erlebnisse und Betrachtungen aus der Zeit des Weltkrieges*, Leipzig 1919

Steiner, Marie, 'Helmuth von Moltke und Rudolf Steiner', *Das Goetheanum*, 5 March 1933

Sturgkh, Josef, *Im Deutschen Großen Hauptquartier*, Leipzig 1921

Tappen, Gerhard, *Bis zur Marne*, Oldenburg 1920

Thaer, Albrecht von, *Generalstabsdienst an der Front und in der O.H.L. Aus Briefen und Tagebuchaufzeichnungen 1915–1919*, Göttingen 1959 (2nd. edn. 1969)

Tirpitz, Alfred von, *Erinnerungen*, Leipzig 1919

Tschuppik, Karl, *Ludendorff. Die Tragödie des Fachmanns*, Vienna and Leipzig 1931

Urbanski, August U. von Ostymiecz, *Conrad von Hötzendorf. Soldat und Mensch*, Graz, Leipzig, Vienna 1938

Wagner, Rudolf, *Kaiserliche Eingriffe in die Weltkriegsführung*, Leipzig 1924

Waldersee, Georg Graf, 'Von Kriegführung, Politik, Persönlichkeiten und ihrer Wechselwirkung aufeinander', *Deutscher Offizier Bund*, Nr. 11, April 1927

'Von Deutschlands militär-politischer Beziehung zu Italien', *Berliner Monatshefte*, 7, 2, 1929

'Über die Beziehungen des deutschen zum österreichisch-ungarischen Generalstabe vor dem Weltkriege', *Berliner Monatshefte*, 8, 1, 1930

'Verfl . . . Kabinettswirtschaft', *Vossische Zeitung*, 18 September 1932

Wegerer, Alfred von (ed.), *Der Ausbruch des Weltkrieges 1914*, 2 vols., Hamburg 1939

Wild von Hohenborn, Adolf, *Briefe und Tagebuchaufzeichnungen des preußischen Generals als Kriegsminister und Truppenführer im Ersten Weltkrieg*, ed. Helmuth Reichold and Gerhard Granier, Boppard/Rhein 1986

Wohlers, Günther, *Die staatsrechtliche Stellung des Generalstabes in Preußen und dem deutschen Reich. Geschichtliche Entwicklung bis zum Versailler Frieden*, Bonn, Leipzig 1921

Wolff, Theodor, *Tagebücher 1914–1918*, ed. Bernd Sösemann, 2 vols., Boppart/Rhein 1984

Wrisberg, Ernst von, *Heer und Heimat 1914–1918*, Leipzig 1921

Xylander, Rudolf Ritter und Edler von, *Die Führung in Lothringen 1914. Wahrheit und Kriegsgeschichte*, Berlin 1935

Zechlin, Egmont, 'Ludendorff im Jahre 1915. Unveröffentlichte Briefe', *HZ*, 211, 1970, pp. 316–353

Zedlitz-Trützschler, Robert, *Zwölf Jahre am deutschen Kaiserhof*, Stuttgart, 1924 (Engl. transl. *Twelve Years at the Imperial German Court*, London 1924)

Ziekursch, Johannes, 'Falkenhayn und Ludendorff in den Jahren 1914–1916', *Forschungen zur Brandenburg-Preußischen Geschichte*, 34, 1922

Zwehl, Hans von, *Erich von Falkenhayn, General der Infanterie. Eine biographische Studie*, Berlin 1926

C. SECONDARY SOURCES

Adams, R. J. Q. (ed), *The Great War, 1914–1918. Essays on the Military, Political and Social History of the First World War*, London 1990

Afflerbach, Holger, *Falkenhayn. Politisches Denken und Handeln im Kaiserreich*, Munich 1994

'Wilhelm II as Supreme Warlord in the First World War', *War in History*, 5, 4, 1998, pp. 427–449

Alf, Wilhelm (ed.), *Deutschlands Sonderung von Europa, 1862–1945*, Frankfurt/M. 1984

Albertini, Luigi, *The Origins of the War of 1914*, 3 vols., Oxford 1952–57

Angelow, Jürgen, 'Vom "Bündnis" zum "Block". Struktur, Forschungsstand und Problemlage einer Geschichte des Zweibundes 1879–1914', *MGM*, 54, 1995, pp. 125–170

Asprey, Robert B., *The German High Command at War. Hindenburg and Ludendorff and the First World War*, paperback edn., London 1994 (First edn. 1991)

Augstein, Rudolf, 'Bismarck', in Wilhelm von Sternburg (ed), *Die deutschen Kanzler. Von Bismarck bis Kohl*, Frankfurt/M. 1994

Bald, Detlev, *Der deutsche Generalstab 1859–1939. Reform und Restauration in Ausbildung und Bildung*, Sozialwissenschaftliches Institut der Bundeswehr, Berichte, Heft 7, Munich 1977

'Zum Kriegsbild der militärischen Führung im Kaiserreich', in J. Dülffer and K. Holl (eds.), *Bereit zum Krieg*, Göttingen 1986

Barlow, Ima Christina, *The Agadir Crisis*, Hamden Conn., reprint 1971
Barnett, Corelli, *The Swordbearers. Studies in Supreme Command in the First World War*, London 1963
Barraclough, Geoffrey, *From Agadir to Armageddon. Anatomy of a Crisis*, London 1982
Beck, Ludwig, 'Besaß Deutschland 1914 einen Kriegsplan?' in idem, *Studien*, ed. Hans Speidel, Stuttgart 1955
 'West- oder Ostoffensive 1914?', in idem, *Studien*, ed., Hans Speidel, Stuttgart 1955
Beck, Walter, *Rudolf Steiner. Sein Leben und Werk. Eine Biographie mit neuen Dokumenten*, Dornach 1997
Becker, Josef *et al.* (eds.), *Lange und kurze Wege in den Ersten Weltkrieg. Vier Beiträge zur Kriegsursachenforschungen*, Munich 1996
Berghahn, Volker R., *Der Tirpitz-Plan. Genesis und Verfall einer innenpolitischen Krisenstrategie unter Wilhelm II*, Düsseldorf 1971
 Germany and the Approach of War in 1914, paperback edn London 1973
Berghahn, Volker R., *Rüstung und Machtpolitik. Zur Anatomie des 'Kalten Krieges' vor 1914*, Mannheimer Schriften zur Politik und Zeitgeschichte, Düsseldorf 1973
 Militarism. The History of an International Debate. 1861–1979, Leamington Spa 1981
 Imperial Germany 1871–1914. Economy, Society, Culture and Politics, Oxford 1994
Blackbourn, David, *The Long Nineteenth Century. Fontana History of Germany, 1870 - 1918*, London 1997
Boetticher, Friedrich von, *Schlieffen*, 2nd edn, ed. Friedrich-Christian Stahl, Göttingen 1973 (1st edn *Graf Schlieffen. Sein Werden und Wirken*, Berlin 1933)
Bosl, Karl *et al.* (eds.), *Biographisches Wörterbuch zur deutschen Geschichte*, vol. 2, Munich 1974
Bredow, Wilfried von, *Moderner Militarismus. Analyse und Kritik*, Stuttgart, Berlin, Cologne, Mainz 1983
Breit, Gotthardt, *Das Staats- und Gesellschaftsbild deutscher Generale beider Weltkriege im Spiegel ihrer Memoiren*, Boppard/Rhein 1973
Brenneke, Adolf, *Archivkunde. Ein Beitrag zur Theorie und Geschichte des Europäischen Archivwesens, bearb. u. ergänzt von Wolfgang Leesch*, Leipzig 1953
Brühl, Reinhard, *Militärgeschichte und Kriegspolitik. Zur Militärgeschichtsschreibung des preußisch-deutschen Generalstabes, 1816–1945*, (East) Berlin, 1973
Bucholz, Arden, *Hans Delbrück and the German Military Establishment: War Images in Conflict*, Iowa City 1985
 Moltke, Schlieffen and Prussian War Planning, Providence, and Oxford 1991
Buijs, J. 'De spoorbrug bij Roermond. Oorzaak van Nederlands neutraliteit in 1914?', *Militaire Spectator*, 161, 1992, pp. 441–415
Burchardt, Lothar, *Friedenswirtschaft und Kriegsvorsorge. Deutschlands wirtschaftliche Rüstungsbestrebungen vor 1914*, Boppard/Rhein 1968
Burkardt, Johannes *et al.* (eds.), *Lange und kurze Wege in den Ersten Weltkrieg*, Munich 1996

Campbell, Frederick Francis, 'The Bavarian Army 1870–1918: The Constitutional and Structural Relations with the Prussian Military Establishment', Ph.D. Dissertation. Ohio State University 1972

Cecil, Lamar, *Wilhelm II.* vol. 1, *Prince and Emperor, 1859–1900*. Chapel Hill, 1989, vol. 2, *Emperor and Exile*, Capel Hill, 1996

Chickering, Roger, 'Der "Deutsche Wehrverein" und die Reform der deutschen Armee 1912–1914', *MGM*, 25, 1/1979, pp. 7–34

'Patriotic Societies and German Foreign Policy', *International History Review*, 1, October 1979, pp. 470–489

Imperial Germany and a World without War. The Peace Movement and German Society 1893–1914, Princeton 1976

Imperial Germany and the Great War, 1914–1918, Cambridge 1998

We Men Who Feel Most German. A Cultural Study of the Pan-German League 1886–1914, London 1984

'Die Alldeutschen erwarten den Krieg', in Dülffer and Holl (eds.) *Bereit zum Krieg*, q.v.

Chickering, Roger (ed), *Imperial Germany. A Historiographical Companion*, Westport, London 1996

Cimbala, Stephen J., 'Steering Through Rapids: Russian Mobilization and World War I', *The Journal of Slavic Military Studies*, 9, 2, 996, 376–398

Clemente, Steven E., *For King and Kaiser! The Making of the Prussian Army Officer, 1860–1914*, New York 1992

Coetzee, Marily S., *The German Army League. Popular Nationalism in Wilhelmine Germany*, Oxford 1990

Cole, Terence F., 'German Decision-Making on the Eve of the First World War. The Records of the Swiss Embassy in Berlin', in Röhl (ed.), *Der Ort Kaiser Wilhelm II in der deutschen Geschichte*, q.v.

Cambridge Ancient History, Vol. 3, 'Rome and the Mediterranean to 133 B.C.', Cambridge 1989

Conze, Werner, *Polnische Nation und Deutsche Politik im Ersten Weltkrieg*, Cologne and Graz 1958

Cornwall, Mark (ed.), *The Last Years of Austria-Hungary: Essays in Political and Military History 1908–1918*, Exeter 1990

Craig, Gordon A., 'The World War I Alliance of the Central Powers in Retrospect: The Military Cohesion of the Alliance', *Journal of Modern History*, 37, 1965, pp. 336–344

Germany 1866–1945, Oxford, paperback edn. 1981 (1st edn. 1978)

The Politics of the Prussian Army 1640–1945, Oxford 1955

Creveld, Martin van, *Supplying War: Logistics from Wallenstein to Patton*, Cambridge 1977

Darby, Graham, *Origins of the First World War*, London 1998

Degreif, Diether, 'Operative Planungen des K.u.K. Generalstabes für einen Krieg in der Zeit vor 1914 (1880–1914)', Ph.D. Dissertation. Mainz 1983

Deist, Wilhelm, 'Die Armee in Staat und Gesellschaft 1890–1914', in Michael Stürmer (ed), *Das kaiserliche Deutschland. Politik und Gesellschaft, 1870–1918*, Düsseldorf 1970

'Armee und Arbeiterschaft 1905–1918', *Francia*, 2, 1974, pp. 485–548

Flottenpolitik und Flottenpropaganda. Das Nachrichtenbüro des Reichsmarineamtes, 1897–1914, Stuttgart 1976

'Zur Geschichte des preußischen Offizierkorps 1888–1918', in Hans Hubert Hofmann, (ed.), *Das deutsche Offizierkorps 1860–1960*, Boppard/Rhein 1980

'Die Reichswehr und der Krieg der Zukunft', *MGM* 1, 1989

'Kaiser Wilhelm II. als Oberster Kriegsherr' in idem, *Militär, Staat und Gesellschaft. Studien zur preußisch-deutschen Militärgeschichte*, Munich 1991

'The German army, the authoritarian nation-state and total war', in John Horne (ed.), *State, Society and Mobilization in Europe during the First World War*, Cambridge 1997

Deist, Wilhelm (ed.), *The German Military in the Age of Total War*, Leamington Spa 1985

Demeter, Karl, *Das Deutsche Offizierskorps in Gesellschaft und Staat, 1650–1945*, Frankfurt/M., 2nd edn 1962 (English translation *The German Officer Corps in Society and State, 1640–1945*, London 1965)

Das Reichsarchiv. Tatsachen und Personen, Frankfurt 1969

Düding, Dieter, 'Die Kriegervereine im Wilhelminischen Reich und ihr Beitrag zur Militarisierung der deutschen Gesellschaft', in J. Dülffer and K. Holl (eds.), *Bereit zum Krieg*, q.v.

Dukes, Jack R., 'Militarism and Arms Policy revisited: the Origins of the German Army Law of 1913', in Jack R. Dukes and Joachim J. Remak (eds.), *Another Germany: A Reconsideration of the Imperial Era*, Boulder and London 1988

Dülffer, Jost, *Regeln gegen den Krieg? Die Haager Friedenskonferenzen von 1899 und 1907 in der internationalen Politik*, Berlin 1981

Dülffer, Jost (ed.), *Parlamentarische und öffentliche Kontrolle von Rüstung in Deutschland, 1700–1970. Beiträge zur historischen Friedensforschung*, Düsseldorf 1992

Dülffer, Jost and Holl, Karl (eds.), *Bereit zum Krieg. Kriegsmentalität im wilhelminischen Deutschland, 1890–1914*, Göttingen 1986

Dülffer, Jost, Kröger, M. and Wippich, R.-H. (eds.), *Vermiedene Kriege. Deeskalation von Konflikten der Großmächte zwischen Krimkrieg und Erstem Weltkrieg (1856–1914)*, Munich 1997

Earle, Edward Mead (ed.), *Makers of Modern Strategy. Military Thought from Machiavelli to Hitler*, Princeton 1943

Echevarria II, Antulio J., 'On the Brink of the Abyss: the Warrior Identity and German Military Thought before the Great War', *War and Society*, 13, 2, 1995, pp. 23–40

'A Crisis in Warfighting: German Tactical Discussions in the Late Nineteenth Century', *MGM*, 55, 1996

'General Staff Historian Hugo Freiherr von Freytag-Loringhoven and the Dialectics of German Military Thought', *The Journal of Military History*, 60, 1996, pp. 471–494

Eggenberger, David, *A Dictionary of Battles*, London 1967

Eibicht, Rolf-Joseph, *Schlieffen. Strategie und Politik. Aus der Unterlegenheit zum Sieg*, Lünen 1991

Eley, Geoff, *Reshaping the German Right. Radical Nationalism and Political Change after Bismarck*, New Haven 1979

Epkenhans, Michael, *Die Wilhelminische Flottenrüstung 1908–1914. Weltmachtstreben, industrieller Fortschritt, soziale Integration*, Munich 1991

' "Wir als deutsches Volk sind doch nicht klein zu kriegen . . ." Aus den Tagebüchern des Fregattenkapitäns Bogislav von Selchow', *MGM*, 55, 1996

Erdmann, Karl Dietrich, 'Zur Beurteilung Bethmann Hollwegs', *Geschichte in Wissenschaft und Unterricht*, 15, 1964

Der Erste Weltkrieg, Munich, 1st edn. 1980

Evans, R. J. W. and Pogge v. Strandmann, H. (eds.), *The Coming of the First World War*, Oxford 1988

Evera, Stephen van, 'The Cult of the Offensive and the Origins of the First World War', *International Security*, 9, 1984, pp. 85–107

Ewert, Gottfried, 'Das Bild des Soldaten im Wandel der Zeit', *Europäische Wehrkunde*, 3, 1984

Farrar, L. L., 'The Short-War Illusion: The Syndrome of German Strategy, August-December 1914', *MGM*, 12, 1972, pp. 39–52

The Short-War-Illusion. German Policy, Strategy and Domestic Affairs August-December 1914, Oxford 1973

'The Strategy of the Central Powers', in Strachan (ed.), *The Oxford Illustrated History of the First Wold War*, q.v.

Feldmann, Gerard D., *Army, Industry and Labour in Germany 1914–1918*, Princeton 1966

Fellner, Fritz, 'Die Mission Hoyos', in Alf (ed.), *Deutschlands Sonderung von Europa*, q.v.

Fellner, Fritz, 'Austria-Hungary' in Keith Wilson (ed.), *Decisions for War, 1914*, London 1995

Ferguson, Niall, 'Germany and the Origins of the First World War: New Perspectives', *Historical Journal*, 35, 3, 1992

'Public Finance and National Security: The Domestic Origins of the First World War Revisited', *Past and Present*, 142, 1994, pp. 141–168

The Pity of War, London 1998

Ferro, Marc, *The Great War, 1914–1918*, London 1995

Fesser, Gerd, *Reichskanzler Bernhard Fürst von Bülow. Eine Biographie*, Berlin 1991

Der Traum vom Platz an der Sonne. Deutsche 'Weltpolitik' 1897–1914, Bremen 1996

Fischer, Fritz, *Griff nach der Weltmacht. Die Kriegszielpolitik des kaiserlichen Deutschlands, 1914/18*, Nachdruck der Sonderausgabe 1967, Düsseldorf 1984 (English translation: *Germany's Aims in the First World War*, London 1967)

Krieg der Illusionen. Die deutsche Politik von 1911–1914, paperback reprint of 2nd edn. 1970 (1st edn. 1969), Düsseldorf 1987

Bündnis der Eliten. Zur Kontinuität der Machtstrukturen in Deutschland 1871–1945, Düsseldorf 1979

Juli 1914: Wir sind nicht hineingeschlittert. Das Staatsgeheimnis um die Riezler Tagebücher, Reinbek 1983

'Kaiser Wilhelm und die Gestaltung der deutschen Politik von 1914', in Röhl (ed.), *Der Ort Kaiser Wilhelm II,* q.v.

Fischer, Jörg-Uwe, *Admiral des Kaisers. Georg Alexander von Müller als Chef des Marinekabinetts Wilhelms II.,* Frankfurt 1992

Foerster, Roland G., *Die Wehrpflicht. Entstehung, Erscheinungsform und politisch-militärische Wirkung,* Munich 1994

Foerster, Roland G. (ed.), *Generalfeldmarschall von Moltke. Bedeutung und Wirkung,* Munich 1991

Förster, Gerhard *et al., Der preußisch-deutsche Generalstab 1640–1965,* (East) Berlin 1966

Förster, Stig, *Der Doppelte Militarismus. Die deutsche Heeresrüstungspolitik zwischen Staus-quo-Sicherung und Aggression, 1890–1913,* Stuttgart and Wiesbaden 1985

'Mit Hurra und vollem Bewußtsein in die Katastrophe. Der Erste Weltkrieg und das Kriegsbild des deutschen Generalstabs', *Frankfurter Rundschau,* 9 August 1994

'Der deutsche Generalstab und die Illusion des kurzen Krieges, 1871–1914. Metakritik eines Mythos', *MGM,* 54, 1/1995, pp. 61–98; also in Becker *et al.* (eds.), *Lange and Kurze Wege,* q.v.

'The Armed Forces and Military Planning', in Roger Chickering (ed.), *Imperial Germany. A Historiographical Companion,* Westport, London 1996

Förster, Stig, (ed.), *Moltke. Vom Kabinettskrieg zum Volkskrieg,* Bonn, Berlin 1992

Förster, Wolfgang, 'Einige Bemerkungen zu Gerhard Ritters Buch "Der Schlieffenplan"', *Wehrwissenschaftliche Rundschau,* 1, 1957, pp. 37–44

Foley, Robert T., 'Schlieffen's last Kriegsspiel', *War Studies Journal,* 4, 1, 1999

'Attrition: Its Theory and Application in German Strategy, 1880–1916', Ph.D. Dissertation, King's College, University of London, 1999

Forsbach, Ralf, *Alfred von Kiderlen-Wächter (1852–1912). Ein Diplomatenleben im Kaiserreich,* 2 vols., Göttingen 1997

Frentz, Hans, *Der unbekannte Ludendorff. Der Feldherr in seiner Epoche,* Wiesbaden 1972

Fricke, Dieter (ed.), *Die bürgerlichen Parteien in Deutschland. Handbuch der Geschichte der bürgerlichen Parteien und anderer bürgerlicher Interessenorganisationen vom Vormärz bis zum Jahre 1945,* 2 vols., Berlin 1968

Friedrich, Otto, *Blood and Iron. From Bismarck to Hitler. The von Moltke Family's Impact on German History,* New York 1995

Fröhlich, Michael, *Imperialismus. Deutsche Kolonial- und Weltpolitik, 1880–1914,* Munich 1994

Galbreath, Robert C., 'Spiritual Science in an Age of Materialism. Rudolf Steiner and Occultism', Ph.D. Dissertation, University of Michigan 1970

Gasser, Adolf, *Deutschlands Entschluß zum Präventivkrieg 1913/14. Sonderdruck aus Discordia consors. Festschrift für Edgar Bonjour,* Basel 1968

Preußischer Militärgeist und Kriegsentfesselung 1914. Drei Studien zum Ausbruch des Ersten Weltkrieges, Basel and Frankfurt/M. 1985

Geinitz, Christian, *Kriegsfurcht und Kampfbereitschaft. Das Augusterlebnis in Freiburg. Eine Studie zum Kriegsbeginn 1914*, Essen 1998

Geiss, Imanuel, *Der Lange Weg in die Katastrophe. Die Vorgeschichte des Ersten Weltkrieges, 1815–1914*, Munich 1990

German Foreign Policy 1871–1914, London and Boston 1976

Das deutsche Reich und die Vorgeschichte des Ersten Weltkrieges, Munich 1978

Gemzell, Carl-Axel, *Organization, Conflict, and Innovation. A Study of German Naval Strategic Planning, 1888–1948*, Lund, Sweden, 1973

Gersdorff, Ursula von, 'Wolfgang Förster 85 Jahre', *Wehrwissenschaftliche Rundschau*, 10, 1960

Geyer, Michael, 'Die Geschichte des deutschen Militärs von 1860–1945. Ein Bericht über die Forschungslage (1945–1975)', in H.-U. Wehler (ed.), *Die moderne deutsche Geschichte in der internationalen Forschung*, Göttingen 1978

Deutsche Rüstungspolitik 1860–1980, Frankfurt/Main 1984

Gilbert, Martin, *The First World War*, London, paperback edn 1995

Glad, Betty (ed.), *Psychological Dimensions of War*, London, New Delhi, 2nd edn 1994 (1st edn 1990)

Goodspeed, D. J., *Ludendorff. Soldier, Dictator, Revolutionary*, London 1966

Görlitz, Walter, *Der Deutsche Generalstab. Geschichte und Gestalt*, Frankfurt 1950

Kleine Geschichte des deutschen Generalstabes, 2nd edn, Berlin, 1977

Granier, Gerhard, 'Deutsche Rüstungspolitik vor dem Ersten Weltkrieg. General Franz Wandels Tagebuchaufzeichnungen aus dem preußischen Kriegsministerium', *MGM*, 2/1985, pp. 123–162

Groh, Dieter, '"Je eher desto besser!" Innenpolitische Faktoren für die Präventivkriegsbereitschaft des Deutschen Reiches 1913/14', *Politische Vierteljahresschriften*, 13, 1972

Grone, Jürgen von, 'Zum Kriegsausbruch 1914', *Die Drei, Zeitschrift für Anthroposophie und Dreigliederung*, Herausgegeben von der Anthroposophischen Gesellschaft, Stuttgart, 1964/1

'Wie es 1914 zur Marneschlacht kam. Oberste Heeresleitung und Armeeführung nach den Grenzschlachten bis zum Beginn der Marneschlacht', *Die Drei, Zeitschrift für Anthroposophie und Dreigliederung*, Herausgegeben von der Anthroposophischen Gesellschaft, Stuttgart, 1964/3

'Marneschlacht. Der jüngere Moltke in den Tagen der Krise', *Die Drei, Zeitschrift für Anthroposophie und Dreigliederung*, Herausgegeben von der Anthroposophischen Gesellschaft, Stuttgart, 1964/5, pp. 361–371

Wie es zur Marneschlacht 1914 kam, Selbstverlag des Autors, Stuttgart 1971

Groote, Wolfgang von, 'Historische Vorbilder des Feldzuges 1914 im Westen', *MGM*, 1/1990, pp. 33–55

Guth, Ekkehard P., 'Der Gegensatz zwischen dem Oberbefehlshaber Ost und dem Chef des Generalstabes des Feldheeres 1914/15. Die Rolle des Majors v. Haeften im Spannungsfeld zwischen Hindenburg, Ludendorff und Falkenhayn', *MGM*, 35, 1984, pp. 113–139

Gutsche, Willibald, *Aufstieg und Fall eines kaiserlichen Reichskanzlers. Theobald von Bethmann Hollweg 1856–1921. Ein politisches Lebensbild*, (East)Berlin 1973

Haffner, Sebastian and Venohr, Wolfgang, *Das Wunder an der Marne. Rekonstruktion der Entscheidungsschlacht des Ersten Weltkrieges*, Bergisch Gladbach 1982

Hahlweg, Werner, *Klassiker der Kriegskunst*, Darmstadt 1960

Hamann, Brigitte, *Hitlers Wien*, Munich 1996

Hauser, Oswald (ed.), *Zur Problematik 'Preußen und das Reich'*, Cologne, Vienna 1984

Hecker, Gerhard, *Walther Rathenau und sein Verhältnis zum Militär*, Boppard/Rhein 1983

Heiber, Helmuth, *Walter Frank und sein Reichsinstitut für Geschichte des neuen Deutschlands*, Stuttgart 1966

Heisterkamp, Jens, 'Helmuth von Moltke – eine Lebensskizze', in Meyer, *Helmuth von Moltke*, q.v.

Hentschel, Volker, *Deutsche Wirtschafts- und Sozialpolitik 1815–1945*, Düsseldorf 1980

Hermann, C. H., *Deutsche Militärgeschichte*, Frankfurt/M. 1966

Hermann, Matthias, 'Das Reichsarchiv (1919–1945): Eine archivalische Institution im Spannungsfeld der deutschen Politik', 2 vols., Ph.D. dissertation, Berlin Humboldt University 1994

Herrmann, David G., *The Arming of Europe and the Making of the First World War*, paperback edn., Princeton 1997

Hertz-Eichenrode, Dieter, *Deutsche Geschichte 1890–1918. Das Kaiserreich in der Wilhelminischen Zeit*, Stuttgart, 1996

Herwig, Holger H., 'Imperial Germany', in Ernest R. May (ed.), *Knowing One's Enemies: Intelligence Assessment before the Two World Wars*, Princeton 1984

'From Tirpitz Plan to Schlieffen Plan: Some Observations on German Military Planning', *Journal of Strategic Studies*, 9, 1986, pp. 53–63

'Disjointed Allies: Coalition Warfare in Berlin and Vienna, 1914', *Journal of Military History*, 54, July 1990, pp. 265–80.

'Clio Deceived', in Steven Miller *et al.* (eds.), *Military Strategy and the Origins of the First World War. An 'International Security' Reader*, Princeton 1991

'Luxury' Fleet. The Imperial German Navy, 1888–1918, London 1991

The First World War. Germany and Austria-Hungary 1914–1918, London, New York, Sydney, Auckland 1997

Herwig, Holger H. (ed.), *The Outbreak of World War I. Causes and Responsibilites*, 5th edn, Lexington, Mass. 1991

Herwig, Holger H. and Heyman, Neil M. (eds.), *Biographical Dictionary of World War I*, Westport, Conn., and London 1982

Herzfeld, Hans, *Der Erste Weltkrieg*, Munich 1968

Hildebrand, Klaus, 'Julikrise 1914: Das europäische Sicherheitsdilemma. Betrachtungen über den Ausbruch des Ersten Weltkrieges', *Geschichte in Wissenschaft und Unterricht*, 7, 1985, pp. 469–503

Deutsche Außenpolitik 1871–1918, Munich 1989

'Saturierheit und Prestige. Das deutsche Reich als Staat im Staatensystem
1871–1918', *Geschichte in Wissenschaft und Unterricht*, 4, 1989, pp. 193–202

'Reich-Großmacht-Nation. Betrachtungen zur Geschichte der deutschen
Aussenpolitik 1871–1945', *HZ*, 2, 1994, pp. 369–389

Das Vergangene Reich. Deutsche Außenpolitik von Bismarck bis Hitler, 1871–1945,
Stuttgart 1995

Hillgruber, Andreas, 'Kurt Riezlers Theorie des "kalkulierten Risikos" und
Bethmann Hollwegs politische Konzeption in der Julikrise 1914', *HZ*, 202,
1966

Höbelt, Lothar, 'Schlieffen, Beck, Potiorek und das Ende der gemeinsamen
deutsch-österreich-ungarischen Aufmarschpläne im Osten', *MGM*,
2/1984, pp. 7–30.

Hölzle, Erwin, *Die Selbstentmachtung Europas. Das Experiment des Friedens vor und im
Ersten Weltkrieg*, Göttingen 1975

Hofmann, Hanns Hubert (ed.), *Das deutsche Offizierkorps 1860–1960*,
Boppard/Rhein 1980

Horne, John (ed.), *State, Society and Mobilization in Europe during the First World War*,
Cambridge 1997

Hossbach, Friedrich, *Die Entwicklung des Oberbefehls über das Heer in Brandenburg,
Preussen und im Deutschen Reich von 1655 bis 1945*, Würzburg 1957

Howard, Michael, 'Men Against Fire: The Doctrine of the Offensive in 1914',
in Paret, (ed.), *Makers of Modern Strategy*, q.v., pp. 510–526.

Hubatsch, Walther, *Der Admiralstab und die obersten Marinebehörden in Deutschland
1848–1945*, Frankfurt/M. 1958

'Die Verwaltung des Militärwesens 1867–1918', in Kurt G. A. Jeserich, Hans
Pohl and Georg-Christoph von Unruh (eds.), *Deutsche Verwaltungsgeschichte*,
vol.3, *Das Deutsche Reich bis zum Ende der Monarchie*, Stuttgart 1984

Huber, Ernst R., *Deutsche Verfassungsgeschichte seit 1789*, 6 vols., Stuttgart
1957–1981: Vol. 3, *Bismarck und das Reich*, Stuttgart, 1963; vol. 4, *Struktur und
Krisen des Kaiserreichs*, Stuttgart 1969

Heer und Staat in der deutschen Geschichte, Hamburg 1943

Hull, Isabel, 'Kaiser Wilhelm II and the Liebenberg Circle', in John C. G. Röhl
and N. Sombart (eds.), *Kaiser Wilhelm II. New Interpretations*, Cambridge 1982

The Entourage of Kaiser Wilhelm II 1888–1918, Cambridge 1982

Isselin, Henri, *The Battle of the Marne*, London 1965

Jäger, Wolfgang, *Historische Forschung und politische Kultur in Deutschland. Die Debatte
1914–1980 um den Ausbruch des Ersten Weltkrieges*, Göttingen 1984

Janßen, Karl-Heinz, *Der Kanzler und der General. Die Führungskrise um Bethmann
Hollweg und Falkenhayn, 1914–1916*, Göttingen 1967

Jany, Curt, *Geschichte der preußischen Armee vom 15. Jahrhundert bis 1914*, vol. 4,
Osnabrück 1967

Jarausch, Konrad, *The Enigmatic Chancellor. Bethmann Hollweg and the Hubris of
Imperial Germany*, New Haven and London 1973

'The Illusion of Limited War: Bethmann Hollweg's Calculated Risk, July
1914', *Central European History*, 2, 1969, pp. 48–76

Jäschke, Gotthard, 'Zum Problem der Marneschlacht 1914', *HZ*, 190, 1960, pp. 311–348

Jäschke, Gotthard, '"Schlieffenplan" und "Marneschlacht"', in Dermont Bradley and Ulrich Marwedel (eds.), *Militärgeschichte, Militärwissenschaft und Konfliktforschung. Festschrift für Werner Hahlweg*, Osnabrück 1977

Jeserich, Kurt GA., Pohl, Hans and Unruh, Georg-Christoph von (eds.), *Deutsche Verwaltungsgeschichte*, vol. 3: *Das Deutsche Reich bis zum Ende der Monarchie*, Stuttgart 1984

Joll, James, *The Origins of the First World War*, 2nd edn, London, 1992

Kaiser, David, 'Germany and the Origins of the First World War', *Journal of Modern History*, 55, 3, 1983

Kaufmann, Stefan, *Kommunikationstechnik und Kriegführung 1815–1945. Stufen telemedialer Rüstung*, Munich 1996

Keegan, John, *A History of Warfare*, paperback edn., London 1993
The First World War, London 1998

Keiger, John, 'Jules Cambon and Franco-German Détente, 1907–1914', *The Historical Journal*, 26, 3, 1983
France and the Origins of the First World War, London 1983
Raymond Poincaré, Cambridge 1997
The Rise of Anglo-German Antagonism, London 1980

Kennedy, Paul M. (ed.), *The War Plans of the Great Powers, 1880–1914*, London 1979
Grand Strategies in War and Peace, New Haven, London 1991

Kessel, Eberhard, *Moltke*, Stuttgart 1957

Kielmansegg, Peter Graf von, *Deutschland und der Erste Weltkrieg*, 2nd edn, Frankfurt/M., 1980

Kitchen, Martin, *The German Officer Corps*, Oxford 1968
The Silent Dictatorship. The Politics of the German High Command under Hindenburg and Ludendorff, 1916–1918, London 1976
'Civil–Military Relations in Germany during the First World War', in R. J. Q. Addams (ed.), *The Great War 1914–1918*, London 1990

Klein, Fritz (ed.), *Deutschland im Ersten Weltkrieg*, 2 vols., vol. 1, *Vorbereitung, Entfesselung und Verlauf des Krieges bis Ende 1914*, (East)Berlin 1968

Koch, Hannsjoachim W. (ed.), *The Origins of the First World War. Great Power Rivalry and German War Aims*, London, 2nd edn 1984

Krafft, Heinz, 'Karl von Bülow', *NDB*, vol. 2, Berlin 1955, pp. 736ff.
Staatsräson und Kriegsführung im kaiserlichen Deutschland 1914–1916: Der Gegensatz zwischen dem Generalstabschef von Falkenhayn und dem Oberbefehlshaber Ost im Rahmen des Bündniskrieges der Mittelmächte, Göttingen 1980

Kramer, Alan, '"Greueltaten". Zum Problem der deutschen Kriegsverbrechen in Belgien und Frankreich 1914', in Gerhard Hirschfeld *et al.* (eds.), *Keiner fühlt sich hier mehr als Mensch. Erlebnis und Wirkung des Ersten Weltkriegs*, Essen 1993

Kronenbitter, Günther, 'Bundesgenossen? Zur militärpolitischen Kooperation zwischen Berlin und Vienna 1912–1914', in W. Bernecker and V. Dotterweich (eds.), *Deutschland in den internationalen Beziehungen des 19. und 20. Jahrhunderts. Festschrift für Josef Becker*, Munich 1996

'"Nur los lassen!" Österreich-Ungarn und der Wille zum Krieg', in Burkhardt *et al.* (eds.), *Lange und kurze Wege in den Ersten Weltkrieg*, q.v., pp. 159–187

'Austria-Hungary and World War I', in Günther Bischof and Anton Pelinka (eds.), *Austrian Historical Memory and National Identity*. Contemporary Austrian Studies, vol. 5, New Brunswick and London 1997

'Die Macht der Illusionen. Julikrise und Kriegsausbruch 1914 aus der Sicht des deutschen Militärattachés in Wien', *MGM*, 57, 1998

Krumeich, Gerd, *Armaments and Politics in France on the Eve of the First World War. The Introduction of the Three-Year Conscription, 1913–1914*, London 1984

Lackey, Scott W., *The Rebirth of the Habsburg Army*, Westport, Connecticut 1995

Lahme, Rainer, 'Das Ende der Pax Britannica: England und die europäischen Mächte 1890–1914', *Archiv für Kulturgeschichte*, 73, 1, 1991, pp. 169–192

Lambi, I., *The Navy and German Power Politics 1862–1914*, Boston 1984

Langdon, John W., *July 1914. The Long Debate 1918–1990*, New York and Oxford 1991

Lange, Karl, *Marneschlacht und deutsche Öffentlichkeit 1914–1939. Eine verdrängte Niederlage und ihre Folgen*, Düsseldorf 1974

Lerman, Kathy, *The Chancellor as Courtier. Bernhard von Bülow and the Governance of Germany, 1900–1909*, Cambridge 1990

Leslie, John, 'Österreich-Ungarn vor dem Kriegsausbruch. Der Ballhausplatz in Wien im Juli 1914 aus der Sicht eines österreichisch-ungarischen Diplomaten', in *Deutschland und Europa in der Neuzeit. Festschrift für Karl Otmar Frh. von Aretin zum 65. Geburtstag*, 2. Halbband, ed. Ralph Melville *et al.*, Stuttgart 1988

'The Antecedents of Austria-Hungary's War Aims. Policies and Policy-Makers in Vienna and Budapest before and during 1914', *Wiener Beiträge zur Geschichte der Neuzeit*, 20, 1993, pp. 307–394

Lieven, Dominic, *Russia and the Origins of the First World War*, London 1983

Lindenberg, Christoph, *Rudolf Steiner*, Hamburg 1992

Linnekohl, Hans, *Vom Einzelschuß zur Feuerwalze. Der Wettlauf zwischen Technik und Taktik im Ersten Weltkrieg*, Koblenz 1990

Liss, Ulrich, 'Graf Schlieffen's [sic] letztes Kriegsspiel', *Wehrwissenschaftliche Rundschau*, 1965, pp. 162–166

Lissau, Rudi, *Rudolf Steiner. Life, Work, Inner Path and Social Initiatives*, Stroud, 1987

Löbel, Uwe, 'Neue Forschungsmöglichkeiten zur preußisch-deutschen Heeresgeschichte', *MGM*, 51, 1992, pp. 143–149

Lorenz, Chris, 'Beyond Good and Evil? The German Empire and Modern German Historiography', *Journal of Contemporary History*, 30, 4, 1995, pp. 729–765

MacGinty, Roger, 'War Causes and Peace Aims? Small States and the First World War', *European History Quarterly*, 27, 1, January 1997

Mai, Gunther, *Das Ende des Kaiserreichs. Politik und Kriegführung im Ersten Weltkrieg*, Munich 1987

Mann, Heinrich, *Der Untertan*, Frankfurt 1991 (1st edn 1919)

Marks, Sally, '"My Name is Ozymandias"'. The Kaiser in Exile', *Central European History*, 16, 1983, pp. 122–170

Martell, Gordon, *The Origins of the First World War*, 2nd edn, London 1996

Maser, Werner, *Hindenburg. Eine politische Biographie*, Rastatt 1989

Maurer, John H., *The Outbreak of the First World War. Strategic Planning, Crisis Decision Making and Deterrence Failure*, Westport, Connecticut and London 1995

May, Ernest R. (ed.), *Knowing One's Enemies: Intelligence Assessment before the two World Wars*, Princeton 1984

Meier-Welcker, Hans, 'Strategische Planungen und Vereinbarungen der Mittelmächte für den Mehrfrontenkrieg', *Österreichische Militärzeitschrift*, Sonderheft II, 1964

Meier-Welcker, Hans and Groote, Wolfgang von (eds.), *Handbuch zur deutschen Militärgeschichte 1648–1939*, 5 vols, vol 5: *Von der Entlassung Bismarcks bis zum Ende des Ersten Weltkrieges, 1880–1918*, Munich 1979

Meisner, H. O., *Der Kriegsminister 1814–1914. Ein Beitrag zur militärischen Verfassungsgeschichte*, Berlin 1940

Militärattachés und Militärbevollmächtigte in Preußen und im Deutschen Reich, Berlin 1957

Menning, Bruce W., *Bayonets before Bullets: The Imperial Russian Army, 1861–1914*, Bloomington 1992

Menning, Ralph R., 'The Collapse of "Global Diplomacy": Germany's Descent into Isolation, 1906–1909', Ph.D. Dissertation, Brown University 1986

Mertens, Lothar, 'Das Privileg des Einjährig-Freiwilligen Militärdienstes im Kaiserreich und seine gesellschaftliche Bedeutung', *MGM*, 39, 1986

Messerschmidt, Manfred, *Militär und Politik in der Bismarckzeit und im Wilhelminischen Deutschland*, Darmstadt 1975

'Die politische Geschichte der preußisch-deutschen Armee', *Deutsche Militärgeschichte in 6 Bänden, 1648–1939*, ed. Militärgeschichtliche Forschungsanstalt, vol. 2, Herrschig 1983

Militärgeschichtliche Aspekte der Entwicklung des deutschen Nationalstaates, Düsseldorf 1988

Meyer, Thomas, *'Endlich eine Tat, eine befreiende Tat…'. Alfred von Kiderlen-Wächters 'Panthersprung nach Agadir' unter dem Druck der öffentlichen Meinung*, Husum 1996

Michalka, Wolfgang (ed.), *Der Erste Weltkrieg. Wirkung, Wahrnehmung, Analyse*, Munich, Zurich 1994

Miller, Steven *et al.* (eds.), *Military Strategy and the Origins of the First World War. An 'International Security' Reader*, Princeton 1991

Model, Hansgeorg, *Der deutsche Generalstabsoffizier. Seine Auswahl und Ausbildung in Reichswehr, Wehrmacht und Bundeswehr*, Frankfurt/Main 1968

Möller-Witten, Hanns, 'General der Infanterie v. Kuhl zum 95. Geburtstag', *Wehrwissenschaftliche Rundschau*, 6/7, 1951, pp. 77–78

Mombauer, Annika, 'A Reluctant Military Leader? Helmuth von Moltke and the July Crisis of 1914', *War in History*, 6, 4, 1999, pp. 417 446

Mommsen, Wolfgang J., 'Domestic Factors in German Foreign Policy before 1914', *Central European History*, 6, 1973, pp. 3–43

'Das Kaiserreich als System umgangener Entscheidungen', in H. Berding, K. Düwell, L. Gall, W. J. Mommsen and H.-U. Wehler (eds.), *Festschrift für Theodor Schieder zum 70. Geburtstag*, Munich 1978

'Der Topos vom unvermeidlichen Krieg: Außenpolitik und öffentliche Meinung im Deutschen Reich im letzten Jahrzehnt vor 1914', in idem, *Der autoritäre Nationalstaat*, q.v

Der autoritäre Nationalstaat. Verfassung, Gesellschaft und Kultur im deutschen Kaiserreich, Frankfurt/M. 1990

Großmachtstellung und Weltpolitik 1870–1914. Die Außenpolitik des Deutschen Reiches, Frankfurt/M. and, Berlin 1993

Moritz, Albrecht, *Das Problem des Präventivkrieges in der deutschen Politik während der 1. Marokkokrise*, Bern and Frankfurt/M. 1974

Müller, Christian, 'Anmerkungen zur Entwicklung von Kriegsbild und operativ-strategischem Szenario im preußisch-deutschen Heer vor dem Ersten Weltkrieg', *MGM*, 57, 2, 1998

Murawski, Erich, 'Die amtliche deutsche Kriegsgeschichtsschreibung über den Ersten Weltkrieg', *Wehrwissenschaftliche Rundschau*, 9, 1959, 2 parts, pp. 513–531, 584–598

Murray, W., Knox, M. and Bernstein, A. (eds.), *The Making of Strategy: Rulers, Strategy, and War*, Cambridge 1994

Neue Deutsche Biographie, vol. 2, Berlin 1955ff.

New Encyclopaedia Britannica, vol.1, *Micropaedia*, 15th edn, London 1991

Nipperdey, Thomas, *Deutsche Geschichte 1866–1918*, 2 vols., Munich 1992

O'Connell, Robert L., *Of Arms and Men. A History of War, Weapons and Aggression*, New York, Oxford 1989

Offer, Avner, *The First World War: An Agrarian Interpretation*, Oxford 1991

'Going to War in 1914: A Matter of Honour?', *Politics and Society*, 1995

Oncken, Emily, *Panthersprung nach Agadir. Die deutsche Politik während der 2. Marokkokrise 1911*, Düsseldorf 1981

Ostertag, Heiger, *Bildung, Ausbildung und Erziehung des Offizierkorps im deutschen Kaiserreich 1871–1918. Eliteideal, Anspruch und Wirklichkeit*, Frankfurt/M., Bern, New York and Paris 1990

Otto, Helmuth, 'Zum strategisch-operativen Zusammenwirken des deutschen und österreichisch-ungarischen Generalstabes bei der Vorbereitung des ersten Weltkrieges', *Zeitschrift für Militärgeschichte*, 2, 1963, pp. 423–440

Schlieffen und der Generalstab. Der preußisch-deutsche Generalstab unter der Leitung des Generals von Schlieffen 1891–1905, Deutscher Militärverlag, (East)Berlin 1966

"Der Bestand Kriegsgeschichtliche Forschungsanstalt des Heeres im Bundesarchiv-, Militärisches Zwischenarchiv Potsdam", *MGM*, 51, 1992, pp. 429–441

Paret, Peter (ed.), *Makers of Modern Strategy from Machiavelli to the Nuclear Age*, Oxford reprint 1994 (1st edn 1986)

Peters, Michael, *Der Alldeutsche Verband am Vorabend des Ersten Weltkrieges (1908–1914)*, Frankfurt/M. 1992

Pogge von Strandmann, Hartmut, 'Staatsstreichpläne, Alldeutsche und Bethmann Hollweg', in Pogge von Strandmann and Geiss (eds.), *Die Erforderlichkeit des Unmöglichen*, q.v.

'Nationale Verbände zwischen Weltpolitik und Kolonialpolitik', in Schottelius, H. and Deist, W. (eds.), *Marine und Marinepolitik im kaiserlichen Deutschland, 1871–1914*, q.v.

Pogge von Strandmann, Hartmut and Geiss, Imanuel (eds.), *Die Erforderlichkeit des Unmöglichen. Deutschland am Vorabend des ersten Weltkrieges*, Frankfurt 1965

Pöhlmann, Markus, 'World War Experience and Future War Images in the Official German Military History', Paper delivered at the 'Shadows of Total War' Conference, Bern, August 1999, forthcoming in Roger Chickering and Stig Förster (eds.), *The Shadows of Total War: Europe, East Asia, and the United States, 1919–1939*, Washington DC and Cambridge, Mass. 2001

Rahne, Hermann, *Mobilmachung. Militärische Mobilmachungsplanung und -technik in Preußen und im deutschen Reich von der Mitte des 19. Jahrhunderts bis zum 2. Weltkrieg*, (East)Berlin, 1983

Rassow, Peter, 'Schlieffen und Holstein', *HZ*, 173, 1952

Rauchensteiner, Manfried, *Der Tod des Doppeladlers. Österreich-Ungarn und der Erste Weltkrieg*, Graz, Vienna, Cologne 1993

Rauh, Manfred, 'Die britisch-russische Militärkonvention von 1914 und der Ausbruch des Ersten Weltkrieges', *MGM*, 41, 1987

Retallack, James, *Germany in the Age of Kaiser Wilhelm II*, London 1996

Rich, Norman, *Friedrich von Holstein. Politics and Diplomacy in the Era of Bismarck and Wilhelm II*, 2 vols., Cambridge 1965

Ritter, Gerhard, 'Die Zusammenarbeit der Generalstäbe Deutschlands und Österreich-Ungarns vor dem ersten Weltkrieg', in Wilhelm Berges and Carl Hinrichs (eds.), *Zur Geschichte der Demokratie: Festgabe für Hans Herzfeld*, Berlin 1958

'Der Anteil der Militärs an der Kriegskatastrophe von 1914', *HZ*, 193, 1961, pp. 72–91

Staatskunst und Kriegshandwerk. Das Problem des 'Militarismus' in Deutschland, 4 vols, Munich 1954–1968

The Schlieffen Plan. Critique of a Myth, London 1958 (*Der Schlieffenplan. Kritik eines Mythos*, Munich 1956)

Ritter, Gerhard A., *Deutsche Parteien vor 1918*, Cologne 1973

(ed.), *Das Deutsche Kaiserreich. Ein Historisches Lesebuch 1871–1914*, Göttingen, 4th edn 1981

Rogge, Helmuth, *Holstein und Harden. Politisch-publizistisches Zusammenspiel zweier Außenseiter des Wilhelminischen Reiches*, Munich 1959

Röhl, John C. G., *Germany without Bismarck. The Crisis of Government in the Second Reich, 1890–1900*, London 1967

'Admiral von Müller and the Approach of War, 1911–1914', *Historical Journal*, 12, 4, 1969, pp. 651–673

'An der Schwelle zum Weltkrieg: Eine Dokumentation über den "Kriegsrat" vom 8. Dezember 1912', *MGM*, 21, 1/1977

'Die Generalprobe. Zur Geschichte und Bedeutung des "Kriegsrates" vom 8. Dezember 1912', in Dirk Stegmann, Bernd-Jürgen. Wendt and Peter-Christian Witt (eds.), *Industrielle Gesellschaft und politisches System. Beiträge zur politischen Sozialgeschichte. Festschrift für Fritz Fischer zum 70. Geburtstag*, Bonn 1978

Kaiser, Hof und Staat. Wilhelm II und die deutsche Politik, Munich 1988 (English translation: *The Kaiser and his Court*, London 1995)

Wilhelm II. Die Jugend des Kaisers 1859–1888, Munich 1993 (English translation: *Young Wilhelm. The Kaiser's Early Years*, Cambridge 1998)

'Germany' in Keith Wilson (ed.), *Decisions for War 1914*, q.v.

(ed.), *From Bismarck to Hitler. The Problem of Continuity in German History*, London 1970

1914: Delusion or Design? The Testimony of Two German Diplomats, London 1973

Der Ort Kaiser Wilhelm II in der deutschen Geschichte, Munich 1991

Röhl, John C. G. and Sombart, Nikolaus (eds.), *Kaiser Wilhelm II. New Interpretations*, Cambridge 1982

Rohkrämer, Thomas, *Der Militarismus der 'kleinen Leute'. Die Kriegervereine im Deutschen Kaiserreich 1871–1914*, Munich 1990

Romeyk, Horst, 'Das ehemalige sowjetische Sonderarchiv in Moskau', *Der Archivar*, 45, July 1992, Heft 3

'Die deutschen Bestände im Sonderarchiv in Moskau', *Der Archivar*, 45, July 1992, Heft 3

Ropponen, Risto, *Italien als Verbündeter. Die Einstellung der politischen und militärischen Führung Deutschlands und Österreich-Ungarns zu Italien von der Niederlage von Adua 1896 bis zum Ausbruch des Weltkrieges 1914*, Helsinki 1986

Rosinski, Herbert, *Die deutsche Armee*, Düsseldorf, Vienna 1970

Rumschöttel, Hermann, *Das bayerische Offizierkorps 1866–1914*, Berlin 1973

Salewski, Michael, 'Moltke, Schlieffen und die Eisenbahn' in Roland G. Foerster (ed.), *Generalfeldmarschall von Moltke. Bedeutung und Wirklichkeit*, Munich 1991

Samuels, Martin, 'The Reality of Cannae', *MGM*, 1/1990, pp. 7–31

Command or Control? Command, Training and Tactics in the British and German Armies, 1888–1918, London 1995

'Directive Command and the German General Staff', *War in History*, 2/1, 1995, pp. 22–42

Scheibe, Friedrich Carl, 'Marne und Gorlice: Zur Kriegsdeutung Hans Delbrücks', *MGM*, 53, 1994, pp. 355–376

Schieder, Wolfgang (ed.), *Erster Weltkrieg. Ursachen, Entstehung und Kriegsziele*, Cologne and Berlin 1969

Schleier, Hans, *Die bürgerliche deutsche Geschichtsschreibung der Weimarer Republik*, Cologne 1975

Schmidt-Richberg, Wiegand, *Die Generalstäbe in Deutschland 1871–1945: Aufgaben in der Armee und Stellung im Staate*, Stuttgart 1962

Schmidt-Richberg,Wiegand, 'Die Regierungszeit Wilhelms II', in Militärgeschichtliches Forschungsamt (ed.), *Handbuch zur deutschen Militärgeschichte 1648–1939*, vol. 5, *Von der Entlassung Bismarcks bis zum Ende des Ersten Weltkrieges (1890–1918)*, Frankfurt 1968

Schoenbaum, David, *Zabern 1913. Consensus Politics in Imperial Germany*, London 1982

'Kriegsgefahr und Krisenmanagement vor 1914. Zur Außenpolitik des kaiserlichen Deutschland', *HZ*, 267, 1998

Schöllgen, Gregor, 'Kriegsgefahr und Krisenmanagement vor 1914. Zur Aussenpolitik des kaiserlichen Deutschlands', *HZ*, 267, 2, 1998

Schöllgen, Gregor (ed.), *Flucht in den Krieg? Die Außenpolitik des kaiserlichen Deutschlands*, Darmstadt 1991

Schottelius, Herbert and Deist, Wilhelm (eds.), *Marine und Marinepolitik im Kaiserlichen Deutschland 1871–1914*, Düsseldorf 1972

Schulte, Bernd-Felix, *Die Deutsche Armee 1900–1914. Zwischen Beharren und Verändern*, Düsseldorf 1977

'Neue Dokumente zum Kriegsausbruch und Kriegsverlauf 1914', *MGM*, 25, 1/1979, pp. 123–185

'Zu der Krisenkonferenz vom 8. Dezember 1912 in Berlin', *Historisches Jahrbuch*, 102, 1982

Europäische Krise und Erster Weltkrieg. Beiträge zur Militärpolitik des Kaiserreichs 1871–1914, Frankfurt/M. 1983

Die Verfälschung der Riezler Tagebücher: ein Beitrag zur Wissenschaftsgeschichte der 50er und 60er Jahre, Franfurt/M. 1985

Schwarzmüller, Theo, *Zwischen Kaiser und "Führer". Generalfeldmarschall August von Mackensen. Eine politische Biographie*, Paderborn, Munich, Vienna and Zürich 1995

Seligmann, Matthew S., 'A View from Berlin: Colonel Frederick Trench and the Development of British Perceptions of German Aggressive Intent, 1906–1910', *Journal of Strategic Studies*, 23/2, 2000, pp. 114–147

'Germany and the Origins of the First World War in the Eyes of the American Diplomatic Establishment', *German History*, vol. 15, 3, 1997, pp. 307–332

Senghaas, Dieter, *Rüstung und Militarismus*, Frankfurt 1972

Shanafelt, Gary W., *The Secret Enemy. Austria-Hungary and the German Alliance, 1914–1918*, New York 1985

Sheehan, James J., *Imperial Germany*, New York 1976

Showalter, Dennis E., 'The Eastern Front and German Military Planning, 1871–1914 – Some Observations', *East European Quarterly*, 15, 1981, pp. 163–180

German Military History 1648–1982. A Critical Bibliography, New York and London 1984

'German Grand Strategy: A Contradiction in Terms?', *MGM*, 48, 1990, pp. 65–102

Tannenberg. Clash of Empires, Hamden, Conn. 1991

Snyder, Jack, *The Ideology of the Offensive. Military Decision-Making and the Disasters of 1914*, Ithaca, New York and London 1984
'Civil–Military Relations and the Cult of the Offensive, 1914–1918', *International Security*, 9, 1, 1984
Stahl, Friedrich-Christian, 'Der große Generalstab, seine Beziehung zum Admiralstab und seine Gedanken zu den Operationsplänen der Marine. Aus Anlaß des 50. Todestages des Generalfeldmarschalls von Schlieffen am 4. Januar 1963', *Wehrkunde*, 1963, pp. 8–12
'Preußische Armee und Reichsheer 1871–1914', in Oswald Hauser (ed.), *Zur Problematik 'Preußen und das Reich'*, Cologne 1984
Stargardt, Nicholas, *The German Idea of Militarism. Radical and Socialist Critics, 1866–1914*, Cambridge 1994
Steinberg, Jonathan, *Yesterday's Deterrent. Tirpitz and the Birth of the German Battle Fleet*, London 1965
'The Copenhagen Complex', *Journal of Contemporary History*, 1/3, July 1966
'Germany and the Russo-Japanese War', *American Historical Review*, 75/4, 1970, pp. 1965–1986
'Diplomatie als Wille und Vorstellung: Die Berliner Mission Lord Haldanes im Februar 1912', in Schottelius and Deist (eds.), *Marine und Marinepolitik im Kaiserlichen Deutschland 1871–1914*, q.v
Steiner, Rudolf, *Mein Lebensgang*, Dornach, Switzerland, 8th edn 1982
Steiner, Zara, *Britain and the Origins of the First World War*, London 1977
Stengers, Jean, 'Guillaume II et le Roi Albert à Potsdam en novembre 1913', *Bulletin de la Classe des Lettres et des Sciences Morales et Politiques*, 7–12, 1993, pp. 227–53
Stern, Fritz, *Bethmann Hollweg und der Krieg: Die Grenzen der Verantwortung*, Tübingen 1988
Sternburg, Wilhelm von (ed.), *Die deutschen Kanzler. Von Bismarck bis Kohl*, Frankfurt 1994
Stevenson, David, *The First World War and International Politics*, Oxford 1988
Armaments and the Coming of War. Europe 1904–1914, Oxford 1996
The Outbreak of the First World War. 1914 in Perspective, London 1997
Stöcker, M., *"Augusterlebnis 1914" in Darmstadt. Legende und Wirklichkeit*, Darmstadt 1994
Stolberg-Wernigerode, Otto Graf zu, *Die Unentschiedene Generation. Deutschlands konservative Führungsschichten am Vorabend des Ersten Weltkrieges*, Munich 1968
Stone, Norman, 'Moltke–Conrad: Relations between the Austro-Hungarian and German General Staffs, 1909–1914', *Historical Journal*, 9, 1966, pp. 201–228 (also in Kennedy, ed., *The War Plans of the Great Powers*, q.v.).
'Die Mobilmachung der österreichisch-ungarischen Armee 1914', *MGM*, 16, 2/1974, pp. 67–95
The Eastern Front 1914–1917, London 1975
Stoneman, Mark R., 'Bürgerliche und adlige Krieger: Zum Verhältnis zwischen sozialer Herkunft und Berufskultur im wilhelminischen Armee-Offizierkorps', in Heinz Reif (ed.), *Bürgertum und Adel im 19. und 20. Jahrhundert*, Berlin 2000

Storz, Dieter, *Kriegsbild und Rüstung vor 1914. Europäische Landstreitkräfte vor dem Ersten Weltkrieg*, Herford, Berlin, Bonn 1992

Strachan, Hew, *European Armies and the Conduct of War*, London 1983

'Germany in the First World War: The Problem of Strategy', *German History*, 12, 2, 1994

The First World War, London 1997

Strachan, Hew (ed.), *The Oxford Illustrated History of the First World War*, Oxford 1999

Stumpf, Reinhard (ed.), *Kriegstheorien und Kriegsgeschichte. Carl von Clausewitz. Helmuth von Moltke*, Frankfurt 1993

Stürmer, Michael (ed.), *Das kaiserliche Deutschland. Politik und Gesellschaft, 1870–1918*, Düsseldorf 1970

Tautz, Johannes, *Walter Johannes Stein. Eine Biographie*, Philosophisch-Anthroposophischer Verlag am *Goetheanum*, Dornach 1989

Teske, Herman, 'Colmar von der Goltz-Pascha', *NDB*, vol 6, Berlin 1964, p. 630

Thompson, Wayne C., 'The September Program: Reflections on the Evidence', *Central European History*, 11, 4, 1978

Trachtenberg, Marc, *History and Strategy*, Princeton 1991

Trumpener, Ulrich, 'War Premeditated?', *Central European History*, 9, 1976

Tucker, Spencer C., *The European Powers in the First World War. An Encyclopedia*, New York, London 1996

Tunstall, Graydon A. Jr., 'The Schlieffen Plan: the Diplomacy and Military Strategy of the Central Powers in the East, 1905–1914', Ph.D. Dissertation. Rutgers University, New Brunswick, NJ 1974

Planning for War Against Russia and Serbia: Austro-Hungarian and German Military Strategies, 1871–1914, New York 1993

Turner, L. C. F., 'The Significance of the Schlieffen Plan', *The Austrian Journal of Politics and History*, 13, 1967, pp. 47–66

'The Role of the General Staffs in July 1914', *The Austrian Journal of Politics and History*, 11, 1965, pp. 305–323

The Origins of the First World War, London 1970

Tyng, Sewell, *The Campaign of the Marne 1914*, Oxford 1935

Uhle-Wettler, Franz, *Erich Ludendorff in seiner Zeit. Soldat, Stratege, Revolutionär. Eine Neubewertung*, Berg 1995

Ullrich, Volker, 'Das deutsche Kalkül in der Julikrise 1914 und die Frage der englischen Neutralität', *Geschichte in Wissenschaft und Unterricht*, 34, 1983

'Der Sprung ins Dunkle – Die Julikrise 1914 und ihre aktuellen Lehren', *Geschichtsdidaktik*, 2, 1984

Die nervöse Großmacht 1871–1918. Aufstieg und Untergang des deutschen Kaiserreiches, Frankfurt/M. 1997

Umbreit, Hans, 'Von der preußisch-deutschen Militärgeschichte zur heutigen Militärgeschichte', in Ursula von Gersdorff (ed.), *Geschichte und Militärgeschichte*, Frankfurt 1974

Valiani, Leo, 'Verhandlungen zwischen Italien und Österreich-Ungarn,

1914–1915', in Wolfgang Schieder (ed.), *Erster Weltkrieg. Ursachen, Entstehung und Kriegsziele,* Cologne and Berlin 1969

Velsen, Stefan von, 'Deutsche Generalstabsoffiziere im Ersten Weltkrieg 1914–18. Erinnerungen', *Die Welt als Geschichte,* 16, 1956, pp. 250ff.

Veltzke, Veit, 'Kaiser and Heer 1888–1914', *Forschungen zur Brandenburgisch-Preussischen Geschichte,* 7/1, 1997, pp. 69–79

Venohr, Wolfgang, *Ludendorff. Legende und Wirklichkeit,* Berlin 1993

Vierhaus, Rudolf (ed.), *Das Tagebuch der Baronin Spitzemberg. Aufzeichnungen aus der Hofgesellschaft des Hohenzollernreiches,* Göttingen 1960

Vietsch, Eberhard von, *Bethmann Hollweg. Staatsmann zwischen Macht und Ethos,* Boppard/Rhein 1969

Vogel, Jakob, *Nationen im Gleichschritt. Der Kult der 'Nation in Waffen' in Deutschland und Frankreich, 1871–1914,* Göttingen 1997

Vogt, Adolf, *Oberst Max Bauer. Generalstabsoffizier im Zwielicht, 1869–1929,* Osnabrück 1974

Waite, Robert G., 'Leadership Pathologies: The Kaiser and the Führer and the Decisions for War in 1914 and 1939', in Betty Glad (ed.), *Psychological Dimensions of War,* London, 2nd edn 1994

Wallach, Jehuda L., *Das Dogma der Vernichtungsschlacht. Die Lehren von Clausewitz und Schlieffen und ihre Wirkungen in zwei Weltkriegen,* Frankfurt/M. 1967

Kriegstheorien. Ihre Entwicklung im 19. und 20. Jahrhundert, Frankfurt/M. 1972

Anatomie einer Militärhilfe. Die preußisch-deutschen Militärmissionen in der Türkei 1835–1919, Düsseldorf 1976

'Feldmarschall von Schlieffens Interpretation der Kriegslehre Moltkes d.Ä.', in Roland G. Foerster (ed.), *Generalfeldmarschall von Moltke. Bedeutung und Wirkung,* Munich 1991

Walle, Heinrich, 'Helmuth von Moltke', *NDB,* vol. 18, 1997

Wegner, Bernd, 'Deutsche Aktenbestände im Moskauer Zentralen Staatsarchiv. Ein Erfahrungsbericht', *Vierteljahreshefte für Zeitgeschichte,* 2, 1992, pp. 311–319

Wehler, Hans-Ulrich, 'Der Fall Zabern. Rückblick auf eine Verfassungskrise des wilhelminischen Kaiserreichs', in H. E. Stier and F. Ernst (eds.), *Die Welt als Geschichte,* Stuttgart 1963

Das Deutsche Kaiserreich 1871–1918, Göttingen 1973

Wehler, Hans-Ulrich (ed.), *Krisenherde im Kaiserreich 1871–1918,* Göttingen 1970

Wende, Frank, *Die belgische Frage in der deutschen Politik des Ersten Weltkrieges,* Hamburg 1969

Wernecke, Klaus, *Der Wille zur Weltgeltung. Außenpolitik und Öffentlichkeit im Kaiserreich am Vorabend des Ersten Weltkrieges,* Düsseldorf, 2nd edn 1970

Williamson, Samuel R. Jr., 'Joffre Reshapes French Strategy', in Paul M. Kennedy, (ed.), *The War Plans of the Great Powers, 1880–1914,* London 1979

'The origins of World War One', *Journal of Interdisciplinary History,* 18/4, 1988, pp. 795–818

Austria-Hungary and the Origins of the First World War, paperback edn., London 1991

Williamson, S. R. Jr. and Pastor, P. (eds.), *Essays on World War I: Origins and Prisoners of War,* New York 1983

Wilson, Keith, 'The Agadir Crisis, the Mansion House speech, and the Double-Edgedness of Agreements', *Historical Journal*, 15, 3, 1972, pp. 513–532

Wilson, Keith (ed.), *Decisions for War 1914*, London 1995

Forging the Collective Memory. Governments and International Historians Through Two World Wars, Providence, Oxford 1996

Witt, Peter-Christian, *Die Finanzpolitik der Deutschen Reiches von 1903 bis 1913. Eine Studie zur Innenpolitik des Wilhelminischen Deutschland*, Lübeck and Hamburg 1970

Yasamee, F. A. K., 'Colmar Freiherr von der Goltz and the Rebirth of the Ottoman Empire', *Diplomacy and Statecraft* 9, 2, 1998

Young, Harry F., *Prince Lichnowsky and the Great War*, Athens, Georgia 1977

Zechlin, Egmont, 'Motive und Taktik der Reichsleitung 1914', *Der Monat*, 209, February 1966, pp. 91–95

Krieg und Kriegsrisiko. Zur Deutschen Politik im Ersten Weltkrieg. Düsseldorf 1979

'Die Adriakrise und der "Kriegsrat" vom 8. Dezember 1912', in idem, *Krieg und Kriegsrisiko*, q.v.

Ziemann, Benjamin, *Front und Heimat. Ländliche Kriegserfahrungen im südlichen Bayern*, Essen 1997

Zilch, Reinhold, 'Zur wirtschaftlichen Vorbereitung des deutschen Imperialismus auf den Ersten Weltkrieg', *Zeitschrift für Geschichtswissenschaft*, 24, 1976

Die Reichsbank und die finanzielle Kriegsvorbereitung 1907–1914, (East)Berlin 1987

Zmarzlik, Hans-Günther, *Bethmann Hollweg als Reichskanzler 1909–1914. Studien zu Möglichkeiten und Grenzen seiner innerpolitischen Machtstellung*, Düsseldorf 1957

Zuber, Terence, 'The Schlieffen Plan Reconsidered', *War in History*, 6, 3, 1999, pp. 262–305

Index

Aehrenthal, Alois Lexa Graf von, Austro-
  Hungarian Foreign Minister 1906–1912,
  110, 111, 127
Afflerbach, Holger, historian, 208
Agadir Crisis, 1911, 86, 106, 108, 121, 122, 124,
  126, 127, 129, 130–133, 140n, 142
Albert I, Belgian King, 1909–1933, 153, 162,
  165
Albrecht von Württemberg, Herzog, 229
Algeciras Agreement, 121
Alsace-Lorraine, 76, 91, 92, 100, 102, 126
Alten, Georg von, Prussian general, 71
Anglo-French Naval Agreement, February
  1913, 126
Antwerp, siege and capture of, 272
Army increases:
  debate between General Staff and
    Ministry of War over, 29, 82, 85, 87, 178,
    180
  problems for General Staff in requesting,
    86, 87, 106
  army bill of 1913, 108
  following Agadir Crisis, 130, 134, 136
  Moltke's requests for, 145, 146, 149, 174, 178,
    180, 285
'Augusterlebnis', 212n.
Auguste Victoria (1858–1921), Queen of
  Prussia, Kaiserin of Germany, 198, 199
Austria-Hungary:
  Austro-Hungarian Ministerial Council, 193
  Dual Alliance with Germany, 82, 107
  mobilization, 214
  relationship between German and
  Austro-Hungarian General Staff, see Great
    General Staff
  ultimatum to Serbia, 190, 193, 198

Baghdad Railway, 120
Balkan Wars 1912/1913, 120, 125, 135–137, 146,
  152, 182
  results of, 144, 171

Bauer, Max Hermann (1869–1929), Prussian
  officer, 156, 157
Beck, Ludwig, historian, 224
Beck-Rzikowsky, Friedrich Freiherr von,
  Austro-Hungarian Chief of the General
  Staff, 43, 81
Belgium:
  threat of future army increases, 162, 172
  violation of neutrality, 8, 76, 77, 92, 94, 153,
    154, 156, 158–160, 163, 166, 197, 203, 204,
    221, 222, 229, 230, 234, 236, 252, 284
Below, Fritz von, Prussian general, 278
Berchtold, Leopold Graf von, Austro-
  Hungarian Foreign Minister 1912–15, 154,
  188, 204, 285
Berghes, Rose-Marie von, Helmuth von
  Moltke's granddaughter, 7n
Bernhardi, Friedrich von (1849–1930), Prussian
  general and military writer, 24, 108, 114, 130
Bertrab, General von, Prussian general, 191, 192
Beseler, Hans Hartwig von (1850–1921),
  Prussian general, 46, 56, 68, 272, 281
Bethmann Hollweg, Theobald von
  (1856–1921), German Chancellor
  1909–1914, 120, 121, 126, 136, 139, 143,
  153, 155, 158, 161, 162, 169, 172, 173, 178,
  181, 184 (illustr.), 185, 190–192, 197–199,
  207, 211, 212, 232, 233, 237, 265, 281, 286
  Reichstag Speech, 4 August 1914, 159, 230
  'September Programme', 252
  hopes for British neutrality, 77, 104, 109, 142,
    200, 210, 219, 220
  intrigues against Falkenhayn, 275–278, 280
  joins demands for army increases, 131, 132,
    134, 136, 149, 152, 285
  fear of potential Russian threat, 188, 189
  demands delay in mobilization, 204, 205, 208
Bethusy-Huc, Astrid Gräfin von, neé Moltke,
  Helmuth von Moltke's daughter, 7
Bethusy-Huc, Marie-Liza, Helmuth von
  Moltke's granddaughter, 7n

Beyens, Eugène Baron de, Belgian envoy in
  Berlin 1912–1914, 166
Bienerth, Karl Graf von (1872–1941), Austro-
  Hungarian Military Attaché in Berlin,
  141, 144n, 233
Bismarck, Otto Fürst von (1815–1898),
  German Chancellor 1871–1890, 15, 21,
  27–29, 77, 78, 85
Bosnian Annexation Crisis, 110–114, 118, 120
Boulanger Crisis, 77
Britain:
  German attitude towards, 77–79, 127, 130,
    145, 146, 172, 209, 210
  Anglo-Russian Entente, 79
  Anglo-Russian naval negotiations, 189
  Irish Question, 178
  Possibility of British neutrality, 104, 109, 116,
    117, 200, 206, 219, 221
  Entry into the War, 153, 164
  British Expeditionary Force, 157, 209
Bronsart von Schellendorf, Paul (1832–1891),
  Prussian Minister of War 1883–1889,
  27
Bronsart, Fritz, Prussian officer, 282
Bucholz, Arden, historian, 109, 110, 112
Bulgaria, as an ally, 171
Bülow, Bernhard Graf von (1849–1929),
  German Chancellor 1900–1909, 42, 44,
  50, 108, 111, 116, 161, 210
Bülow, Karl von (1846–1921), Prussian general,
  46, 46, 68, 69, 229, 242 (illustr.), 243, 252,
  253, 256, 257, 276
Burchardt, Lothar, historian, 95

Cadorna, Luigi Conte de (1850–1928), Italian
  Chief of the General Staff, 170
Cannae, Battle of, 5, 72, 251
Capelle, Eduard von (1855–1931), German
  admiral, 191
Carlowitz, Carl von, Saxon Minister of War,
  187, 214
Carlyle, Thomas, historian, 51
Chamberlain, Houston Stewart, writer, 51
Class, Heinrich, Leader of the Pan-German
  League, 129
Clausewitz, Karl von, German general and
  military writer, 85
Commanding Generals, Corps Commanders,
  14, 22, 24, 25, 34, 56
Conrad von Hötzendorf, Franz Graf
  (1852–1925), Austro-Hungarian Chief of
  the General Staff 1906–1911, 1912–1917,
  82, 109, 111, 113–116, 119, 162, 169, 174,
  188, 194, 205, 214, 215, 251, 269, 274
Craig, Gordon, historian, 216, 224

Delcassé, Théophile, French Foreign Minister
  1898–1905, 42
Dohna-Schlobitten, Alfred Graf von, military
  plenipotentiary in St. Petersburg
  1912–1914, 198
Dommes, Wilhelm von, Prussian officer,
  Moltke's adjutant, 6, 8, 12, 45, 46, 149,
  150, 209, 222, 223, 255, 257–259
Dual Alliance, 82, 107, 111
'Dual Militarism', 83, 106

Eastern Deployment Plan, scrapping of, April
  1913, 100–102, 104, 105, 109, 120, 164, 167,
  225
East Prussia, in danger from Russian offensive,
  158, 245–247
Eckardstein, Hermann Freiherr von
  (1864–1933), First Secretary at German
  Embassy in London, 209
Edward VII (1841–1910), British King, 137
Eibicht, Rolf-Joseph, historian, 4
Einem, Karl von (1853–1934), Prussian Officer,
  Prussian Minister of War 1903–1909,
  Commander of Third Army, 21, 50, 59,
  64n, 68, 84, 155, 250n, 254
Eisendecher, Karl J.G., Prussian envoy in
  Karlsruhe, 139
Emmich, General von, 231, 232
Endres, Karl von, 71
Entente Cordiale, 78, 126, 130, 151
Esebeck, Walter Freiherr von, 250n.
Eulenburg-Hertefeld, Philipp zu:
  Spiritualism, 53
  Influence on Moltke's appointment, 71, 71

Fabeck, Karl von, 50, 255
Fabeck, Max von, Chief of Central Dept in
  German General Staff, 150
Falkenhayn, Erich von (1861–1922), Prussian
  Minister of War 1913–1915, Chief of the
  General Staff 1914–1916, 10, 126, 143,
  150, 178–181, 188, 190–193, 196, 198–200,
  202–205, 207, 208, 216, 219, 220, 235, 237,
  257, 261, 266, 267, 268 (illustr.), 269, 270,
  272, 273, 276–278, 281
  attitude towards Britain, 180
  intrigues against Falkenhayn, 275, 279, 280,
    287
Fischer, Fritz, historian, Fischer controversy, 1
Fischer, Jörg-Uwe, historian, 19
Fleischmann von Theissruck, Hauptmann,
  Austrian liaison officer in Berlin, 204,
  214
Flügeladjutanten, 23, 67
Förster, Stig, historian, 95, 211, 288

Förster, Wolfgang (1875–1963), Prussian officer and military writer, last president of Reichsarchiv, 1937–1945, 12n
France:
　army increases, 108
　German opinion of French army, 112, 115, 119, 145, 175, 177, 179
　revanche idea, 126
　French attitude to Belgian neutrality, 162, 165
　Plan XVII, 238, 252
Franco-Prussian War 1870/71, 74, 163, 260
Franz Ferdinand (1863–1914), Austro-Hungarian Archduke, 61 (illustr.), 187
　assassination at Sarajevo, 173, 174, 178, 182, 186, 191, 208
Franz Joseph I (1830–1916), Austrian Emperor and Hungarian King, 137, 194, 215
Freytag-Loringhoven, Hugo Freiherr von (1855–1924), Prussian officer and military writer, 94
'Frontiers, Battles of the', 14–25 August 1914, 238, 252

Gasser, Adolf, historian, 103, 105
Gebsattel, Konstantin Freiherr von, Leader of Pan-German League, 144
Gebsattel, Ludwig von, Bavarian military attaché, 122, 129
Geiss, Imanuel, historian, 197, 202
German Army:
　allegiance/oath to monarch, 20, 21, 30
　contingent armies, 16, 17, 29, 35
　continuities from Second to Third Reich, 13
　influence in Prussia, 15
　lack of cooperation between Army and Navy, 20
　polycratic structure, 14, 22, 24, 25, 33, 56, 142, 143
German Army League, 88, 127, 131, 146
German deployment in 1914, 215, 227, 228
German 'encirclement', 79, 130, 178
German military headquarters (OHL), 189, 232–234, 237, 256, 265, 272
German Mobilization, 201–204, 206, 208, 216, 217 (illustr.), 219, 220, 227, 228
German Mobilization Plan, 38–40
German Navy, 57, 87
　introduction of dual command structure, 19
　secrecy vis-à-vis the army, 83
　end of Navy's predominance, 134
German Navy League, 128
German public opinion, 117, 126, 127, 131, 150, 212

Goltz, Colmar von der (1843–1916), Prussian officer and military writer, 24, 43, 46, 51, 56, 68, 69, 70 (illustr.), 71, 113, 118, 275, 281
Graevenitz, Fritz von (1861–1922), Württemberg's military plenipotentiary in Berlin, 189
Great General Staff:
　as an institution, 2, 34ff.
　secret connections with the Reichsarchiv, 12
　role vis-à-vis other military institutions, 14, 41, 83, 236
　establishes its independence, 25ff.
　relationship with Austro-Hungarian General Staff, 80–82, 107, 113, 167, 205, 213–216, 269
　secrecy/security concerns, 39, 83, 89, 235, 236, 269
Grone, Jürgen von, Anthroposophist writer, 6
Groener, Wilhelm (1867–1939), Württemberg officer, Head of General Staff railway department, 2, 4, 12n, 18, 35, 45, 68, 95, 97, 99, 100, 102, 150, 192, 235, 240 (illustr.), 246, 250, 255, 272
Grey, Sir Edward, British Foreign Minister 1905–1916, 219
Gumbinnen, 246, 247

Haeften, Hans von (1870–1937), Prussian officer, military writer, President of Reichsarchiv 1931–1937, 12, 206, 207, 212, 220, 223, 226, 234, 265
Hahnke, Wilhelm von (1833–1901), Chief of Military Cabinet 1888–1901, 32, 33
Hahnke, Wilhelm von, Prussian officer, Schlieffen's son-in-law, 3, 22, 42–44, 78, 84, 85, 101
Haldane of Cloan, Richard Burdon Lord, British Minister of War 1905–1912, 139
Haldane Mission, February 1912, 130
Hamman, Otto, press officer in German Foreign Office, 122
Harbou, Christian von, Prussian officer, 101
Harden, Maximilian, German publicist/journalist, 53
Hart, Basil Henry Liddell, historian, 84
Hasse, Hauptmann, German liaison officer in Vienna, 214
Hausen, Generaloberst von, 229, 250n
Haussmann, Conrad (1857–1922), politician and member of Reichstag, 189
Heeringen, August von, Chief of Reich Navy Office 1911–1913, 139
Heeringen, Josias von (1850–1926), Prussian Minister of War 1909–1913, 87, 131, 133, 136, 139n, 149, 158

Helfferich, Karl Theodor (1872–1924), banker
and politician, 249
Heligoland, 140, 144*n*
Hentsch, Richard (1869–1918), Saxon officer,
35, 150, 250, 255, 257–260, 263
Hertling, Georg Friedrich Graf von
(1843–1919), Bavarian Minister President
1912–1917, German Chancellor
1917–1918, 190, 193
Herwig, Holger, historian, 85, 186, 243
Hindenburg, Paul von Beneckendorff und von
(1847–1934), Prussian general, leader of
OHL 1916–1918, 247, 262 (illustr.),
276–280
Höfer, General von, Conrad's deputy as Chief
of the Austro-Hungarian General Staff,
194
Hoffmann, Max (1869–1927), Prussian officer,
231, 245, 276
Holland:
violation of neutrality, 8, 93, 94, 96, 210,
284
as 'windpipe', 94, 95
Holstein, Friedrich von (1837–1909), 24, 44
Hopman, Albert, German admiral, 139*n*, 187
House, Edward, American Special Envoy in
London, 174
Hoyos, Alexander Graf von, Chief of Cabinet
in Austro-Hungarian Foreign Ministry,
188, 213
Huber, E. R., historian, 31, 32
Hubertusstock, meeting of 13 October 1912,
136, 138, 142
Hülsen-Haeseler, Dietrich von (1852–1908),
Chief of the Military Cabinet 1901–1908,
32, 33, 43, 52, 65 (illustr.), 68, 84
Humbert, Charles, French senator, 189, 194

Immediatstellen/Immediatsrecht, 21, 22
'Imminent Danger of War', state of, 206
Italy:
as an ally, 115, 125, 144, 167–169, 178
conquers Tripoli, 125, 132, 167

Jagow, Gottlieb von (1863–1935), Secretary of
State in German Foreign Office
1913–1916, 159–161, 172, 192, 193, 196,
197, 199, 206, 237, 265
Jarausch, Konrad, historian, 286
Jäschke, Gotthard, historian, 99, 100
Joffre, Joseph Jacques (1852–1931), French
Chief of the General Staff from 1910, 96,
160, 253
July Crisis of 1914, 4, 77, 102, 104, 106, 116,
142, 170, 174, 180ff., 190, 215, 223, 286

pretended ignorance of events of, by main
decision-makers, 192–194

Kageneck, Karl Graf von, German military
attaché in Vienna 1908–1914, 137, 194,
195, 214, 215
Kaltenborn-Stachau, Hans von, Prussian
Minister of War, 27
Karlsbad, 173, 185, 190–193, 214, 274
Keim, August, Founder of German Army
League, 128, 131
Kessel, Gustav von, 233
Keyserlingk, Freiherr von, 20
Kiderlen-Wächter, Alfred von (1852–1912),
State Secretary in German Foreign
Ministry, 121, 122, 126–128, 136, 141, 143,
159
Kiel Canal, 140, 144*n*
Kleist, Oberstleutnant von, German military
attaché in Rome 1912–1913, 169, 170
Klewitz, Oberst von, 210
Krafft von Dellmensingen, Konrad, Bavarian
general, 149, 150, 199, 233, 235, 239, 255,
256, 272
Kreisau, 51, 245
Kress von Kressenstein, Friedrich Freiherr,
(1870–1948), Bavarian Minister of War,
200
Kriegsgeschichtliches Forschungsamt, see
Reichsarchiv
Kluck, Alexander von, 113, 168, 229, 241
(illustr.), 243, 252, 253, 256
Knobelsdorff, General Schmidt von, 278
Kuhl, Hermann von (1856–1958), Prussian
general, 3*n*, 38

Lerchenfeld-Koefering, Hugo Philipp Graf
von und zu (1843–1925), Bavarian envoy
in Berlin 1880–1919, 172, 190, 209, 211,
228
Lichnowsky, Karl Max Fürst von (1860–1928),
German ambassador in London
1912–1914, 104, 138, 139, 141, 142, 155,
173, 188, 216, 219, 220, 223, 224
Liège:
coup de main on, 95, 96, 98, 154, 158, 161, 203,
204, 207, 208, 220, 226, 230–233, 237,
238, 272, 281
initial failure to take, 225
Lloyd George, David (1863–1945), Mansion
House Speech, 126
London, Pact of, 1914, 260, 261
Lorraine, Battle of, 20–23 August 1914, 238, 248
Ludendorff, Erich (1865–1937), Prussian
general, 3*n*, 88, 90, 93, 97, 99, 100, 126,

Ludendorff, Erich (*cont.*)
128, 131, 134, 136, 136, 148, 150, 174, 203, 231, 232, 247, 259–264, 262 (illustr.), 275–280
alleged influence over Moltke, 147
dismissal, 1913, 148, 149
Luxembourg, violation of neutrality of, 76, 77, 153, 158, 220, 222, 223, 229, 230, 284
Lyncker, Baronin von, 144
Lyncker, Moriz Freiherr von (1853–1932), Chief of the Military Cabinet 1908–1918, 33, 111, 113, 139n, 148, 190, 196, 219, 253, 157, 266, 267, 280

Mackensen, August von (1849–1945), Prussian general, Field Marshal, 11
Marschall, Ulrich Freiherr von (1863–1925), Chief of Military Cabinet July–November 1918, 267
manoeuvres, 34, 35, 38, 39, 48, 60 (illustr.), 66, 78, 88, 89, 151, 168, 223
improvements under Moltke, 19, 58, 59, 88
interference by the Kaiser, 18, 58, 59, 64, 88, 223
Manstein, Erich von, Prussian officer, 21
Mantey, Friedrich von, Prussian officer, 3, 49, 92, 165
Marne, Battle of the, 2, 100, 226, 249–253, 256, 258–261, 264–267, 270, 271, 273
Mertz von Quirnheim, Hermann Ritter von (1866–1947), first president of the Reichsarchiv, 11, 12n
Mewes, Major, 264
Military Cabinet, 31–33, 56, 71, 149, 246n., 267
Military Plenipotentiaries, 17
Ministry of War, Prussian, 14, 28ff.
Moltke, Adam von, son of younger Moltke, 6, 57, 224, 225, 273
Moltke, Eliza von, wife of younger Moltke, 7, 40, 52, 54, 197, 222, 233, 234, 263, 272, 282
connection with Rudolf Steiner, 8, 52, 54, 263
Moltke, Helmuth Karl Bernhard Graf von (1800–1891), the 'elder' Moltke, Generalfeldmarschall and Chief of the General Staff, 16, 25, 28, 47–49, 56, 74, 75, 80, 81, 99, 222, 255, 282
Moltke, Helmuth Johannes Ludwig von (1848–1916), Chief of the German General Staff, 1906–1914:
reputation and character, 2, 51, 52, 56
alleged weakness and mistakes, 48, 124, 203, 207, 248, 251, 258, 286
political role, 6

relationship with Wilhelm II, 6, 22, 23, 32, 53, 55, 56, 58, 59, 64, 110, 112, 139, 219, 220, 222, 223, 226, 234, 273, 274, 278, 283
downfall and dismissal, 216, 220, 234, 257, 261, 264–267, 269–271, 273, 274, 277
attempts to regain position, 275–280
death, 6, 281, 282, 289
Erinnerungen and papers, 8, 274
appointment, 42, 46ff., 54–71
early army career, 48
family background, 47
fear of Russia, 133, 179, 181, 188, 189, 285
Social Darwinist beliefs, 152, 176, 282, 285, 287
and Occultism/Spiritualism, 51, 53, 263, 287, 289
economic considerations in military planning, 102, 280, 281, 284
belligerence, 106, 109, 114–116, 118, 122, 135, 136, 140, 142, 143, 146, 152, 154, 166, 169, 172, 187, 195, 201, 202, 203, 206, 208, 211, 219, 225, 228, 229, 283, 286, 288, 289
views on importance of public opinion, 107, 117, 129, 141, 151, 152, 285
doubts regarding British neutrality, 109, 116, 117, 124, 146, 155, 157, 159, 163, 164, 206, 209, 210, 221
attitude towards Belgium, 157, 161–164, 166
attitude towards France, 119, 164, 165, 179
demands for army increases, 130, 131, 133, 134, 136, 146, 147, 149, 174, 175, 179, 285
as scapegoat for lost war, 98, 271
pessimism, 145, 211, 281
Moltke Plan, 5, 101, 108, 158, 176, 186, 203, 204, 216, 225, 229, 238, 243, 245, 251, 284
in Karlsbad, 173, 185, 190–193, 214, 274
absence during July Crisis, 190–193, 196
drafting of note to Belgium, 197
belief in long war, 211, 285, 287
war-time decision-making, 237, 239, 243, 246, 247, 249, 253–255, 257–259
alleged adulteration of Schlieffen Plan, 243, 245, 251, 255, 256, 267
dismissal, 270
as Chief of Deputy General Staff, 274, 281
receives Pour le Mérite, 281
Moltke, Wilhelm von, son of younger Moltke, 6
Mommsen, Theodor, historian, 51
Moroccan Crisis 1905, 42, 44, 45, 71, 78, 79, 107
Mudra, Bruno von, Prussian officer, 43, 68, 71, 72, 118
Müffling, Karl Freiherr von (1775–1851), Prussian officer, 25

Müller, Georg Alexander von (1854–1940),
    German admiral, Chief of Navy Cabinet
    1906–1918, 122, 139, 140, 141, 143, 153,
    207, 220, 226, 232, 237, 238, 246, 249,
    264, 267, 272, 274
Münster, Count, Ambassador at German
    Embassy in Paris, 24
Mutius, Oberst von, 222

Natzmer, Oberstleutnant von, 232, 233, 235
Naumann, Victor, journalist, 188
Navy, *see* German Navy
Navy Cabinet, 32
Nicolai, Walter, 192, 251
Nicholas II (1868–1918), Russian Tsar, 108,
    120
Nida, Major von, 227

Oberkommando Ost (OberOst), 276, 280
origins of the First World War:
    debate, 1
    war-guilt question, 7, 8

Pan-German League, 128, 129
Parliamentary Commission, 191
Plessen, Hans von (1841–1929), Prussian
    officer, Commandant of the Kaiser's
    Headquarters, 43, 62 (illustr.), 84, 190,
    219, 238, 246–249, 253, 264–267, 270, 277,
    279, 281, 282
Podolsk, 9
Pohl, Hugo von (1855–1916), Chief of
    Admiralty Staff 1913–1915, Chief of
    High Sea Fleet 1915–1916, 198
Pollio, Alberto, Italian Chief of the General
    Staff 1908–1914, 167, 168
    death, 170
preventive war, 108n, 180, 181
Prittwitz und Gaffron, Max von (1858–1917),
    Prussian General, Leader of Eighth
    Army 1914, 229, 244, 246, 247
Prussia:
    constitution, 16
    tensions with other German states, 17

Railway Department, 38, 40, 232, 233, 235
Rassow, Peter, historian, 44
Redern, Major von, 274
Reichsarchiv, 9–13, 86, 114, 147, 155, 156, 159,
    160, 161, 186, 228, 251, 258–260, 284
Riezler, Kurt (1882–1955), 188, 189, 198, 212,
    213, 237
Ritter, Gerhard, historian, 4, 72, 75, 80, 82, 83,
    119, 164, 214, 224, 279
Röhl, John C. G., historian, 142

Rupprecht of Bavaria, Crown Prince
    (1869–1955), 107, 229, 239, 255
Russia:
    Anglo-Russian Entente, 79
    German fear of, 137, 173, 175, 179, 189, 285
    German opinion of Russian army, 112, 122,
        145, 186, 200
    army increases, 103, 108, 122, 133, 172, 177
    mobilization, 77, 199, 200–204, 206
    Russian Revolution 1905, 78
    Russo-Japanese War, 78, 79

Sanders, Liman von, 171
Santen, Hermann von, Prussian officer, 37, 39,
    40, 88, 89, 212, 265
Sazonov, Sergej (1860–1927), Russian Foreign
    Minister 1910–1916, 120
Schäfer, Theobald von, Prussian officer and
    military writer, member of the
    Reichsarchiv, 86, 156
Schemua, Blasius von, Austro-Hungarian
    Chief of the General Staff 1912, 137
Schlichting, Sigismund von, Prussian general,
    24
Schlieffen, 'Alice von', fictional granddaughter
    of Alfred von Schlieffen, 4n
Schlieffen, Alfred Graf von (1833–1913),
    Prussian Generalfeldmarschall, Chief of
    the General Staff 1891–1905, 2, 4, 5, 20,
    22, 28, 42–44, 46, 49, 59, 64, 67, 68, 75,
    78–80, 84, 98, 99, 127, 131, 146, 165, 243,
    245, 251, 252, 255, 267, 280, 282, 284
    dealings with Austria, 80–82
    demands preventive war in 1905, 44, 45, 78
    attitude towards Moltke, 44, 46, 47, 56
    Schlieffen's final memorandum, 80
'Schlieffen myth', 3, 12, 42, 43, 74, 80, 85, 92,
    97, 98, 251, 283, 284
Schlieffen Plan, 2, 3, 8, 68, 72ff. 86, 92, 100,
    103, 141, 154, 176, 238, 252, 260, 271, 283,
    283
    changes under Moltke, 3, 80, 90, 94–97,
        100, 102, 103, 104, 109, 119, 243, 245, 285
    planned encirclement of Paris, 76, 84, 108,
        142, 238, 248, 252, 260
    see also Moltke Plan
'Schlieffen school', 2, 4, 67, 100, 110, 252, 280,
    284
Schlieffenverein, 12, 13
Schmidt-Richberg, Wiegand, historian, 32
Schoen, Hans von, Bavarian *chargé d'affaires*,
    193
Schulenburg, Graf von der, German military
    attaché in London, 78
Seidler, Lisbeth ('Heeres-Sybille'), 263, 264

'September Programme', 252
Sonderweg, 15
Spitzemberg, Hildegard Baronin von, 50, 66, 144
Stahl, Friedrich-Christian, historian, 35
Stein, Hermann von (1854–1927), Prussian general, 67, 90, 97–100, 148–150, 244, 253, 267
Steiner, Rudolf (1861–1925):
  and Anthroposophy/Theosophy, 52, 53
  connection with Helmuth von Moltke, 7*n*, 52, 53, 263, 264, 274
  connection with Eliza von Moltke, 8, 52, 54, 263
  Rudolf Steiner Nachlassverwaltung, 8
Stumm, Wilhelm von, Head of Political Department in German Foreign Office 1911–1916, 213, 236
Stürgkh, Josef Graf (1862–1945), Austro-Hungarian military plenipotentiary in German military headquarters, 233, 269, 274
Suttner, Bertha von, German pacifist, 127
Szögyény-Marich, Ladislaus Graf von, Austro-Hungarian ambassador in Berlin 1892–1914, 190, 191

Tannenberg, Battle of, 27–30 August 1914, 247, 276
Tappen, Gerhard (1866–1953), Prussian officer, 12, 40, 93, 98, 102, 149, 150, 157, 159, 175, 192, 193, 196, 227, 230, 235, 236, 238, 243, 248, 249, 254, 255, 257–259
Tieschowitz von Tischowa, Hans, Prussian officer, Moltke's adjutant, 150
Tirpitz, Alfred von (1849–1930), German admiral, State Secretary of the Reich Navy Office 1897–1916, 20, 78, 84, 86, 106, 117, 128, 132, 135, 139, 140, 142, 150, 187, 205, 216, 219, 251, 269, 271, 280
Treitschke, Heinrich von, historian, 51
Trench, Frederick, British military attaché, 90
Tschirschky und Bögendorff, Heinrich von (1858–1916), German ambassador in Vienna 1907–1916, 107, 108, 114
Turkey, as possible German ally, 120, 137, 171, 172
Turner, L. C. F., historian, 124, 125, 194

Uhle-Wettler, Franz, historian, 148
Ulmansky, Milan, Austro-Hungarian General Staff Officer, 122
universal military conscription, demands for, 146, 147, 148, 176

Varnbüler, Axel Freiherr von, member of 'Liebenberg Circle', 50, 225
Verdy du Vernois, Julius Ludwig von (1832–1910), Prussian Minister of War 1889–1890, 27
Versailles, Treaty of, 8, 12, 155, 284
Vistula, 246, 247
Voigt, Wilhelm, 'Hauptmann von Köpenick', 15
Volkskrieg, 229, 260

Waldersee, Alfred Graf von (1832–1904), Chief of the German General Staff 1888–1891, 22, 26, 27, 32, 47, 58, 67, 75, 80, 81, 99
  relationship with Wilhelm II, 26
  dismissal, 27, 28
Waldersee, Georg Graf von, Prussian officer, 33, 102, 103, 150, 159, 167, 171, 173, 177, 178, 187, 190, 192, 194, 195, 197, 215, 244, 245–247
Wallach, Jehuda, historian, 79
Wandel, Franz von (1858–1921), Prussian officer, 30, 133, 134, 146, 147
War Academy, Berlin, 37, 48, 50
War Council Meeting, 8 December 1912, 104, 135, 142, 143, 146
Wars of Unification, 15, 16, 26
Wenninger, Karl Ritter von (1861–1917), Bavarian military attaché in Berlin 1912–1914, and in German military headquarters 1914/1915, 140, 149, 170, 172, 200, 227, 232, 234, 236, 246, 269, 270, 272
Wermuth, Adolf (1855–1927), State Secretary of Reich Treasury, 134
Wild von Hohenborn (1860–1925), Prussian Minister of War 1915–1916, 279, 280
Wilhelm II (1859–1941), Prussian King and German Kaiser 1888–1918, 6, 8, 32, 42–44, 49, 107, 111, 122, 136, 138, 141, 162, 165, 169, 185, 215, 232, 233, 249, 254, 265, 266, 270, 272, 276, 279
  as 'Supreme War-Lord', 16, 17, 222, 223, 226, 259
  influence over the army, 14–16, 18, 19, 23, 25, 27, 31, 45, 67, 72, 148, 199, 219, 220, 222, 237, 266, 267, 269, 287
  contempt for civilians, 18, 82
  interference in army manoeuvres, 18, 58, 59, 64, 88, 223
  relationship with his military entourage, 23, 24
  'Halt-in-Belgrade' suggestion, 199, 208
  in exile in Amerongen, 8
  North Sea Cruises, 49, 192
  for relationship with Moltke *see* Moltke

Wilhelm, Prussian Crown Prince (1882–1951), 117, 229

Winterfeldt, Detlev von, German military attaché in Paris, 124, 162

Wolff, Theodor, journalist, editor of *Berliner Tageblatt*, 161, 213

Zabern Affair, 1913, 269

Zedlitz und Trützschler, Graf Robert von (1837–1914), Prussian officer, 18, 59, 111, 112, 117

Zenker, Hans, Kapitän, 190

Zimmermann, Arthur (1864–1940), Under-Secretary of State in German Foreign Ministry 1911–1916, 173, 191, 193, 196, 206, 213

Zuccari, Italian general, 168